THE BIBLE AMONG RUINS

Biblical writers lived in a world that was already ancient. The lands familiar to them were populated throughout by the ruins of those who had lived 2,000 years previously. References to ruins abound in the Hebrew Bible, attesting to widespread familiarity with the material remains by those who wrote these texts. Never, though, do we find a single passage that expresses an interest in digging among these ruins to learn about those who lived before. Why? In this book, Daniel Pioske offers the first study of ruination in the Hebrew Bible. Drawing on scholarship in biblical studies, archaeology, contemporary historical theory, and philosophy, he demonstrates how the ancient experience of ruins differed radically from that of the modern era. For the biblical writers, ruins were connected to temporalities of memory, presence, and anticipation. Pioske's book recreates the encounter with ruins as it was experienced during antiquity and shows how modern archaeological research has transformed how we read the Bible.

DANIEL PIOSKE is Assistant Professor of Theology at the University of St. Thomas, Minnesota. He is the author of *David's Jerusalem: Between Memory and History* and *Memory in a Time of Prose: Studies in Epistemology, Hebrew Scribalism, and the Biblical Past.*

THE BIBLE AMONG RUINS

TIME, MATERIAL REMAINS, AND THE WORLD OF THE BIBLICAL WRITERS

DANIEL PIOSKE

University of St. Thomas

Shaftesbury Road, Cambridge CB2 8EA, United Kingdom

One Liberty Plaza, 20th Floor, New York, NY 10006, USA

477 Williamstown Road, Port Melbourne, VIC 3207, Australia

314–321, 3rd Floor, Plot 3, Splendor Forum, Jasola District Centre, New Delhi – 110025, India

103 Penang Road, #05–06/07, Visioncrest Commercial, Singapore 238467

Cambridge University Press is part of Cambridge University Press & Assessment, a department of the University of Cambridge.

We share the University's mission to contribute to society through the pursuit of education, learning and research at the highest international levels of excellence.

www.cambridge.org
Information on this title: www.cambridge.org/9781009412605

DOI: 10.1017/9781009412612

© Cambridge University Press & Assessment 2023

This publication is in copyright. Subject to statutory exception and to the provisions of relevant collective licensing agreements, no reproduction of any part may take place without the written permission of Cambridge University Press & Assessment.

First published 2023

Printed in the United Kingdom by CPI Group Ltd, Croydon CR0 4YY

A catalogue record for this publication is available from the British Library.

Library of Congress Cataloging-in-Publication Data
NAMES: Pioske, Daniel D., 1982– author.
TITLE: The Bible among ruins : time, material remains, and the world of the biblical writers / Daniel Pioske, University of St. Thomas, Minnesota.
DESCRIPTION: Cambridge, United Kingdom ; New York, NY, USA : Cambridge University Press, 2023. | Includes bibliographical references and index.
IDENTIFIERS: LCCN 2023022877 (print) | LCCN 2023022878 (ebook) | ISBN 9781009412605 (hardback) | ISBN 9781009412582 (paperback) | ISBN 9781009412612 (epub)
SUBJECTS: LCSH: Bible. Old Testment–Antiquities. | Bible. Old Testament–Historiography. | Cities and towns, Ancient–Middle East. | Middle East–Antiquities. | Urban archaeology–Middle East. | Archaeology. | Israel–Antiquities.
CLASSIFICATION: LCC BS1196.5 .P56 2023 (print) | LCC BS1196.5 (ebook) | DDC 220.9/3–DC23/eng/20230710
LC record available at https://lccn.loc.gov/2023022877
LC ebook record available at https://lccn.loc.gov/2023022878

ISBN 978-1-009-41260-5 Hardback

Cambridge University Press & Assessment has no responsibility for the persistence or accuracy of URLs for external or third-party internet websites referred to in this publication and does not guarantee that any content on such websites is, or will remain, accurate or appropriate.

To my daughters – Eve, Esther, and Ella
*The Book of Jeremiah speaks of hope for the future,
and you are mine, my loves*

CONTENTS

List of Figures	*page* ix
Preface	xi
Acknowledgments	xiii
INTRODUCTION: AMONG THE RUINS	1
1 ON RUINS, THEN AND NOW	18
2 SHILOH AND THE RUINS OF MEMORY	88
3 THE RUINS OF RACHEL'S TOMB AND THE PRESENCE OF THE PAST	146
4 JERUSALEM AND THE RUINS OF TOMORROW	203
CONCLUSION	253
Bibliography	269
Subject Index	301
Scripture Index	305

FIGURES

1	Reproduction of Torso Belvedere	*page* 3
2	Furniture plaque carved in relief with a "Woman at the Window"	7
3	Ruins of Alte Synagoge, Aachen	9
4	Magdalenenklause exterior	19
5	Portrait of Ruinenberg (foreground)	20
6	Cruciform Monument of Maništušu	22
7	Map of sites of ruins	32
8	Tel Arad	34
9	Bronze Age ruins of Tel Yarmuth	35
10	Tel Lachish	38
11	Tel Nagila	39
12	Cyclopean stones used in Middle Bronze Age II wall and tower	40
13	Gezer Stelae	41
14	Cyclopean wall	45
15	Replica of inscribed Ramses Gate among Egyptian ruins, Jaffa	48
16	Ruin mound of Beth-Shean (background), ruins of Scythopolis (foreground)	49
17	Ruins of Late Bronze Age Egyptian governor residence, Beth-Shean	49
18	Ruins of entrance to Late Bronze Age ceremonial center, Hazor	50
19	Ruins of Early Iron Age gate complex, Khirbet Qeiyafa	55
20	Iron Age fortifications of the lower city in Area D East, Gath (Tell es-Safi)	56
21	Assyrian siege of Lachish relief panel	60
22	Ruins of Iron Age pillared house, Jerusalem	61
23	*Alexanderschlacht*	69
24	Temple of Isis at Pompeii	78
25	Catharine Wolfe expedition to Sippar (Tell Abu Habba)	86
26	Lion Gate, Mycenae	89
27	Mask of Agamemnon	90
28	Map of Shiloh's location in the highlands	96
29	View from Tel Shiloh	97
30	Map of Tel Shiloh	98
31	View of Shiloh's ruins	102
32	Plan of Tanis from *Description de l'Egypte*	148
33	Ruins of Tanis	150
34	Great Sphinx (twenty-sixth century BCE) found at Tanis	153

35	Garden Tomb (eighth–seventh centuries BCE), Jerusalem	158
36	Tomb of Pharaoh's Daughter (ca. ninth–seventh centuries BCE), Jerusalem	162
37	Seated deity figurines	169
38	Monumental remains of Pella Temple	170
39	Mt. Ebal complex	172
40	Arad Sanctuary with standing stone (background) and incense stands (foreground)	173
41	Replica of Stela of Seti I, Beth-Shean	176
42	Image of Assyrian royal monument (right) with stone carvers (left)	180
43	Fallen capital among ruins, Palmyra	206
44	Temple of Baal Shamin, Palmyra	206
45	Excavation sites, southeastern hill, Jerusalem	214
46	Late Iron Age broad wall, Jewish Quarter, Jerusalem	216
47	Paul Klee, *Angelus Novus*	242
48	Aerial View of Tel Megiddo	254
49	Area BB, Megiddo	256
50	Excavation of royal cemetery at Ur	266

PREFACE

It is a truism that history always has to do with time.[1]

This book is the third and last in a series of connected monographs, each volume bound to certain questions that emerge when investigating the relationship between the biblical writings and ancient Israel's past. The first of these studies (*David's Jerusalem: Between Memory and History*) examines theoretical issues of historical representation, focusing on the biblical portrayals of Jerusalem's Davidic past and the distinct means by which we write the history of that location today. The second volume (*Memory in a Time of Prose*) probes these differences further by turning to the history of knowledge. Driven by the premise that the claims we make about the past are contingent on the eras in which they are realized, *Memory in a Time of Prose* draws out and explores certain modes of knowing that contributed to the stories the biblical writers told in antiquity. The present book looks to move upstream, so to speak, from these considerations of historiography and epistemology to that of phenomenology, guided by an interest in how those in the ancient world experienced time through the material remains they encountered. The task is to persuade you of the value of this approach.

It is well demonstrated that every work of history is produced through the lens of the present. The study that follows is no different. This monograph on ruins and biblical storytelling is an outcome of a longstanding interest in how archaeological excavations over the past century have transformed the ways in which we read the Bible. But a preoccupation with ruins and the meanings they convey is about more than an interest in archaeology alone. The recent upsurge in studies devoted to ruins and, more broadly, to issues of temporality, is, as Hannah Arendt once observed, likely an attempt to come to terms with what she described as the "law of ruin"[2] that took hold among the catastrophes

---

[1] "Es ist eine Binsenwahrheit, dass die Geschichte immer mit Zeit zu tun hat." Reinhart Koselleck, "Moderne Sozialgeschichte und historische Zeiten," in *Zeitschichten: Studien zur Historik* (Frankfurt: Suhrkamp, 2000), 321.
[2] Hannah Arendt, "Franz Kafka: A Revaluation – On the Occasion of the Twentieth Anniversary of His Death," in *Essays in Understanding, 1930–1954*, ed. J. Kohn, 69–80. (New York: Harcourt, Brace & Company, 1994 [1944]), 74–75.

of the previous century. Still more, such works reflect a sense that further ruin looms very much before us. Laurent Olivier writes in this vein of a "crisis in history," which is "symptomatic of a crisis in time that the cataclysms of the 20th century, such as those involving mass destruction, have brought to the surface of the present." He comments further that our moment is defined by a "field of ruins," haunted by the past and immobilized by a future in which more ruin appears to be at hand.[3]

On this book's cover is Andrea di Lione's *Tobit Burying the Dead*, produced sometime in the 1640s. Meaningful about this painting for my purposes is its dramatic vision of ruins, presumably of Nineveh, which occupy this portrait but are never referred to in the Book of Tobit itself. Di Lione's decision to portray this particular scene of the illicit internment of the dead carries further meaning for this book, however, framed, as this study is, by W. H. Auden's two poems, one on archaeology and the other on Brueghel's painting, *The Fall of Icarus*.

---

[3] Laurent Olivier, *The Dark Abyss of Time: Archaeology and Memory*, trans. A. Greenspan (Lanham, MD: AltaMira Press, 2011), 86.

ACKNOWLEDGMENTS

This book is the culmination of a decade of research that would have been impossible apart from a community of scholars and friends who have supported this journey, one that has led from Princeton to New York, south to Savannah, and now, finally, home among the northern waterways and prairies of Minnesota. Odysseus is distinguished on his return to Ithaca by the famous scar he bears. We bear our scars, too, but mine are the fainter for the care of those who have accompanied me.

Among them are a number who read various pieces of this work. Peter Altmann, Elizabeth Bloch-Smith, Chip Dobbs-Allsopp, Janling Fu, Eric Jarrard, Mahri Leonard-Fleckman, Aren Maeir, Vic Matthews, Andrew Tobolowsky, and Ian Wilson all offered incisive comments on particular chapters. I offer special thanks to Prof. Maeir for an invitation to Bar Ilan University to workshop some of these thoughts at a conference on Iron Age urbanism and to Dr. Bloch-Smith for rich conversations over the years regarding our mutual interests in ruins and how the biblical writings relate to recent archaeological discoveries. But above all I thank Elaine James and Paul Kurtz, who read and commented on nearly all aspects of this work and without whom it would not have been attempted, much less completed.

Others require thanks. The first soundings into these ideas were eventually published in the journal *Revue Biblique*, some passages of which, revised and reworked, will be found in certain sections of Chapter 1. This project was initially undertaken within the Department of Philosophy and Religious Studies at Georgia Southern University and received warm support from its chair, Dr. Karin Fry, and found its end within the Department of Theology at the University of St. Thomas under the direction of its chair, Dr. Mark DelCogliano. And I reserve special thanks to Beatrice Rehl at Cambridge University Press for taking an early interest in this project and shepherding it to completion. The many words of gratitude one finds among CUP volumes to Beatrice, across many disciplines, reflect her editorial care and breadth of interests. I add my own voice to that chorus.

These acknowledgments find their end, however, where all my acknowledgments do: with my wife Suzette. If Browning's *Love Among the Ruins* inspired this work's title, it resonates in other ways for us more deeply, and more truly. Three daughters eventually came to accompany us in these travels. It is to them that this book is dedicated, their wild joy and untamable spirits refusing to let a book on ruins and loss be the last word.

INTRODUCTION

Among the Ruins

> The archaeologist's spade
> delves into dwellings
> vacancied long ago,
>
> unearthing evidence
> of life-ways no one
> would dream of leading now[1]

Sometime in the 1430s the *Torso Belvedere* reappears in the historical record after centuries of being lost from view. Its discovery was not the result of an archaeologist's spade, however, nor the eye of a Renaissance master who saw in it something worthy of safekeeping. Rather, the first mention of the sculpture appears in the notebook of the well-traveled antiquarian Cyriac of Ancona, whose interest in artifacts and ancient inscriptions led him to the residence of the Colonna family located somewhere in the lower Quirinal Hill area of Rome.[2] It was there that Cyriac encountered the sculpture and documented the type of information an amateur epigrapher would find

---

[1] W. H. Auden, "Archaeology," in *Collected Poems*, ed. E. Mendelson, 893–94 (New York: Vintage International, 1991).

[2] Nancy Thompson de Grummond, "Belvedere Torso," in *An Encyclopedia of the History of Classical Archaeology*, Vol. I, ed. N. de Grummond, 146–48 (Westport: Greenwood Press, 1996); Phyllis Pray Bober and Ruth Rubinstein, *Renaissance Artists and Antique Sculpture: A Handbook*, 2nd ed. (London: H. Miller, 2010), 166–68.

meaningful, providing no details other than what was written on the front of the base: "Apollonius son of Nestor, Athenian, made it."[3]

Seven decades pass before the *Torso Belvedere* receives further mention. Around the turn of the century the statue finds its way into the possession of Andrea Bregno and into the sketchbooks of friends and fellow artists in Rome who visit his personal collection of antiquities.[4] Its fragmentary character, however, appears to forestall any widespread popularity. It is not until Michelangelo comes across the sculpture and finds in it something exemplary – patterning later frescoes of the Sistine Chapel and images on the Medici tombs after it – that the *Torso Belvedere* will gain the fame as a masterpiece that it still enjoys today.[5]

But of those decades before Michelangelo's study, little is known about the statue. How it made its way from the Colonna residence to Bregno's studio and, in time, to the Belvedere Court of the Vatican, is still unclear. As Leonard Barkan observes in his landmark study, "the *Torso Belvedere*, for us one of the definitive examples of the inspired and inspiring ancient masterpieces, was probably above ground for nearly a century before it received much attention."[6]

For perhaps a century one of the most renowned sculptures from the Greco-Roman world was visible and yet went mostly unnoticed. But how? How is it that during an era when Renaissance figures were captivated by classical antiquity there was not a more concerted effort to locate and secure artifacts like the *Torso Belvedere*? Or, as Barkan puts it,[7]

> Given the hundreds of accidental discoveries of ancient art during the Renaissance, and given the historical importance assigned to these objects as well as their monetary value, why is it that the discoveries remained *accidental*? How could it be that such an enormous industry of intellect, aesthetics, politics, and economy in a city notorious for poor intrinsic resources should *not* give rise to the professional enterprise of archaeology such as awaited another two centuries to be born?

Barkan's response is that this prevailing disinterest toward material remains had something to do with the "conditions"[8] of thought that contributed to how the

---

[3] The inscription reads: ΑΠΟΛΛΩΝΙΟΣ ΝΕΣΤΟΡΟΣ ΑΘΗΝΑΙΟΣ ΕΠΟΙΕΙ. On the inscription and sculpture, see Walter Amesung, *Die Sculpturen des Vaticanischen Museums*, Band II, 2 (Berlin: Reimer, 1908), 11–13.

[4] Leonard Barkan, *Unearthing the Past: Archaeology and Aesthetics in the Making of Renaissance Culture* (New Haven, CT: Yale University Press, 1999), 190–200.

[5] Ibid., 198–200. On the famous description of the Torso by J. Winkelmann, including its characterization as one of "the most perfect examples of ancient sculpture," see Johann Winkelmann, "Description of the Torso in the Belvedere in Rome (1759)," in *Johann Joachim Winckelmann on Art, Architecture, and Archaeology*, trans. D. Carter, 143–48 (Rochester: Camden House, 2013).

[6] Barkan, *Unearthing the Past*, 1–2.   [7] Ibid., 18–19. (italics original)   [8] Ibid., 17.

INTRODUCTION: AMONG THE RUINS

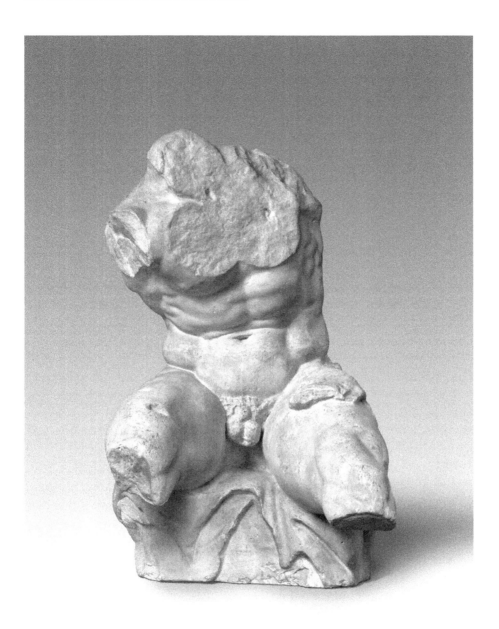

1 Reproduction of Torso Belvedere, 1875–1925 CE. Louvre, Paris. Hervé Lewandowski, photograph. https://collections.louvre.fr/en/ark:/53355/c1010270747

past was experienced among those who ventured to Rome or lived there in the fifteenth century CE, a collective sense of the past that was informed by a distinct "set of predispositions" and a "different mentality" about ruins than what would take hold in the era that followed.[9] For those of this period, Barkan

---

[9] Ibid., 18–19.

contends, ancient Rome was a symbolic space more than a historical one, a city whose former grandeur could be appreciated through the accounts of Pliny or Cicero but which was not, indeed could not be, conceived as lying beneath the rather depressed and dilapidated city with which they were familiar. "Archaeology does not develop in 1480," Barkan writes, because "you cannot travel through symbolic space with a shovel."[10] There is no reason to excavate, in other words, if one believes that underfoot there is little to be found.

§

1.1 PATHWAYS

But what of other time periods and places whose populations came across the ruins of a more distant past? After two centuries of excavations across hundreds of sites in the eastern Mediterranean region, we now know that the landscapes familiar to the biblical writers enclosed the ruins of numerous cities, many already centuries, if not millennia, old. It is perhaps not surprising, then, that within the Hebrew Bible ruins feature prominently among a number of texts. References to ruins abound within these documents, in fact, appearing in poems and prose stories, prophetic oracles and discussions of law, numbering well over two hundred citations spread across nearly all twenty-four scrolls that would come into the canon. The Hebrew Bible is in many ways a book of ruins, written in a world where wreckage and loss – or the threat thereof – were common.

But never do we come across a single passage that expresses an interest in unearthing these remains. In the study that follows, I ask why. Why, that is, in a collection of ancient writings pervaded with references to ruins, is there no mention of any attempt to dig among these sites and explore them in an effort to learn about those who lived before? Why, among texts that otherwise exhibit such a fascination with the past, is there not more curiosity about what ruins might disclose about former times? And what meanings did ruins then hold for the biblical writers if they were not viewed as evidence of practices, beliefs, or behaviors from previous ages?

Such are the questions that give rise to this volume. Straightforward as they seem, the pathways taken in response will prove more oblique and demanding. Similar to Barkan's intuitions, the answers offered in this book are those that will be occupied with certain predispositions toward the meanings that ruins convey, those shared convictions and mindsets about ruination that contribute to how material remains are regarded within the writings of the Hebrew Bible. What results from this approach is something more than an investigation into certain

---

[10] Ibid., 25.

INTRODUCTION: AMONG THE RUINS

ruined sites or artifacts from the eastern Mediterranean world, as important as this evidence will be for the study at hand. It is also an examination of the experience of ruins expressed within the biblical writings that refer to them.

A key argument of this book is that this experience has been recast since the eras in which these documents took form. How we identify and ascribe meaning to ruins familiar to us today, I maintain, is something distinct from the impression ruins leave on those who portray them in the Hebrew Bible. The clearest evidence of this divide is the relatively recent birth of the discipline of archaeology, which systematically excavates sites of ruin in ways never imagined in times previous to its emergence.[11] The development of modern archaeological practice, in short, signals a rupture. Its rise demonstrates that the way we think about ruins is something historically specific, a product of the time period in which these thoughts have taken hold.

This book investigates the history of this unfolding. In part, *The Bible Among Ruins* is a title that highlights a historical interest in how the experience of ruins is inflected within the texts the biblical writers composed in antiquity – their stories and poems being formed, I contend, among a landscape in which ruins were a salient and suggestive phenomenon. What I aim through this manner of study is to investigate the world that imprinted itself on the writings of the Hebrew Bible, being attentive to the ways in which these texts are responsive to the ruined terrain in which they were created.[12] In short, it is a study that strives to locate these writings in the ancient environs in which they were produced so as to draw closer to those individuals who stand behind them.[13]

Nevertheless, this pursuit of intimacy is encumbered at the outset by how remote our world has come to be.[14] *The Bible Among Ruins* also appeals to this

---

[11] On the development of modern archaeological practice, see Julian Thomas, *Archaeology and Modernity* (London: Routledge, 2004); Bruce Trigger, *A History of Archaeological Thought*, 2nd ed. (Cambridge: Cambridge University Press, 2006); Margarita Díaz-Andreu, *A World History of Nineteenth Century Archaeology: Nationalism, Colonialism, and the Past* (Oxford: Oxford University Press, 2007); Eric Cline, *Three Stones Make a Wall: The Story of Archaeology* (Princeton, NJ: Princeton University Press, 2017). For a study centered on the rise of archaeology with the Bible in view, see Thomas W. Davis, *Shifting Sands: The Rise and Fall of Biblical Archaeology* (Oxford: Oxford University Press, 2004).

[12] On landscapes and literature, Elaine James writes, "There is a meaningful circle of influence between human cultures and their physical environs," and a landscape "is not merely a material fact, but also a cultural product that encodes meaning and promotes values." Elaine T. James, *Landscapes of the Song of Songs: Poetry and Place* (New York: Oxford University Press, 2017), 2. This works draws on a similar sensibility toward landscape and meaning within the biblical writings.

[13] "How, indeed," Ricoeur writes, "could one ignore the simple fact that in history one is concerned with practically nothing but the dead of other times?" Paul Ricoeur, *Memory, History, Forgetting*, trans. K. Blamey and D. Pellauer (Chicago: University of Chicago Press, 2004), 364.

[14] For a rich analysis of the dialectic between "closeness and distance" within nineteenth century CE philological studies, see Constanze Güthenke, *Feeling and Classical Philology:*

sense of distance. What becomes evident when studying ancient remains, that is, is how removed we are from the experiences these artifacts disclose.[15] In turning to the archaeological record in an effort to surmount the expanse of time that divides us from those in antiquity, what can result instead is a further hollowing out of the gulf between us, intensifying a sense of separation that is the result not only of the millennia that have transpired but also of distinct worldviews and practices that were lost long ago. What the title of this work seeks to capture, then, is an inescapable tension running throughout the pages that follow: a desire for proximity bound to a sense of loss.

The history that follows is a history of how ruins have been perceived across time. The impetus for this approach stems from a renewed interest in the phenomenological within historical theory and practice. What this perspective endeavors to restore, as Gabrielle Spiegel describes it in her incisive methodological study,[16] is "the historical actor and his or her consciousness of the world, however thoroughly mediated by discourses of one sort or another, to the center of historical concerns."[17] From this vantage point, the historian's interests are oriented toward feelings, perceptions, and atmospheres, on the subjective, often embodied, responses to certain phenomena that are inscribed textually but also materially through the traces that have endured. It is these "involvements and interactions" with material environments that a history attentive to the phenomenological has as its primary subject matter,[18] an investigation that asks "how people in the past experienced their world and

---

Knowing Antiquity in German Scholarship 1770–1920 (Cambridge: Cambridge University Press, 2020).

[15] Paul Kurtz, in his study of the rise of modern philological interests, underscores this point well: "The amassing of more material engendered a greater sense of what once was and, with it, a keener sense of loss: in the irrecoverable, inaccessible past and in the incompleteness of knowledge." Paul Michael Kurtz, "The Philological Apparatus: Science, Text, and Nation in the Nineteenth Century," *Critical Inquiry* 47.4 (2021): 761.

[16] Spiegel writes further, "It is this actor-centered perspective, a belief in individual experience and perception as the agent's own source of knowledge about, and action in, the world – a perception mediated and perhaps constrained but *not* wholly controlled by the cultural scaffolding or conceptual schemes within which it takes place – that I see as the return of a modified phenomenology." Gabrielle Spiegel, "The Future of the Past: History, Memory, and the Ethical Imperatives of Writing History," *Journal of the Philosophy of History* 8 (2014): 155–56.

[17] Ibid., 153. Cf. Gabrielle Spiegel, "The Limits of Empiricism: The Utility of Theory in Historical Thought and Writing," *The Medieval History Journal* 22:1 (2019): 1–22.

[18] David Carr, *Experience and History: Phenomenological Perspectives on the Historical World* (Oxford: Oxford University Press, 2014), 1. Carr comments further of this approach: "A phenomenology of history inquires into history as a phenomenon, and into the experience of the historical. How does history present itself to us, how does it enter our lives, and what are the forms of experience in which it does so?" Ibid., 1.

INTRODUCTION: AMONG THE RUINS

2 Furniture plaque carved in relief with a "Woman at the Window." Assyrian, ninth–eighth century BCE. The Metropolitan Museum of Art, New York. Fletcher Fund, 1957. www.metmuseum.org

in what way this experience may differ from how we relate to our own world," as Frank Ankersmit characterizes this historical pursuit.[19] The focus,

---

[19] Frank Ankersmit, *Sublime Historical Experience* (Stanford, CA: Stanford University Press, 2005), 3–4.

Ankersmit comments further, "is on what may seem to us strange or even simply impossible to imagine in the *experience vécue* of our ancestors."[20]

What the study of ruins affords is the possibility of examining these lived experiences through the remains that have been left behind. Interactions that would otherwise prove fleeting are made more lasting and available to study, that is, by attending to how these engagements are inscribed in ancient documents still available to us and shaped in response to a physical terrain that can be investigated archaeologically today. Because ruins persist, in other words, encounters with them provide one of the few points of possible contact between us and those who lived in antiquity, where certain landscapes once visible to them are, at moments, still visible to us.

But what is also meaningful about a study of ruins is how it converges with a growing interest in such sites of disrepair among a diverse collection of scholarship that offers further, comparative insights into what ruins signify across distinct contexts and time periods. "We seem to be in the midst of a contemporary *Ruinenlust*,"[21] Caitlin DeSilvey and Tim Edensor remark in an article devoted to this theme, a preoccupation spurred by the catastrophes of the century that preceded ours, it is argued, and also by the logic of our late capitalist moment and its commodification of nearly all forms of life.[22] A study of ruins is not a parochial concern reserved for scholars burrowed away in some corner of their field, this is to say, but rather connects to something larger, to a yawning sense that ruins indicate something desperately meaningful to us, aware as we are, too, that we have not escaped the possibilities of our own ruination.[23]

---

[20] Ibid., 4.

[21] Caitlin DeSilvey and Tim Edensor, "Reckoning with Ruins," *Progress in Human Geography* 37.4 (2012): 465.

[22] On this point, see also Andreas Huyssen, "Nostalgia for Ruins," *Grey Room* 23 (2006): 6–21; Julia Hell and Andreas Schönle, "Introduction," in *Ruins of Modernity*, eds. J. Hell and A. Schönle, 1–16 (Duke, NC: Duke University Press, 2010); Þóra Pétursdóttir and Bjørnar Olsen, "An Archaeology of Ruins," in *Ruin Memories: Materialities, Aesthetics, and the Archaeology of the Recent Past*, ed. B. Olsen and Þ Pétursdóttir, 1–29 (New York: Routledge, 2014), 3–4.

[23] In addition to those cited in Footnote 22, significant studies of ruins have appeared in disparate disciplines, including, for example, Anna Laura Stoler, "Imperial Debris: Reflections on Ruins and Ruination," *Cultural Anthropology* 23.2 (2008): 191–219; Nicholas Halmi, "Ruins Without a Past," *Essays in Romanticism* 18 (2011): 7–27; Dariusz Gafijczuk, "Dwelling Within: The Inhabited Ruins of History," *History and Theory* 52 (2013): 149–70; Dora Apel, *Beautiful Terrible Ruins: Detroit and the Anxiety of Decline* (New Brunswick, NJ: Rutgers University Press, 2015); Andrew Hui, *The Poetics of Ruins in Renaissance Literature* (New York: Fordham University Press, 2017); Alain Schnapp, "What is a Ruin? The Western Definition," *Know* 2.1 (2018): 155–73; Julia Hell, *The Conquest of Ruins: The Third Reich and the Fall of Rome* (Chicago: University of Chicago Press, 2019); Susan Stewart, *The Ruins Lesson: Meaning and Material in Western Culture* (Chicago: University of Chicago Press, 2020); Maia Kotrosits, *The Lives of Objects: Material Culture, Experience, and the Real in the History of Early Christianity* (Chicago: University of Chicago Press, 2020), esp. 42–66.

INTRODUCTION: AMONG THE RUINS

3 Ruins of Alte Synagoge. Aachen, Germany, 1938. United States Holocaust Memorial Museum, courtesy of Stadtarchiv Aachen. Public domain

But what does the experience of ruins involve? An array of impressions, to be sure, whose meanings are multiple and varied. Left behind in the material record are expressions of aesthetic values from previous ages that confront our own ideas of beauty and form, glimpses of past political and religious ideologies, and mundane vestiges of daily life that were once commonplace at a site.

But above all ruins have to do with time. "The ruin's extensive relation to time, stretching beyond the span of not only a human lifetime but also the extent of the rise and fall of particular cultures," Susan Stewart writes in her elegant study, "gives it a certain power."[24] This potency is similarly accented by Felix Ó Murchadha in his phenomenological discussion of ruination, where it is observed that "[t]he power of time shows itself in the ruin," displaying a fading of form that attests to how "the ruin belongs to the passing of the past."[25] Or, as Andreas Huyssen puts it succinctly, "In the ruin, history appears spatialized and built space temporalized."[26]

The strong association between ruins and time similarly finds expression in the famous essay by Georg Simmel on "The Ruin" from a century ago.[27] Within it, Simmel contends that a pivotal experience of ruination resides in how these remains capture "the past with its destinies and transformations,"[28] preserving a historical trajectory or duration that can somehow be experienced by an onlooker in the present. In these reflections, Simmel directs our attention to how time becomes tangible among places of ruin, those sites "of life from which life has departed," as he describes them, in whose remnants are preserved "the entire span of time since its formation."[29] And Paul Ricoeur, too, describes how the phenomena of ruins are an "intratemporal" feature of our surroundings that convey a fundamental sense of "within-time-ness" to us, disclosing how we are "in" time and enclosed among the trappings of its various temporalities, so to speak, and cannot escape it.[30] Elsewhere, Ricoeur will draw attention to the image of the ruin itself in his philosophical discussion – "the remains of a Greek temple" – and pose a question that will be asked in various ways throughout this study: "What were, at another time, the things we see before us, deteriorated but yet still visible?"[31]

The capacity of ruins to mediate a sense of temporality through their duration, to waken within us impressions about the past, present, and future, is the experience that forms the heart of this study. This book joins others,

---

[24] Stewart, *The Ruins Lesson*, 15.
[25] Felix Ó Murchadha, "Being as Ruination: Heidegger, Simmel, and the Phenomenology of Ruins," *Philosophy Today* 46 (2002): 10–11.
[26] Huyssen, "Nostalgia," 13.
[27] Georg Simmel, "Die Ruine," in *Philosophische Kultur: Gesammelte Essais*, 125–33 (Leipzig: Kröner, 1919).
[28] Ibid., 132.   [29] Ibid.
[30] Paul Ricoeur, *Time and Narrative*, Vol. III, trans. K. Blamey and D. Pellauer (Chicago: University of Chicago Press, 1988), 122. In these observations, Ricoeur draws on a significant passage from Heidegger's *Being and Time*: "Remains, monuments, and records that are still present-at-hand, are *possible* 'material' for the concrete disclosure of the Dasein which has-been-there." Martin Heidegger, *Being and Time*, trans. J. Macquarrie and E. Robinson (London: Blackwell, 1962), 446. (italics original) The "disclosure" of what "has been" by way of the ruins left behind will be a theme that resounds throughout this work.
[31] Ricoeur, *Time and Narrative*, III, 78.

then, that participate in what Sarit Gribetz and Lynn Kaye have recently described as a temporal turn in ancient Judaism and Jewish Studies.[32] Yet even this turn, as Gribetz and Kaye observe, is more of an aftereffect, one that took hold in response to the great philosophical and literary works on time that were produced in the late nineteenth and early twentieth centuries CE, including those of Bergson,[33] Proust,[34] Heidegger,[35] Woolf,[36] and Ricoeur,[37] among others, who all reflected on the tectonic shift in the experience of time that, in German, was named the "*Neuzeit*" – literally, the "new time," or, for us Anglophones, "modernity."[38] This work has therefore learned from and accompanies those historians who have recently pursued similar studies on experience and time, particularly Zachary Schiffman's nuanced exploration of when the idea of "the past" took hold in Western thought,[39] François Hartog's provocative investigation into varying "regimes of historicity" that have crystallized over the centuries,[40] and, somewhat closer to home, Paul Kosmin's erudite history of time in the Seleucid Empire, wherein a "revolution in chronological thought and historical experience" is discerned.[41]

This work departs from these with its focus on the writings of the Hebrew Bible and their relationship to the archaeological remains of the southern Levant. Of the many contributions that archaeology affords to our study of the biblical corpus, one of the most important is how it brings to light the landscapes in which these texts were once realized, offering insights into what Elizabeth Bloch-Smith terms the "tangible experience of the world of ancient Israel" that informs these writings.[42] Reading the Bible among ruins left

---

[32] Sarit Kattan Gribetz and Lynn Kaye, "The Temporal Turn in Ancient Judaism and Jewish Studies," *Currents in Biblical Research* 17.3 (2019): 332–95.

[33] Henri Bergson, *Matière et mémoire: essai sur la relation du corps a l'esprit*, 5th ed. (Paris: F. Alcan, 1908).

[34] Marcel Proust, *In Search of Lost Time*, trans. C. K. S. Moncrieff, T. Kilmartin, and A. Mayor (New York: Modern Library, 2003 [1913–1927]).

[35] Heidegger, *Being and Time* [1927].

[36] Virginia Woolf, *Mrs. Dalloway* (New York: Harcourt, Brace & World, 1925).

[37] Paul Ricoeur, *Time and Narrative*, 3 vols., trans. K. Blamey and D. Pellauer (Chicago: University of Chicago Press, 1984–88 [1983–1985]).

[38] See Reinhart Koselleck, "'Neuzeit:' Remarks on the Semantics of Modern Concepts of Movement," in *Futures Past: On the Semantics of Historical Time*, trans. K. Tribe, 222–54 (New York: Columbia University Press, 2004).

[39] Zachary Schiffman, *The Birth of the Past* (Baltimore: Johns Hopkins University Press, 2011).

[40] François Hartog, *Regimes of Historicity: Presentism and Experiences of Time* (New York: Columbia University Press, 2015).

[41] Paul Kosmin, *Time and Its Adversaries in the Seleucid Empire* (Cambridge, MA: Harvard University Press, 2018).

[42] Elizabeth Bloch-Smith, "Archaeology: What It Can Teach Us," in *The Wiley Blackwell Companion to Ancient Israel*, ed. S. Niditch, 13–27 (Malden, MA: Wiley, 2016): 25. Cf. Elizabeth Bloch-Smith, "A Stratified Account of Jephthah's Negotiations and Battle: Judges 11:12033 from an Archaeological Perspective," *JBL* 134.2 (2015): 291–311. This perspective on the relationship between archaeology and ancient texts draws near that of Susan Sherratt's

behind from antiquity draws our attention to a palpable world of sights and sounds, tastes and smells, that are presumed in the biblical writings but which can go unnoticed by us, we who are now separated from their composition by over two millennia.

Attentiveness to the archaeological record thus makes us more attentive readers. In her study of literature, Rita Felski similarly accents the importance of material objects referred to within literary works, especially in those "transhistorical encounters" that find us engaging writings from regions and time periods distant from our own, demanding from us a "cross-temporal leap, a destabilizing shift from one time frame and cultural sensibility to another."[43] How to gain our footing in these foreign worlds is bolstered by a mindfulness toward the items that appear within them, intimating "what it feels like to be inside a particular habitus," Felski comments, and "to experience a world that is self-evident, to bathe in the waters of a way of life."[44] A sensitivity to the materials that these writings draw to our attention, Felski contends, promotes a mode of "seeing as" rather than "seeing that," prompting us to look at a world through the eyes of an author in a manner that confronts and challenges our sense of the way things are.[45] From this vantage point, the remains archaeologists unearth make us more attuned to what ancient texts disclose about the worlds they represent, and, in doing so, make us more alert to the possible meanings these texts convey.

This book investigates these past worlds by bringing together archaeological research and the ways in which the biblical writings portray the ruins that were located among them. The numerous and varied references to ruins in the Hebrew Bible indicate that the biblical writers were familiar with such sites of disrepair and the once formidable locations connected to them. But from our standpoint today, what is striking is that this familiarity did not elicit a subterranean interest in what lay buried. Though the biblical writers knew that they were latecomers to a world inhabited long before, the presence of ruins left behind from these earlier communities did not compel these authors to dig among them and reflect on what they found. Instead, ruins provoked different responses.

---

notion of "archaeological contexts" for ancient Greek epic. On this methodological stance, see Susan Sherratt, "Archaeological Contexts," in *A Companion to Ancient Epic*, ed. J. M. Foley, 119–41 (Malden, MA: Blackwell, 2009).

[43] Rita Felski, *The Uses of Literature* (Malden, MA: Blackwell, 2008), 92.

[44] Ibid., 92. Felski terms this framework a "social phenomenology," whose ambition is to "register the importance of things." Ibid., 98.

[45] Ibid., 93. On the "world" of a text that we are invited to enter on its reading, see also the discussion in Paul Ricoeur, *Time and Narrative*, Vol. I, trans. K. McLaughlin and D. Pellauer (Chicago: University of Chicago Press, 1984), 77–82. Ricoeur writes, "I will say that, for me, the world is the whole set of references opened by every sort of descriptive or poetic text I have read, interpreted, loved ... what is interpreted in a text is the proposing of a world that I might inhabit and into which I might project my inmost powers" (80–81).

To better understand them, I concentrate on the experience of time associated with material remains in the biblical writings. To be sure, other historical explanations could be pursued for why the biblical writers express such little interest in what lay buried, including significant factors wedded to what was absent in antiquity with regard to technological developments and colonial ambitions that, quite suddenly in the decades surrounding the turn of the nineteenth century CE, led to a transformation in how ruins were appraised.[46] But as will be argued at length in this book, even these necessary considerations are derivative of something more fundamental, of profound changes in the experience of time that began to take hold in the period after the *Torso Belvedere* came into public view.

This study of ruins in the Hebrew Bible draws us near, then, to experiences of ruination that are often distinct from our own. By entering into the ancient world of the Hebrew writers who composed these documents, we come across impressions of ruination that depart from the dominant historical interests in material remains that still guide our scholarly pursuits today. Our awareness of a disconnect between the present and the past, of "life-ways" in previous times that "no one would dream of living now," as W. H. Auden puts it in the epigraph to this chapter, suggests an experience of ruins that is more recent, a product of the "archaeologist's spade" that has exposed remains "from long ago." To explore the perspectives of ruination in the Hebrew Bible is an inquiry that resonates, consequently, with an approach Johann Gottfried Herder once described as a *sich hineinfühlung in*, a "feeling oneself into" the experiences of those who lived so differently in ages before.[47]

§

---

[46] For rich studies in this vein, see again Díaz-Andreu, *A World History of Nineteenth Century Archaeology: Nationalism, Colonialism, and the Past;* Donald Malcolm Reid, *Whose Pharaohs? Archaeology, Museums and Egyptian National Identity from Napoleon to World War I* (Berkeley: University of California Press, 2002); Stephen Dyson, *In Pursuit of Ancient Pasts: A History of Classical Archaeology in the Nineteenth and Twentieth Centuries* (New Haven, CT: Yale University Press, 2006); and Billie Melman, *Empires of Antiquities: Modernity and the Rediscovery of the Ancient Near East, 1914–1950* (Oxford: Oxford University Press, 2020).

[47] So Herder: "In order to share in feeling this, do not answer on the basis of the word but go into the age, into the clime, the whole history, feel yourself into everything [*fühle dich in alles hinein*] – only now are you on the way towards understanding the word." Johann Gottfried Herder, "This Too a Philosophy of History for the Formation of Humanity," in *Philosophical Writings*, ed. and trans. M. N. Forster, 272–358 (Cambridge: Cambridge University Press, 2002 [1774]), 292. On this method, Forster writes, "First of all, the metaphor implies (once again) that the interpreter faces radical difference, a gulf, between his own mentality and that of the interpreted subject, making interpretation a difficult, laborious task." Michael Forster, *After Herder: Philosophy of Language in the German Tradition* (Oxford: Oxford University Press, 2010), 19. For a further discussion of this interpretive principle, see Michael Forster, *Herder's Philosophy* (Oxford: Oxford University Press, 2018), 100–10.

1.2 TRAJECTORY

This study begins in the ancient world. Chapter 1 ("Among the Ruins: Then and Now") opens in antiquity, where we examine the landscapes that would have been familiar to the scribes behind the biblical writings. What comes to light through this archaeological investigation is a terrain where an encounter with older ruins would have been commonplace, some connected to sites that had fallen long before the biblical writings were composed and others destroyed more proximate to the period when these documents were formed. The writings of the Hebrew Bible were produced in a world where the ruins of past populations were visible and lasting, including from a number of locations that are referred to explicitly within these texts.

But what is absent from these writings is any indication that ruins could be investigated to learn about those who had lived before. During an era that Reinhart Koselleck terms the *Sattelzeit* (1750 CE–1850 CE),[48] however, I argue that ruins come to be thought about differently, now being viewed as dense with history. The second movement of this chapter is focused on this development, when systematic excavations begin to be carried out at a number of locations in the eastern Mediterranean region. Following the insights of Koselleck and Ricoeur,[49] among others, this interest in the historical character of ruins is connected to a more acute awareness of the discontinuities that mark the passing of time. This section proceeds by retracing how moral and aesthetic valuations of ruins give way to a perspective that historicizes them, the remains of antiquity now offering its onlookers historical information about those who once lived at these fallen sites. Our study encounters a series of vignettes that illustrates this turn, from Edward Robinson's travels across Palestine in 1838 to the appearance of Sir Flinders Petrie at the site of Tel el-Hesi in 1890,[50] Petrie's visit occurring after a heavy rain had washed away part of the ancient mound and left it exposed. Petrie's recognition of archaeological strata and their importance for situating ruins in history will bring us into the present, with this chapter's study concluding by attending to the theoretical reflections of Koselleck and Ricoeur, both of whom contend that impressions of time had been reshaped during the centuries traversed in this chapter. Koselleck, for his part, describes this occurrence as a widening chasm between the

---

[48] Reinhart Koselleck, "Einleitung," in *Geschichtliche Grundbegriffe: Historisches Lexikon zur politisch-sozialen Sprache in Deutschland*, Vol. I, eds. O. Brunner, W. Bonze, and R. Koselleck, XIII–XXVII(Stuttgart: Klett-Cotta, 1972), XV–XVII.

[49] Koselleck, *Futures Past: On the Semantics of Historical*; Reinhart Koselleck, *Sediments of Time: On Possible Histories*, trans. S. Franzel and S. L. Hoffmann (Stanford, CA: Stanford University Press, 2018); Paul Ricoeur, *Memory, History, Forgetting*, esp. 281–411.

[50] Edward Robinson, *Biblical Researches in Palestine, 1838–1852*, Vols. I–III (Boston: Crocker & Brewster, 1856). W. M. Flinders Petrie, *Tell el Hesy (Lachish)* (London: Palestine Exploration Fund, 1891).

"space of experience" and the "horizon of expectation";[51] Ricoeur as our "historical condition."[52]

Chapters 2–4 explore how ruins were experienced otherwise by the biblical writers. What is developed in these chapters are three case studies that examine different modes of temporality connected to ruination in the Hebrew Bible. A much more integrated sense of time elicited through an encounter with material remains is separated artificially in these chapters, consequently, with certain impressions unbound from one another in an effort to draw out and account for the complexity with which these landscapes are described in the Hebrew Bible. The heuristic character of this separation is foregrounded here at the outset so as to acknowledge that such experiences did not occur in isolation from one another. The ruins of Jerusalem, to cite one example, could evoke memories of former times (Amos 9:11), pose deep questions about the present (Jer 44), and give rise to prophetic claims about the time ahead when the ruins of Jerusalem would, perhaps, be ruins no more (Is 44:26). But, in order to elaborate the richness and polysemy of ruination found in the Hebrew Bible, this investigation will disentangle certain impressions of time in order to examine their claims in greater detail.[53]

The first of these studies ("Shiloh and the Ruins of Memory") investigates the relationship between ruins and remembrance. Spurred by theoretical discussions on the attachments between places, material remains, and memory, Chapter 2 investigates how the ruins of Shiloh contributed to stories told about it in the Hebrew Bible. Shiloh is of particular interest with regard to memory and ruination because of the relatively early period of the location's destruction (ca. 1050–1000 BCE) and its abandonment, aside from moments of small-scale occupation, until late in the Hellenistic era a thousand years later. During this millennium of lying in ruin, this chapter contends, a collection of stories and poems were written about Shiloh's past, ranging from Priestly (P) references to Shiloh's import at the beginning of Israel's life in Canaan (Josh 18–22) to the Book of Jeremiah's allusions to the location that were written at least four centuries after Shiloh was destroyed (Jer 7:12; 26:6, 9). What comes to light through this investigation is how the ruins of Shiloh called to mind a medley of references to the past that came to be preserved in the biblical corpus, its ruins giving rise to distinct and at times competing claims of what once transpired at

---

[51] Koselleck, *Futures Past*, 255–76.   [52] Ricoeur, *Memory, History, Forgetting*, 281–86.
[53] The modes of temporality treated here are modeled, in large measure, on Augustine's famous discussion of the experience of time in Book XI of the *Confessions*. "It might be correct to say that there are three times," Augustine writes, "a present of past things, a present of present things, and a present of future things ... The present of past things is memory; the present of present things is direct perception; and the present of future things is expectation."
Augustine, *Confessions*, ed. C. Hammond (Cambridge, MA: Harvard University Press, 2016), 252–53.

the site. The full force of this association between ruins and remembrance will only be felt when it is countervailed by our attempts to excavate both this location and others, a quest whereby memory's past is eclipsed by the critical methods of modern historical inquiry. The "unending competition" between memory and history, as Ricoeur describes it,[54] forms the final theme of this chapter's investigation.

This study of remembrance leads to one of presence. Drawing on recent historical studies oriented toward the afterlife of ruins, Chapter 3 ("The Ruins of Rachel's Tomb") investigates how ruins elicit an experience of immanence in the here and now within the biblical writings, the meanings of certain material remains determined not only by a retrospective interest in the past but also by the ways in which these remnants continue to haunt the present. This sense of immediacy is examined by way of references to various items referred to in the Hebrew Bible, encompassing tombs, altars, pillars, and heaps of stone, among other objects, many of which are characterized as persisting "until this day" in the terrain familiar to the ancient writers who make mention of them. In the Book of Genesis, for example, we come across the titular passage of this chapter's study, where the narrator remarks, "Jacob set up a pillar at her grave; it is the pillar of Rachel's tomb, which is there to this day" (Gen 35:40). The possibility of a past becoming present through an encounter with ruins forms the focus of this chapter's study, an impression of time produced by a sense of simultaneity brought about through material remains that have endured over long stretches of time. To conclude, the sense of presence connected to ruination in the biblical writings is set against the theme of discontinuity and temporal dissonance, which, as discussed in Chapter 1, characterized a key feature of modern historical thought.

The final case study of this book ("Jerusalem and the Ruins of Tomorrow") examines how ruins are associated with the future. What so often distinguishes the biblical writings, Chapter 4 argues, is that sites of disrepair frequently presage something about the time ahead. This prospective temporality, as I term it, is examined by way of the biblical descriptions of Jerusalem's ruins, particularly those texts written with the location's destruction by the Neo-Babylonian empire (586 BCE) in view. Ruins are frequently described in these passages as forerunners of events to come, referred to in order to warn contemporaries of what may soon come to pass. But what is also found in these references to ruins is a future that holds out the possibility of restoration, culminating in the remarkable claims in the Books of Isaiah and Ezekiel that the ruins of Jerusalem will one day "become like the Garden of Eden" (Ezek 36:35; Is 51:3). Such claims about the future lead to a consideration of the

---

[54] Ricoeur, *Memory, History, Forgetting*, 500.

INTRODUCTION: AMONG THE RUINS

writings of Walter Benjamin and his "Theses on the Philosophy of History," composed not long before his tragic death in 1940. Within these "Theses" Benjamin elaborates a "messianic" order of time, a temporal framework that, like many claims in the prophetic writings, conceives of a different future in response to a present world come undone.[55]

This book's Conclusion revisits the questions that open the discussion. As to why the biblical writers exhibit such little interest in unearthing the ruins that surrounded them, the responses developed in this study concentrate chiefly on the impressions of time that ruins conveyed to these ancient storytellers and poets. The temporalities of ruination these writings disclose prove to be beyond or other than our historical intuitions, I contend, our architecture of historical thought constructed on a more recent, acute awareness of pronounced asymmetries between past, present, and future. The ramifications of this argument are far reaching. But one implication, with the subject of ruins in view, is that our contemporary sense of material remains may in some ways be diminished when situated alongside more ancient understandings of such remnants. To probe the meanings that ruins signified in antiquity would offer something to our historical habits and mindsets, consequently, we "latecomers and epigones," as Friedrich Nietzsche calls us, perhaps more aware than any of those before that "history must itself resolve the problem of history, knowledge must turn its sting against itself."[56] This study of ruins gestures throughout toward this Nietzschean impulse, where the historical interest in ruination that animates this work is itself historicized and problematized, reflecting a specific *agon* surrounding history's aims that, in the final moments of this book, will be placed under the sign of a predicament.[57]

---

[55] Walter Benjamin, "Theses on the Philosophy of History," *Illuminations: Essays and Reflection*, ed. H. Arendt, 253–64 (New York: Mariner, 2019 [1968]).

[56] Friedrich Nietzsche, "On the Uses and Disadvantages of History for Life," in *Untimely Meditations*, ed. D. Breazeale, 57–124 (Cambridge: Cambridge University Press, 1997), 103.

[57] "But as the youth races through history, so do we modern men race through art galleries and listen to concerts. We feel that one thing sounds different from another, that one thing produces a different effect from another: increasingly to lose this sense of strangeness, no longer to be very much surprised at anything, finally to be pleased with everything – that is then no doubt called the historical sense, historical culture." Ibid., 98.

ONE

ON RUINS, THEN AND NOW

> Rooftops in ruin, towers tumbled down.
> Gate-locks lie broken, frost chokes the lime,
> Ceilings sapped with age, the high hall loftless.
> The mortar is moldy, the master-builders are gone,
> Buildings and brave men in the clutch of the grave.
> A hundred generations have passed away,
> Princes and peoples now forgotten
> The ruddy wall-stones are stained with gray,
> Rocks that have outlived the reign of kings,
> The crash of storms, the crush of time.[1]

On the grounds of the Nymphenburg Schloß in Munich lies a small hermitage, the Magdalenenklause, nestled within a grove of trees among the well-manicured gardens that surround the palace. Though somewhat hidden away along the winding paths of the park's pavilions, the building itself is unmistakable when one draws near. Composed of a disarranged collection of tiles, plaster, and stone masonry, the hermitage gives the impression of being quite antiquated, its slow decay offset by the repairs made to it over the centuries that have left its façade dilapidated but sound. The interior of the building is no less peculiar, with its southern quarter placed on what appears to be an ancient grotto and its northern end modeled on monastic chambers edged into the

---

[1] Anonymous, "The Ruin," in *The Complete Old English Poems*, trans. C. Williamson, 582–83 (Philadelphia: University of Pennsylvania Press, 2017 [ca. 8th–9th centuries CE]).

4 Magdalenenklause exterior. Nymphenburg Schloß, Munich. Wikimedia Commons, Creative Commons CC0 1.0 universal public domain

rock. One imagines that perhaps the Bavarian rulers of old built their palace adjacent to what had been a sacred site long before their arrival, their piety expressed by preserving the venerable sanctum near the royal estate that was soon to emerge.

Or so it seems. The hermitage's history is rather a more recent one, having been built in 1725 CE after much of the nearby palace was complete. Designed as a place of contemplation for the elector of Bavaria by the court architect, Joseph Effner, the Magdalenenklause represents the "artificial ruin" or "folly" architectural form that had gained popularity among rulers throughout Europe at the time.[2] Some examples, such as Frederick the Great's Ruinenberg at Sanssouci or the Ruin of Carthage at Schloß Schönbrunn in Vienna, could even draw on a more ancient, Greco-Roman past in their designs, though

---

[2] Kai-Uwe Nielsen, *Die Magdalenenklause im Schlosspark zu Nymphenburg* (München: Tuduv Verlag, 1990), 18–26. For broader studies of these architectural forms, see especially Susan Stewart, *The Ruins Lesson: Meaning and Material in Western Culture* (Chicago: University of Chicago Press, 2020), esp. 212–25; Reinhard Zimmerman, *Künstlichen Ruinen: Studien zu ihrer Bedeutung und Form* (Wiesbaden: Reichert, 1989); and Andrew Siegmund, *Die romantische Ruine im Landschaftsgarten: Ein Beitrag zum Verhältnis der Romantik zu Barock und Klassik* (Würzburg: Königshausen & Neumann, 2006).

5 Portrait of Ruinenberg (foreground) at Sanssouci Palace. Potsdam, Germany. Carl Daniel Freydanck, 1847. Wikimedia Commons. Public domain

such architectural remains had never been unearthed at these locations and were not indigenous to the regions in which they now stood.

Made to look ancient in spite of their recent appearance, the forged ruins of European estates convey a number of sentiments and impressions. Prominent among them is the aspiration to display connections with a world of ancient predecessors, affiliating the authority of a ruler to an idealized past. To take in the remains of supposedly distant ages was to be mindful of the great works of imagined forebears, above all those of Rome, and to be proximate to the power – political, cultural, aesthetic – that their ruins still conveyed to the audiences who would view them.[3] But fake ruins were also designed to be didactic, intimating the lesson that time attenuates what is created, even the most monumental and opulent of our achievements. This theme of loss would soon resonate among the Romantic poets,[4] perhaps most famously in Percy Shelley's

---

[3] On this theme, see especially Julia Hell's reflections on ruins, mimesis, and power in *The Conquest of Ruins: The Third Reich and the Fall of Rome* (Chicago: University of Chicago Press, 2020), 10–32. Cf. Stewart, *The Ruins Lesson*, 220–25.

[4] Nicholas Halmi, "Ruins Without a Past," *Essays in Romanticism* 11 (2011): 7–27; Thomas McFarland, *Romanticism and the Forms of Ruin: Wordsworth, Coleridge, and the Modalities of*

"Ozymandias," which was composed during this era: "Look on my Works, ye Mighty, and despair!" the crumbling inscription of the great pharaoh declares in the poem, though all that remains of the ruler's accomplishments, the speaker tells us, are a statue's two trunkless legs and its head half sunken in the sand.[5]

Though the manufacture of counterfeit ruins would reach its height in the eighteenth century CE, the practice of faking antiquities was already an ancient one. A striking example comes to us from the site of Tell Abu Habba, known in antiquity as the city of Sippar, located approximately 30km southwest of Baghdad in modern Iraq. On February 8, 1881, the eminent Iraqi-Assyrian archaeologist Hormuzd Rassam had a letter sent to the British Museum in London, on whose behalf Rassam was leading his excavation at the time. In his dispatch, Rassam writes of the recovery of a collection of inscribed objects found enclosed in a brick construction located in a palatial room made conspicuous by its bitumen floor.[6] The finds consisted of two terracotta cylinders nearly flawlessly preserved and, located beneath them, an "inscribed black stone, 9 inches long cut into the shape of a wheel of a treadmill, and ends [sic] at the top and bottom in the shape of a cross."[7]

When the writings on the item and associated cylinders were deciphered, the latter were found to be clearly from the time of Nabonidus, a Neo-Babylonian ruler of the sixth century BCE. But the stone object was more mysterious. Written on it was a text attributed to a ruler named Maništušu, third king of the Old Akkadian dynasty, who reigned in the late third millennium BCE – or some 1,500 years before the time of Nabonidus.[8] The purpose of the cruciform object, it appeared, was to commemorate details surrounding renovations made to the great Ebabbar temple at Sippar – a sanctuary that served as the domain of the region's solar deity, Shamash. Preserved in the inscription were details surrounding the extensive construction measures undertaken at the site during Maništušu's reign, including the generous funds and offerings bestowed on its priesthood by the ancient Akkadian ruler. For such reasons, the item came to be known among scholars as the "Cruciform Monument of Maništušu," an artifact valued as an important witness to the language and history of the era surrounding this lesser-known figure of the Old Akkadian period.

Fragmentation (Princeton, NJ: Princeton University Press, 1981); Sophie Thomas, *Romanticism and Visuality: Fragments, History, Spectacle* (London: Routledge, 2007).
[5] Percy Bysshe Shelley, "Ozymandias," in *The Works of Percy Bysshe Shelley*, Vol. II, 62 (New York: Gordian, 1965 [1818]).
[6] For a recent overview of this discovery, see Irving Finkel and Alexandra Fletcher, "Thinking outside the Box: The Case of the Sun-God Tablet and the Cruciform Monument," *Bulletin of the American Schools of Oriental Research* 375 (2016): 215–48.
[7] Excerpts from Rassam's letter are quoted in Ibid., 218.
[8] For translation and discussion, see Leonard King, "The Cruciform Monument of Manishtushu," *Revue d'assyriologie* 9 (1912): 91–105.

6 Cruciform Monument of Maništušu. Neo-Babylonian, sixth century BCE. Creative Commons Attribution-Noncommercial-Share Alike 4.0 international (CC BY-NC-SA 4.0) license. © The Trustees of the British Museum

Three decades after its initial publication, however, a series of studies demonstrated that the object was a forgery fabricated long after Maništušu would have ruled.[9] In a detailed discussion of how the Cruciform Monument may have emerged, Irving Finkel and Alexandra Fletcher write of how the item was likely manufactured by the Sippar priesthood at a moment when Nabonidus' personal devotion to Sîn, the lunar deity, was viewed as a potential threat to their sanctuary and livelihood. During a renovation to the Ebabbar sanctuary, those who worked at the temple seized on the moment to bring to Nabonidus' attention an ancient item they had "found" during the building's restoration. On it was a venerable inscription from a distant king that happened to document strong royal financial support for the Sippar cult.[10] To further the ploy, the object was intentionally distressed to make it look antiquated, though enough of the cuneiform signs, carefully excised in an archaic cuneiform script, were safeguarded from impairment so that the claims of the inscription could still be read aloud by expert scribes before the ruler.[11] By all accounts, the gambit was successful. Nabonidus made extensive renovations to the temple and circulated copies of the monument's inscription throughout the region, suggesting that the object's authenticity had been accepted and, in time, even promoted by the ruler.[12]

But the ruse was also successful because it was realized before Nabonidus. Of all the great rulers of the long history of the kingdoms located in regions of Mesopotamia, it is Nabonidus who stands out for his fascination with the ruins of his predecessors.[13] Nabonidus even takes on the title as the one "into whose hands [the deity] Marduk entrusted the abandoned tells ($DU_6^{meš}$ na-du-ti),"[14] identifying himself as the divinely appointed caretaker of the ancient ruins

---

[9] I. J. Gelb, "The Date of the Cruciform Monument of Manishtushu," *Journal of Near Eastern Studies* 8 (1949): 346–48; Edmond Sollberger, "The Cruciform Monument," *Jaarbericht Ex Oriente Lux* 20 (1968): 50–70. Cf. Marvin A. Powell, "Naram-Sin, Son of Sargon: Ancient History, Family Names, and a Famous Babylonian Forgery," *Zeitschrift für Assyriologie* 81 (1991): 20–30; F. N. H. Rawi and A. R. George, "Tablets from the Sippar Library. III. Two Royal Counterfeits," *Iraq* 56 (1994): 135–48.

[10] Finkel and Fletcher, "Thinking outside the Box," 241. The connections between the production of this text and the famous book-finding incident during King Josiah's reign in 2 Kings 22–23 have been noted by scholars. See, for example, Nadav Na'aman, "The 'Discovered Book' and the Legitimation of Josiah's Reform," *Journal of Biblical Literature* 130.1 (2011): 47–62.

[11] Finkel and Fletcher, "Thinking outside the Box," 242–43.   [12] Ibid., 245.

[13] For a discussion, see G. Goossens, "Les recherches historiques à l'époque néo-babylonienne," *Revue d'assyriologie* 42 (1948): 149–59; Paul-Alain Beaulieu, *The Reign of Nabonidus King of Babylon 556–539 B.C.* (New Haven, CT: Yale University Press, 1989), 137–43; Irene Winter, "Babylonian Archaeologists of the(ir) Mesopotamian Past," in *Proceedings of the First International Congress of the Archaeology of the Ancient Near East*, Vol. 2, eds. P. Matthiae et al., 1787–1800 (Rome: La Sapienza, 2000).

[14] Stephen Langdon, *Die Neubabylonischen Königsinschriften* (III:8) (Leipzig: J. C. Hinrichs, 2012), 274.

strewn across the Babylonian empire. At over a dozen cities Nabonidus fulfilled this vow by renovating nearly thirty buildings during his relatively brief reign (556–539 BCE)[15] – a preoccupation with restoration that was driven by a strong interest in the past and in his royal predecessors. Among the cylinders that Rassam discovered near the Cruciform Monument, for example, we read of Nabonidus' efforts at the Ebabbar temple at Sippar:[16]

> He [Nebuchadnezzar II] rebuilt that temple but after forty-five years the walls of that temple were caving in. I became troubled, I became fearful, I was worried and my face showed signs of anxiety ... I cleared away that temple, searched for its old foundation deposit, dug to a depth of eighteen cubits, and the foundation of Narām-Sîn, the son of Sargon, which for 3200 years no king before me had seen – the god Shamash, the great Lord, revealed to me the [foundation of the] Ebabbar, the temple of his contentment.

For our purposes, a number of details stand out from this section of Nabonidus' inscription. The first is the lengths to which Nabonidus' workers went in an effort to rebuild the sanctuary. Though the ancient renovators lacked our technological capacity, the inscription claims that the massive structural remains from the large building site were cleared away, and the location was excavated to a depth of around 10m. This undertaking followed those from a generation before, it is further reported, when Nebuchadnezzar II had similarly attempted to renovate the ancient temple but, apparently, had done so unsuccessfully – a recurrent problem for rulers attending to temples that were already well over a millennium old and structurally unsound.[17] Lastly, what is perhaps of most interest is the expressed aim of the operation. The inscription describes Nabonidus' primary intent as one of locating an ancient artifact, the *temennu*, or foundation deposit of the sanctuary, which no ruler had viewed for over 3,000 years. Even if this calculation substantially misses the mark (the distance between Narām-Sîn and Nabonidus was around 1,700 years), what is clearly conveyed in this text is an awareness that buried beneath the ground were artifacts from distant predecessors that could be unearthed and recovered.

---

[15] Beaulieu, *The Reign of Nabonidus*, 1; Hanspeter Schaudig, "The Restoration of Temples in the Neo- and Late Babylonian Periods: A Royal Prerogative as the Setting for Political Argument," in *From the Foundations to the Crenelations: Essays on Temple Building in the Ancient Near East and Hebrew Bible*, eds. M. Boda and J. Novotny, 141–64 (Münster: Ugarit-Verlag, 2010).

[16] Hanspeter Schaudig, *Die Inschriften Nabonids von Babylon und Kyros' des Großen samt den in ihrem Umfeld entstandenen Tendenzschriften*, 2.12 (Münster: Ugarit-Verlag, 2001), 422–38.

[17] For a discussion of the many renovations made to the Ebabbar temple in the first millennium BCE, for example, see Gerdien Jonker, *The Topography of Remembrance: The Dead, Tradition and Collective Memory in Mesopotamia*, trans. H. Richardson (Leiden: Brill, 1995), 153–71.

Such discoveries and their attachments to previous ages were not restricted to Sippar alone. Nabonidus states that, at the city of Ur, he undertook similar renovations to those taking place nearly simultaneously at the temple of Sîn.[18] Once more, his workers came across items from many centuries before. Unearthed among the temple remains was a (presumably authentic) stele from the time of Nebuchadnezzar I (late twelfth century BCE) with an elaborate image of the high priestess who had once served the sanctuary, in addition to descriptions of rites and ceremonies that had been connected to the venerable temple. A further inscription details that when Nabonidus learns of the artifact and examines the image, he orders the long-abandoned office of the high priestess to be restored, installs his own daughter in the role, and gives her an archaic, ancient Sumerian name: En-nigaldi-Nanna.[19]

That a putative monument from long ago could deceive the king is not then surprising, so sensitive was Nabonidus to the possibility that items from the past were resonant with meaning for the present. Nabonidus' numerous digs have even led scholars to label him an early "archaeologist,"[20] driven by a fascination with more distant periods and predecessors that had especially taken hold among rulers in the Neo-Babylonian period (ca. 626–539 BCE). This "antiquarian interest," as Paul-Alain Beaulieu terms it in his study of Nabonidus' reign, could be expressed through different activities and representations, including what was one of the first recorded restorations of an ancient artifact when a nearly two-millennia-old statue of Sargon the Great was refurbished.[21] Though Nabonidus is known as the "Mad King" who famously withdrew from Babylon at the height of his reign to reside at the oasis of Teyma, he was nevertheless also a scrupulous ruler who exercised vast resources to recover and safeguard materials from former times, often in an attempt to connect himself with more venerable forebears.[22]

At the outset to this study, the example of Nabonidus reminds us that we are not the first to be drawn to ruins and to wonder about what they signify, nor are we the first to locate traces of previous generations beneath the ground. And, though there is nothing in the Hebrew Bible that corresponds to the rich descriptions offered by Neo-Babylonian rulers of their attempts to unearth older structures and collect their relics, a similar fascination with distant

---

[18] Schaudig, *Die Inschriften Nabonids*, P4, 590–94. [19] Ibid., 2.7, 373–77.
[20] Winter, "Babylonian Archaeologists," 1792; Francis Joannès, *The Age of Empires: Mesopotamia in the First Millennium BC* (Edinburgh: Edinburgh University Press, 2004), 131–32.
[21] Beaulieu, *Reign of Nabonidus*, 139.
[22] Winter, "Babylonian Archaeologists," 1794. On this point, see also Beaulieu, *Reign of Nabonidus*, 137–43; Paul-Alain Beaulieu, "Nabonidus the Mad King: A Reconsideration of His Steles from Harran and Babylon," in *Representations of Political Power: Case Histories and Times of Change and Dissolving Order in the Ancient Near East*, eds. M. Heinz and M. Feldman, 137–66 (Winona Lake, IN: Eisenbrauns, 2007).

ancestors and origins is also found across the biblical writings, as is a recognition that individual mounds (תל) and sites of wreckage (חרבת) among other ruins, are the vestiges left behind by former populations. The Hebrew scribes responsible for the biblical writings, as with the Neo-Babylonians, and as with us, were aware that they were latecomers to a world inhabited long before.

There is much, then, that connects our experience of ruins with experiences from antiquity.[23] But the divide between then and now that this chapter pursues also pertains to the example of Nabonidus, one whose attempts to disinter older buildings and recover relics can feel so similar to our own efforts at archaeological excavation today. A usurper to the throne, Nabonidus was confronted by questions of legitimacy that dogged him throughout his reign. He was also by all accounts pious, a devotee of the deity Sîn in ways that could make him politically vulnerable within a capital city and empire whose chief god of the pantheon was Marduk.[24] The motivations at work in Nabonidus' renovation efforts, accordingly, were often driven by political calculation and personal devotion rather than by a historical interest in how previous populations – whether at Sippar, Ur, or elsewhere – once lived.[25] Having ascended to the throne via a coup, Nabonidus was eager to demonstrate his royal authority by situating himself among the great rulers of old, rebuilding what they had built and carefully attending to those remains – inscriptions, sculptures, temples – that they had left behind. Materials from the past were drawn on by Nabonidus to solidify claims of being able to rule in the present.

But what we do not find expressed within Nabonidus' inscriptions is what Hanspeter Schaudig, in his extensive study of these texts, terms an "awareness" of historical development and change.[26] Instead, Schaudig argues that what permeates these writings is a mostly "unhistorical worldview" rendered "anachronistically," whereby past and present are depicted as predominantly coincident and deeply connected, with Nabonidus' rule portrayed in such a way as to foreground an abiding continuity with more ancient rulers of the region.[27] It is for such reasons that Nabonidus resolves to reinstate the practices described

---

[23] On this point, see again the rich discussion in Winter, "Babylonian Archaeologists," 1787–1800.

[24] Beaulieu, *Reign of Nabonidus*, 183–85, 203.

[25] On the religious dimensions of Nabonidus' renovation efforts, see Goossens, "Les recherches historiques," 149–59. On the political, see especially Schaudig, "The Restoration of Temples," 155–61.

[26] Hanspeter Schaudig, "Nabonid, der 'Archäologe auf dem Königsthron': Zum Geschichtsbild des ausgehenden neubabylonishcen Reiches," in *Festschrift für Burkhart Kienast*, ed. G. Selz, 447–97 (Münster: Ugarit-Verlag, 2003), 492. Schaudig writes, "Even in our own culture it took a long time until an awareness emerged of the changes that occurred in times past." ("Auch in unserer eigenen Kultur hat es lange gedauert, bis sich aus dem Bewußtsein über vergangene Zeit eine Erkenntnis der dadurch entstandenen Veränderungen ergeben hat.")

[27] Schaudig remarks, "The worldview was at its core unhistorical and 'history' was often perceived with an anachronistic displacement of the present to the past." ("Das Weltbild war

in the Cruciform Monument at Sippar and to reestablish the role of the high priestess at Ur, rather than relegating these conventions to past societies whose practices are now obsolete.

From this perspective, the similarities between Nabonidus' digging activities and those excavations undertaken today, Schaudig argues, are superficial.[28] Nowhere in these royal writings is there a historical sense of the asymmetries in lived experience that distinguish past from present, of how different life under the Sargonids in the third millennium BCE would have been, for example, from that of the sixth century BCE when Nabonidus ruled. Instead, these inscriptions view the distant past as an exemplar for the present, the practices and customs of previous ages serving as an ideal to which the present should return. In short, what induced Nabonidus' efforts to excavate old buildings were desires and motivations other than those that would arise in the eighteenth through nineteenth centuries CE, a period that developed a distinct historical mindset toward material remains not long after the time when the Magdalenenklause's fake ruins had been completed.[29]

The intent of this chapter is to chart these changing attitudes toward ruins by investigating the worlds in which they arose. This study begins in antiquity, where I draw on past decades of archaeological research to survey the landscapes that would have been visible to the biblical writers and their contemporaries. What comes to light through this investigation is an ancient terrain that enclosed ruins from two millennia of settlement activity, leaving the lands familiar to the biblical writers populated by the remains of both distant and more recent societies. Of course, passages scattered throughout the Hebrew Bible recognize the belatedness of the Israelite people and their communities in Canaan (i.e., Num 13–14; Deut 26:1–9; Judges 1; Pss 78, 105). Yet only with the advent of archaeological research has it become clear that these texts were written down within an already ancient landscape, of fallen Bronze and Iron Age settlements that still bore the traces of those communities who had once inhabited them.

---

im Kern unhistorisch und 'Geschichte' wurde oft mit anachronistischer Übertragung der damaligen Gegenwart auf die Vergangenheit wahrgenommen.") Schaudig, "Nabonid," 491.

[28] Ibid., 492. Trigger, in his expansive overview of archaeological thought, concludes in a similar vein that in antiquity "nothing resembling a discipline of archaeology emerged in any of these civilizations." Bruce Trigger, *A History of Archaeological Thought*, 2nd ed. (Cambridge: Cambridge University Press, 2006), 31. This argument is also found in Rojas's recent study of Anatolian remains examined and unearthed by later Roman inhabitants: "Referring to situations in antiquity as evidence of 'archaeology' (and, as is also frequently done, labeling ancient individuals 'archaeologists') obscures cultural and historical specifics and poses a teleological trap." Felipe Rojas, *The Pasts of Roman Anatolia: Interpreters, Traces, Horizons* (Cambridge: Cambridge University Press, 2019), 6.

[29] Schaudig, "Nabonid," 492.

But, though these writings depict cities and objects of ruination that archaeologists – thousands of years later – would unearth, their descriptions of these remains depart from our understanding of them in a fundamental detail. This point of disconnect, I will argue, is the temporal framework within which ruined sites are situated in the biblical accounts. Despite the recognition in these writings of the venerable character of many ruined settlements, how ruins are located in time is frequently opposed to how we think about the history of these remains today.

The final movement of this chapter is focalized on an era when an understanding of ruins takes a decisive turn. Following what Reinhart Koselleck describes as the *Sattelzeit* period,[30] this investigation examines a transitional or bridgelike era that stretched from roughly 1750–1850 CE, when pivotal new experiences of time and history emerged. This century finds significance for our study because it also marks the moment when ruins came to be thought about differently. François René de Chateaubriand, whom we will encounter later on a visit to Pompeii, describes this experience vividly in his memoirs from the early nineteenth century CE, remarking, "I have found myself caught between two ages as in the conflux of two rivers, and I have plunged into their waters"[31] What awaited Chateaubriand and those of his generation across this waterway was unknown, but what was clear to these individuals was that there was no retreat to a time before: "Turning regretfully from the old bank upon which I was born," Chateaubriand writes, he advances "towards the unknown shore at which the new generations are to land."[32]

For Koselleck, the significance of this timeframe resides in how those who lived within it expressed a feeling of dramatic acceleration in the spheres of economics, politics, and technology, wherein the "space of experience" and "horizon of expectation" were felt to be increasingly torn apart.[33] Said differently, the past became progressively unbound from the present during this century, Koselleck contends, no longer able to serve as a paradigm for how future societies should order themselves and flourish. The lives of those in previous generations became ever more detached from contemporary

---

[30] Reinhart Koselleck, "Einleitung," in *Geschichtliche Grundbegriffe: Historisches Lexikon zur politisch-sozialen Sprache in Deutschland*, Vol. I, ed. O. Brunner, W. Bonze, and R. Koselleck, XIII–XXVII (Stuttgart: Klett-Cotta, 1972), XV. From a much different theoretical vantage point but with arguments about this time period that are in many ways similar to Koselleck's, see Michel Foucault, *The Order of Things: An Archaeology of the Human Sciences* (London: Routledge, 2002 [1966]), esp. pp. xii, xxv, 235–39, and 400–6.

[31] François René de Chateaubriand, *The Memoirs of François René, Vicomte de Chateaubriand*, trans. A. Teixeira de Mattos (London: Freemantle, 1902), xxiv.

[32] Ibid., xxiv.

[33] See "'Space of Experience' and 'Horizon of Expectation'" in Reinhart Koselleck, *Futures Past: On the Semantics of Historical Time*, trans. K. Tribe, 26–42 and 255–76 (New York: Columbia University Press, 2004).

experiences, it is maintained, reduced to something distant and unfamiliar. This chapter concludes by reflecting on what Paul Ricoeur terms, in his own reading of Koselleck, our "historical condition," a horizon against which the remaining chapters of this book, devoted to the experience of the ruins in antiquity, will be set.[34]

§

The lands the biblical writers inhabited were already ancient. Among the remains left behind from populations come and gone were those of monumental cities that had fallen long ago, their appearance – like the Roman ruins described by Anglo-Saxon poets in the poem that begins this chapter – conveying a world of "master-builders" from distant times, whose practices could appear more advanced than those of the present. Other remnants were of ancient temples built for deities no longer worshipped and of cultic objects whose meanings had been lost. Visible, too, was the wreckage left behind of the many kingdoms and empires who sought to control the narrow strip of land in which the biblical stories are set, a region positioned on the strategic crossroads located between the Mediterranean Sea and the Arabian Desert. Remains from the lengthy periods of Egyptian involvement in the southern Levant would have been apparent, for example, as were the traces of Aramean campaigns from the north and local resistance to these incursions. But most resonant for those behind the biblical writings were the ruins that arose from the later Assyrian and Babylonian invasions of the region, their conquests bringing the Iron Age to a close and, with that, the end of the kingdoms of Israel and Judah.

In the current chapter, we journey amid this landscape of ruins, taking in the remains that would have been visible to those who wrote and revised those texts that came to be included in the Hebrew Bible. Because these documents were composed over the course of a thousand years – extending, roughly, from the beginning of the first millennium BCE to its end – this investigation proceeds by considering key sites of ruin that existed during these centuries. We begin by examining Bronze Age ruins (ca. 3100 BCE–1175 BCE) that would have endured into the first millennium BCE, including at several locations that are referred to in the Hebrew Bible itself. This circuit then leads to another, where we investigate Iron Age ruins (ca. 1175 BCE–586 BCE) that arose nearer to the time when the biblical writings were first being composed, culminating with the destruction of Jerusalem by the Babylonian Empire.

---

[34] Paul Ricoeur, *Memory, History, Forgetting*, trans. K. Blamey and D. Pellauer (Chicago: University of Chicago Press, 2004), 281–342. On this concept, see also the penetrating remarks of Hayden White, "Guilty of History? The *Longue Durée* of Paul Ricoeur," *History and Theory* 46 (2007): 233–51.

That ruins were familiar to those behind the Hebrew Bible is evident throughout their writings. With hundreds of references scattered across nearly every scroll now included in this corpus, the frequency and variety of allusions to older remains in these texts attest to a widespread awareness among its authors of older locations and objects that had fallen into disrepair.[35] It is a persistent feature of these writings, furthermore, that the ruins described are not vestiges of a mythic past or located among the domains of the gods,[36] such as when the messengers of Baal descend to the ruin mounds that mark the entrance to the Kingdom of Death in the Ugaritic epic that bears this deity's name (*CAT* 1.4, viii 4).[37] Rather, in the Hebrew Bible ruins are portrayed consistently as the remains of human activity, affiliated most often with what has been left behind from the destruction or abandonment of inhabited sites.

My aim here is to consider the ruined terrain that is reflected in these writings. In turning to what archaeologists have unearthed in the lands of the southern Levant, we are offered a more robust and detailed impression of the landscapes that the biblical writers and their contemporaries would have known, landscapes that will feature as well in Chapters 2–4.[38] What becomes

---

[35] There are fourteen distinct lexemes in the Hebrew Bible that have connotations associated with ruins or material remains the biblical writers identify with destruction or decay. Some are *hapax legomena*, such as in Amos 9:11, where it is proclaimed that the sukkah of David will be raised up at a moment in the future, including the rebuilding of "its ruins" (הרסתיו), a nominal form of the more common verbal expression "to tear, break down (הרס)" that occurs only in this passage. Other terms appear sparingly, as in Psalm 89, where the poet speaks of how Yahweh had "broken down the walls" of the anointed one and "laid his strongholds in rubble" (מחתה) [Ps 89:41]), and, in another psalm (74:3), where a request is made that this deity be directed toward the "enduring ruins" (משאות נצח)of Mt. Zion. Both expressions, though rare, nevertheless share affiliations with emotions of dismay (חתת)or devastation (שאה) that appear with more frequency in biblical writings. The bulk of references to ruins in the Hebrew Bible are, however, expressed through words derived from three roots, √חרב √שמם and √שחת, and three terms that appear only as nouns (√עוה)עי, תל(√תלל), and גל(√גלל). For further discussion, see Daniel Pioske, "'And I Will Make Samaria a Ruin in the Open Country': On Biblical Ruins, Then and Now," *Revue Biblique* 129.2 (2022): 161–82.

[36] On the various mythic understandings of ruins among Greco-Roman societies, for example, see the discussion in Rojas, *The Pasts of Roman Anatolia*, 61–103.

[37] For a study of this passage, see Matthew Suriano, "Ruin Hills at the Threshold of the Netherworld: The Tell in the Conceptual Landscape of the Ba'al Cycle and Ancient Near Eastern Mythology," *Die Welt des Orients* 42.2 (2012): 210–30. On this broader distinction, see Robert Kawashima, "Covenant and Contingence: The Historical Encounter between God and Israel," in *Myth and Scripture: Contemporary Perspectives on Religion, Language, and Imagination*, ed. D. Callender, Jr., 51–70 (Atlanta: SBL Press, 2014).

[38] Elizabeth Bloch-Smith makes the crucial point that the ruins visible to the biblical writers were assuredly more prevalent and encompassing than what we can ascertain through our current knowledge established by way of archaeological surveys and excavations (personal communication). That is, in addition to the many sites discussed below, the ruins of further settlements would have also been apparent in antiquity. What we perceive of the ruined landscapes visible in the first millennium BCE, in other words, is only a partial glimpse into a world that featured far more remains than what we currently know.

apparent through this survey is that the depictions of ruins found in the biblical corpus are a product of lived experience, of real and meaningful encounters with the remains of past communities strewn throughout the terrain of the southern Levant.

1.1 BRONZE AGE RUINS

1.1.1 *The Early Bronze Age II–III (ca. 3100–2500 BCE)*

The antiquity of the ruins encountered by those living in the first millennium BCE could be considerable, reaching back into even the Neolithic and Chalcolithic eras, when some of the first settlements in the region, such as that at Jericho, were founded. But many of the oldest ruins still visible to the biblical writers would have descended from the Early Bronze Age (EBA) II–III periods (ca. 3100–2300 BCE). Around 3100 BCE a new settlement network appeared for the first time in the history of the southern Levant, one characterized, as Raphael Greenberg describes it, by a "permanent, fortified entity separated from its surroundings."[39] Some of these early locations were marked by simple mud-brick walls set on stone foundations – a type of architecture that was either replaced in later centuries or slowly weathered over time.

But at certain sites more impressive fortifications persisted. At Tell el-Far'ah (North) (biblical Tirzah), a stone rampart was positioned alongside an older mud-brick one in the EBA II period, creating walls 6m thick that were further augmented with a city gate flanked by towers that reached 7m high.[40] At Tel Beth Yerah, located just southwest of the Sea of Galilee, three successive walls enclosed an impressive 20ha settlement with paved streets situated on a grid pattern.[41] And the EBA fortifications at Tel Yarmuth (biblical Jarmuth) exceed even these.[42] In the most expansive EBA fortification system unearthed from the region, an initial stone wall came to be modified in time to include another enclosure built 20–30m in front of it, creating a massive rampart that stretched to 40m wide in certain sections. In the final phase of the EBA site, monumental stone platforms were placed in the space between the two walls, most likely

---

[39] Raphael Greenberg, *The Archaeology of the Bronze Age Levant: From Urban Origins to the Demise of City-States, 3700–1000 BCE* (Cambridge: Cambridge University Press, 2019), 71.
[40] Pierre de Miroschedji, "Far'ah, Tell el-(North)," in *New Encyclopedia of Archaeological Excavations in the Holy Land*, Volume II, 437.
[41] Raphael Greenberg, Sarit Paz, David Wengrow, and Mark Iserlis, "Tel Bet Yerah: The Hub of the Early Bronze Age Levant," *Near Eastern Archaeology* 75.2 (2012): 88–107; 91–95.
[42] Pierre de Miroschedji, "Yarmuth: The Dawn of City-States in Southern Canaan," *Near Eastern Archaeology* 62.1 (1999): 2–19; Pierre de Miroschedji, "Excavations at Tel Yarmouth: Results of the Work from 2003 to 2009," *Comptes-rendus des séances de l année – Académie des inscriptions et belles-lettres* (2013): 759–804.

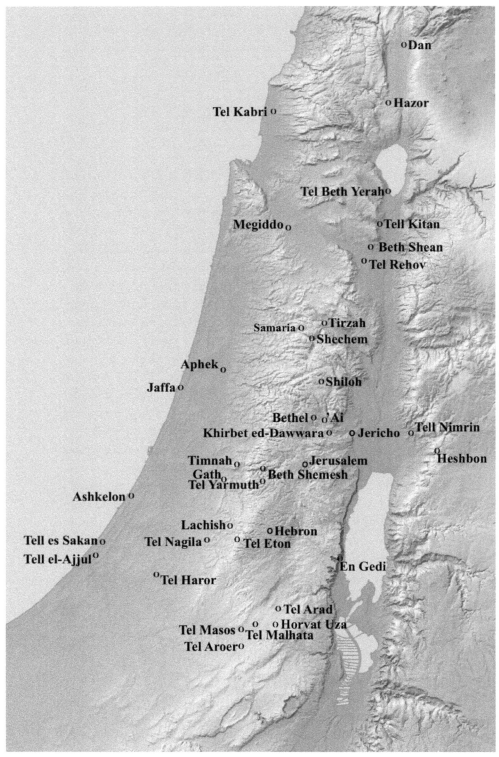

7 Map of sites of ruins discussed in this study. Author map

supporting citadels or large towers that helped guard the city. To this day, the plastered, outer wall stands to a height of 7m.[43]

Tel Yarmuth is of particular interest because it is abandoned at the end of the EBA period and left to ruin. Around a thousand years later the acropolis of the site experiences some traces of settlement activity and more definite architectural features in the Iron I period, but the extensive lower city bears few indications of rebuilding after it was deserted.[44] The small Late Bronze Age (LBA) and Iron Age communities that existed at the location would have therefore lived among the ruins of the imposing EBA center, including the remains of the impressive Palace B and the old fortifications that enclosed this lower area of the city.[45] For these later residents who came to live atop the ruin mound, daily affairs would have been shaped by the monumental debris left behind from communities who had settled Tel Jarmuth a thousand years before, and whose building projects and public architecture far exceeded what early Iron Age communities were able to muster.

Encounters such as these with ruins from an EBA past would have been a widespread phenomenon among later populations in the southern Levant. The large city of Tel Beth Yerah mentioned above, for example, is abandoned for over 2,000 years, apart from a brief moment in the Middle Bronze Age (MBA) period when archaeological evidence suggests that a potter's community plied their trade among the ruins from many centuries before.[46] The impressive site of Tell es Sakan, located just south of Gaza near the Mediterranean coast, is similarly abandoned after the EBA when new settlements are founded nearby within view of its ruins.[47] To the east, Khirbet ez-Zeraqun, situated on the Irbid Plateau in the Transjordan region and protected by walls over 3m thick, shares a similar fate, being abandoned along with its palace around 2700 BCE and never resettled.[48]

That these EBA ruins left an impression on later populations is evident in the fact that a number of these sites are referred to in the Hebrew Bible. Jarmuth, for example, is characterized in the Book of Joshua as one of the great Amorite cities of Canaan (Josh 10:3, 5, 23; 12:11; 15:35; 21:29) even though the location would have only been a modest town in the Iron Age and Persian period when the biblical stories about it were first written and revised. Two other EBA settlements also mentioned in the Hebrew Bible stand out. The first is the city of Arad, situated at the site of Tel Arad in the eastern Negev region and referred to

---

[43] de Miroschedji, "Yarmuth: Dawn of the City-States," 6.   [44] Ibid., 3, 17.
[45] Ibid., 10–12.   [46] Greenberg et al., "Tel Bet Yerah," 104.
[47] Pierre de Miroschedji et al., "Les fouilles de Tell es-Sakan (Gaza): nouvelles données sur les contacts égypto-cananéens aux IVe–IIIe millénaires," *Paléorient* 27.2 (2001): 75–104.
[48] Ibrahim Moawiyah and Siegfried Mittmann, "Zeiraqun (Khirbet El)," in *Archaeology of the Jordan II.2: Field Reports, Sites L–Z*, eds. D. Homès-Rederiq and J. B. Hennesy (Leuven: Peeters, 1989), 641–46; Greenberg, *Archaeology of the Bronze Age*, 97, 102.

8 Tel Arad. Ruins of Iron Age fortress (background) and Bronze Age Arad (foreground). Wikimedia Commons. Released into the public domain by its author, אסף.צ at the Wikipedia Project

in a number of biblical texts that describe it as a prominent Canaanite city (i.e., Num 21:1; 33:40; Josh 12:14; Judges 1:16). Over the course of eighteen seasons of excavation a large EBA settlement came into view at the location, its community flourishing in conjunction with the copper trade that passed by it during these centuries.[49] EBA Arad was enclosed by an impressive double-gated city wall that ran 1,200m in length and featured at least eleven semi-elliptical towers to guard the settlement. One of the great fortified cities of the Levant, Arad oversaw a key trade route that coursed through the region.

But as with those other EBA locations, Arad was finally abandoned around 2600 BCE and was not resettled for over 1,500 years, until, ca. 950 BCE, a small Iron Age community arose amid its ruins.[50] The LBA city referred to at moments in the Hebrew Bible, much like the city of Jarmuth, did not then exist. But what was present at these locations were monumental ruins from an EBA past.

[49] Ruth Amiran and Ornit Ilan, *Early Arad: The Chalcolithic and Early Bronze 1B Settlements and the Early Bronze II City: Architecture and Town Planning* (Jerusalem: Israel Exploration Society, 1996), 140–47; Ruth Amiran and Ornit Ilan, "Arad," in *New Encyclopedia of Archaeological Excavations in the Holy Land*, Volume I, 76–82.

[50] Amiran and Ilan, *Early Arad*, 147; Amiran and Ilan, "Arad," 82.

9 Bronze Age ruins of Tel Yarmuth. Bukvoed, photograph. Licensed under Creative Commons Attribution 4.0 International license

A similar relationship between ruins and biblical storytelling occurs in conjunction with the site of 'Ai (et-Tell). Situated 15km to Jerusalem's northeast and mentioned in a number of biblical texts, 'Ai features most prominently in an extended narrative in Josh 7–8 that recounts how it was destroyed by Israelite forces. As with other EBA cities, 'Ai was settled initially in the EBA I era and subsequently grew into a large, fortified location at the beginning of the EBA II period.[51] Remains of monumental public architecture, both palaces and temples, were located on the acropolis of the city, and in time the walls of 'Ai expanded in successive building phases to become 8m wide. During this time, 'Ai was the principal city of a region that, a thousand years later, Jerusalem would come to control.

Yet – much like Jarmuth, Arad, and other EBA centers – 'Ai was destroyed around 2500 BCE and abandoned for well over a thousand years. In the Iron I period a small settlement came to be built on the old terraces along the ruins of the acropolis, but this village was also soon deserted, and 'Ai was never again resettled. The biblical stories told about a great LBA city refer, therefore, to a legendary settlement that was abandoned long before the period when these biblical stories were set. But once more what prevailed at 'Ai when the biblical writers told stories about it were monumental ruins from a distant past – ruins that came to define even the location's name in Hebrew: 'Ai, the city of "the ruins" (העי), built and fallen long ago.

Remains unearthed across disparate regions of the southern Levant indicate that "prominent ruins" from the EBA "were visible to the inhabitants of the country in later periods," as Amihai Mazar observes in his overview of this

---

[51] Joseph Callaway, "New Evidence on the Conquest of 'Ai," *Journal of Biblical Literature* 87.3 (1968): 312–20; Joseph Callaway, "Excavating Ai (Et-Tell): 1964–1972," *Biblical Archaeologist* 39.1 (1976): 18–30; Joseph Callaway, "Ai," in *New Encyclopedia of Archaeological Excavations in the Holy Land*, Volume I, 39–45.

era.[52] The biblical references to Jarmuth, Arad, and 'Ai offer further evidence of this visibility, attesting to how the biblical writers were familiar with the ruins of EBA locations. Their descriptions of these sites as imposing fortified cities suggest that these stories were shaped by the EBA remains that persisted at these locations – the remnants of ancient city walls, palaces, and temples, amid other debris, giving rise to narratives that recounted how these locations had fallen in a more distant past. Though these cities were abandoned at least a thousand years before any biblical text was written down, their monumental ruins left a deep and lasting impression on those later populations who came across them, a point apparent in the fact that the biblical writers told stories about these locations long after their demise. The distance in time between 'Ai's downfall in the EBA and the Book of Joshua's story of its destruction likely approached two thousand years, or a similar distance that separates us from the Roman conquest of Britain.

But what these biblical references to EBA cities also reveal is that the actual antiquity of these settlements was lost on their later storytellers. The scribes who composed these narratives appear to have been unaware that the ruins located at these sites preceded even the era of Abraham, according to biblical chronology. None of these accounts, that is, depict EBA cities as sites that came to ruin in the mid-third millennium BCE. Even 'Ai's name suggests that the original identification of the site fell out of local memory, lost in the millennium that passed after its EBA destruction and abandonment. When stories were told about these ancient locations, the time period when these sites were destroyed was conflated with much later eras, a point to which we will turn below. Unable to distinguish between historical periods on the basis of stratigraphy, as archaeologists do today, the blurred and vague temporal framework attached to these ruins arose because knowledge of how to date these remains did not exist in antiquity, nor, for that matter, did a depth of historical time needed to account for these ancient predecessors.

1.1.2 *The Middle Bronze Age II (ca. 1800–1600 BCE)*

Though EBA ruins would have been part of the visible landscape of the first millennium BCE in the southern Levant, it is the ruins of the MBA II period that would have been most distinct. "If the second millennium can, in its entirety, be characterized as the Canaanite millennium," Greenberg writes, "then the MB II must be its high-water mark, in terms of settlement expansion and the flowering of a recognizable and distinct cultural idiom."[53] Indeed, what

---

[52] Amihai Mazar, *Archaeology of the Land of the Bible 10,000–586 BCE* (New York: Doubleday, 1990), 144.
[53] Greenberg, *Archaeology of Bronze Age Levant*, 224.

is significant about this era for our purposes is that it represents the "zenith of urban development" in the long Bronze Age period,[54] a timeframe when impressive monumental urban centers emerged that would, at many locations, not be surpassed until the Roman era over fifteen hundred years later.

Among MBA sites, it is once again the ruins of their fortifications that would have been most conspicuous.[55] Mazar comments,[56]

> During the eighteenth and seventeenth centuries B.C.E. the art of fortification reached a level of unparalleled sophistication ... The idea was to surround the city with steep artificial slopes which will raise the level of the city wall high above the surrounding area and locate it as far as possible from the foot of the slope so that siege devices such as battering rams, ladders, and tunneling methods would not be effective. Two major types of fortifications were adopted, both of which were intended to achieve the same effect: the earth rampart and the glacis.

The result of these immense construction projects was the utter transformation of the southern Levant's landscape, where city walls came to be elevated on artificial earthen embankments that rose above the terrain and appeared across the horizon as settlements set on artificial hills.

At Shechem (Tel Balatah), for example, a massive earthen rampart was created by the site's engineers that still stands to the height of nearly 10m in its northwestern sector.[57] At Hazor, the city expanded to a remarkable 80ha during this time, or roughly twice the size of Vatican City, with its new MBA rampart rising 30m above the plain in which it sits.[58] Timnah (Tel Batash), also situated on a low alluvial plain, had its nearly precise square rampart carefully oriented toward the cardinal directions,[59] and a massive rampart, 70m in width, enclosed the city of Ashkelon on the Mediterranean coast.[60]

---

[54] William Dever, "The Middle Bronze Age: The Zenith of the Urban Canaanite Era," *Biblical Archaeologist* 50 (1987): 149–77; 150.

[55] For a detailed study of these fortifications, see Aaron Burke, *Walled up to Heaven: The Evolution of Middle Bronze Age Fortification Strategies in the Levant* (Winona Lake, IN: Eisenbrauns, 2008), esp. 48–73. Cf. Joel Uziel, "Middle Bronze Age Ramparts: Functional and Symbolic Structures," *Palestine Exploration Quarterly* 142.1 (2010): 24–30.

[56] Mazar, *Archaeology of the Land of the Bible*, 198.

[57] Edward Campbell, *Shechem III: The Stratigraphy and Architecture of Shechem Tell Balâtah*, Vol. 1 (Boston: American Schools of Oriental Research, 2002), 105–43; Edward Campbell, "Shechem," *New Encyclopedia of Archaeological Excavations in the Holy Land*, Volume IV: 1349–51; Dever, "The Middle Bronze Age," 155–56.

[58] Burke, *Walled up to Heaven*, 65–70; David Ussishkin, "Notes on the Middle Bronze Age Fortifications of Hazor," *Tel Aviv* 19 (1992): 274–81.

[59] Amihai Mazar, *Timnah (Tel Batash) I: Stratigraphy and Architecture* (Jerusalem: Hebrew University Press, 1997), 249–50.

[60] Lawrence Stager, "Introduction," in *Ashkelon 6: The Middle Bronze Age Ramparts and Gates of the North Slope and Other Fortifications*, eds. L. Stager, J. D. Schloen, and R. Voss, 3–23 (North Park, PA: Eisenbrauns, 2018).

10 Tel Lachish, 1936 CE. G. Eric and Edith Matson Photograph Collection. Library of Congress. Public domain

At other sites, too, including even those of a more modest size, such as Shiloh (Khirbet Seilun) or Tel Nagila, we find the construction of substantial earthen works to support new walls that encircled these settlements.[61] The result of these monumental construction projects was a landscape that suddenly featured great mounds, artificially built, on which cities now stood.

Remains of these monumental cities would have therefore endured long after they had come to ruin. Prominent among these ruins was the cyclopean masonry used to construct city walls. Consisting of stones that could reach 3m in length and over a ton in weight, Hazor, Shechem, Jerusalem, Jericho, and Hebron – among other sites[62] – all incorporated these massive boulders into walls built during the MBA period, many of which, because of their sheer size, can still be found at these locations today. In addition, new monumental gates and towers were constructed that far outpaced their EBA antecedents in terms of size and the sophistication of their engineering.[63] Flanking these gates were often large bastions or towers, though both architectural forms could appear throughout the course of a location's city wall. At Gezer, a half-dozen towers

---

[61] Ruth Amiran and Amir Eitan, "A Canaanite-Hyksos City at Tel Nagila," *Archaeology* 18 (1966): 113–23; Israel Finkelstein and Zvi Lederman, "Area H–F: Middle Bronze III Fortifications and Storerooms," in *Shiloh: The Archaeology of a Biblical Site*, ed. I. Finkelstein, 49–64 (Tel Aviv: Tel Aviv University Press, 1993).

[62] Burke, *Walled up to Heaven*, 55, 234, 271, 282, 307; Dever, "The Middle Bronze Age," 154.

[63] The six-pier gate is most typical of MBA cities, constructed on a direct-axis passageway and typically incorporating two sets of doors that permitted entry into these sites, such as examples recovered from Gezer, Megiddo, and Shechem. On this gate, see Burke, *Walled up to Heaven*, 68.

11 Tel Nagila. Amos Meron, photograph. Creative Commons Attribution-Share Alike 3.0 unported

were unearthed along its lengthy MBA enclosure, though it originally included many more,[64] and the remains of a number of impressive towers were also recovered from the MBA fortifications at Beth Shemesh, Hebron, and Jericho.[65]

---

[64] Ibid., 260–63; Dever, "Middle Bronze Age," 156–57; Joe Seger and James Hardin, "Cultural and Historical Summary: Synchronic and Diachronic Study of the Fortifications at Gezer," in *Gezer VII: The Middle Bronze and Later Fortifications in Fields II, IV, and VIII*, eds. J. Seger and J. Hardin, 12–36 (Winona Lake, IN: Eisenbrauns, 2013), 13–15.

[65] Shlomo Bunimovitz and Zvi Lederman, "Solving a Century-Old Puzzle: New Discoveries at the Middle Bronze Age of Tel Beth-Shemesh," *Palestine Exploration Quarterly* 145.1 (2014): 6–24; Burke, *Walled up to Heaven*, 276–81; Jeffrey Chadwick, "Hebron in Early Bronze III and Middle Bronze Age II: Fortification Walls in Area I.3 of the American Expedition to Hebron (Tell er-Rumeide)" in *Tell It in Gath: Studies in the History and Archaeology of Israel. Essays in Honor of Aren M. Maeir on the Occasion of His Sixtieth Birthday*, eds. J. R. Chadwick et al., 167–86 (Münster: Zaphon, 2018); Nicolo Marchetti, "A Century of Excavations on the Spring Hill at Tell es-Sultan, Ancient Jericho: A Reconstruction of Its Stratigraphy," in *The Synchronisation of Civilisations in the Eastern Mediterranean in the Second Millennium B.C. II*, ed. M. Bietak, 295–321 (Wien: Verlag der Österreichischen Akademie der Wissenschaften, 2003), 312.

12 Cyclopean stones used in Middle Bronze Age II wall and tower. Hebron (Tell er-Rumeideh). Jeffrey Chadwick, photograph. Used by permission

Within the confines of these MBA cities, the ruins of elite residences and temples would have been conspicuous. Frequently built on a monumental scale, such public architecture contributed to the idea of these settlements as an "*axis mundi*," Greenberg remarks, "linking the nether worlds to the celestial through the mediation of the man-made (or at least improved) mountain."[66] At Tel Kabri in the western Galilee region, an elaborate 6,000m^2 palace, larger than the White House, was constructed in the eastern part of the city and was notable, in part, for its large audience hall adorned with rich frescoes and paintings that bear a relationship to Minoan and Theran forms.[67] Excavations at Lachish have similarly located a large MBA palace with walls 2m thick, ashlar masonry used in its design, and rooms built with cedar wood imported from

---

[66] Greenberg, *Archaeology of the Bronze Age Levant*, 226.
[67] Assaf Yasur-Landau and Eric Cline, "The Four-Dimensional Palace: The Middle Bronze Age Palace of Kabri through Time," in *Space and Time in Mediterranean Prehistory*, eds. S. Souvatzi and A. Hadji, 231–46 (New York: Routledge, 2014); Assaf Yasur-Landau and Eric Cline, "Looking Ahead: Strategies for Moving forward and Synthesis of Stratigraphic Sequences," in *Excavations at Tel Kabri: The 2005–2011 Seasons*, eds. A. Yasur-Landau and E. Cline, 335–40 (Leiden: Brill, 2020), 336–38.

13 Gezer Stelae. Mboesch, photograph. Creative Commons Attribution-Share Alike 4.0 international license.

the far north in Lebanon.[68] Large palatial buildings were similarly located at Aphek, Megiddo, Tell Ajjul, and Jericho, among other sites.[69]

Of the temples constructed during this era, the most famous are the *migdal* or tower-temples that were positioned on raised platforms and could be seen from a great distance.[70] Examples include those unearthed at Hazor, Megiddo, and Shechem, the latter of which had walls 5m wide that supported two large towers at its entrance hall.[71] At Tel Haror, located on the Wadi esh-Sharia, a fine temple of similar form had features that were partially preserved in situ

---

[68] David Ussishkin, "Area P: The Middle Bronze Age Palace," in *The Renewed Excavations at Lachish (1973–1994)*, Vol. 1, ed. D. Ussishkin, 140–87 (Tel Aviv: Tel Aviv University Press, 2004).

[69] Moshe Kochavi, "The History and Archaeology of Aphek-Antipatris," *Biblical Archaeologist* 44.2 (1981): 75–86; 77; Lorenzo Nigro, "The 'Nordburg' of Megiddo: A New Reconstruction on the Basis of Schumacher's Plan," *Bulletin of the American Schools of Oriental Research* 293 (1994): 15–29; Holly Winter, "Tell el-'Ajjul Palaces I and II: Context and Function," *Palestine Exploration Quarterly* 150.1 (2018): 4–33; Lorenzo Nigro, "The Built Tombs on the Spring Hill and the Palace of the Lords of Jericho ('dmr Rha) in the Middle Bronze Age," in *Exploring the Longue Durée: Essays in Honor of Lawrence E. Stager*, ed. J. Schloen, 261–76 (Winona Lake, IN: Eisenbrauns, 2009).

[70] Matthew Sussnow, *The Practice of Canaanite Cult: The Middle and Late Bronze Ages* (Münster: Zaphon, 2021), 54–65.

[71] Campbell, *Shechem III*, 145–51; Campbell, "Shechem," *New Encyclopedia of Archaeological Excavations in the Holy Land*, Volume IV: 1349–51. Dever, "Middle Bronze Age," 166–68.

because of an earthquake that collapsed the structure. But Hazor stands out, once again, not only for its large "Southern Temple" that stems from this period but also for a cultic precinct located to the southeast of this building that featured more than thirty standing stones in what appears to be an open-air sanctuary.[72] A large open-air sanctuary was also present at Gezer, featuring ten imposing megalithic stelae, some over 3m tall, coordinated along a north-south axis.[73]

For our purposes, the great cities of the MBA find significance because of how their remains left a lasting imprint on the southern Levant's terrain. Aaron Burke observes how the ruins of this era are distinguished by being "still visible across the landscape," surviving "like the pyramids of Egypt" four thousand years later due to their "impressive size" and the "enormous quantity of material and labor" that were required for their formation.[74] But, as with the demise of EBA cities, so, too, did the MBA period come to a close through a series of widespread destructions and abandonments, most occurring during the decades around 1600 BCE.[75] At a few sites, such as Aphek,[76] Jaffa,[77] Hazor,[78] and Jerusalem,[79] renewed or continued settlement persisted in the centuries after. Yet, as with a number of EBA settlements, many MBA sites went unoccupied for hundreds of years after their downfall, and some for millennia, leaving their monumental ruins lying largely uninhabited. Geographically, these deserted sites could be found across the southern Levant: The large palatial estate at Tel Kabri is destroyed in the seventeenth century BCE and is not resettled until a small fortress appears in the Iron IIA period some seven centuries later;[80] Tell Nimrin, a prominent site in the Jordan valley located 16km east of Jericho, is abandoned for over five centuries

---

[72] Sharon Zuckerman, "The Temples of Canaanite Hazor," in *Temple Buildings and Temple Cult*, ed. J. Kamla, 99–125 (Wiesbaden: Harrasowitz Verlag, 2012), 111–13. Sussnow, *Practice of Canaanite Cult*, 52.

[73] William Dever, "The Middle Bronze Age 'High Place' at Gezer," *Bulletin of the American Schools of Oriental Research* 371 (2014): 17–57.

[74] Burke, *Walled up to Heaven*, 3.   [75] Greenberg, *Archaeology of the Bronze Age Levant*, 263.

[76] Moshe Kochavi, "The Aphek Acropolis in Context," in *Aphek-Antipatris II: The Remains on the Acropolis*, 592–603 (Tel Aviv: Emery and Claire Yass Publications, 2009).

[77] Aaron Burke, "Early Jaffa: From the Bronze Age to the Persian Period," in *The History and Archaeology of Jaffa*, Vol. 1, 63–78 (Los Angeles: Cotsen Institute of Archaeology Press, 2011).

[78] Amnon Ben-Tor et al., "The Late Bronze Age Strata XV–XIII (Strata XV–XIII)," in *Hazor VII: The 1990–2012 Excavations, The Bronze Age*, ed. A. Ben-Tor et al., 66–144 (Jerusalem: Israel Exploration Society, 2017).

[79] Joe Uziel, Yuval Baruch, and Nahshon Szanton, "Jerusalem in the Late Bronze Age – The Glass Half Full," in *The Late Bronze and Early Iron Ages of Southern Canaan*, ed. A. Maeir et al., 171–84 (Berlin: De Gruyter, 2019).

[80] Meir Edrey et al., "The Iron Age Lower Settlement at Kabri Revisited," *Palestine Exploration Quarterly* 152.2 (2020): 94–120.

after its MBA destruction;[81] and the MBA fortifications at Tel Malhata and Tel Masos, both situated in the Beersheba Valley in the Negev, are also destroyed and deserted for half a millennium.[82]

Yet from the perspective of the biblical writings, the most meaningful MBA site is that of Jericho. Though preceded by a number of earlier settlements in the long history of the location, in the MBA Jericho was rebuilt on a more massive scale, expanding well beyond the confines of the EBA settlements that had once resided there. Like other locations of its time, Jericho came to be encircled by a rampart built of cyclopean stones, creating a fortification line that included the spring on which Jericho was originally founded ('Ain es-Sultan) and which enclosed a large palatial building, termed the "Hyksos Palace" in earlier excavations.[83] An impressive temple from the Spring Hill area of the settlement has also been recovered just inside the city gate of the upper city, as has a domestic quarter from the lower area of the city.[84]

The history of Jericho was nevertheless a volatile one. Destroyed three different times in the MBA, the city was much reduced in the centuries that followed the final assault against it. An administrative text suggests that some activity was carried out at the site a few hundred years later in the fourteenth century BCE,[85] though physical remains of this settlement are modest and much reduced from its previous MBA stature.[86] After this period of occupation, Jericho was again abandoned apart from faint traces of activity in the Iron I period and not rebuilt until sometime in the tenth through ninth centuries BCE, or well over half a millennium after the large MBA city had been destroyed.[87]

---

[81] James Flanagan et al., "Tell Nimrin: Preliminary Report on the 1993 Season," *Annual of the Department of the Antiquities of Jordan* 38 (1994): 205–44.

[82] Izthaq Beit-Arieh and Liora Freud, *Tel Malḥata: A Central City in the Biblical Negev*, Vol. 1 (Tel Aviv: Amery and Claire Yass Publications in Archaeology, 2015), 739; Itamar Singer, "The Middle Bronze Age Fortified Enclosure," in *Ergebnisse der Ausgrabungen auf der Ḥirbet el-Mšaš (Tel Masos), 1972–75*, 186–97 (Wiesbaden: Otto Harrassowitz, 1983).

[83] Burke, *Walled up to Heaven*, 275–82; Lorenzo Nigro, "The Built Tombs on the Spring Hill and the Palace of the Lords of Jericho," 361–76; Lorenzo Nigro, "Tell es-Sultan 2015: A Pilot Project for Archaeology in Palestine," *Near Eastern Archaeology* 79:1 (2016): 4–17; 5, 14–15; Lorenzo Nigro, "The Italian-Palestinian Expedition to Tell es-Sultan, Ancient Jericho (1997–2015): Archaeology and Valorisation of Material and Immaterial Heritage" in *Digging up Jericho: Past, Present and Future*, ed. R. T. Sparks et al., 175–214 (Oxford: Archeopress, 2020), 196–202.

[84] Marchetti, "A Century of Excavations on the Spring Hill at Tell es-Sultan," 312–14; Nigro, "Tell es-Sultan 2015," 14–16; Nigro, "The Italian-Palestinian Expedition to Tell es-Sultan," 202.

[85] S. Smith, "Report on a Tablet from Jericho," *Annals of Archaeology and Anthropology* 21 (1934): 116–17.

[86] So Burke: "To date there has been no evidence for the fortifications of Jericho during the Late Bronze Age." Burke, *Walled up to Heaven*, 282.

[87] Nigro, "Tell es-Sultan," 16–17. In the Iron IIC period (late eighth–early sixth centuries BCE), Jericho flourished, expanding beyond its walls for the first time in its lengthy history. Nigro, "The Italian-Palestinian Expedition to Tell es-Sultan," 206.

For the biblical writers, Jericho was therefore a site of ruins. These remains would have descended from successive cities built and destroyed over the course of two thousand years prior to when the biblical stories about the location were first written down. Even the notable late Iron Age settlement that eventually arose at Jericho would have been surrounded by prominent ruins from a MBA past, particularly from the massive rampart and defensive fortifications that had once guarded the city. If the large and monumental city of the LBA portrayed in the famous story about its downfall in the Book of Joshua did not, then, exist (Josh 6), what was apparent at Jericho during the time of the biblical writers were ancient ruins from a distant past.[88] The stories told about the conquest of this site would have been in keeping with those told about the EBA cities whose ruins also gave rise to biblical accounts of how they came to be.

Among locations that continued to be occupied in the centuries after the MBA ended, the ruins of this period would have stood out to later inhabitants. Many such settlements, in fact, were located in the heart of the central hill country where a number of biblical stories are set. Shechem, Shiloh, Bethel, Jerusalem, and Hebron, for example, all contained communities who lived among the ruins left behind from the MBA period. At Shechem, later residents attempted to reuse what they could salvage of the MBA fortification system in the centuries that followed,[89] and recent excavations from Hebron suggest that the large MBA rampart was still in use in the Iron Age II period many centuries later, with new fortification elements added to it at this time.[90] Shiloh's Iron I community built into the ruins of the MBA wall that encompassed the site to support their new structures,[91] and later residents of Jerusalem inhabited a location whose "very large" MBA wall would have been a striking feature of the landscape, attesting to Jerusalem's importance hundreds of years before Iron Age populations occupied the site.[92] When stories were told about Israel's early past in Canaan, this is to say, they were often performed and written

---

[88] Nigro writes in a similar vein, "The ruins at Tell es-Sultan are far older than the alleged date of Joshua's conquest ... Nonetheless, the already famous ruins of Jericho were exploited by the biblical author giving them an everlasting fame." Nigro, "The Italian-Palestinian Expedition to Tell es-Sultan," 204.

[89] Campbell, *Shechem III*, 169.

[90] David Ben-Shlomo, "New Evidence of Iron Age II Fortifications at Tel Hebron," in *The Last Century in the History of Judah: The Seventh Century BCE in Archaeological, Historical, and Biblical Perspectives*, eds. F. Capek and O. Lipschits, 63–88 (Atlanta: Society of Biblical Literature Press, 2019).

[91] Israel Finkelstein, "Conclusion," in *Shiloh: The Archaeology of a Biblical Site*, 383–84 (Tel Aviv: Institute of Archaeology of Tel Aviv, 1993).

[92] Aren Maeir, "Assessing Jerusalem in the Middle Bronze Age: A 2017 Perspective," *New Studies in the Archaeology of Jerusalem and Its Region* 11 (2017): ★64–★74. Cf. Ronny Reich and Eli Shukron, "A New Segment of the Middle Bronze Fortification in the City of David," *Tel Aviv* 37 (2010): 141–53; Alon De Groot and Hannah Bernick Greenberg, *Excavations at the*

14 Cyclopean wall. Jericho (Tell es-Sultan), 1900 CE. G. Eric and Edith Matson Photograph Collection. Library of Congress. Public domain

down in the shadows cast by the ruins of the region's Middle Bronze Age centers. The impression left by these physical remains is perhaps most evident in the story recalled about the fall of Jericho in Joshua 6 and the miraculous collapse of its great wall. But the lesser-known accounts of the Anakim at Hebron (Num 13:22; Josh 11:21), the covenant renewal ceremony at Shechem (Josh 24), or Samuel's early career at Shiloh (1 Sam 1–3) were stories also set at

City of David 1978–1985 Directed by Yigal Shiloh, Vol. VIIA (Jerusalem: Hebrew University of Jerusalem, 2012), 148–54.

sites where monumental ruins from the MBA period endured.[93] When David conquers Jerusalem (2 Sam 5:6–9), later audiences of this story could have envisioned David surmounting the city's old walls and occupying what remained of ruined structures from long ago, though these individuals would not have known who was actually responsible for the ruins that were visible at the site or how they came to be. Of the great cities of the MBA, the biblical writers knew little of their origins or their demise.

1.1.3 The Late Bronze Age (ca. 1550–1175 BCE)

The settlements that appeared in the centuries that followed the MBA were often much diminished from their predecessors, both in terms of their infrastructure and the size of their populations. The traces these locations left on the landscape of the southern Levant were therefore more sporadic and less evident than those of their predecessors, at moments enclosed within the larger EBA or MBA ruins that surrounded them or lodged at sites that would become more imposing during later centuries. Nevertheless, certain remains from LBA sites would have been visible in the centuries that followed.

Some of these ruins were those left behind from Egyptian rule. During the course of the fifteenth century BCE, Egyptian incursions into the Levant brought much of the region under its control, its jurisdiction continuing for three centuries until Egyptian power finally receded with the waning of the LBA international system of which it was involved.[94] It is a feature of Egyptian policy during this era, however, that, though an Egyptian presence "was pronounced" culturally, it was "structurally limited," its authority often exercised via intermediaries and local leaders loyal to Egypt rather than through the destruction and reconstruction of locations that Egypt sought to command.[95] The result of this strategy was that the material assemblages found among LBA sites in Canaan could evince an abundance of Egyptian wares or those

---

[93] Ronald Hendel, for example, has called attention to biblical stories that identify giants located at sites where monumental Bronze Age remains were present, thus accounting for the massive building projects from centuries before. Ronald Hendel, "The Landscape of Memory: Giants and the Conquest of Canaan," in *Collective Memory and Collective Identity: Deuteronomy and the Deuteronomistic History in Their Context*, eds. J. Ro and D. Edelman, 263–88 (Berlin: De Gruyter, 2021). For a similar argument about the early Iron Age period and the great ruins at Gath, see Aren Maeir, "Memories, Myths, and Megalithics: Reconsidering the Giants of Gath," *Journal of Biblical Literature* 139.4 (2020): 675–90.

[94] Aaron Burke, "Canaan under Siege: The History and Archaeology of Egypt's War in Canaan during the Early Eighteenth Dynasty," in *Studies on War in the Ancient Near East: Collected Essays on Military History*, ed. J. Vidal, 43–66 (Munster: Ugarit Verlag, 2010); Mario Liverani, "The Great Powers Club," in *Amarna Diplomacy: The Beginnings of International Relations*, eds. R. Cohen and R. Westbrook, 15–27 (Baltimore: Johns Hopkins, 2000).

[95] Greenberg, *Archaeology of the Bronze Age Levant*, 262.

influenced by them but provide less evidence of more pronounced Egyptian architectural forms.[96]

At two sites familiar to the biblical writers, however, the material footprint of Egypt was more apparent. The first is the port city of Jaffa on the Mediterranean coast (Josh 19:46; 2 Chron 2:16; Jonah 1:3; Ezra 3:7). Conquered by the Egyptians during the reign of Thutmose III (ca. 1482–1428 BCE), Jaffa was turned into an Egyptian harbor in the late fifteenth century BCE and remained under Egyptian control for the next three hundred years.[97] Of the remains left behind from the Egyptian garrison stationed there, the most significant known to us is the large gatehouse attached to a fortress that existed at the city during this time. The monumental façade is the most striking feature of this structure, bearing a large inscription of Ramesses II that was positioned along a passageway over 4m high and guarded by two large towers. After its destruction ca. 1125 BCE, the Ramesses Gate area evinces few traces of settlement activity until the Persian Period many centuries later, though some ephemeral Philistine material remains suggest these new inhabitants constituted a "squatter occupation" among the ruins that followed Egyptian withdrawal.[98]

The second LBA city that preserved Egyptian ruins is that of Beth-Shean. Located at the confluence of the Jordan River and Jezreel Valley, the site came under Egyptian control in the fifteenth century BCE and was used as the principal administrative center for Egyptian activities in Canaan at the time.[99] In the Ramesside period of the thirteenth century BCE, Beth-Shean was rebuilt on a more monumental scale with new temples, public buildings, and

---

[96] Ibid., 282. Cf. Anne Killebrew, "New Kingdom Egyptian-Style and Egyptian Pottery in Canaan: Implications for Egyptian Rule in Canaan during the 19th and Early 20th Dynasties," in *Egypt, Israel, and the Ancient Mediterranean World: Studies in Honor of Donald B. Redford*, eds. G. Knoppers and A. Hirsch, 309–43 (Leiden: Brill, 2004); M. A. S. Martin, "Egyptian and Egyptianized Pottery in Late Bronze Age Canaan," *Egypt and the Levant* 14 (2004): 265–84; Bernd Schipper, "Egypt and Israel: The Ways of Cultural Contact in the Late Bronze and Iron Age," *Journal of Ancient Egyptian Interconnections* 4 (2012): 30–47; Katharina Streit, "Archaeological Evidence for the Presence of Egyptians in the Southern Levant during the Late Bronze Age – A Reappraisal," *Journal of Ancient Egyptian Interconnections* 21 (2019): 68–87.

[97] Burke, "Early Jaffa," 68–70; Aaron Burke and Krystal Lords, "Egyptians in Jaffa: A Portrait of Egyptian Presence in Jaffa during the Late Bronze Age," *Near Eastern Archaeology* 73.1 (2010): 2–30.

[98] Aaron Burke et al., "Excavations of the New Kingdom Fortress in Jaffa, 2011–2014: Traces of Resistance to Egyptian Rule in Canaan," *American Journal of Archaeology* 121.1 (2017): 85–133; 128.

[99] Amihai Mazar, "Tel Beth-Shean: History and Archaeology," in *One God – One Cult – One Nation. Archaeological and Biblical Perspectives*, eds. R. G. Kratz and H. Spieckermann, 238–71 (Berlin: De Gruyter, 2010); Amihai Mazar, "The Egyptian Garrison Town at Beth-Shean," in *Egypt, Canaan and Israel: History, Imperialism, Ideology and Literature*, eds. S. Bar, D. Kahn, and J. J. Shirley, 155–89 (Leiden: Brill, 2011).

15 Replica of inscribed Ramses Gate among Egyptian ruins. Jaffa. Ricardo Tulio Gandelman, photograph. Creative Commons Attribution 2.0 generic license.

a residential quarter, featuring monuments erected on behalf of Seti I and, later, of Ramesses II. The final phase of the Egyptian center (twelfth century BCE) was characterized by still more widespread Egyptian monuments and inscriptions – "unparalleled elsewhere in Canaan,"[100] its excavator observes – that may have been fashioned in an effort to promote strength and authority during a period when Egyptian power was actually under threat.

The twelfth century BCE garrison town would soon fall, but the ruins left behind of the Egyptian center remained: In the eleventh century BCE Canaanite settlement that followed, Egyptian monuments were carefully preserved and situated within and outside the northern temple of the site, including a large statue of Ramesses III, established, perhaps, to venerate the location's past Egyptian heritage among inhabitants who, nevertheless, were no longer Egyptian.[101]

---

[100] Mazar, "Egyptian Garrison Town," 171.
[101] Mazar, "Tel Beth-Shean," 260–61; Robert Mullins, "The Late Bronze and Iron Age Temples at Beth-Shean," in *Temple Building and Temple Cult Architecture and Cultic Paraphernalia of Temples in the Levant (2.–1. Mill. B.C.E.)*, ed. J. Kamlah, 127–58 (Wiesbaden: Harrassowitz Verlag, 2012).

16 Ruin mound of Beth-Shean (background), ruins of Scythopolis (foreground). Author photograph

17 Ruins of Late Bronze Age Egyptian governor residence. Beth-Shean. Author photograph

But the most impressive LBA city is that of Hazor. One of a handful of MBA sites in the southern Levant to escape destruction, the city transitioned into the LBA period rather seamlessly, it appears, and without major disruption.[102] The acropolis of the site was, however, reorganized in the LBA, with two of the temples in the ceremonial precinct intentionally put out of use and carefully filled with earth, including the open-air sanctuary of standing stones situated outside of the South Temple, in addition to an earlier palace.[103] In their place a massive ceremonial residence was constructed in Area A of the site, replete with a fine colonnaded courtyard, basalt orthostats that lined the main hall's inner walls, and cedar beams that were incorporated into the brickwork throughout the structure. Nearby, another monumental building has been unearthed in the adjacent Area M, most likely a further palatial building.[104] These grand structures of the acropolis overlooked a city that retained its impressive 80ha size from centuries before, with Hazor easily the largest LBA settlement in the southern Levant.

18 Ruins of entrance to Late Bronze Age ceremonial center. Tel Hazor. Author photograph

---

[102] Amnon Ben-Tor, "The Ceremonial Precinct in the Upper City of Hazor," *Near Eastern Archaeology* 76.2 (2013): 81–83; Amnon Ben-Tor, *Hazor: Canaanite Metropolis, Israelite City* (Jerusalem: Israel Exploration Society, 2016), 78–89.

[103] Ben-Tor, "Ceremonial Precinct," 81–83; Ben-Tor, *Hazor*, 88–89.

[104] Ben-Tor, "Ceremonial Precinct," 85–91. Sharon Zuckerman, "'The City, Its Gods Will Return There . . .': Toward an Alternative Interpretation of Hazor's Acropolis in the Late Bronze Age," *Journal of Near Eastern Studies* 69.2 (2010): 163–78.

Nevertheless, the public buildings of the upper city came to a fiery end in the latter half of the thirteenth century BCE, at which time the extensive lower city was also abandoned.[105] Hazor became a monumental city of ruins in the time that followed, its acropolis strewn with remains of its massive buildings and its lower city never reoccupied. When later communities came to the city, they preserved the burnt remains of the acropolis, living among the ruins from centuries before. For five centuries, it appears, "the ruins of the Canaanite palace remained standing as a desolate hilltop,"[106] with Hazor's later residents carefully safeguarding the ruins by prohibiting any new building activity in this area of the site.

The fall of Hazor coincided with the destruction of a number of other LBA sites in the southern Levant, including both Jaffa and Beth-Shean, but also areas of Megiddo, Aphek, and Bethel, among others.[107] Lachish, the dominant city of the southern Shephelah – and one that flourished under Egyptian influence – also falls around 1130 BCE and is abandoned for over 200 years.[108] Located to Lachish's southwest, the fortified site of Tel Nagila is deserted near the same time, later becoming only a "hamlet or village" that was positioned amid the ruins of the old mound.[109] At Tell Kitan, located along the west bank of the Jordan River 12km north of Beth-Shean, monumental temples built near the center of the site were of such a size that there was little room for homes at the location, suggesting that the location may have functioned as a "ritual center for the surrounding settlements."[110] During the LBA, however, Tell Kitan was destroyed, perhaps by Egyptian forces, and lay in ruins for two thousand years until it was resettled in the Early Arabic period.

---

[105] Sharon Zuckerman, "Anatomy of a Destruction: Crisis Architecture, Termination Rituals and the Fall of Canaanite Hazor," *Journal of Mediterranean Archaeology* 20 (2007): 3–32; Amnon Ben-Tor and Sharon Zuckerman, "Hazor at the End of the Late Bronze Age: Back to Basics," *Bulletin of the American Schools of Oriental Research* 350 (2008): 1–6.

[106] Doron Ben-Tor, "Hazor at the Beginning of the Iron Age," *Near Eastern Archaeology* 73.2 (2013): 104. Cf. Sharon Zuckerman, "Ruin Cults at Iron Age I Hazor," in *The Fire Signals of Lachish: Studies in the Archaeology and History of Israel in the Late Bronze Age, Iron Age, and Persian Period in Honor of David Ussishkin*, eds. I. Finkelstein and N. Na'aman, 387–94 (Winona Lake, IN: Eisenbrauns, 2010).

[107] For Megiddo, see David Ussishkin, "The Destruction of Megiddo at the End of the Late Bronze Age and Its Historical Significance," *Tel Aviv* 22.2 (1995): 240–67; on Aphek, Yuval Gadot, "The Late Bronze Egyptian Estate at Aphek," *Tel Aviv* 37 (2010): 48–66; for Bethel, see Israel Finkelstein and Lily Singer-Avitz, "Reevaluating Bethel," *Zeitschrift des Deutschen Palästina-Vereins* 125.1 (2009): 33–48.

[108] David Ussishkin, "A Synopsis of the Stratigraphical, Chronological, and Historical Issues," in *The Renewed Archaeological Excavations at Lachish (1973–1994)*, Vol. I, Part I, ed. D. Ussishkin, 50–122 (Tel Aviv: Emery and Claire Yass, 2004), 62–70.

[109] Itzhaq Shai, David Ilan, Aren M. Maeir, and Joe Uziel, "The Iron Age Remains at Tel Nagila," *Bulletin of the American Schools of Oriental Research* 363 (2011): 25–43.

[110] Emmanuel Eisenberg, "The Temples at Tell Kittan," *Biblical Archaeologist* 40.2 (1977): 77–81; Emmanuel Eisenberg, "Tell Kitan," *New Encyclopedia of Archaeological Excavations in the Holy Land*, Volume III: 878–81.

At certain locations scattered throughout the southern Levant, then, ruins from the LBA would have been part of the visible landscape for those who lived in the centuries that followed. Some of these sites would have borne the traces of earlier Egyptian involvement in the region, from monuments to past pharaohs[111] to the more ubiquitous Egyptian scarabs, glyptics, faience, and pottery remains. Other locations, such as at Hazor or Tell Kitan, would have enclosed monumental remains that lay undisturbed for many centuries after the LBA ended.

In terms of the biblical writings, two features of the LBA stand out. The first is the complete absence in the Hebrew Bible of references to Egyptian control of Canaan during these centuries. Though the exodus from Egypt is the pivotal narrative of the entire biblical corpus, and though the Hebrew Bible contains a number of stories that are set in the LBA spanning from the Books of Numbers to Judges, there is not a single mention in these writings of an Egyptian presence in the Levant. This omission may be the result of the more ephemeral footprint of the Egyptians in a region that was permitted to act under the impress of local authorities and harbored few monumental Egyptian buildings outside of the administrative centers the Egyptians established. Yet, in light of the lengthy period of Egyptian hegemony in the region, the dearth of allusions to Egyptian rule among the stories told in the Hebrew Bible is remarkable. It may be that knowledge about much of this period, too, was lost by the era when the biblical writings were being formed.[112] How residents of the region understood the Egyptian ruins they would have come across in the centuries that followed Egyptian withdrawal is not conveyed in these later texts, unless these experiences were somehow woven into the strains of storytelling that pertained to the exodus story, which was said to have taken place centuries before.[113]

But alongside this absence are faint glimmers of a LBA horizon that perhaps can be discerned in these writings. Stories surrounding Hazor (Josh 11), Shechem (Judges 9), Bethel (Judges 1), and Lachish (Joshua 10), for example, all situate the destruction of these locations, roughly, within the closing moments of the LBA in which they fell. Such narratives do not demonstrate that the biblical stories communicate information about what had once taken place at these sites, particularly given that the agents behind the destruction are

---

[111] Giulia Tucci, "Egyptian Royal Statues and Stelae from Late Bronze Public Buildings in the Southern Levant," in *Proceedings of the 9th International Congress on the Archaeology of the Ancient Near East*, ed. S. Bickel, 87–102 (Wiesbaden: Harrassowitz Verlag, 2016).

[112] On this point, see Nadav Na'aman, "The 'Conquest of Canaan' in the Book of Joshua and History," in *From Nomadism to Monarchy: Archaeological and Historical Aspects of Early Israel*, eds. N. Na'aman and I. Finkelstein, 218–81 (Jerusalem: Israel Exploration Society, 1992), 223, 241–47.

[113] See, for example, the argument of Nadav Na'aman, "The Exodus Story: Between Historical Memory and Historiographical Composition," *Journal of Ancient Near Eastern Religions* 11 (2011): 38–69.

historically unknown and that the fall of Hazor and Lachish, to cite only one example, took place a century apart and not months, as the narrative in Joshua 10–11 suggests.[114] Unlike the ruins of EBA and MBA sites, however, it may be that remnants of a few LBA locations were associated with vague memories of a past that had endured with the ruins and persisted over time at these locations, memories pertaining to a violent end long ago that brought down impressive cities in the region.[115]

1.2 IRON AGE RUINS

When we enter the Iron Age period, we encounter a time when many biblical texts were first written down.[116] The ruins that arose in this era would have been more immediate to the storytellers behind these writings and, consequently, the outcome of events was often experienced by societies of which the biblical writers were part or had more recently descended. Nevertheless, it is the case that Iron Age texts would have been revised and reworked further in the generations that followed this period, whether these writers resided in the Persian (ca. 530–330 BCE) or Hellenistic (ca. 330–60 BCE) eras. And for these later communities, the ruins of Jerusalem, destroyed in 586 BCE, would be the most significant for the texts they developed.

1.2.1 *The Early Iron Age (Iron I–IIA, ca. 1175–830 BCE)*

In the wake of Egyptian withdrawal from the Levant in the twelfth century BCE, the settlements that emerged in the early Iron Age featured predominantly small, unwalled towns and villages set apart from the larger centers located on or near the coastal plain.[117] The ruins left behind from these sites would have been mostly negligible, therefore, particularly in comparison to monumental Bronze Age remains that persisted throughout the region. And though these centuries would witness unrest, the skirmishes that occurred

---

[114] For Hazor, see Zuckerman, "Anatomy of a Destruction," 3–32; on Lachish, see Ussishkin, "Synopsis," 70–72.

[115] For this argument, see especially Zuckerman, "Ruin Cults," 393; cf. Brendon Benz, "The Destruction of Hazor: Israelite History and the Construction of History in Israel," *Journal for the Study of the Old Testament* 44.2 (2019): 262–78. This point on memory and ruins will be developed at length in Chapter 2.

[116] See, for example, discussions in William Schniedewind, *How the Bible Became a Book: The Textualization of Ancient Israel* (Cambridge: Cambridge University Press, 2004), 48–63; Seth Sanders, *The Invention of Hebrew* (Urbana: University of Illinois Press, 2009), 103–56; David Carr, *The Formation of the Hebrew Bible: A New Reconstruction* (New York: Oxford University Press, 2011), 355–85; Konrad Schmid, *The Old Testament: A Literary History*, trans. L. Maloney (Minneapolis: Fortress, 2012), 53–70.

[117] For summary, see Israel Finkelstein, *The Archaeology of the Israelite Settlement* (Jerusalem: Israel Exploration Society, 1988), 237–91; Mazar, *Archaeology of the Land of the Bible*, 335–48.

were typically of a local variety rather than by the design of larger empires, the terrain of the Levant being less marked by these hostilities than by those that would take place in the centuries to follow.

For our purposes, a few ruins from this period are nevertheless meaningful. Megiddo, Shechem, and Bethel, for example, were all destroyed in the Iron I period.[118] Though Megiddo was quickly resettled, Shechem and Bethel would not be rebuilt for at least a century. And even after, neither settlement would regain its monumental stature from the centuries of the MBA.[119] At Shiloh, an Iron I community arose on the MBA ruin mound that had been abandoned since the sixteenth century BCE. This Iron Age settlement would be short-lived, however, as it was destroyed in the late eleventh century BCE after perhaps only a few decades of existence.[120] Remnants of other small, abandoned highland sites may have also endured in the region, such as the modest Iron I/early Iron IIA fortress at Khirbet ed-Dawwara[121] or the fortification tower at Giloh,[122] both situated not far from Jerusalem but also, like Shiloh, abandoned after this time. Tel Rehov, a comparatively large 10ha settlement located just south of Beth-Shean, falls in the mid-ninth century BCE, and is finally abandoned a century later.[123] In the Shephelah region further to the west, the fortified site of Khirbet Qeiyafa is destroyed in the early tenth century BCE and is thereafter deserted,[124] and the impressive Iron I city of Ekron falls near the same time, with its extensive lower city not resettled for 250 years.[125]

---

[118] Israel Finkelstein, David Ussishkin, and Baruch Halpern, "Archaeological and Historical Conclusions," in *Megiddo IV: The 1998–2002 Seasons*, Vol. 2, eds. I. Finkelstein, D. Ussishkin, and B. Halpern, 848–51 (Tel Aviv: Emery and Claire Yass Publications, 2006); Israel Finkelstein, "Shechem in the Late Bronze and Iron I," in *Timelines: Studies in Honor of Manfred Bietak*, Vol. 2, eds. E. Czerny et al., 348–56 (Leuven: Peeters, 2006); Finkelstein and Singer-Avitz, "Reevaluating Bethel," 37–38.

[119] On the possibility that a MBA temple continued in use until the Iron I period, see L. E. Stager, "The Fortress-Temple at Shechem and the 'House of El, Lord of the Covenant,'" in *Realia Dei: Essays in Archaeology and Biblical Interpretation in Honor of Edward F. Campbell, Jr. at His Retirement*, eds. P. H. Williams, Jr., and T. Heibert, 228–49 (Atlanta: Scholars Press, 1999).

[120] Finkelstein, *Shiloh*, 168–73.

[121] Israel Finkelstein, "Excavations at Khirbet ed-Dawwara: An Iron Age Site Northeast of Jerusalem," *Tel Aviv* 17 (1990): 163–208.

[122] Amihai Mazar, "An Early Israelite Settlement Site near Jerusalem," *Israel Exploration Journal* 31 (1981): 1–36.

[123] Amihai Mazar, "The Ladder of Time at Tel Rehov: Stratigraphy, Archaeological Context, Pottery and Radiocarbon Dates," in *The Bible and Radiocarbon Dating*, ed. T. Levy (London: Equinox, 2005), 193–255; Amihai Mazar, "Tel Reḥov in the Tenth and Ninth Centuries BCE," *Near Eastern Archaeology* 85.2 (2022): 110–25.

[124] Yosef Garfinkel et al., "King David's City at Khirbet Qeiyafa: Results of the Second Radiocarbon Dating Project," *Radiocarbon* 57.5 (2015): 881–90.

[125] Seymour Gitin, "Philistia in Transition: The Tenth Century and Beyond," in *Mediterranean Peoples in Transition: Thirteenth to Early Tenth Centuries BCE*, eds. S. Gitin et al., 162–83 (Jerusalem: Israel Exploration Society, 1998), 167.

19 Ruins of Early Iron Age gate complex. Khirbet Qeiyafa. Author photograph

But it is the city of Gath (Tell es-Safi) that would have left behind the most impressive ruins from this era. Located 45km southwest of Jerusalem, Gath flourished during the EBA, MBA, and Iron I–IIA periods.[126] Of these eras, however, it would be during the early Iron Age when Gath would reach its greatest prominence, becoming one of the largest cities of its time at around 40–50ha in size.[127] Recent archaeological evidence suggests that Gath's status in the early Iron Age was derived from its role in the copper trade that originated in the Arabah region and flowed through the Elah Valley to the coast,[128] in addition to the extensive tracts of agricultural land Gath commanded from atop the hill on which it was positioned, some of which were used for olive oil production.[129] From this perspective, not only was Gath an

---

[126] For an overview of these remains, see Aren Maeir, "The Tell es Safi/Gath Archaeological Project 1996–2010: Introduction, Overview, and Synopsis of Results," in *Tell es Safi/Gath I: The 1996–2005 Seasons, Part I: Texts*, ed. A. Maeir, Ägypten und Altes Testament 69, 1–88 (Wiesbaden: Harrassowitz Verlag, 2012); Aren Maeir, "Introduction and Overview," in *Tell es Safi/Gath II: Excavations and Studies*, eds. A. Maeir and J. Uziel, 3–54 (Münster: Zaphon, 2020).

[127] Maeir, "Introduction and Overview," *Tell es Safi/Gath II*, 21; Aren Maeir, "Memories, Myths, and Megalithics: Reconsidering the Giants of Gath," *Journal of Biblical Literature* 139.4 (2020): 675–90.

[128] Ibid., 28–29.

[129] Assaf Yasur-Landau, *The Philistines and Aegean Migration at the End of the Late Bronze Age* (Cambridge: Cambridge University Press, 2010), 288.

20 Iron Age fortifications of the lower city in Area D East, Gath (Tell es-Safi). M. Eniukhina, photograph. Courtesy of the Tell el-Safi Archaeological Project and Aren Maeir. Used by permission

imposing fortified city during an era when few existed in the southern Levant, but it was also an affluent one.

For such reasons, Gath was targeted by the kingdom of Damascus when its ruler, Hazael, swept south in the ninth century BCE and ravaged regions of the southern Levant. After laying siege to the location, the Arameans finally conquered Gath and destroyed it ca. 830 BCE, ending its long history of regional authority.[130] Throughout the site, evidence of Gath's destruction has been unearthed, where an 80cm layer of ash and debris has preserved vestiges of Gath's downfall.[131] After the Aramean conquest, Gath is abandoned for around a century until a smaller settlement emerges in the upper reaches of the ruined city toward the end of the eighth century BCE. This community, however, is also quickly ended when the Assyrian Empire invades the Levant at this time.[132] Subsequently, Gath is deserted once more and never rebuilt.

The ruins of Gath would lie exposed for centuries after the city was destroyed and abandoned, taking their place among the monumental remains

---

[130] Maeir, "Introduction," *Tell es Safi/Gath I*, 47–49.

[131] Dvory Namdar et al., "The 9th Century BCE Destruction Layer at Tell es-Safi/Gath, Israel: Integrating Macro- and Microarchaeology," *Journal of Archaeological Science* 38.12 (2011): 3471–82.

[132] Maeir, "Introduction," *Tell es Safi/Gath I*, 50–56.

of the great Bronze Age centers that had been overthrown before. Some Bronze Age fortifications at Gath, as at Hebron, appear, in fact, to have continued in use into the Iron Age, making the city's defenses a composite of formidable architectural features from many centuries.[133] Aren Maeir writes of how the city's former status would have been apparent to later visitors, who would have been able to view the "impressive and still visible physical remains of the city's extent, its massive fortifications, and other architectural features."[134] Among the wreckage present at the site would have been the remains of these fortifications and the debris of homes left exposed to the windblown sediments that had accumulated on them, the deep trenches and other remains of the siege system implemented by the Arameans at the time of Gath's fall, and scattered human remains of those who were not buried after Gath was overrun.[135]

Gath's stature before its fall is also apparent in the biblical writings, particularly in relation to stories surrounding David in the Book of Samuel, whose connections with the city of Gath and Gittite individuals form a significant theme in his rise to power (e.g., 1 Sam 21, 27; 2 Sam 6, 15).[136] Gath's destruction after the long period of its dominance would have been a seismic event in the early Iron Age, demonstrating to later visitors that even the largest and wealthiest of cities in the region could be overrun. Much like references to Shiloh's former standing (e.g., Josh 18–22; 1 Sam 1–4) or the brief account of Bethel's capture (Judges 1:22–26), stories connected to early Iron Age locations can be found within the biblical writings, even if the accounts as we have them now are more the creation of the centuries that followed Gath's destruction than when it stood.[137]

But one explanation for the appearance of these narratives is the ruins that prevailed. At both Gath and Shiloh, monumental remains stood among locations otherwise mostly abandoned, both also positioned on key transit routes that cut through the terrain of the southern Levant. It is perhaps not surprising,

---

[133] Maier, "Introduction and Overview," *Tell es Safi/Gath II*, 21.
[134] Maier, "Memories, Myths, and Megalithics," 686.
[135] Maeir, "Introduction," *Tell es Safi-Gath I*, 43–49.
[136] Yigal Levin, "Philistine Gath in the Biblical Record," in *Tell es Safi/Gath I: The 1996–2005 Seasons, Part I: Texts*, ed. A. Maeir, 141–52 (Wiesbaden: Harrassowitz Verlag, 2012); Daniel Pioske, "Material Culture and Making Visible: On the Portrayal of Philistine Gath in the Book of Samuel," *Journal for the Study of the Old Testament* 43.1 (2018): 3–27. On the role and identity of Gath in biblical storytelling, see also the incisive observations in the forthcoming work of Mahri Leonard-Fleckman, *Scribal Representations and Social Landscapes of the Iron Age Shephelah* (New York: Oxford University Press).
[137] Edward Greenstein, "The Formation of the Biblical Narrative Corpus," *Association for Jewish Studies Review* 15.2 (1990): 165–78; Na'aman, "The 'Conquest of Canaan,'" 218–23; Schniedewind, *How the Bible Became a Book*, 64–90; and Daniel Pioske, *Memory in a Time of Prose: Studies in Epistemology, Hebrew Scribalism, and the Biblical Past* (New York: Oxford, 2018), 30–54.

then, that the remains of both sites are referred to explicitly in later biblical texts. In the Book of Amos, for example, the leaders of Israel and Judah are summoned to "go down to Gath of the Philistines" to see what had become of it a century after its fall (Amos 6:2), its great ruins serving as a warning of what might become of Jerusalem and Samaria. Later, the Book of Jeremiah provides a similar directive to visit Shiloh and take in its remains, the already ancient ruins of the city offering a sign of Jerusalem's impending fate (Jer 7:12).

But what the archaeological record also discloses is that other remains of the early Iron Age left less of an impression on the stories that would be told about this time, particularly of an Iron I (1175–980 BCE) landscape that featured smaller settlements and villages. If Shiloh is recalled as an important settlement in the biblical writings, we are nonetheless never told how Shiloh was destroyed or by whom, nor, for that matter, are we told who resided at the fortresses of Khirbet Qeiyafa, Khirbet ed-Dawwara, or Giloh, or the circumstances surrounding the fall of Iron I Megiddo. Even an event as pivotal as David's capture of Jerusalem in the early tenth century BCE comes to us in rather cryptic form, voiced in proverbs and difficult sayings that make it challenging to reconstruct how the biblical writers understood David's acquisition of the city.[138] The impact registered by the ruins of smaller early Iron Age sites on biblical storytelling was often, in this sense, a rather modest one.

1.2.2 *The Late Iron Age (Iron IIB–IIC, ca. 830–586 BCE)*

The ruins of the late Iron Age mark the final stage of this overview. The remains left behind from this era were the result of two empires and their incursions into the southern Levant that took place a century apart. The first was that of Assyria. Beginning in the mid-eighth century BCE, the Assyrian Empire pursued a more aggressive policy under Tiglath-Pileser III toward lands in the Levant, culminating in the conquest of the kingdoms of Aleppo, Hadrach, and Damascus, among others, during the decade of the 730s BCE.[139] Israel, resisting Assyrian rule alongside Damascus in a coalition they had formed, lost the northern part of its kingdom (Galilee) in 734/733 BCE and, after a subsequent revolt, was finally conquered in 721 BCE.[140] Left in the wake of the Assyrian advance was a decimated kingdom. Avraham Faust observes that nearly all settlements in Israelite territory "show signs of

---

[138] Daniel Pioske, "Prose Writing in an Age of Orality: A Study of 2 Sam 5:6–9," *Vetus Testamentum* 66 (2016): 261–79.
[139] Amélie Kuhrt, *The Ancient Near East c. 3000–300 BC*, Vol. 2 (London: Routledge, 1995), 458–72.
[140] Bob Becking, *The Fall of Samaria: An Historical and Archaeological Study* (Leiden: Brill, 1992), 95–104.

destruction, damage, and decline, and most did not recover at all."[141] Of forty-two excavated sites, a full twenty-seven were not reoccupied or were occupied only by a handful of squatters among the ruins after the Assyrian invasion, and a further twelve locations were vastly reduced in size and population in the decades after.[142] It appears that well over 90 percent of sites in Israel were affected by the Assyrian campaign, resulting in substantial demographic upheaval and the depopulation of entire regions. For those who journeyed through Israelite lands in the aftermath of Assyria's attack, the former kingdom would have appeared, as the Book of Jeremiah describes it, like a kingdom "in ruins" (Jer 2:15).

The fallen remains of this territory would have been apparent in all quarters of its former holdings. The city of Hazor is destroyed once more at this time and evinces only "sporadic" occupation in the subsequent centuries, with a few later residents constructing poor, flimsy homes among the wreckage of the ancient city.[143] Beth-Shean is set aflame and is not settled again until the Hellenistic period half a millennium later.[144] Bethel, too, is "sparsely settled"[145] after the Assyrian advance, being rebuilt on a larger scale only centuries later during the Hellenistic period. After being subdued, Dan, Megiddo, and Tirzah are rebuilt and reoccupied afterward, though what dominates these locations are large Assyrian residences constructed by the victors to oversee the region.[146]

Two decades later, the Assyrians would attack Judah. Spurred once more by revolt among their vassals in the southern Levant, the Assyrian ruler Sennacherib invaded territories in Phoenicia, Philistia, and Judah in the final years of the eighth century BCE to bring them back into the Assyrian orbit.[147] The campaign in Judah was particularly devastating. In the fertile Shephelah region in the western part of the kingdom, Sennacherib claims to have destroyed forty-six fortified settlements in an inscription recounted about this

---

[141] Avraham Faust, "Settlement, Economy, and Demography under Assyrian Rule in the West: The Territories of the Former Kingdom of Israel as a Test Case," *Journal of the American Oriental Society* 135.4 (2015): 765–89; 774.

[142] Ibid., 775.

[143] Débora Sandhaus, "Hazor in the Ninth and Eighth Centuries BCE," *Near Eastern Archaeology* 76.2 (2013): 110–17; Ben-Tor, *Hazor*, 167–70.

[144] Mazar, "Tel Beth-Shean," 266.

[145] Finkelstein and Singer-Avitz, "Reevaluating Bethel," 41–42.

[146] Faust, "Assyrian Rule in the West," 768–71. On the Neo-Assyrian governor's residence at Dan, for example, see Yifat Thareani, "Imperializing the Province: A Residence of a Neo-Assyrian City Governor at Tel Dan," *Levant* 48.3 (2016): 254–83.

[147] Mordechai Cogan, "Cross-examining the Assyrian Witnesses to Sennacherib's Third Campaign: Assessing the Limits of Historical Reconstruction" in *Sennacherib at the Gates of Jerusalem: Story, History and Historiography*, eds. I. Kalimi and S. Richardson, 51–74 (Leiden: Brill, 2014).

21 Assyrian siege of Lachish relief panel, Southwest Palace. Nineveh. Creative Commons Attribution-Noncommercial-Share Alike 4.0 international (CC BY-NC-SA 4.0) license. © The Trustees of the British Museum

campaign. Azekah,[148] Beth-Shemesh,[149] and Tel Eton (Eglon),[150] among others, all bear witness to Sennacherib's invasion. The most prominent site to be overrun was, however, that of Lachish,[151] with its grim downfall depicted among the famous reliefs found in the Assyrian royal palace at Nineveh.[152]

But it would be the Babylonian Empire that would finally bring Judah and its royal center, Jerusalem, to an end.[153] With the fall of Nineveh in 612 BCE and the defeat of Egypt at the battle of Carchemish in 605 BCE, Babylon took control of the Levant, including the kingdom of Judah, which was made its vassal. After a rebellion by the Judahite king, Jehoiakim, the Babylonians laid

---

[148] Oded Lipschits, Yuval Gadot, and Manfred Oeming, "Four Seasons of Excavation at Tel Azekah: The Expected and (Especially) Unexpected Results," in *The Shephelah during the Iron Age: Recent Archaeological Studies*, eds. O. Lipschits and A. Maeir, 1–26 (Winona Lake, IN: Eisenbrauns, 2017).

[149] Shlomo Bunimovitz and Zvi Lederman, "The Final Destruction of Beth Shemesh and the Pax Assyriaca in the Judean Shephelah," *Tel Aviv* 30.1 (2003): 3–26.

[150] Hayah Katz and Avraham Faust, "The Assyrian Destruction Layer at Tel 'Eton," *Israel Exploration Journal* 62.1 (2012): 22–53.

[151] Ussishkin, "Synopsis," 88–90.

[152] David Ussishkin, "The 'Lachish Reliefs' and the City of Lachish," *Israel Exploration Journal* 30 (1980): 174–95.

[153] For a detailed discussion of the destruction of Jerusalem, see Chapter 4.

ON RUINS, THEN AND NOW 61

22 Ruins of Iron Age pillared house. Jerusalem. Author photograph

siege to Jerusalem in 597 BCE, resulting in the deportation of an elite contingent of the city's residents but not in the destruction of the city itself. Ten years later, a further rebellion brought Babylon to the gates of Jerusalem once more. This time, the city was not spared. Archaeological evidence for the destruction of Jerusalem has been found throughout different areas of the ancient city,[154] from the Jewish Quarter excavations[155] to a number of sites unearthed in the City of David.[156] As the biblical description of the destruction suggests (2 Kings 25; Jer 39), much of Jerusalem was burned to the ground at the time and its fortifications dismantled. The royal city that had stood for over a thousand years in the highlands was, finally, laid waste.

In addition to Jerusalem, large swaths of Judah were also either destroyed or abandoned, joining those ruined sites in the Shephelah that had been devastated a century before. Consequently, nearly every Judahite settlement was

---

[154] For summary, see Oded Lipschits, *The Fall and Rise of Jerusalem: Judah under Babylonian Rule* (Winona Lake, IN: Eisenbrauns, 2005), 210–11.

[155] Hillel Geva, *Jewish Quarter Excavations in the Old City of Jerusalem Conducted by Nahman Avigad 1969–1982. Vol. I: Architecture and Stratigraphy: Areas A, W, and X-2, Final Report* (Jerusalem: Israel Exploration Society, 2000), 155–59.

[156] See, for example, Yigal Shiloh, *Excavations at the City of David*, Vol. I (Jerusalem: Hebrew University, 1984), 18–19; Margreet Steiner, *Excavations by Kathleen Kenyon in Jerusalem, 1961–1967, Vol. III: The Settlement in the Bronze and Iron Ages* (Sheffield: Sheffield Academic Press, 2001), 108–15.

affected during these late Iron Age invasions, from the lowlands in the west to the central hills south of Jerusalem to fortified settlements located still further south in the Negeb region. Hebron,[157] Arad,[158] Lachish,[159] Jericho,[160] and En-Gedi[161] were all destroyed or abandoned near the time of Jerusalem's downfall, with much more modest populations reoccupying these ruined sites in the century after. To the far southwest, Kadesh Barnea is overrun,[162] and, across the Jordan to the east, the city of Heshbon also falls,[163] both of which are sparsely settled in the Persian period. But other locations were abandoned far longer. The southern fortresses of Aroer[164] and Horvat Uza,[165] for example, were deserted for many centuries after Judah's end. The result of the Babylonian campaign was that most of the Iron Age kingdom of Judah, save the settlements just to the north of Jerusalem in the Benjamin region, was destroyed and depopulated. Demographically, the territories of Judah were so depleted that they would not recover to their former Iron Age levels for five hundred years. Much like Israel after the Assyrian campaigns of the late eighth century BCE, Judah also became a land of ruins.

The devastation wrought by the Assyrian and Babylonian empires brought the era of the Iron Age to a close. To those living in the time that followed, the landscape of the southern Levant must have appeared forlorn, its terrain featuring scores of ruined settlements that had arisen over the course of the previous two thousand years. Many of the biblical references to ruins are informed by this late Iron Age era of widespread destruction, including those in Jeremiah and Ezekiel, whose visions often surround Jerusalem's fall. Descriptions of Jerusalem's ruins are, in fact, the most abundant in the biblical corpus, found in the Books of Kings, Lamentations, Isaiah, Jeremiah, Ezekiel, Haggai, Nehemiah, Ezra, and certain Psalms. In the Book of Nehemiah,

---

[157] Jeffrey Chadwick, "Discovering Hebron," *Biblical Archaeology Review* 31.5 (2005): 70.
[158] Ze'ev Herzog, "The Fortress Mound at Tel Arad: An Interim Report," *Tel Aviv* (2002): 3–109; 102.
[159] Ussishkin, "Synopsis," 90–95.
[160] On the few remains from the settlement in the early Persian period, see the discussion in Lipschits, *Fall and Rise*, 232–33.
[161] Benjamin Mazar, "En Gedi," in *New Encyclopedia of Archaeological Excavations in the Holy Land*, Volume II, 402.
[162] Israel Finkelstein, "Kadesh Barnea: A Reevaluation of Its Archaeology and History," *Tel Aviv* 37 (2010): 111–25.
[163] Lawrence Geraty, "Hesban," in *Oxford Encyclopedia of Archaeology in the Near East*, Vol. III, 18–22 (Oxford: Oxford University Press, 1997).
[164] Yifat Thareani, "The Judean Frontier in the Seventh Century BCE: A View from 'Aroer,'" in *Unearthing the Wilderness: Studies on the History and Archaeology of the Negev and Edom in the Iron Age*, ed. J. Tebes, 227–65 (Leuven: Peeters, 2014).
[165] Itzhaq Beit-Arieh, *Horvat 'Uza and Horvat Radum: Two Fortresses in the Biblical Negev* (Tel Aviv: Emery and Claire Yass Publications, 2007), 48–56.

written at least 150 years after the Babylonian campaign, Jerusalem is portrayed as still "in ruins" and its gates "burned with fire" (Neh 2:3, 17).

1.3 THE HEBREW BIBLE AND THE RUINS THAT REMAIN

It is within this world of ruins that the biblical writers worked and lived. As with other ancient authors, such as Herodotus or Pausanias,[166] the texts composed by the biblical writers are imprinted with their descriptions of older landscapes. Perhaps the most salient feature of the ruins identified is their venerable character. This association with the past is imparted in a number of passages, such as in the references to the "ruins of old" (חרבות עולם) mentioned in Is 58:12 and 61:4, or the "enduring ruins" (משאות נצח) named in Ps 74:3. In Jer 44:6, the "waste and ruined" spaces from earlier in Jerusalem's history are said to have persisted "still to this day" (כיום הזה), and in Amos 9:11 the promise is made to rebuild certain ruins so that their restored structures would appear "as in the days of old" (כימי עולם). In Ps 9, the enemies of Yahweh are described as having "disappeared into lasting ruins (חרבות לנצח), their cities you [Yahweh] have uprooted," the destruction of these sites being so total and lasting that the memory of them had, much like those who had resided at 'Ai, "perished" (Ps 9:7).

This sense of the past is also framed by the storyteller's present. The large rock on which the ark once rested in the field of Joshua of Beth-Shemesh (1 Sam 6:18) or the altar fashioned by Gideon at the village of Ophrah (Judges 6:24), among many other artifacts, are described in these writings as being visible "to this day" (עד היום הזה), suggesting that some time had passed between when these objects had been in use and the narrator's own later context when stories about them were written down.[167] In Josh 11:13 and Jer 30:18 we come across depictions of ruin mounds that had formed long before the accounts that mention them, and in the great poem of Job 3 the poet evokes the rulers and counselors of the earth "who rebuild ruins for themselves" (Job 3:14), the renovated structures composed by the affluent couched in the language of death and degeneration that calls attention to how these

---

[166] For an overview, see Alain Schnapp, "The Poetics of Ruin in Ancient Greece and Rome," in *The Archaeology of Greece and Rome: Studies in Honour of Anthony Snodgrass*, eds. J. Bintliff and K. Rutter, 382–401 (Edinburgh: Edinburgh University Press, 2016); James Porter, "Ideals and Ruins: Pausanias, Longinus, and the Second Sophistic," in *Pausanias: Travel and Memory in Roman Greece*, eds. S. Alcock, J. Cherry, and J. Elsner, 63–92 (New York: Oxford: 2001). For an incisive account of how later Roman and Greek writers reflected on ruination, see Julia Hell, *The Conquest of Ruins: The Third Reich and the Fall of Rome* (Chicago: University of Chicago Press, 2019), 37–108.

[167] On these descriptions of ruins and the language of "to this day," see the discussion on "presence" in Chapter 3.

restored ruins will, nevertheless, come to ruin once more.[168] But even those stories that recall the settlements that once existed at Hazor or Shiloh or Gath (e.g., Josh 11; Josh 18; 1 Sam 1; 1 Sam 27), each destroyed and abandoned in a more distant past, attest to an awareness of older locations that were in ruin when these documents were produced.[169]

It is significant that those behind the biblical writings also recognized that a ruin mound (תל) is a product not of nature but of a settlement destroyed and, at moments, rebuilt over time.[170] This practice of building on a formerly ruined settlement is attested in the Book of Jeremiah, where the promise is made that "the city will be rebuilt atop its ruin mound" (עיר על תלה) (Jer 30:18). But more frequently the biblical writings call attention to ruin mounds that remain uninhabited. In Deut 13:17 the Israelites are commanded to burn down towns that apostatize against Yahweh, leaving them a "perpetual ruin mound" (תל עולם) never to be rebuilt, and in Josh 8:28 its eponymous leader "burned 'Ai" and made the city, once more, a "perpetual ruin mound." In Num 21:1–3, a Canaanite city is renamed "utter destruction" (Hormah) after the invading Israelites destroy it (cf. Judges 1:17), a name that continued in use for some time afterward, it appears, or which was applied to other sites that had come to a similar end (Deut 1:44; 1 Chr 4:30). Micah's famous prophecy of Jerusalem's future downfall demonstrates, too, an awareness that ruin mounds not resettled could be given over to agriculture and that a number of such locations in the southern Levant were likely used for this purpose. Thus, Zion is envisioned as one day being "plowed as a field" (Micah 3:12), and, in a later vision from the Book of Isaiah, Jerusalem becomes the place where the "fatlings and kids shall feed among the ruins" (Is 5:17).

The ruins the biblical writers depict are most frequently those of a location's defenses. Fortresses (מבצר) are repeatedly brought to such an end, not only those of foreign locations such as Moab (Is 25:12; Jer 48:18) or Edom (Is 34:13) but also the strongholds of Judah (Lam 2:2; Jer 5:17) and Israel (Is 17:3; Hosea 10:14). The walls (חומה) that comprise fortifications are also depicted in a state of ruin across a number of biblical texts, perhaps most famously at Jericho (Josh

---

[168] On this reading, see especially Choon-Leong Seow, *Job 1–21* (Grand Rapids, MI: Eerdmans, 2013), 358–60.

[169] This awareness is also found in Assyrian and Babylonian texts. In a royal text from Ashurnasirpal II (883–859 BCE), for example, the ruler mentions "abandoned cities, which during the time of my predecessors had turned into ruins (*a-na* DU$_6$ GUR-*ru*)." RIMA 2, A.0.101.30, 79. This retrospective sense of ruination will be taken up further in Chapter 2.

[170] "Ruin hills" (*tillu*) are also referred to in a wide collection of Akkadian texts, and the term is also used adverbially, both as *tillāniš* and *tillišam*, as in making a site "into a tell." All derivations are written either syllabically or with the logogram DU$_6$, corresponding to Sumerian DUL. On this, see CAD T, 405, 408–10; AHw, 1359. In addition to this term, *ḫarābu/ḫarbu* (to lay waste/devastated) and *anāḫu/anḫūtu* (to be in disrepair/dilapidated) also appear with some frequency.

6:20), though a similar fate awaits the great walls of Tyre (Ezek 26:4) and Babylon (Jer 51:44) and, of course, the city wall brought down around Jerusalem when it was destroyed (2 Kings 25:10). Dismantled, too, are the battlements (פנה) (Zeph 3:16) and towers (מגדל) that would have projected above these ramparts (i.e., Judges 8:17; Is 30:25; Ezek 26:9), including the greatest tower of them all at Babel, left to ruin after its builders had been scattered across the earth (Gen 11:8).

Within the confines of settlements, the phenomena most commonly associated with ruins are temple and cult. Already in 1 Kgs 9:8 we read of a warning voiced to Solomon that if he or those of future generations should not keep the commandments and ordinances set forth by Yahweh, then the temple in Jerusalem would come to ruin.[171] Indeed, throughout the Hebrew Bible threats are levied against cultic features and sanctuaries, such as those built for the worship of Baal (Judges 6:25) or used among what is described as other, foreign religious practices (Ex 34:13; Judges 2:2). In a striking example, Jehu is said to have brought down the Temple of Baal in Samaria atop its worshippers and turned it into a "latrine, as it is to this day" (2 Kgs 10:27).[172] Yet even cultic items connected specifically to the worship of Yahweh, such as the altar at Bethel (2 Kgs 23:15), or ostensibly wedded to its cult, such as those features recorded in Leviticus (Lev 26:30), are characterized as falling into ruin or potentially coming to such an end. In Amos 7:9 it is declared that the "high places of Isaac will be made desolate, and the sanctuaries of Israel ruined" (מקדשי ישראל יחרבו), and in Hosea (12:12) it is announced that the altars of Gilgal will become "like heaps of stones" (כגלים) in an alliterative wordplay on the location's name. An extended description of the destruction of putative Yahwistic cultic items is found in the story of Hezekiah's reign in 2 Kings (18:4), and in Is 64:10 the warning voiced to Solomon long before becomes realized, with the "holy and beautiful" temple being burned with fire and all the pleasant places of Zion turned to ruins.

Finally, it is significant that older material remains are also portrayed as part of the broader countryside within these writings. Saul, David, and Absalom are all said to have erected monuments (יד, מצבת) at various sites earlier in Israel's history (Mt. Carmel, 1 Sam 15:12; the "river," 2 Sam 8:3; King's Valley,

---

[171] A number of traditions, including the MT and OG, preserve "exalted" (עליון) in place of ruins (עיין), though this term, as M. Cogan points out, is "contextually impossible" at this moment in the narrative (Mordechai Cogan, *1 Kings* [AB 10; New York: Doubleday, 2001], 296). The Targum, however, offers a double reading that harmonizes these elements: "and this house that was exalted will be ruins" (וביתא הדין דהוה עילאי יהי חריב).

[172] The desecrated shrine area recently recovered at Lachish, dated to the era of Hezekiah and replete with a toilet seat positioned in the inner sanctuary, offers archaeological evidence of such practices. Saar Ganor and Igor Kreimerman, "An Eighth Century BCE Gate Shrine at Tel Lachish, Israel," *Bulletin of the American Schools of Oriental Research* 381 (2019): 211–36.

Jerusalem, 2 Sam 18:8), and in 2 Kings 23:17 King Josiah spots a large grave marker (ציון) near Bethel that would have been nearly three centuries old when he comes across it, according to the chronology of the story. Furthermore, pillars and heaps of stone are frequently raised by various figures to commemorate past events – from the monoliths established by Moses at Sinai (Ex 24:4) to those boulders that marked the crossing of the Jordan River by the Israelites (Josh 4:5–7). In addition, the ruins of tombs (1 Sam 10:2; 2 Sam 3:32), altars (Josh 8:30, 22:10; Judges 6:24), and old, deserted towns (Is 17:9; Ezek 36:4) are depicted in the biblical writings as part of the countryside that could be encountered by those traversing this territory.

For our purposes, what matters about these biblical references is that they provide descriptions of ruins that we would recognize as ruins today. Whether in terms of the material remains archaeologists have recovered from the southern Levant (i.e., buildings, cultic items, monuments) or in these writings' awareness of the antiquity of certain sites (i.e., being "of old" or "persisting to this day"), portrayals of ruins in the Hebrew Bible conform to our own encounters with older remains. There are even instances when we can be reasonably confident that certain ruins now in view – the MBA wall of Shechem, the LBA remains of Hazor's acropolis – were also visible during the centuries when the biblical writings were being composed, providing a point of contact between ancient experiences of the southern Levant's landscape and our own. Though we are separated from the composition of the Hebrew Bible by over two millennia, we can nevertheless experience something of the world behind these writings by encountering the ruins that their authors also encountered.

1.3.1 Ruins and the "Temporalization of History"

Such points of affinity, however, give way to a key disparity between how ruins are represented in the Hebrew Bible and our current understanding of them. Already in the discussion of Bronze Age sites in Sections 1.1.1 and 1.1.2, it became apparent that the biblical stories of Arad or Jericho's downfall, for example, were fundamentally at odds with how we now date the destruction of these locations. Though these Bronze Age settlements and a number of others referred to in the Hebrew Bible (e.g. Jarmuth, 'Ai, Shechem, Hebron) came to ruin at various moments in the EBA and MBA periods, the biblical accounts collapse some fifteen hundred years of ruination into essentially one era – that of the LBA II period (ca. thirteenth–twelfth centuries BCE) – when, according to accounts in the Books of Numbers, Joshua, and Judges, the Israelites conquered and settled the land of Canaan. This tendency to locate so many sites of ruin to a particular LBA horizon is all the more arresting in light of the fact that EBA and MBA sites would often have been more impressive than those that had appeared during later centuries. The thirteenth through twelfth centuries BCE were not some watershed moment, in other words, that witnessed the downfall of numerous monumental cities whose remains displaced or sublimated what had survived from earlier eras. If one period were to be singled out for its ruins, we would expect it to be located by the biblical writers in the centuries of the MBA. But of the ruins from this era, the Hebrew Bible says little.

How we date the ruins of ancient settlements in the southern Levant often diverges from how the biblical writers account for these remains. Rather than locating ruins in distinct ages that stretch ever further back in history (EBA, MBA, etc.), as is our practice, the biblical writings tend toward a more uniform vision.[173] Apart from those late Iron Age destructions that occurred closer to the time when these texts were initially produced, the more venerable remains described in the Hebrew Bible occupy a temporal framework that frequently resists our manner of sequencing. Even sites that we know had been destroyed more recently, such as Kadesh Barnea and Heshbon in the late Iron Age, could be cast back in time by the biblical writers (Josh 10:41; Num 21:25–30) so as to correspond to that late LBA horizon when so many other settlements were said to have been destroyed. Accounts of Shechem's downfall (Judges 9) or Bethel's (Judges 1:22–26), furthermore, can have an almost timeless quality about them, devastated long ago, according to biblical storytelling, but without reference to a specific chronological marker that would help us situate these stories in time. The result of this practice is that ruins from EBA, MBA, LBA, and even certain Iron Age contexts appear as the outcome of one epoch.

What becomes clear when reading the biblical references to ruins is that the time attributed to them by the biblical writers can depart substantially from how we conceive of their duration. If we theorize this point of disconnect, what is absent in these ancient accounts is a more acute sense of what Reinhart Koselleck, in his study of the semantics of historical time, terms the "temporalization of history" (*Verzeitlichung der Geschichte*).[174] By this phrase, Koselleck

---

[173] My focus here is on the dating of ruins. To be sure, a sense of periodization can be expressed in the biblical writings, perhaps most famously in the Book of Daniel and its vision of a statue made of differing materials that represent successive kingdoms across time (Dan 2:31–46). But even the impression of the era of the patriarchs and matriarchs, the exodus, the judges, etc., expresses some awareness of ages in the past (see, for example, Gary Knoppers, "Periodization in Ancient Israelite Historiography: Three Case Studies," in *Periodisierung und Epochenbewusstein im Alten Testament und in seinm Umfeld*, eds. J. Wiesehöfer and T. Krüger, 121–45 [Stuttgart: Franz Steiner, 2012]). The issue, as will be taken up below, is not the idea of periodization, but how these periods are distinguished in time.

[174] Reinhart Koselleck, *Vergangene Zukunft: Zur Semantik geschichtlicher Zeiten* (Frankfurt: Suhrkamp Verlag, 1979), esp. 19, 188–207; Reinhart Koselleck, *Futures Past: On the Semantics of Historical Time*, trans. K. Tribe (New York: Columbia University Press, 2004), 4, 11, 137–42.

describes a perspective in which time "gains a historical quality,"[175] as he puts it, defined not according to the movement of heavenly bodies or the reigns of rulers, as was frequently done in antiquity, but of human developments that could be distinguished as time advanced. Conceiving of time in this manner afforded the possibility of locating human activity "in time," so to speak, whether our interest lay in technology (i.e., the Neolithic period), politics (i.e., the Roman Empire), culture (i.e., the Renaissance), or some amalgamation of these interests and others. Crucially, what this framework afforded was the possibility of discerning discontinuities in lived experience that arose between eras, guided by the conviction that successive ages could be differentiated from what had preceded them and what would come after, including one's own. When we situate the biblical writings in the Iron Age, Persian Period, or Hellenistic era, we are driven by this assumption, one that holds that these epochs are separate, distinct, and identifiable. But this outlook would have held little meaning to the biblical writers themselves.

For Koselleck, the key assumption that we share is that as the centuries progress significant transformations occur in lived experience. The forward flow of time is for us a "dynamic and historical force in its own right,"[176] Koselleck comments, producing futures that we presume will be far different from the presents we happen to occupy. This premise is informed by our own space of experience (*Erfahrungsraum*) that has given rise to the belief that what the future holds (*Erwartungshorizont*) is unforeseeable, made uncertain by rapid technological and social developments.[177] To cite one small example of the phenomenon that Koselleck details, those of us born in the 1980s began our childhood educations in classrooms with typewriters and chalkboards, and now as adults we conduct classes fully online through technology that even a decade ago would have been unimaginable.[178] The pace of change has been breathtaking. And we are conditioned to assume that other advancements will soon take hold, further fracturing past experiences from future ones.

But this sense of the relationship between past and present has not always been so. In the opening pages to *Futures Past*, Koselleck draws our attention to the famous portrait of the *Alexanderschlacht* by Albrecht Altdorfer (1529 CE). What is curious about this painting is how images of sixteenth century CE

---

[175] Koselleck, *Futures Past*, 236. [176] Ibid., 236. [177] Ibid., 255–76.

[178] This sense of acceleration has been felt throughout the modern period, of course, and is not restricted to our own technological moment. In a famous observation from 1933, Walter Benjamin writes: "A generation that had gone to school on a horse-drawn streetcar now stood under the open sky in a countryside in which nothing remained unchanged but the clouds." Walter Benjamin, "The Storyteller," in *Illuminations: Essays and Reflection*, ed. H. Arendt, 83–110 (New York: Mariner, 2019 [1968]), 84. Hartog, too, draws attention to those who experienced World War II and their similar sense of an acceleration of time. François Hartog, *Regimes of Historicity: Presentism and Experiences of Time*, trans. S. Brown (New York: Columbia University Press, 2015), 3–7.

23 *Alexanderschlacht*. Albrecht Altdorfer, 1529. Public domain

combatants from the Holy Roman and Ottoman Empires are found fighting alongside fourth century BCE Persian and Macedonian forces.[179]

[179] Koselleck, *Futures Past*, 8–11.

The effect of this rendering, Koselleck writes, is an impression of time in which the "present and the past were enclosed within a common historical plane," producing an image of the ancient Battle of Issus that was "at once historical *and* contemporary" for Altdorfer's audience.[180] To further this temporal effect, statistics of those who fell in battle are detailed in faint numbered columns that appear on banners, but one number is omitted: the year the Battle of Issus actually took place (333 BCE). Altdorfer's "battle thus is not only contemporary," Koselleck comments, but also "simultaneously appears to be timeless."[181]

Yet it is precisely the "timelessness" of Altdorfer's work that is so jarring to those of us who view it today. Though Altdorfer was aware that the Battle of Issus took place long ago in regions far away from Vienna, his painting is often indifferent to such matters of historical context. Depictions of Alexander, Darius, battle formations, and dress are instead clearly transposed onto a sixteenth century CE setting. "Temporal difference was not more or less arbitrarily eliminated," Koselleck remarks on this feature of Altdorfer's portrait. "It was not, as such, at all apparent."[182] Past and present are woven tightly together in this portrayal, bound without regard for the obvious historical inaccuracies that would inevitably arise through such a depiction or for the concerns of misrepresentation that might occur. To our knowledge, none of Altdorfer's contemporaries were troubled by the manifest historical errors that were strewn throughout the painting. But when Friedrich Schlegel comes across the portrait three centuries later, he is astonished at the "marvel" of Altdorfer's work, of how it captured the mindset of a previous age that no longer existed. "[T]here was for Schlegel, in the three hundred years separating him from Altdorfer, more time," Koselleck writes, "than appeared to have passed in the eighteen hundred years or so that lay between the Battle of Issus and his painting."[183]

The *Alexanderschlacht* becomes meaningful for our study because it represents a perspective of time similar to that found in the biblical portrayals of ruins. In both, temporal difference is effectively elided by collapsing distinct eras into a vision that is more uniform. The biblical description of Arad's destruction (ca. 2500 BCE), for example, as occurring near the same time as Hazor's (ca. 1250 BCE) and Heshbon's (ca. 600 BCE), produces a narrative effect that is akin to Altdorfer's portrait and his blurring of Hellenistic and late Medieval worlds. In these renderings, historical disparities between time periods are effaced in a manner that is noticeable to us today who are sensitive to these differences, we who are aware of the many dissimilarities that would have separated fourth century BCE Persian forces from sixteenth century CE

---

[180] Ibid., 10. (my italics)   [181] Ibid., 10.   [182] Ibid.   [183] Ibid.

Ottoman fighters, or who date the ruins of cities in the southern Levant to much different centuries in time on the basis of variations in their material remains. But in both the biblical narrative and in Altdorfer's portrait, this temporalization of history is absent.

Less absorbed with the asymmetries in lived experience that arise as time unfolds, Koselleck's theory of temporalization offers a constructive explanation for the disinterest expressed in the biblical writings about those who had once inhabited the ruins they describe. Nowhere in these ancient texts, that is, is there any indication that one could examine these remains to discover how cultic practices or the design of buildings, beliefs about the dead or the defense of settlements, food consumption or the production of textiles, may have been practiced and experienced *differently* in the past. To be sure, various biblical accounts can refer to those who once resided at destroyed sites as being distinct from Israelite populations, presumably carrying out cultural and religious practices that were believed to deviate from the biblical writers' own. But at no place in these texts do we read of the possibility, much less the act, of digging among ruined sites to learn about those who had once resided at Jericho or 'Ai or Shiloh.

But this idea is so commonplace to us that we rarely reflect on why we hold to it, or when it came to be. Our lack of reflection on this development is in some sense an outcome of the incredible success of archaeological fieldwork over the past two centuries, in which manifest differences between populations have been revealed again and again. These remains attest to how the affairs of small highland settlements of the Iron I period, to cite one example, were quite distinct from those in the larger MBA cities that preceded them or, again, from the late Iron Age centers that would emerge hundreds of years later.[184] Apart from brief comments on sporadic religious reforms, the biblical writers, however, rarely discuss broader social or cultural changes that had transpired during these centuries, and never do they draw attention to idiosyncratic or peculiar material artifacts – an Egyptian inscription in Jerusalem, a cyclopean stone at Shechem – that would suggest past experiences at odds with the present. When celebrants walk by a "house of David" in Jerusalem in the Book of Nehemiah (Neh 12:37), no mention is made of how this structure would have been at least five centuries old when the procession occurs, a remnant of a past world that had been mostly lost by the time of Nehemiah's governorship. The Jerusalem temple was refurbished on a number of occasions according to a collection of biblical texts,[185] but no passage reflects on how much different

---

[184] See, for example, Elizabeth Bloch-Smith, "Israelite Ethnicity in Iron I: Archaeology Preserves What Is Remembered and What Is Forgotten in Israel's History," *Journal of Biblical Literature* 122.3 (2003): 401–25.

[185] Peter Dubovsky, *The Building of the First Temple: A Study in Redactional, Text-Critical and Historical Perspectives* (Tübingen: Mohr Siebeck, 2015), esp. 28–108.

the sanctuary must have appeared during the time of Zedekiah (597–586 BCE) in contrast to the period of Solomon's reign (ca. 950 BCE) from nearly four centuries before. The careful reader will be hard pressed to notice any differences between the portrayal of David's Jerusalem in the Book of Samuel from Josiah or Jehoiakim's capital depicted in the Book of Kings or the Book of Jeremiah, though the former city had roughly one-tenth the population that occupied an inhabited area not half the size of the latter.[186] Tenth century BCE Jerusalem was a much different place than its seventh or fifth century BCE successors, in other words, but no biblical text considers what these differences would have meant for how life was experienced within the highland city over the generations.[187]

What is key to Koselleck's theory of the temporalization of history, then, is a sensitivity to anachronism that emerged in tandem with it. By anachronism, I mean an awareness of time being "out of joint," as Annette Barnes and Jonathan Barnes describe it, such as when "a clock strikes in *Julius Caesar*" or when the Virgin and Child "receive devotions from fifteenth century Venetians" in a painting that adorns a cathedral wall.[188] To draw on Zachary Schiffman's definition in his study of this phenomenon, our sense of anachronism derives from the realization that "the past is not simply *prior* to the present but *different* from it,"[189] with our predecessors living in a world disparate from what we experience today.[190] This awareness drives our historical desire to situate phenomena from the past into their specific historical contexts and to identify those moments – Moses commenting on Twitter, Esther responding to Mordechai by quoting Sartre – when something has been misplaced, dislodged from its proper historical period and situated elsewhere in a time that it does not belong in. Our pronounced sensitivity to anachronism – the great "sin against the holy spirit of history"[191] – is "second nature" to us, Schiffman writes – an outcome of a presupposition we hold about how the past is utterly distinct from the present. But as Schiffman's book-length study

---

[186] Jane Cahill, "Jerusalem at the Time of the Monarchy: The Archaeological Evidence," in *Jerusalem in Bible and Archaeology: The First Temple Period*, eds. A. Vaughn and A. Killebrew, 13–80 (Atlanta: Society of Biblical Literature, 2003).

[187] For a study of these different Jerusalems and the influence of their landscapes on biblical storytelling, see Daniel Pioske, *David's Jerusalem: Between Memory and History* (New York: Routledge, 2015).

[188] Annette Barnes and Jonathan Barnes, "Time out of Joint: Some Reflections on Anachronism," *The Journal of Aesthetics and Art Criticism* 47.3 (1989): 253–61; 253.

[189] Zachary Schiffman, *The Birth of the Past* (Baltimore: Johns Hopkins University Press, 2011), 2. (author's italics)

[190] For the classic treatment of "the sense of anachronism," see Peter Burke, *The Renaissance Sense of the Past* (New York: St. Martin's Press, 1969), esp. 1–2, 138–45.

[191] Constantine Fasolt, *The Limits of History* (Chicago: University of Chicago Press, 2004), 6.

makes clear, this presupposition has a history, ours being the product of a much more recent mindset.[192]

This argument, however, requires some nuance.[193] In the Hebrew Bible there are, in fact, a number of passages where older customs or terminology is recognized as outmoded or even obsolete. In 1 Sam 9:9 the narrator remarks in an aside that "formerly in Israel, anyone who went to inquire of God would say, 'Come, let us go to the seer,' for the one who is now called a prophet was once called a seer." A similar comment appears in Ruth 4:7 ("now in former times this is how redeeming and exchanging happened") and in 2 Kings 17:34, 40 ("to this day they continue to practice their former traditions"). In addition, various biblical texts comment on how certain locations had been renamed in the past, such as Hebron ("Now the name of Hebron formerly was Kiriath-arba" [Josh 14:15; Judges 1:10]) or Debir ("the name of Debir was formerly Kiriath-sepher" [Judges 1:11]). Older texts not found in the biblical writings are also alluded to in a number of passages (e.g., Num 21:14–15; Josh 10:13), perhaps detailing a past that was distinct from the biblical writers' present, particularly given the possibility that some of these documents were older royal annals that recorded information from generations before.[194]

The biblical writers were aware, then, of certain practices that belonged to a bygone world. Yet, as with the ancient Greek writers Schiffman examines, the appearance of these references in the Hebrew Bible are quite isolated and never lead to a more concentrated reflection on what these older ways of life might indicate for the relationship between the past recounted in biblical storytelling and the biblical authors' present.[195] Instead, Schiffman observes, texts from antiquity note incidents of anachronism "only in passing, for specific rhetorical purposes, after which the ancient authors set them aside, effectively relegating them to oblivion."[196] It is not, then, that the biblical writers were unaware of anachronisms. It is that they did not find them meaningful.

It is perhaps for similar reasons that other examples of anachronism receive such little attention within these writings. It is rather unsettling from our

---

[192] Schiffman, *Birth of the Past*, 144–52.

[193] From a comparative perspective, see also the important arguments that Greco-Roman authors did exhibit a sensitivity toward anachronism in Tim Rood, Carol Atack, and Tom Phillips, *Anachronism and Antiquity* (London: Bloomsbury, 2020), esp. 8–32. However, as these authors admit, the idea of anachronism present among these ancient authors succumbed to a "radical transformation of the concept in the course of the nineteenth century" (22). It is that transformation that is at issue here.

[194] There are thirty-four references to older annals or royal writings in the Hebrew Bible, most found in the Book of Kings.

[195] See also Burke's strong thesis: "Their [Jewish] linear interpretation of history was a metaphysical one ... which did not involve any empirical sense of anachronism or change." Burke, *Renaissance Sense of the Past*, 141.

[196] Schiffman, *Birth of the Past*, 6.

historical perspective, for example, to read of Philistine populations appearing on the coastal plain (Gen 21:32, 26:1) half a millennium before we know, archaeologically speaking, they had settled in the southern Levant,[197] or to find Abraham saddling his camels (Gen 24:10) centuries prior to when they were domesticated in the region.[198] In Deuteronomy the narrator refers to an Israelite conquest that had already been completed before it began (Deut 2:12), and certain "cities of Samaria" (1 Kings 13:32) are referred to in the time of Jeroboam I, decades before Samaria is said to have been built as the royal center of the Omrides (1 Kings 16:24). In Samuel, Israelites make payments to Philistines in a weight system that would not exist until hundreds of years after the time period in which the story is set (1 Sam 13:21),[199] and later David walks into a Jerusalem temple that had not yet been built (2 Sam 12:20). In the Book of Chronicles, David receives money for the sanctuary in a coinage introduced by the Persian Empire five hundred years after he died (1 Chr 29:7),[200] and Asaph sings a hymn on behalf of exilic populations (1 Chr 16:35) when the exile was still four hundred years in the future. Later in the book, temple personnel and liturgical practices are carefully ordered by David (1 Chr 23–27) in ways that reflect practices of the Second Temple and not those of the early Iron Age cult that would have been more familiar to those living half a millennium before. And to these instances can be added our study of ruins that appeared over the course of nearly two thousand years but are portrayed largely as the outcome of one era in the biblical corpus, without comment on the differences that would have marked their appearance and forms to those who encountered them.

This rather indifferent attitude toward anachronism matters because it provides further insight into why the biblical writers make no mention of digging among the ruins they describe. If past and present were experienced as deeply connected by those behind the Hebrew Bible, if ways of life were

---

[197] On the appearance of the Philistines, see Lawrence Stager, "Forging an Identity: The Emergence of Ancient Israel," in *The Oxford History of the Biblical World*, ed. M. Cogan, 152–71 (New York: Oxford, 1998); Aren Maeir and Louise Hitchcock, "The Appearance, Formation and Transformation of Philistine Culture: New Perspectives and New Finds," in *The Sea Peoples Up-to-Date: New Research on the Migration of Peoples in the 12th Century BCE*, eds. P. Fischer and T. Bürge, 149–62 (Vienna: Verlag der Österreichischen Akademie der Wissenschaften, 2017).

[198] Lidar Sapir-Hen and Erez Ben-Yosef, "The Introduction of Domestic Camels to the Southern Levant: Evidence from the Aravah Valley," *Tel Aviv* 40 (2013): 277–85; Lidar Sapir-Hen, "Human–Animal Relationship with Work Animals: Symbolic and Economic Roles of Donkeys and Camels during the Bronze and Iron Ages in the Southern Levant," *Zeitschrift des Deutschen Palästina-Vereins* 136 (2020): 83–94.

[199] Raz Kletter, *Economic Keystones: The Weight System of the Kingdom of Judah* (Sheffield: Sheffield Academic Press, 1998), 42–48.

[200] Christine Mitchell, "David and Darics: Reconsidering an Anachronism in 1 Chronicles 29," *Vetus Testamentum* 69 (2019): 748–54.

thought to exhibit some coherence across the generations, then the impulse to excavate ruins and index what was distinctive about conditions in previous times would have been muted. Old debris strewn beneath the ground and the present buildings above it could be viewed as predominantly complementary, as materials of a world, past and present, that held much in common. If we think otherwise, it is because we are bound to a particular impression of time, whereby "expectations have distanced themselves evermore from all previous experience,"[201] as Koselleck describes it. This sense of the past as distant and alien has been reinforced by two centuries of archaeological excavations that have demonstrated, in a decisive manner, the discontinuities that separate one period from the next.

If we return to the ancient site of Sippar and examine once more Nabonidus' attempt to excavate the great Ebabbar temple with his team of workers, a similar set of questions can be posed. Schaudig had already pointed the way forward, as noted in the opening to this chapter, by remarking that Nabonidus' efforts at excavation were not driven by an interest in learning about the past as such but by a desire to demonstrate continuity between more ancient rulers and his present, granting him legitimacy at a moment when it may have been in question. Nabonidus' "worldview," Schaudig argues, was fundamentally "unhistorical," with the connection between past and present being maintained in a manner that was "anachronistic."[202] This was a worldview that sought cohesion across time and space in spite of the substantial changes that had transpired in the two millennia that separated the reign of Sargon the Great from Nabonidus' own. The past was once experienced as unbroken and repeatable, Koselleck argues in this vein, functioning as the *magistra vitae* that offered lessons to be imitated in the present, a past that was to be returned to and emulated whenever possible.[203] From this perspective, Nabonidus did not dig in order to discover foreign cultic practices and ancient beliefs that separated the Old Akkadian period from his own Neo-Babylonian context. He wanted to demonstrate that his rule was akin to those of the great rulers of old, consistent with their practices and ways of life.

Though there is no mention of it in their writings, it cannot be discounted, then, that contemporaries to the biblical writers or the biblical writers themselves sifted among the ruins that surrounded them. It is apparent that individuals in the first millennium BCE could reuse older materials found at ruined sites (*spolia*).[204] The famous Tel Dan inscription, for example, was found in

---

[201] Koselleck, *Futures Past*, 11, 263. [202] Schaudig, "Nabonid," 491.
[203] See "Historia Magistra Vitae: The Dissolution of the Topos into the Perspective of a Modernized Historical Process," in Koselleck, *Futures Past*, 26–42.
[204] On this point, see the extended discussion in Chapter 3.

three pieces,[205] each fragment located in secondary construction contexts. The builders who reused these stones were apparently "unaware" that the pieces were "part of a broken stele erected by an Aramean king," the excavators write,[206] or, at the very least, they had little interest in the historical significance such fragments held. After Jerusalem's fall, archaeological evidence suggests that squatters lived among the ruins of the capital in the decades after and reused materials from destroyed buildings[207] – a phenomenon also witnessed elsewhere in the region after various calamities.[208] Items of value could also be buried and returned to, such as the silver hoards found at Ekron or Eshtemoa.[209] Perhaps, like Nabonidus, relics from the past were similarly sought at certain locations, even if for destruction, as when Josiah is said to have demolished the old altar at Bethel and those cultic items connected to it (2 Kings 23:15), including certain graves in Bethel's vicinity.

But such practices are not what archaeologists undertake today. Beyond the retrieval or reuse of specific items of value found buried in the ground, the aims of contemporary excavations are now more encompassing and systematic, given over to exposing broad swaths of a settlement so as to better understand the lives of those who inhabited it across centuries and even millennia.[210] "The archaeologist's use of his [sic] stratified relics depends on his conceiving them as artifacts serving human purposes," R. G. Collingwood writes, "and thus expressing a particular way in which men [sic] have thought about life."[211]

---

[205] Avraham Biran and Joseph Naveh, "An Aramaic Stele Fragment from Tel Dan," *Israel Exploration Journal* 43 (1993): 81–98; Avraham Biran and Joseph Naveh, "The Tel Dan Inscription: A New Fragment," *Israel Exploration Journal* 45 (1995): 1–18.

[206] Biran and Naveh, "The Tel Dan Inscription," 8.

[207] De Groot and Bernick-Greenberg, *Excavations at the City of David 1978–1985, Volume VIIA*, 176.

[208] E.g., Amihai Mazar, "Tel Rehov in the Assyrian Period: Squatters, Burials, and a Hebrew Sea," in *The Fire Signals of Lachish: Studies in the Archaeology and History of Israel in the Late Bronze Age, Iron Age, and Persian Period in Honor of David Ussishkin*, eds. I. Finkelstein and N. Na'aman, 265–80 (Winona Lake, IN: Eisenbrauns, 2011); Maeir, "Introduction and Overview," 21; Ido Koch, "Religion at Lachish under Egyptian Colonialism," *Die Welt des Orients* 49.2 (2019): 161–82; 163. On this phenomenon, see more detailed comments in Chapter 3.

[209] Raz Kletter and Etty Brand, "A New Look at the Iron Age Silver Hoard from Esthemoa," *Zeitschrift des Deutschen Palästina-Vereins* 114.2 (1998): 139–54; Amir Golani and Benjamin Sass, "Three Seventh-Century BCE Hoards of Silver Jewelry from Tel Miqne-Ekron," *Bulletin of the American Schools of Oriental Research* 311 (1998): 57–81.

[210] Commenting on Nabonidus, among other examples from antiquity, Thomas writes: "Yet while these cases demonstrate an awareness of the remains of the past surviving into the present, there is no sense in which these remains were being used as evidence in the construction of a systematic knowledge of a past society, or of the diversity of humankind ... they were not practicing archaeology." Julian Thomas, *Archaeology and Modernity* (London: Routledge, 2004), 4.

[211] R. G. Collingwood, *The Idea of History*, rev. ed., ed. J. Van Der Dussen (London: Oxford University Press, 2005 [1946]), 212.

But this interest in a "particular way" of conceiving the world is dependent on a fundamental assumption, one that presumes historical particularity and a belief that how we understand ourselves and our environment is contingent on the places and periods in which specific human purposes are carried out. To us, ruins are evidence of these particularities and contingencies, illustrating the divisions in technology, taste, and lifeways that separate one era from the next. But nowhere in the biblical writings are ruins described as such.

The question is when this sense of ruins transforms. In Section 1.3.2, we turn to a period that Koselleck terms the *Sattelzeit*. In this era, stemming from roughly 1750 CE–1850 CE, Koselleck contends that overarching impressions of time, drawn out from the writings of leading figures of this era, begin to be described differently, including the identification of the present as a "new time" (*neue Zeit*) that is severed from all that came before. For our purposes, what matters about this era is that it coincides with novel understandings of ruins that also emerge.

1.3.2 *Ruins Now*

On January 11, 1804, François René de Chateaubriand visited the ruins of Pompeii.[212] In a journal he would later publish as *Travels in America and Italy*,[213] Chateaubriand describes the excavations being carried out at the site, now already in their fifth decade by the time of that warm January day. It is within these journal entries that Chateaubriand records what areas of Pompeii had been uncovered and what structures unearthed, providing us with a snapshot of how the location appeared at this time. But what makes Chateaubriand's journal of special interest are his reflections on the techniques used by the laborers to dig up the site's remains. Of these efforts, Chateaubriand writes that the men "remove whatever they discover" in the buildings they clear, from simple household utensils to the more elaborate furniture and statuary they have retrieved within the settlement's ancient enclosures.[214]

Though such practices were commonplace at the time,[215] Chateaubriand is nevertheless troubled by what he witnesses. "What is present done seems to me lamentable" he remarks, a sentiment precipitated, it appears, by how

---

[212] For a rich discussion of Chateaubriand's visit and its implications, see Peter Fritzsche, *Stranded in the Present: Modern Time and the Melancholy of History* (Cambridge, MA: Harvard University Press, 2004), 92–139. See also the discussion of ruins and Chateaubriand in Hartog, *Regimes of Historicity*, 88–96.

[213] François René de Chateaubriand, *Travels in America and Italy*, Vol. II (London: Henry Colburn, 1828), 248–54.

[214] Chateaubriand, *Travels*, 252.

[215] For an overview of these early excavation techniques, see Trigger, *History of Archaeological Thought*, 52–67.

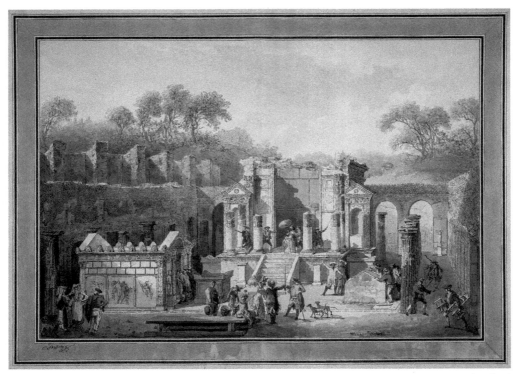

24 *Temple of Isis at Pompeii*. Francesco Piranesi, 1788. Creative Commons (CC0 1.0). Cleveland Museum of Art

Pompeii's artifacts were "promiscuously carried" off to the royal palace at Portici to be stored away for its benefactors to possess, "buried in cabinets where they are no longer in keeping with surrounding objects."[216] Rather than extracting antiquities from the site and sending them away, Chateaubriand writes that these items should be "preserved on the spot," the structures' roofs and ceilings, floors and windows, "being carefully restored" in an effort to safeguard these remains.[217] The result of such practices would be to preserve a Roman city in its entirety, offering insights into "the domestic history of the Roman people" that would surpass in its details "all the books of antiquity."[218] Yet, unable to prevent the workers from their pilfering, Chateaubriand stands removed, voicing a final question for an audience whose time had not yet come: "Why not have left these things as they found them, and where they found them?"[219]

Chateaubriand's writings have received considerable scholarly attention because of the turning point they represent,[220] exhibiting "a rather more

---

[216] Chateaubriand, *Travels*, 252, 54.   [217] Ibid., 252–53.   [218] Ibid., 253.
[219] Ibid., 253.
[220] See, for example, Fritzsche, *Stranded in the Present*, 92–139; Peter Fritzsche, "Chateaubriand's Ruins: Loss and Memory after the French Revolution," *History and Memory* 10.2 (1998):

complex relationship to the past than had been seen before,"[221] as Peter Fritzsche remarks in his study of this era. Much of what makes Chateaubriand's discussion of ruins peculiar for their time is their sensitivity to what we would now describe as these remains' archaeological context, or the desire to understand artifacts in situ, interpreted historically within the broader, undisturbed framework in which certain objects are found. What matters about Pompeii's ruins, from this vantage point, is the historical information they convey. Rather than seeing items of high worth wrested from excavations to be sold to wealthy benefactors or clients, as was the dominant practice at the time, Chateaubriand expresses the desire to study Pompeii's ruins in order to learn about the more mundane details of how the ancient inhabitants of the city once lived. Such insights, as Chateaubriand describes them, are necessary for understanding the "domestic history" of the Roman population that had perished at Pompeii, a history that required the city's material remains to be left in place so that they could be examined where they were found.

Though nothing had changed about Pompeii's ruins in the decades since their discovery, Chateaubriand suddenly sees them differently than did those who came before.[222] Why he does so is connected to the broader historical circumstances in which Chateaubriand was embroiled, above all the French Revolution and the transformations to French society that Chateaubriand and his royalist allies had attempted to halt.[223] Fritzsche writes,[224]

> What is crucial here are not the ruins themselves, for they did not change, but the new historical field in which they were seen and apprehended. Like Simmel's stranger, the ruins appeared all at once, and they stayed in view. They were rendered visible by *new structures of temporality* based on

---

102–17. For a further assessment of Chateaubriand's importance for new conceptions of historical thought in the nineteenth century, see Hartog, *Regimes of Historicity*, 65–96; Ivanna Rosi and Jean-Marie Roulin, eds., *Chateaubriand, penser et écrire l'histoire* (Saint-Étienne: Publications de l'Université de Saint-Étienne, 2009).

[221] Fritzsche, *Stranded in the Present*, 101.

[222] The great art historian Johann Winckelmann had also critiqued the haphazard and secretive collection of artifacts from Herculaneum and Pompeii, writing a highly popular "letter" that publicized the finds to a broader European audience. But never did Winckelmann suggest that the remains of these sites be left in place to be studied, nor did he evince much interest in the mundane, daily life of these locations' residents. See Johann Winckelmann, *Letter and Report on the Discoveries at Herculaneum*, trans. C. Mattusch (Los Angeles: Getty Publications, 2011 [1764]).

[223] See also the argument of Hartog, who also emphasizes the experience of the rupture of time at this moment: "This man, so squarely on the losing side in the French Revolution, nevertheless had a deeper understanding, when all is said and done, of the emergent temporal order of modernity than many of his contemporaries. And he managed to transform his experience of a break, rift, or breach in time into the very mainspring of his writing." Hartog, *Regimes of Historicity*, 65–66.

[224] Fritzsche, *Stranded*, 106. (my italics)

disorder and rupture, concealment and half-life, that emerged with revolution in France. The power of ruins in the nineteenth century was to depict the violence of historical movement without imputing necessity to its direction. They challenged the absoluteness of the present with counterfactuals of the past.

Witnesses to a movement that sought a sundering with France's past, Chateaubriand and his contemporaries began to consider ruins from perspectives that had not been regarded before. In part, Fritzsche argues, this new lens for contemplating material remains was occasioned by how ruins were affected by the French Revolution. The National Convention's decision to destroy old castles, estates, and churches left an indelible impression on those who sought to safeguard France's past, a practice that perhaps reached its height when the royal tombs at Saint-Denis were exhumed so that the cadavers could be desecrated and dumped in a common trench.[225] The attempt to erase the past, in other words, suddenly brought it sharply into relief for those such as Chateaubriand, giving rise to a new "historical field" and novel "structures of temporality" that enabled individuals to look at older remains in ways no one had looked at them before.

To these ruins of revolution would be added those that arose in the wake of Napoleon's advances in Europe soon thereafter, where territories outside of France also experienced ruination at a scale not before encountered. The manufacture of artificial ruins such as the Magdalenenklause, so common on royal estates in the early decades of the eighteenth century CE, now gives way to a new sensibility a century later. What emerges in the nineteenth century is an interest in the historical provenance of ruins and their preservation, the material remains of locations valued for their connections to a national heritage and their capacity to shed light on how forebears once lived at a particular site or within a territory, as Chateaubriand's journal intimates. Ruins become dense with history in this period, their materials seen as traces of singular and unrepeatable past events that offered "evidence of counter lives"[226] who occupied ages other than one's own. Ruins can no longer be faked and found meaningful. They need to be excavated, studied, and conserved. It is only now, in the nineteenth century, that widespread efforts at the preservation of ruins takes hold.[227] Work on the Cologne Cathedral, abandoned to ruin in 1473 CE, is suddenly resumed in 1842 CE.[228]

---

[225] Ibid., 97–98. [226] Ibid., 104.

[227] Pope Pius II issued the first decree (bull) for the protection of ancient ruins (in 1462 CE), but broader regional and national efforts at preservation do not appear until the nineteenth century CE. See "Bulle de Pie II relative à la conservation des monuments antiques (28 avril 1462)," in *Les Arts á la cour des papes endant le XVe et le XVIe siècle: Recueil de documents inédits tirés des archives et des bibliothèques romaines*, 3 vols., ed. Eugène Müntz, 1:352 (Paris, 1878–1882).

[228] Fritzsche, *Stranded*, 108–10.

Why Chateaubriand and those who followed began to look at ruins differently is a phenomenon that is certainly more complex than what one catalyst can explain, however momentous. To political revolution can be added rapid industrialization and the maturation of capitalist market economies, intensive practices of colonialism by European powers, and the rise of technologies that would forever alter lived experience (e.g., synchronized clocks, international railway systems, the telegraph). But more important for our study than the reasons for this change in perspective is the perspective itself that took hold. An interest in ruins, Fritzsche observes, was now "marked by a new historical sensibility that scrutinized differences" among the remains encountered, galvanized by a "concern with context and curiosity about 'how people lived.'"[229]

Chateaubriand's long life spanned nearly the entirety of Koselleck's *Sattelzeit*, from his birth in 1768 to his death in Paris in 1848. For those from this era, Koselleck argues, a displacement or rupture in the sense of time became a central part of their experience.[230] In the writings of Immanuel Kant, one reads of a new conception of "progress" (*Fortschritt*) by which the future is increasingly distanced from past practices and ideas; for de Lamartine, the "rapidity of time" (*La rapidité du temps*) contributed to the sense that "there is no more contemporary history," his present era made immediately obsolete due to the dramatic social and political changes that were occurring in such quick succession.[231] In this period, German writers begin to speak of a "new time" (*neue Zeit*), characterized as more than one of simple succession but qualitatively novel, a time never experienced before, and, by the last quarter of the nineteenth century CE, the composite expression *Neuzeit* is used widely as the term that signifies the modern period in its entirety.[232]

There was something about this era that was "new" to those who lived during it, in other words, and what was novel was the experience of time itself. Koselleck, for his part, describes this moment as the "dawning of a new temporality."[233] In his reading of accounts from this era, Koselleck writes,[234]

> Progress thus combined experiences and expectations, both endowed with a temporal coefficient of change. As part of a group, a country, or finally, a class, one was conscious of being advanced in comparison with

---

[229] Ibid., 100–1.
[230] On this point, Foucault similarly writes of the "Age of History," "The last years of the eighteenth century are broken by a discontinuity similar to that which destroyed Renaissance thought ... a discontinuity as enigmatic in its principle, in its original rupture, as that which separates the Paracelsian from the Cartesian order." Foucault, *Order of Things*, 235.
[231] Koselleck, *Futures Past*, 267, 210.   [232] Ibid., 225.
[233] Ibid., 31; Koselleck, *Vergangene Zukunft*, 47.
[234] Koselleck, *Vergangene Zukunft*, 266–67.

> the others ... What was new was that the expectations that reached out for the future became detached from all that previous experience had to offer. Even the new experience gained from the annexation of lands overseas and from the development of science and technology was still insufficient for the derivation of future expectations. From that time on, the space of experience was no longer limited by the horizon of expectations; rather, the limits of the space of experience and of the horizon of expectations diverged.

Born into a world whose future was increasingly unknown and whose past was becoming increasingly unrecognizable, new perspectives on ruins arose in tandem with lived experience coming undone and being recast afresh.[235] With time experienced as accelerating at ever greater speed, leaving a long series of obsolete cultural and political formations in its wake, a sensitivity toward historical differences emerges that elicited novel understandings of ruins and the archaeological record. Our desire "to investigate those past lives through the medium of material remains," Julian Thomas observes in his study of the rise of archaeological practices, "is itself distinctively modern."[236] If we were not descendants of this particular period and its experiences, "it might not occur to us to do archaeology at all."[237]

For Koselleck, it is in this period that a sense of the temporalization of history begins to solidify, and with it a more acute sensitivity to anachronism and historical sequencing. Even the very terminology for history transforms during this time, Koselleck observes, from a concept that posits a plurality of past experiences specific and unique to various territories, to history as a collective singular, a notion of "history itself" (*die Geschichte selber*) that is universal and global, encompassing all events within a shared human past.[238] "This is the master category, the condition under which the time of history can be thought," Ricoeur remarks in his reading of Koselleck. "There is a time of history insofar as there is one single history."[239] The idea of history we hold today, and our experience of its specific temporality, is born in this moment.

It is perhaps not surprising, then, that toward the end of the *Sattelzeit* period the ruins of the southern Levant come to be explored in ways never witnessed

---

[235] Koselleck comments further: "Two specific temporal determinants characterize the new experience of transition: the expected otherness of the future and, associated with it, the alteration in the rhythm of temporal experience: acceleration, by means of which one's own time is distinguished from what went before." Koselleck, *Futures Past*, 241.

[236] Thomas, *Archaeology and Modernity*, xi.   [237] Ibid., xi.

[238] Koselleck, *Futures Past*, 33–42. Koselleck quotes Droysen to this effect, "Beyond histories there is History" (33). For a similar argument from the perspective of the advent of absolute, Newtonian time, see the classic study of Donald Wilcox, *The Measure of Times Past: Pre-Newtonian Chronologies and the Rhetoric of Relative Time* (Chicago: University of Chicago Press, 1987), esp. 16–82.

[239] Ricoeur, *Memory, History, Forgetting*, 298.

before.[240] In 1838 CE, we find Edward Robinson and Eli Smith setting out for Palestine to document the region and investigate sites of ruin that may represent locations named in the Bible, driven by a curiosity to recover an ancient landscape they believed had been lost.[241] In the words of Robinson, their efforts were[242]

> *a first attempt* to lay open the treasures of Biblical Geography and History still remaining in the Holy Land – treasures which *have lain for ages unexplored*, and had become so covered with the dust and rubbish of many centuries, that their very existence was forgotten.

The sense of novelty underscored by Koselleck in his theory of temporalization is, in this passage, readily apparent. Standing on the threshold of "scientific exploration," Thomas Davis comments in his study of these travelers, but still of a mindset beholden to "the days of pilgrimage" from centuries before,[243] these liminal figures provide the first historical geography of eras associated with the Bible, identifying a number of locations that, in time, would come to be excavated. Robinson and Smith's remarkable achievements were however hampered by their inability to understand what the terrain could at moments indicate. Encountering strange hills without visible ruins on their surface, Robinson and Smith bypassed a number of these mounds because they failed to fathom a defining feature of the landscape that the biblical writers had recognized millennia in the past: namely, that certain hills were artificial, the creation of successive cities built and destroyed.[244]

When this insight was recovered is debated. Some link it to the excavations carried out at Hissarlik by Heinrich Schliemann in the early 1870s, where various strata were exposed and differentiated in order to locate the specific layer that represented Homer's Troy.[245] But in Palestine, a clear recognition of how ruin mounds preserve the layered remains of distinct settlements is found in the writings of Sir Flanders Petrie. In 1890, after a number of seasons of excavation in Egypt, Petrie arrived at the site of Tel el-Hesi, 25km east of Gaza.[246] Drawing

---

[240] On the explosion of interest in the lands of Palestine, including the establishment of institutions (such as the Palestine Exploration Fund in 1865) devoted to their study, see Paul Michael Kurtz, "The Silence on the Land: Ancient Israel versus Modern Palestine in Scientific Theology," in *Negotiating the Secular and the Religious in the German Empire*, ed. R. Habermas, 56–100 (New York: Berghahn Books, 2019).

[241] On this expedition, see Haim Goren, *"The Loss of a Minute Is Just So Much Loss of Life": Edward Robinson and Eli Smith in the Holy Land* (Turnhout: Brepols, 2020).

[242] Edward Robinson, *Biblical Researches in Palestine, Mount Sinai and Arabia Petraea: A Journal of Travels in the Year 1838*, Vol. I (Boston: Crocker & Brewster, 1841), xii–xiii. (my italics)

[243] Thomas Davis, *Shifting Sands: The Rise and Fall of Biblical Archaeology* (Oxford: Oxford University Press, 2004), 4.

[244] Davis, *Shifting Sands*, 7.   [245] Trigger, *History of Archaeological Thought*, 291.

[246] W. M. Flinders Petrie, *Tell el Hesy (Lachish)* (London: Palestine Exploration Fund, 1891). Cf. William Dever, "Archaeological Method in Israel: A Continuing Revolution," *Biblical Archaeologist* 43 (1980): 42.

near the site after a heavy rain had washed away an edge of the mound, Petrie observes striations that have become visible. In this moment, Petrie comes to the realization of something that will be essential to all archaeological efforts in the region that follow, writing that the "mound, for over 60 feet of its height, *consists of successive ruins of towns piled one on the other.*"[247] A sensitivity to historical difference is now applied to the material remains of the southern Levant through the idea of archaeological strata, forever altering how excavations will be carried out in the region.

The early efforts of Robinson, Smith, and Petrie give rise to an ever-increasing number of digs in the early decades of the twentieth century CE. Alongside Petrie's observations on stratigraphy will be added W. F. Albright's refined analyses of ceramic typology,[248] and, in time, the Wheeler-Kenyon method of excavation that still prevails today.[249] But with these advancements in archaeological method will come the realization that what had been unearthed could depart from how the biblical writers once described these same ruins in antiquity, a point drawn out at a number of moments in our discussion of Bronze and Iron Age settlements (Sections 1.1.2 and 1.1.3). So it is that we come once more to the site of 'Ai (et-Tell) in the 1960s and find Joseph Callaway struggling to understand the historical implications of what the location's archaeological evidence suggested. Rather than a great city conquered and destroyed in the waning moments of the LBA by the Israelites, as the Book of Joshua suggests, the archaeological evidence from 'Ai indicates instead that its downfall took place a thousand years before in the EBA period. "'Ai is simply an embarrassment,'" Callaway writes in an unguarded moment of reflection, to those who take "the biblical and archaeological evidence seriously."[250] Ruins then, ruins now.

§

The ruins have not changed, but how we look at them has.[251] This shift in perception is most apparent in our inclination today to excavate the remains of ancient settlements in order to learn about the lives of those who once inhabited them – an act and interest not found in any of the many references to ruins located in the Hebrew Bible. The divide around which this chapter is organized centers on this discrepancy, and how to account for it.

---

[247] Petrie, *Tell el Hesy*, 12. (my italics)
[248] For an overview, see the chapter on the "Albright Watershed," in Davis, *Shifting Sands*, 47–94.
[249] For discussion, see P. R. S. Moorey, "Kathleen Kenyon and Palestinian Archaeology," *Palestine Exploration Quarterly* 111 (1979): 3–10; Dever, "Archaeological Method," 44–45.
[250] Joseph Callaway, "New Evidence on the Conquest of 'Ai," *Journal of Biblical Literature* 87.3 (1968): 312.
[251] Fritzsche, *Stranded in the Present*, 106.

What our survey of Bronze and Iron Age settlements demonstrated is that the biblical writers inhabited a world in which ruins were visible throughout the landscapes familiar to them. It does not matter where these scribes were located nor, for that matter, the specific time period in which they were active. From Hazor in the north to Arad in the south, from the city of Jericho in the Jordan Valley to sites scattered along the coastal plain, those living in the southern Levant in the first millennium BCE occupied a terrain in which the remains of numerous Bronze and Iron Age sites were in view. Even at locations that had not been destroyed, more venerable ruins, centuries old, would have often featured as part of the urban landscape, such as at Hebron, Jerusalem, and Megiddo, among other settlements. If the biblical writings express little interest in what lay buried, it is not because material remains of past populations were unknown to them.

Rather, what is striking about these biblical accounts is their consistent recognition of ruins and their antiquity. Frequently, ruins are depicted as the outcome of wanton acts of destruction that took place in the past or simply as remains left behind from former events or practices, wearing away as time progresses. Whether in the fallen fortifications of a settlement or buildings long abandoned, the ruins the biblical writers depict are frequently the items that archaeologists, today, unearth.

These points of continuity dissipate, however, when turning to matters of time. What separates our experience of ruins from those behind the biblical writings, I have argued, is how we locate material remains within the sweep of history. To us, it is the variations of material forms preserved in the archaeological record that provide the possibility of situating their remains within distinct eras, the forward flow of time giving rise to new developments that can be distinguished from what came before. Changes in architectural style and ceramic assemblages, foodways and ritual practices, among other instances, allow us to peg these remains within certain periods in the Bronze or Iron Age, and at moments even in specific centuries.

The biblical writings, however, conceive of the temporality of ruins differently. Like Altdorfer's portrait, the biblical writings are less sensitive to the discontinuities that mark the passing of time, where the world in which David acquired Jerusalem is not too distant from the ones Jeremiah or Ezekiel knew many centuries later. In the Hebrew Bible, the material remains that arose in the past are principally attached to one age, an age whose ways of life are mostly consistent with the biblical writers' own. The time that ruins convey to these scribes is something other than our sense of the depth of history and the developments that have taken place across the millennia. To us, the MBA is a decisive moment in the history of the southern Levant, leaving behind monumental ruins that are some of the most impressive remains from antiquity. The collapse of this society then gives way to centuries of Egyptian hegemony and the construction of Egyptian outposts at Jaffa and Beth-Shean, among other instances of Egyptian involvement. But of the great cities of the MBA or Egyptian control of the region during the LBA, much less the eras that came before, the biblical writings show little awareness or interest.

At work in a world in which past experiences and present ones were believed to have much in common, the inclination to scour ruins for the differences that marked out the lives of forebears was, I contend, less pronounced for the biblical writers. Yet for us this impulse is a guiding presupposition, our sense of the past marked above all by an awareness of discontinuity, of time fractured into distinct periods by changes in technology, taste, politics, and commerce. Ruins are evidence of the developments that have taken hold over the course of time, the EBA II ruins of ca. 2500 BCE being distinct from MBA and LBA settlements that arose hundreds of years after them, let alone from the still later Iron Age, Persian, or Hellenistic communities that would emerge. But this way of looking at ruins is quite recent. The point is straightforward but no less meaningful: The discipline of archaeology is born late, the product of a rupture in the experience of time.

For Ricoeur, this experience speaks to our "historical condition." By *condition*, Ricoeur writes of a twofold meaning: the first, that of being situated, implicated, enclosed; the second, that of something that makes possible a way

25 Catharine Wolfe expedition to Sippar (Tell Abu Habba). John Henry Haynes, photograph, 1884. Sterrett Collection of Archaeological Photographs. Photographs of Asia Minor, #4776. Division of Rare and Manuscript Collections, Cornell University Library. Public domain

of being in the world. In contrast to those who came before, "[w]e make history, and we make histories," Ricoeur writes, "because we are historical."[252] The claim is not triumphant. Ricoeur will write of the "burden" of history and later of the "devastating effect" that the "*historicization* of all human experience" occasions, drawing near to the arguments of Friedrich Nietzsche from a century before.[253] Nevertheless, this condition is ours, something that is "insurmountable," Ricoeur writes, unable, as we are, to think otherwise or beyond it.[254] Our "ambivalence" to this mode of temporality, Koselleck writes in a similar vein, is an experience we cannot outpace.[255]

But if our understanding of ruins is inescapably historical and our practices of excavation recent, the question that emerges is how ruins were experienced otherwise by those behind the biblical writings. In Chapters 2, 3, and 4, we take up this question.

---

[252] Ricoeur, *Memory, History, Forgetting*, 284.
[253] Ibid., 303. Italics original. For Ricoeur's reading of Nietzsche on this theme, see 287–92. "One can wonder," Ricoeur comments later in a key passage, "if the idea of truth, but also the ideas of the good and the just, can be radically historicized without disappearing." Ibid., 304. On this point, see the final reflections in Chapter 4.
[254] Ibid., 284.   [255] Koselleck, *Futures Past*, 104.

TWO

SHILOH AND THE RUINS OF MEMORY

> Scaling little ladders with glue pots and pails of lysol
> I crawl like an ant in mourning
> Over the weedy acres of your brow
> To mend the immense skull plates and clear
> The bald, white tumuli of your eyes.
>
> A blue sky out of the Oresteia
> Arches above us. O father, all by yourself
> You are pithy and historical as the Roman Forum.
> I open my lunch on a hill of black cypress.
> Your fluted bones and acanthine hair are littered
>
> In their old anarchy to the horizon-line.
> It would take more than a lightning-stroke
> To create such a ruin.[1]

Heinrich Schliemann returned to the ruins of Mycenae on August 19, 1876.[2] The excavations he now had permission to undertake were motivated by similar convictions to those that had led him to Hissarlik six years before, driven by a confidence that there was more to Homer's poems than myth and fable. There on the Aegean coast and against scholarly consensus he had

---

[1] Sylvia Plath, "The Colossus," in *The Colossus and Other Poems*, 20–21 (New York: Vintage Books, 1957), 20.

[2] Heinrich Schliemann, *Mycenae: A Narrative of Researches and Discoveries at Mycenae and Tiryns* (New York: Scribner, Armstrong & Company, 1878), 24.

26 Lion Gate, Mycenae. Zde, photograph. Creative Commons Attribution-Share Alike 4.0 international license

located the ancient site of Troy,[3] even if his vulgar digging methods led him to destroy large swaths of the location he intended to find, misidentifying the stratum most closely connected to the period of the *Iliad* by one thousand years.[4] Caution and restraint were not traits Schliemann typically exhibited, however, and so with Homer's poems in hand he once again embarked with his personal fortune and team of workers further west to the Argolis, this time with a new objective in mind: to unearth Agamemnon's ancient capital.[5]

Unlike Troy, the site of Mycenae had been known for centuries. The famous Lion Gate and the cyclopean walls of the site, visible since antiquity, had attracted visitors long before Schliemann's arrival. But in a time when few excavations were funded by governments or universities, Schliemann's personal wealth afforded him the opportunity to dig in ways others could not.

---

[3] A. H. Sayce, "Preface," in Heinrich Schliemann, *Troja: Results of the Last Researches and Discoveries on the Site of Homer's Troy*, v–xxx (London: John Murray, 1884), v–vi. On Schliemann's cool reception among the German classicists and philologists of his time, see Suzanne Marchand, *Down from Olympus: Archaeology and Philhellenism in Germany 1750–1970* (Princeton, NJ: Princeton University Press, 1996), 118–24.

[4] Charles Brian Rose, *The Archaeology of Greek and Roman Troy* (Cambridge: Cambridge University Press, 2014), 2–7, 17–43; Eric Cline, *Three Stones Make a Wall: The Story of Archaeology* (Princeton, NJ: Princeton University Press, 2018), 24–34.

[5] On this campaign, see Leo Deuel, *Memoirs of Heinrich Schliemann* (New York: Harper & Row, 1977), 215–52.

27 Mask of Agamemnon. National Archaeology Museum, Athens. Creative Commons CC0 1.0 universal public domain

After a few months at Mycenae, the news was once again sensational: Five monumental shaft graves had been discovered within the walls of the ancient site, their occupants numbering seventeen adults and two children, including an adult male who wore a gold funeral mask that preserved his bearded features.[6] On November 28, a telegraph written in French arrived for the King of Greece: "With great joy I announce to your majesty that I have discovered the tombs ... of Agamemnon, Cassandra, Eurymedon, and their comrades."[7] The graves were those of Agamemnon and the others

---

[6] Schliemann, *Mycenae*, 333–62; Cathy Gere, *The Tomb of Agamemnon* (Harvard, MA: Harvard University Press, 2012), 7–10; Lena Papazoglou-Manioudaki et al., "Mycenae Revisited Part 3: The Human Remains from Grave Circle A. Behind the Masks: A Study of the Bones of Shaft Graves I–V," *The Annual of the British School at Athens*, 105 (2010): 157–224.

[7] "Avec une extrême joie j'annonce à Votre Majesté que j'ai découvert les tombeaux ... d'Agamemnon, de Cassandra, d'Eurymédon et de leurs camarades." A reprint of the telegraph is found in Schliemann, *Mycenae*, 365.

murdered alongside him on his return from Troy (*Od.* 11.405–35), the mask Agamemnon's own.

Neither claim was true. In time, further excavations at Mycenae revealed that those interred in the shaft graves lived in an era (ca. sixteenth century BCE) that predated the period in which Homer's poems were set by at least three centuries.[8] Grave Circle A, where these tombs were found, attested to a history of Mycenae that far preceded the Homeric age, much as Schliemann's discovery of Troy II in the years before offered evidence of an ancient community no Homeric poet would have known existed.

But Schliemann's "great joy" in unearthing what he believed was Agamemnon's tomb offers us a pointed example of how readily the material remains of Mycenae could elicit associations with a Homeric past, long remembered in the *Iliad*, most of all,[9] but also in the later texts of Athenaeus, Clement of Alexandria, and in the *Oresteia* of Aeschylus. For Schliemann, the ruins of Mycenae could only be those left behind from its most famous ruler, bodying forth Agamemnon once more by way of the location's ruined citadel and the royal tomb in which his corpse lay. Though a "definite opinion" of these artifacts, Schliemann admits, might be out of reach, "an imagination enlightened by the vivid descriptions of Homer and the tragedians" would nevertheless recognize these remains as those left behind from Agamemnon's rule.[10] If we now know that these impressions were mistaken, the power of Mycenae's ruins to evoke Agamemnon's past nevertheless persists. Even today, the grave goods and funeral mask recovered by Schliemann are some of the most visited items on display at the National Museum of Archaeology in Athens,[11] the latter still labeled with the name Schliemann gave to it: the "Mask of Agamemnon."

---

[8] Spyros Iakovidis, *Late Helladic Citadels on Mainland Greece* (Leiden: Brill, 1983), 37–39; Elizabeth French, "Mycenae," in *The Oxford Handbook of the Bronze Age Aegean*, ed. E. Cline, 671–79 (Oxford: Oxford University Press, 2012).

[9] On the role of memory and orality in the formation of Homeric epic, see the penetrating observations in F. A. Wolf's *Prolegomena to Homer, 1795*, trans. A. Grafton, G. Most, and J. Zetzel (Princeton, NJ: Princeton University Press, 1985), 108–11. For more recent studies, see Barry Powell, *Homer and the Origin of the Greek Alphabet* (Cambridge: Cambridge University Press, 1996), 221–37; Elizabeth Minchin, *Homer and the Resources of Memory: Some Applications of Cognitive Theory to the Iliad and Odyssey* (Oxford: Oxford University Press, 2001), 1–31; Elizabeth Minchin, "Spatial Memories and the Composition of the Iliad," in *Orality, Literacy, Memory in the Ancient Greek and Roman World*, ed. E. A. Mackay, 9–34 (Leiden: Brill, 2008); Jonathan Ready, *Orality, Textuality, and the Homeric Epics: An Interdisciplinary Study of Oral Texts, Dictated Texts, and Wild Texts* (New York: Oxford University Press, 2019).

[10] Schliemann, *Mycenae*, 149.

[11] On the exhibition and history of these remains, see Gere, *The Tomb of Agamemnon*, 1–24. As Gere observes, "The Tomb of Agamemnon may not exist, but it has nonetheless had a highly productive career" (23).

Schliemann was not the first, however, to visit the ruins of Mycenae with thoughts of Agamemnon in mind. Well over two thousand years before, Thucydides refers to the ruins of the city at the outset of his great work (*Thuc.* 1.9–10), offering a brief description of the dilapidated settlement in an opening section devoted to what could be known of an age before the Peloponnesian War.[12] Commenting on the "testimony of Homer," Thucydides turns to the reign of Agamemnon and the ruins of his city, to temples apparently still standing and the foundation of buildings visible at the time. Much of what was present at Mycenae must have been the remains of the site destroyed by the Argives in 468 BCE, but no attempt is made in this work to distinguish the ruins of a more distant past from a more recent one.[13] For Thucydides, like Schliemann after him, what is found at the city are traces of Agamemnon's undertakings from a distant time, a location where a Homeric past can still be visited and reflected on because its ruins endure. Indeed, the "small place" that Thucydides encounters at Mycenae attests to the greatness of Agamemnon, demonstrating that power resides not in opulent and monumental works, as Herodotus once suggested, but rather in political vision.[14] Agamemnon is a formidable ruler in spite of a city whose ruins are not the equal of Thucydides' Athens.

The orbital pull of Mycenae's ruins would continue to draw visitors to the site after Thucydides. In the second century CE, some five hundred years after the *History of the Peloponnesian War* was written, Pausanias travels to the location and provides us with the most detailed description of the site's remains from antiquity. Among the features that Pausanias spotlights, we read once more of the Lion Gate and the cyclopean walls, now already quite ancient. But what distinguishes Pausanias' account are the remains he observes "inside the ruins of Mycenae," where, among other features, he comes across the "tombs of those who returned with Agamemnon from Troy" (*Paus.* 2.16.6). What it is that Pausanias observes and how he makes this connection to the ill-fated travelers is uncertain. But it would be these tombs and their presumed victims, the latter sung about by Homeric bards a thousand years before, that would so captivate Schliemann's imagination seventeen hundred years later.

§

---

[12] On Thucydides' discussion of these ruins, see R. M. Cook, "Thucydides as Archaeologist," *The Annual of the British School at Athens*, 50 (1955): 266–70; Simon Hornblower, *A Commentary on Thucydides*, Vol. 1: Books I–III (Oxford: Clarendon Press, 1991), 33–36.

[13] In a point that finds agreement with Koselleck's theory of temporalization discussed in Chapter 1, Cook writes, "Thucydides, and indeed the ancients generally, believed that *Greek culture had continued from Heroic times to their own without any serious break or revolution*; and so Agamemnon's Mycenae and fifth-century Mycenae could be thought of as one city." Cook, "Thucydides," 467. (my italics)

[14] Hornblower, *Commentary on Thucydides*, 33–35.

This study examines the connection between ruins and impressions of the past in the Hebrew Bible. A defining feature of the biblical discourse on ruination, it was maintained in Chapter 1, is that ruined sites are frequently portrayed as remains left behind from former times. The venerable character of these locations can be described through language that explicitly expresses their antiquity, such as references to the "ruins of old" (חרבות עולם) in Is 58:12 or the "perpetual ruins" (חרבות לנצח) of Ps 9:7. But more frequently, the association between ruins and the past is conveyed through narratives that refer to ruined sites or tell stories about how these ruins came to be.

The past affiliated with ruins in the Hebrew Bible can nevertheless depart from our historical understanding of these remains today. This disparity is felt most acutely in our dating of ruins, a practice whereby we assign artifacts to distinct periods on the basis of stratigraphy and typological developments. To return to a key argument from Chapter 1, we are highly sensitive to differences that demarcate one age from the next, where lived experience is presumed to exhibit asymmetries as the centuries advance. Ruins are evidence of these variances realized across time. Domestic architecture in the highlands of the southern Levant, to cite one example, increasingly exhibits the "pillared" form with the onset of the Iron Age in a manner that separates these homes from earlier antecedents and from those that would be built later in the centuries of the Persian period.[15] But no biblical text reflects on these changes of architectural style, nor are there any indications in these writings that ruins could be investigated to better understand what separates life in the past from life in the present.

Our distinct appraisal of ruins suggests that how we experience them is something historically specific, a product of a particular "space" or "order of time," to draw again from the works of Reinhart Koselleck and François Hartog.[16] In Chapter 2, we examine how this past was experienced otherwise in antiquity. The point of departure for our study is the site of Shiloh, a location familiar to those behind the biblical corpus and in ruins when their texts about it were written down. Much like the representation of Mycenae in later Greek accounts, then, what Shiloh offers us is the opportunity to investigate how a ruined site factored into stories and poems written down in

---

[15] Lawrence Stager, "The Archaeology of the Family in Ancient Israel," *Bulletin of the American Schools of Oriental Research* 260 (1985): 1–35; Avraham Faust and Shlomo Bunimovitz, "The Four Room House: Embodying Iron Age Israelite Society," *Near Eastern Archaeology* 66 (2003): 22–31. For more recent discussion with bibliography, see James Hardin, *Lahav II: Households and the Use of Domestic Space at Iron II Tell Halif: An Archaeology of Destruction* (Winona Lake, IN: Eisenbrauns, 2010), 44–74.

[16] Reinhart Koselleck, *Futures Past: On the Semantics of Historical Time*, trans. K. Tribe (New York: Columbia University Press, 2004), 26–42, 255–76; François Hartog, *Regimes of Historicity: Presentism and Experiences of Time*, trans. S. Brown (New York: Columbia University Press, 2015), xv–xvii.

antiquity about a time previous to its destruction. The questions raised by these writings is what pasts were recalled about this ruined site and how they came to be.

My response to these questions begins with an overview of the archaeological evidence from Khirbet Seilun (biblical Shiloh), a settlement located approximately 30 km north of Jerusalem.[17] What comes to light through this investigation is Shiloh's fluorescence in the Middle Bronze Age (MBA) II and Iron I periods, after which time the location is destroyed and mostly abandoned, with only limited occupation at the site until it is fully rebuilt in the late Hellenistic period nearly one thousand years later. What is meaningful about these archaeological remains for our purposes is the relatively early date of Shiloh's destruction in the Iron I period, an event that occurred sometime in the latter half of the eleventh century BCE. Given this timeframe, the biblical stories and poems composed about the location would have been written down in the aftermath of Shiloh's destruction when the ruins of the settlement were still in view.[18]

Though Shiloh had fallen before the biblical texts about it were written down, the settlement is nevertheless depicted in a number of pivotal narratives. These portrayals begin during the period when the Israelites were already said to have first settled in Canaan and extend centuries later into the era after Jerusalem was destroyed. Some of these passages associate Shiloh with the final resting place of the tabernacle (Josh 18–22; Ps 78:60). Other texts portray Shiloh as the home of an important Yahweh temple and where the prophet Samuel was raised (Judges 18:31; 1 Sam 1–4). And still other writings relate Shiloh to developments that occur later in time, both when Jerusalem is said to have supplanted Shiloh as the sanctuary of this deity (Ps 78:68) and when Jerusalem was on the precipice of its own downfall (Jer 7, 26).

How to explain these rich accounts of Shiloh's past when the location itself was in ruins is the key historical question that confronts us. Absent the forms of representation so common to our time – museums carefully curated to offer information about previous eras; archaeological sites to explore; vast archives of

---

[17] On the archaeological remains of the site, see Marie-Louise Buhl and Svend Holm-Nielsen, *Shiloh: The Danish Excavations at Tall Sailun, Palestine, in 1926, 1929, 1932, and 1963: The Pre-Hellenistic Remains* (Copenhagen: National Museum of Denmark, 1969); Israel Finkelstein et al., "Excavations at Shiloh 1981–1984: Preliminary Report," *Tel Aviv* 12 (1985): 123–80; Israel Finkelstein, Shlomo Bunimovitz, and Zvi Lederman, *Shiloh: The Archaeology of a Biblical Site* (Tel Aviv: Institute of Archaeology of Tel Aviv, 1993). See also the discussion of these remains in Donald Schley, *Shiloh: A Biblical City in Tradition and History* (Sheffield: JSOT Press, 1989), 67–79; Ann-Kathrin Knittel, *Das erinnerte Heiligtum: Tradition und Geschichte der Kultstätte in Schilo* (Göttingen: Vandenhoeck & Ruprecht, 2019), 31–54.

[18] This point is self-evident in terms of Jeremiah's references and Ps 78, both of which refer to Shiloh's ruination as having taken place in the past. For other references to Shiloh, see Section 2.2.

images, photographs, and recordings; libraries filled with large quantities of texts[19] – Shiloh's past, I contend, would have been accessed and intuited differently by the ancient individuals behind the biblical references to it. To account for Shiloh's representation in the Hebrew Bible, this study turns to more recent theoretical discussions on the attachments that obtain between ruins and remembrance. By virtue of the strong associations between memory and material remains, I maintain that a crucial reason why we possess such an array of stories about Shiloh in the biblical writings is that the ruins of the settlement endured for centuries after its destruction, unrestored and largely uninhabited.

In the Book of Jeremiah, this bond between ruins and remembrance is apparent. In that work, the prophet commands his contemporaries to visit the remains of Shiloh four hundred years after its downfall so as to draw lessons for what its demise might mean (Jer 7:12; 26:9). But for other biblical passages, too, I argue, the experience of Shiloh's ruins framed a spectrum of memories associated with its past. The ruins of the location would have been an evocative feature of the landscape for those behind these writings, its remains scattered just to the east of the main north-south road that ran through the central highlands (Judges 21:19),[20] calling to mind Shiloh's former importance, and its end.

2.1 SHILOH: AN ARCHAEOLOGICAL PERSPECTIVE

Khirbet Seilun is situated on a hill 714m above sea level at a distance of around 2km east of what is today the Jerusalem-Nablus road that runs through the central highlands. To the south of the settlement is a broad valley suitable for agriculture and to its northeast a spring, the 'Ein Seilun, that watered the site in antiquity.[21]

For the biblical writers, Shiloh was located within the tribal lands of Ephraim, positioned between Shechem to the north and Bethel to the south, both of which were also situated on the important transit route that continued on to Tirzah and, eventually, the Jezreel Valley. The modern identification of Shiloh with Khirbet Seilun was made during Edward Robinson's travels

---

[19] Of our time and the "incessant need to authenticate the 'real'", Roland Barthes writes of "the photograph (immediate witness of 'what was here'), reportage, exhibitions of ancient objects (the success of the Tutankhamen show makes this quite clear), the tourism of monuments and historical sites," all of which emerge near the same moment when the discipline of archaeology also appears. Roland Barthes, "The Reality Effect," in *The Rustle of Language*, trans. R. Howard, 141–48 (Berkeley: University of California Press, 1989), 146.

[20] David Dorsey, *The Roads and Highways of Ancient Israel* (Baltimore: Johns Hopkins University, 1991), 132–40.

[21] Finkelstein et al., "Excavations at Shiloh 1981–1984," 125; Israel Finkelstein, "Introduction," in *Shiloh: The Archaeology of a Biblical Site*, 1–14 (Tel Aviv: Tel Aviv University Press, 1993), 1.

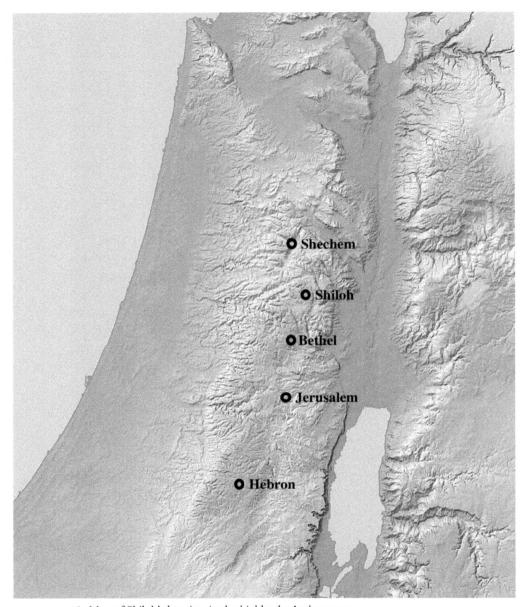

28 Map of Shiloh's location in the highlands. Author map

through Palestine in 1838,[22] an identification secured through descriptions of the site's location in Eusebius' *Onomasticon* and in the Madaba Map, both of which refer to the location, in addition to biblical references (e.g., Judges

[22] Edward Robinson, *Biblical Researches in Palestine, Mount Sinai and Arabia Petraea: A Journal of Travels in the Year 1838*, Vol. III (Boston: Crocker & Brewster, 1841), 84–89. "We came at 7 o'clock to the ruins of Seilûn, surrounded by hills, but looking out through the small valley we had traversed ... As we came up, three startled owls flew off in dismay." Ibid., 85–86.

29 View from Tel Shiloh. Ron Almog, photograph. Creative Commons Attribution 2.0 generic license

21:19) and the site's Arabic name. The settlement was first excavated by a Danish team led by Hans Kjaer from 1926 to 1932 with the assistance of W. F. Albright and included an additional one-season dig in 1963 by Svend Holm-Nielsen.[23] From 1981 to 1984 four seasons of excavation were carried out under the direction of Israel Finkelstein on behalf of Bar-Ilan University. Currently, excavations are being pursued by the Associates of Biblical Research (ABR), led by Scott Stripling.[24]

Though traces of settlement activity precede it,[25] it was in the MB IIC period (ca. 1650–1550 BCE; Stratum VII) when Shiloh became a settlement of some standing in the region. Much like a number of highland sites at this time – including those at Tirzah (Tell el-Far'ah [North]), Shechem (Tel Balatah), Jerusalem, and Hebron (Tell Rumeideh) – an impressive wall was

---

[23] Buhl and Holm-Nielsen, *Shiloh: The Danish Excavations at Tall Sailun*.
[24] The express intent of ABR is "a Christian apologetics ministry dedicated to demonstrating the historical reliability of the Bible through archaeological and biblical research" (http://biblearchaeology.org). For the purposes of this study, our focus will be on the Danish and Israeli excavations.
[25] Israel Finkelstein, "Conclusion," in *Shiloh: The Archaeology of a Biblical Site*, 371–72.

30 Map of Tel Shiloh. Deror Avi, photograph. Creative Commons Attribution-Share Alike 4.0 international license

erected around Shiloh that was composed of large field stones and a massive glacis that supported it.[26] The wall itself was built according to a "sawtooth" technique of separate components 5–7m in length that were bonded together so as to adapt to the contours of the mound and offer the structure further stability. In light of the ruins that Shiloh would become, what is significant about this enclosure for our purposes is that at points it was found to be more than 5m thick; in Area D of the excavations, it still stands at a height of 6.7m.[27] Large portions of the wall complex would have been visible in antiquity, therefore, long after the MBA period. As Zvi Lederman comments in his overview of the bulwark, the impressive MB IIC remains of this enclosure, including evidence of a "massive tower built of enormous field stones" in Area K, attest to "the great architectural and engineering skill of its builders both in planning and construction."[28]

---

[26] Zvi Lederman, "The Middle Bronze Age IIC Defense System," in Finkelstein et al., "Excavations at Shiloh 1981–1984," 140–46; Israel Finkelstein and Zvi Lederman, "Area H–F: Middle Bronze III Fortifications and Storerooms," in *Shiloh: The Archaeology of a Biblical Site*, 49–64 (Tel Aviv: Tel Aviv University Press, 1993).

[27] Zvi Lederman, "The Middle Bronze Age IIC Defense System," 140–46; Finkelstein, "Conclusion," 374.

[28] Lederman, "Defense System," 144.

The wall that surrounded Shiloh encompassed a settlement 17 dunams in size, or approximately 4 acres. For the MBA location, what emerged in the northern precincts, where excavations were most viable, were a series of rooms adjoined to the wall of the city, filled "almost exclusively with storage jars" and, in Room 1527, the remains of axes, scarabs, and a silver pendant.[29] Curiously, other than these storage rooms that abutted the wall, no other MBA architectural features were located from this era. In light of cultic items recovered from rooms in Area F (cult stands, votive bowls), depositional remains from Area D that were interpreted as possible remnants of a *favissa* from the Late Bronze Age (LBA) I era, and on analogy with the layout of MBA Shechem, Finkelstein contends that a cultic structure likely once stood at the location, perhaps on or near the summit of the site, and that the location thus served predominantly as a sanctuary.[30] He writes,[31]

> We should not dismiss out of hand the possibility ... that MBIIC Shiloh was primarily a sacred *temenos*. If we accept this theory, we may further postulate that its enormous stone and earthworks were intended to enhance the special character of the place: a temple at the summit, earthen fills sloping down to the edges of the tell, a massive *temenos* wall (the "city" wall) surrounding this and beyond it the continuation of the earthworks (the glacis).

Such an interpretation, archaeologically speaking, can only be pressed so far, given the absence of evidence connected explicitly to the ruins of a sanctuary. But, at minimum, the enormous effort that went into building the wall and glacis of the location, in addition to the storage facilities built into them, indicates that Shiloh was a settlement whose significance was worth such an undertaking. The MBA settlement that emerges before us through the lens of its archaeological remains is, therefore, somewhat enigmatic: a highland site encircled by an impressive wall that nevertheless enclosed no remains of domestic buildings but rather storage facilities for what was likely a public building or buildings located at the summit of the site.

Shiloh is destroyed at the end of the MBA period (ca. 1550–1500 BCE) and is thereafter abandoned. In Area D, as noted above, a deposit was unearthed with a large amount of LBA I sherds and bones, suggesting that some activity at the location persisted during this time, likely cultic in nature, though no

---

[29] Israel Finkelstein, "Excavations Results in Other Areas," in Finkelstein et al., "Excavations at Shiloh 1981–1984," 152; Finkelstein, "Conclusion," 375–76.

[30] Finkelstein, "Summary and Conclusions," in Finkelstein et al., "Excavations at Shiloh 1981–1984," 162–63; Finkelstein, "Conclusion," 377; Israel Finkelstein, *The Forgotten Kingdom: The Archaeology and History of Northern Israel* (Atlanta: SBL Press, 2013), 24–25.

[31] Finkelstein, "Summary and Conclusions," 164.

architectural features can be linked to this era.[32] It is only in the Iron I period (ca. 1175–980 BCE) that Shiloh is rebuilt (Stratum V). At this moment, the location consists of a town that may have approached 24 dunams in size, or slightly more expansive than its MBA predecessor.[33] The most meaningful remains from this era were discovered in Area C, where on the western slope of the site a number of pillared buildings were unearthed. Situated against the old MBA wall that served as the back of these edifices and which was used as a terrace for the second story, these structures were found to contain a large number of storage jars but, as with the MBA settlement, produced less evidence of domestic ceramic wares (i.e., kitchen ware).[34] For such reasons, these buildings were also interpreted as being public in nature, used predominantly for storage at the settlement and not as homes.[35] The number of silos carved into the northern and eastern sectors of the location at this point also suggests storage activity within Shiloh's precincts, perhaps in conjunction with the collection of small villages (around twenty-five sites within a 5km radius) that emerged in Shiloh's vicinity during this era.[36] In light of these remains, Iron I Shiloh likely functioned as a hub of administrative and economic activity within a region positioned between Shechem in the north and Bethel and Jerusalem to the south.

Finkelstein also holds out the possibility of cultic activity taking place at Shiloh during this era. Given the intensive labor needed to erect the buildings in Area C and their orientation, Finkelstein writes that "there is a high degree of probability that the Iron Age sanctuary was located on or near the summit of the tell and that the pillared buildings of Area C were some of its auxiliary structures."[37] Such an interpretation presumes that a cultic structure (rather than other types of public buildings) must have resided at the site – a premise that depends largely on biblical references to the location. Nevertheless, the preponderance of storage facilities and wares, in addition to small finds that intimate possible continued cultic activity at the site over the centuries, are, once more, suggestive.

---

[32] Finkelstein suggests continued cultic activity at the site based on these remains. Finkelstein, "Conclusion," 381. Vic Matthews (personal communication) makes the important observation that Shiloh is not mentioned in the Amarna Letters (fourteenth century BCE), again suggesting, perhaps, that the site had fallen into disrepair during the LBA period.

[33] For a more recent reflection on the size of the Iron I site, see Israel Finkelstein, "First Israel, Core Israel, United (Northern) Israel," *Near Eastern Archaeology* 82.1 (2019): 8–15; 11.

[34] Finkelstein, "Conclusion," 384.

[35] Shlomo Bunimovitz, "Area C: The Iron Age I Buildings and Other Remains," in Finkelstein et al., "Excavations at Shiloh 1981–1984," 135–36.

[36] Finkelstein, "Conclusion," 386–87; Finkelstein, *The Forgotten Kingdom: The Archaeology and History of Northern Israel* (Atlanta: SBL Press, 2013), 26.

[37] Finkelstein, "Summary and Conclusions," 169; Finkelstein, "Conclusion," 385–87; cf. Finkelstein, *Forgotten Kingdom*, 25. For a similar interpretation, see Amihai Mazar, *Archaeology of the Land of the Bible 10,000–586 B.C.E.* (New York: Doubleday, 1990), 348.

Much like its MBA predecessor from centuries before, the Iron I community at Shiloh evidently possessed enough standing to be targeted for attack. Carbon-14 dating of remains from Area C indicates that the settlement came to an end sometime between 1050–1000 BCE,[38] its downfall marked by evidence of fire found throughout Stratum V of the city.[39] Since the Iron I site was founded sometime in the late twelfth/early eleventh century BCE, it appears that the community at Shiloh was short-lived, perhaps existing for only fifty years.[40]

Why Shiloh was rebuilt during in the Iron I period, and why it was destroyed shortly thereafter, cannot be determined archaeologically. Shechem's destruction and abandonment around 1150 BCE may have been a catalyst to Shiloh's rise.[41] The ruins of the old MBA city at Shiloh, furthermore, perhaps including those of a cultic area that continued in use in the LBA, may have also contributed to the decision to build there once again.[42] More definitively, what can be said is that for an era (Iron I) marked by mostly small, unwalled villages scattered throughout the central highlands, the "high level of planning and construction at Shiloh" and evidence of "intensive economic and administrative activity" at the location all point toward the site's historical importance at this moment.[43] Iron I Shiloh was a sizable location in an era when few existed in the highlands, built upon the remains of its Bronze Age predecessors – its pillared buildings, ceramic assemblage, and storage installations attesting to the meaningful role it played in the lives of those who populated this area.

After Shiloh's destruction in the eleventh century BCE, it is abandoned once more. A few traces of Iron IIA remains were located at the settlement (Stratum IV), such as the reuse of a cistern in Area C that was accessed by ancient individuals digging through the ruins of the Iron I site.[44] Apart from squatters living among the debris of the town during this time and a few

---

[38] Israel Finkelstein and Eliazer Piasetzky, "The Iron I–IIA in the Highlands and Beyond: 14C Anchors, Pottery Phases and the Shoshenq I Campaign," *Levant* 38 (2006): 45–61; 48–49; Finkelstein, *Forgotten Kingdom*, 24.
[39] Finkelstein, "Summary and Conclusions," 173; Finkelstein, *Forgotten Kingdom*, 24.
[40] Finkelstein, "Summary and Conclusions," 168.
[41] Edward Campbell, *Shechem III: The Stratigraphy and Architecture of Shechem/Tell Balatah*, Vol. 1 (Boston: American Schools of Oriental Research, 2002), 231–33; Edward Campbell, "Shechem," in *New Encyclopedia of Archaeological Excavations in the Holy Land*, Volume IV, 1349–51 (Jerusalem: Israel Exploration Society, 1993), 1352. At Pella, for example, successive temples were built atop one another, including Iron Age sanctuaries above the ruins of previous Bronze Age temples. See Stephen Bourke, "The Six Canaanite Temples of Ṭabaqat Faḥil. Excavating Pella's 'Fortress' Temple (1994–2009)," in *Temple Building and Temple Cult: Architecture and Cultic Paraphernalia of Temples in the Levant (2.–1. Mill. B.C.E.)*, ed. J. Kamlah, 159–201 (Wiesbaden: Harrassowitz Verlag, 2012).
[42] Finkelstein, "Summary and Conclusions," 172; Finkelstein, "Conclusion," 388.
[43] Finkelstein, "Conclusion," 387.   [44] Finkelstein et al., "Excavations at Shiloh," 138.

31 View of Shiloh's ruins. Bukvoed, photograph. Creative Commons Attribution 4.0 international license

structures built some distance away from where the MBA and Iron I remains were recovered, little more can be said. A couple of centuries later some building activity at the location appears once more in the eastern and southern areas of the location, but the remains suggest only a "tiny, insignificant settlement,"[45] with few traces found in the northern and western sectors of the site that had produced most of the remains from the MBA and Iron I eras. It would be another five hundred years, and nearly a millennium after the Iron I settlement had been destroyed, before Shiloh is rebuilt, with "full-scale occupation of the site" being "resumed only in the late Hellenistic period."[46]

With these remains in view, a number of details stand out for our study. The first is the lengthy period of Shiloh's ruination. For nearly a millennium, it appears, Shiloh was left mostly in disrepair. The limited building activity that can be discerned at the site in the Iron Age II (ca. 980–586 BCE) or Persian period (550–330 BCE) seems to have been carried out among ruins that were never fully cleared or restored. It would matter little, then, if an individual came to Shiloh a generation after its destruction in the tenth century BCE or some five centuries later when the region was under Persian control. Throughout the Iron Age and after, what remained of Shiloh was a "large ruin,"[47] as Finkelstein describes it.

[45] Finkelstein, "Conclusion," 389. Cf., Finkelstein, *Forgotten Kingdom*, 24.
[46] Finkelstein, "Conclusion," 389.   [47] Finkelstein, *Forgotten Kingdom*, 50.

But what is also meaningful about these remains is the early date in which they appear. In contrast to the late ninth century BCE destructions in Israel attributed to the Arameans,[48] for example, or the devastations wrought by the Assyrian Empire a century later,[49] Shiloh's downfall preceded these invasions by at least two centuries. From the perspective of Jerusalem's history, Shiloh's destruction was of an even more remote past, preceding David's acquisition of Jerusalem by a generation, according to biblical storytelling, and antedating the eventual Babylonian conquest of the kingdom of Judah (586 BCE) by over four hundred years. Shiloh was one of the earliest Iron Age locations of some size in the highlands to have been overthrown and disestablished, coming to ruin "long ago" from the perspective of later biblical writers.[50] Its fate ran counter to other prominent sites in the highland region that endured throughout the centuries of the early Iron Age, accordingly, made conspicuous for how long its ruins stood.

What those in the Iron Age and centuries after would have encountered when they came across the settlement cannot, of course, be fully known. The most prominent ruins, it appears, would have been the monumental remains left behind from the old MBA wall and glacis. The eleventh century BCE inhabitants of Shiloh built structures into and atop this enclosure, often reusing what components they could of this imposing architectural feature. In addition to the remains of this wall, the burnt-out ruins of Iron I structures with their large storage jars and other wares, such as those found in Area C, would have persisted into the centuries that followed the site's demise, particularly for those rooms that were built adjacent to the MBA bulwark that offered them some stability. And though we can only infer what may once have been present at the summit of the location, there is little doubt that the wreckage of some buildings – likely the largest and most impressive of the site – were

---

[48] See, for example, the discussions in Nadav Na'aman, "The Northern Kingdom in the Late 10th–9th Centuries BCE," in *Understanding the History of Ancient Israel*, ed. H. G. M. Williamson, 399–418 (Oxford: British Academy, 2007); Assaf Kleinman, "The Damascene Subjugation of the Southern Levant as a Gradual Process (ca. 842–800 BCE)," in *In Search for Aram and Israel: Politics Culture, Identity*, eds. O. Sergi, M. Oeming, and I. de Hulster, 57–78 (Tübingen: Mohr Siebeck, 2016).

[49] William Dever, "Archaeology and the Fall of the Northern Kingdom: What Really Happened?" in *"Up to the Gates of Ekron": Essays on the Archaeology and History of the Eastern Mediterranean in Honor of Seymour Gitin*, ed. S. W. Crawford et al., 78–92 (Jerusalem: W. F. Albright Institute of Archaeological Research); Avraham Faust, "Settlement, Economy, and Demography under Assyrian Rule in the West: The Territories of the Former Kingdom of Israel as a Test Case," *Journal of the American Oriental Society* 135.4 (2015): 765–89.

[50] A number of Iron I rural villages and smaller sites in the highlands were abandoned or destroyed, such as Khirbet Raddana or Izbet Sartah (on this point, see Avraham Faust, *Israel's Ethnogenesis: Settlement, Interaction, Expansion, and Resistance* [London: Equinox, 2006], 116–27). But larger settlements in the highlands – Tirzah, Mizpah, Bethel – persisted and increased in size, as Faust also points out, during the Iron II period.

positioned there. If Finkelstein's theory is correct, the ruins of an Iron I temple, possibly built atop or near a previous Bronze Age cultic area, would have featured among Shiloh's fallen landscape. At the very least, texts in Jeremiah presuppose that a place where the name of Yahweh once "dwelled" (Jer 7:12) was present at the location and could still be visited many hundreds of years after it was destroyed.

What is of consequence about the ruins of Shiloh for our purposes is their duration and visibility. Finkelstein observes that, "In contrast to the decline of Shiloh, settlement in southern Samaria flourishes during the Iron Age II and the number of sites almost doubled."[51] Indeed, when one turns to other locations in the highlands – such as Tirzah, Shechem, Bethel, or, further south still, to Gibeon, Jerusalem, and Hebron – what we find is that many settlements in the Iron II period flourished at this time, increasing in size and population. Yet at Shiloh, such growth did not take hold. Instead, Shiloh persisted for centuries in a state of ruination during an otherwise prosperous era that witnessed an upsurge in settlement activity among the kingdoms of Israel and Judah.

Why Shiloh was not rebuilt on a more impressive scale in the Iron II period is unknown. It may be that other locations in its vicinity, such as Bethel or Shechem, became the focus of settlement activity after Shiloh was destroyed, or that the location, existing only briefly after its MBA florescence, was no longer deemed a viable site for more lasting occupancy. Perhaps, like the ruins on the acropolis of Hazor, Shiloh's remains were safeguarded and preserved, as Ezekiel, it appears, desired for Jerusalem's later ruins (Ezek 33:23–29). But as the kingdoms of Israel and Judah grew around it, Shiloh remained in disrepair, joining a collection of other sites in the southern Levant that were left in ruins after their fall. The question, then, is what the biblical writings recount about this location – a site that had gone to ruin in a more distant past.

2.2 SHILOH IN THE HEBREW BIBLE

Understanding Shiloh's appearance in the Hebrew Bible is complicated by the fact that we cannot date these writings with any historical precision. In contrast to the archaeological remains of the settlement that can be situated within a span of around fifty to seventy-five years on the basis of carbon-14 evidence,[52] the biblical texts that make mention of Shiloh resist attempts to locate their composition within even a specific century. In large measure, our inability to locate these texts more precisely is the result of the anonymity of the storytellers behind these writings. In contrast to our practices, the ancient Hebrew

---

[51] Finkelstein, "Conclusion," 389.
[52] See again Finkelstein and Piasetzky, "The Iron I–IIA in the Highlands," 45–49.

scribes who produced these writings revealed little about themselves or the worlds in which they produced their documents, effectively disappearing into the documents they composed and taking with them historical traces of the eras in which they wrote.[53] In addition, it is apparent that the biblical writings we now possess were revised over a lengthy period of time, meaning that the Books of Samuel or Jeremiah, for example, where Shiloh features prominently, appear different in their current forms than those earlier versions of these works that preceded them. For these two books in particular, the complex history of their composition is borne out by the differences, sometimes substantial, between the Masoretic (MT) and Septuagint (LXX) recensions of these works. The manuscripts discovered from Qumran (DSS), furthermore, depart from even these.

But for our study, two points matter most about the complex compositional history of these writings. First, the texts that refer to Shiloh are not eyewitness accounts. Though the biblical scribes situate their stories about Shiloh primarily in what we today would term the LBA (Book of Joshua) and the Iron I period (Judges and Samuel), there is little evidence that these individuals lived and wrote during these times.[54] What era the biblical writers did inhabit is a matter of enormous debate.[55] But for this investigation, what matters is that these scribes lived in a world that post-dated Shiloh's destruction.

Second, the stories these scribes told were often shaped by older sources. The form these sources took (oral, written) and the information they conveyed about Shiloh's past are, once again, matters of debate. Given the relatively early date in which Shiloh is destroyed (ca. 1050 BCE), it is reasonable to surmise

---

[53] See more recently Brennan Breed, *Nomadic Text: A Theory of Biblical Reception History* (Bloomington: Indiana University Press, 2014), 75–92; Steven Weitzman, "Text and Context in Biblical Studies: A Brief History of a Troubled Relationship," in *The Wiley Blackwell Companion to Ancient Israel*, ed. S. Niditch, 67–83 (London: John Wiley & Sons, 2016).

[54] Alphabetic texts are clearly present in the epigraphic record already in the LBA, attesting to the presence of writing in this script tradition during these centuries. But the appearance of lengthy narrative prose works such as those found in the Hebrew Bible emerge, as in other literary cultures, centuries after a writing system develops, likely around the ninth century BCE. On this point, see Christopher Rollston, "Scribal Education in Ancient Israel: The Old Hebrew Epigraphic Evidence," *Bulletin of the American Schools of Oriental Research* 344 (2006): 47–74; Ryan Byrne, "The Refuge of Scribalism in Iron I Palestine," *Bulletin of the American Schools of Oriental Research* 345 (2007): 1–31; Seth Sanders, *The Invention of Hebrew* (Champaign: University of Illinois Press, 2009), 130–33; William Schniedewind, *A Social History of Hebrew: Its Origins through the Rabbinic Period* (New Haven, CT: Yale University Press, 2013), 31–48; and Daniel Pioske, *Memory in a Time of Prose: Studies in Epistemology, Hebrew Scribalism, and the Biblical Past* (New York: Oxford University Press, 2018), 25–38.

[55] See, for example, the discussions in Reinhard Kratz, *The Composition of the Narrative Books of the Old Testament*, trans. J. Bowden (London: T&T Clark, 2005); David Carr, *The Formation of the Hebrew Bible: A New Reconstruction* (Oxford: Oxford University Press, 2011); Konrad Schmid, *The Old Testament: A Literary History*, trans. L. Maloney (Minneapolis: Fortress, 2012).

that much of the source material available about the location was oral in form.⁵⁶ Nevertheless, it cannot be discounted that certain anecdotes and references about Shiloh's past were preserved in writing.⁵⁷ More important for this study, however, is that the biblical writers would have drawn on older source material to tell stories about Shiloh at a time when the location itself was in ruins.

In the following, we examine these biblical portrayals of Shiloh. What comes to light are varied and, at times, competing images of the location in the Hebrew Bible, a site that comes to prominence when the Israelites enter Canaan and that continues to have some standing until the location fades from narrative view somewhat abruptly and enigmatically shortly before the rise of David to the throne. How to account for these distinct representations of Shiloh's past is the question pursued in the subsequent discussion, where the biblical depictions of the location are situated alongside what we know about Shiloh's archaeological remains.

2.2.1 *The Book of Joshua*

References to Shiloh appear in a number of works within the Hebrew Bible, the earliest of which, both canonically and in terms of the era in which its stories are set, are found in the Book of Joshua.⁵⁸ The scribes behind this work

---

⁵⁶ By way of orientation to studies of orality and narrative storytelling, see the important works of Ruth Finnegan, *Oral Traditions and the Verbal Arts: A Guide to Research Practices* (London: Routledge, 1992), 106–15; David Rubin, *Memory in Oral Traditions: A Cognitive Psychology of Epics, Ballads, and Counting-Out Rhymes* (New York: Oxford University Press, 1995), 6–13; Minchin, *Homer and the Resources of Memory*, 1–31; John Foley, "Memory in Oral Tradition," in *Performing the Gospel: Orality, Memory, and Mark*, eds. R. Horsely et al., 83–96 (Minneapolis: Fortress, 2011); David Carr, "Orality, Textuality, *and* Memory: The State of Biblical Studies," in *Contextualizing Israel's Sacred Writings: Ancient Literacy, Orality, and Literary Production*, ed. B. Schmidt, 161–73 (Atlanta: SBL Press, 2015). Haun Saussy, *The Ethnography of Rhythm: Orality and Its Technologies* (New York: Fordham University Press, 2016), 63–85. On the "informing orality" that impressed itself on the formation of the biblical writings, see F. W. Dobbs-Allsopp, *On Biblical Poetry* (New York: Oxford, 2015), 233–325.

⁵⁷ For a discussion of the development of a native Hebrew narrative prose tradition, see Pioske, *Memory in a Time of Prose*, 16–54; Daniel Pioske, "The Appearance of Prose and the Fabric of History," in *The Hunt for Ancient Israel: Essays in Honour of Diana V. Edelman*, eds. C. Shafer Elliott et al., 313–35 (London: Equinox, 2022). Cf. Frank Polak, "The Oral and the Written: Syntax, Stylistics and the Development of Biblical Prose Narrative," *Journal of Near Eastern Studies* 26 (1998): 59–105; Sanders, *Invention of Hebrew*, 103–56; Susan Niditch, "Hebrew Bible and Oral Literature: Misconceptions and New Directions," in *The Interface of Orality and Writing: Speaking, Seeing, Writing in the Shaping of New Genres*, eds. A. Weissenrieder and R. Coote, 3–18 (Tübingen: Mohr Siebeck, 2015), 13–17; Dobbs-Allsopp, *On Biblical Poetry*, 243–46; Raymond Person, "Biblical Historiography as Traditional History," in *The Oxford Handbook of Biblical Narrative*, ed. D. Fewell, 73–83 (Oxford: Oxford University Press, 2016).

⁵⁸ It may be that Gen 49:10 preserves a reference to Shiloh, though a number of difficulties surround this passage, including the orthography of Shiloh itself, which appears as שִׁילֹה in the

situate their narratives sometime in the late thirteenth to early twelfth centuries BCE, or roughly the waning moments of the LBA.[59] Apart from the Book of Samuel, Shiloh appears more often in Joshua than anywhere else in the Hebrew Bible.

What distinguishes references to Shiloh in the Book of Joshua is that they occur only in the later sections of this work, enclosed among chapters 18–22 (and Josh 24 in LXX), which offer details about events that take place after the subjugation of Canaan by Israelite forces. Because these narratives center primarily on depictions of tribal land allocation and the establishment of the tent of meeting, the allusions to Shiloh in Joshua have long been associated with the Priestly tradition (P), whether in direct connection with Priestly writers or under the influence of their worldview and literary style.[60] When these stories were written down is a question bound up with the thorny issue of how to date the Priestly writings, a question whose responses vary from the late Iron Age to the Persian/early Hellenistic period.[61] But even a very early

---

MT and ἀποκείμενα in LXX (Leningrad and others). If this text does indeed hold Shiloh in view, however, then we possess a further memory of Shiloh from another distinct tradition in the Hebrew Bible, one that links it to Judah and the Davidic line in a manner that resembles the references to the location in Ps 78. On these issues, see Serge Frolov, "Judah Comes to Shiloh: Genesis 49:10bα, One More Time," *Journal of Biblical Literature* 131.3 (2012): 417–22. For our purposes, however, we focus on better attested allusions to the location.

[59] For a recent and updated overview of the chronology of the exodus and conquest accounts, see Lawrence Geraty, "Exodus Dates and Theories," in *Israel's Exodus in Transdisciplinary Perspective*, eds. T. Levy et al., 55–64 (New York: Springer, 2015).

[60] See Wellhausen's influential analysis that attributed Joshua 18:1, 11–25; 19:10–48, 51; 20; 21, and 22:9–34 to P (Julius Wellhausen, *Die Composition des Hexateuchs und der historischen Bücher des Alten Testaments*, 2nd ed. [Berlin: G. Reimer, 1899], 116–33, esp. 127–28). This point was also conceded in M. Noth's commentary on Joshua that was otherwise so focused on the redactional efforts of his Deuteronomistic Historian (Martin Noth, *Das Buch Josua*, 2nd ed. [Tübingen: J. C. B. Mohr, 1953], 10–11). See also Haran's important observations on the connection between P and Shiloh in Menahem Haran, "Shiloh and Jerusalem: The Origin of the Priestly Tradition in the Pentateuch," *Journal of Biblical Literature* 81.1 (1962): 19–24; and observations in Blum, *Pentateuch*, 225–28. For a fine overview of this orientation of scholarship, see Schley, *Shiloh*, 101–26. For a more recent discussion, see Knittel, *Das erinnerte Heiligtum*, 204–7. For a broader overview of this compositional history, see also Thomas Dozeman, *Joshua 1–12* (New Haven, CT: Yale University Press, 2015), 5–31. For further discussions of P in Joshua, see Volkmar Fritz, *Das Buch Josua* (Zürich: Theologischer Verlag Zürich, 2008), 19–20; Ernst Axel Knauf, *Josua* (Zürich: Theologischer Verlag, 2008), 17–21; and Dozeman, who finds "P styled language" in these passages (Dozeman, *Joshua*, 26–27).

[61] The dating of P and its influence on other biblical traditions is an enormous topic that cannot be addressed in detail here, but for helpful overviews see Erhard Blum, *Studien zur Komposition des Pentateuch* (Berlin: De Gruyter, 1990), 219–85; Jacob Milgrom, "The Antiquity of the Priestly Source: A Reply to Joseph Blenkinsopp," *Zeitschrift für die alttestamentliche Wissenschaft* 111 (1999): 10–22; Jacob Milgrom, *Leviticus 1–16. A New Translation with Introduction and Commentary* (New York: Doubleday, 1991), 3–13; Sarah Shectman and Joel Baden, eds., *The Strata of the Priestly Writings: Contemporary Debate and Future Directions* (Zürich: Theologischer Verlag Zürich, 2009); Philippe Guillaume, *Land and Calendar: The Priestly Document from Genesis 1 to Joshua 18* (New York: T&T Clark, 2009), esp.

dating of these texts in the eighth or seventh centuries BCE places their composition many centuries after Shiloh was destroyed. If we follow a later dating for the development of these texts, Shiloh may have been in ruin for half a millennium or more when they were composed.

For such reasons, what is remarkable about Shiloh's appearance in the Book of Joshua is that it appears at all. For the scribes behind the composition of this work, Shiloh's brief florescence in the Iron I period and abrupt destruction were events from a remote, distant past. Yet not only does Shiloh surface in these later writings, but it is also accorded substantial importance within them. Already in the first reference to Shiloh in Josh 18:1, for example, we read that "the entire assembly of the children of Israel gathered at Shiloh and they set up the tent of meeting there" (Josh 18:1). At this moment in the narrative, we come across the tent sanctuary also known as the tabernacle (e.g., Ex 25–31, 35–40) – a portable shrine that served as the central site of worship for the Israelites during their wanderings in the wilderness and that housed the ark of the covenant. The erection of the tabernacle at Shiloh is consequently a pivotal moment, effectively making the location the dominant cultic site for the Israelite tribes once they have settled in Canaan. The religious significance of the site is underscored later in Josh 18:8 and 18:10 where a casting of lots for tribal lands is performed "before Yahweh" at the location, and again in the closing verse of Josh 19 (v.51) when the inheritances of the priest Eleazar and Joshua are rendered once more by way of the casting of lots "before Yahweh, at the entrance of the tent of meeting." Shiloh's cultic centrality is also emphasized in the last references to the location found in Josh 22:9–34, when a war nearly erupts over the eastern, Transjordanian tribes' decision to set up an altar "of great size" somewhere near the Jordan River (Josh 22:10). In response to this act the "entire assembly of the children of Israel" musters once more at Shiloh (Josh 22:12) – the battle avoided only when the Gadites and Reubenites explain that the altar was not meant for sacrifice or to challenge Shiloh's status but only as a "witness" of solidarity with the Cisjordanian tribes (Josh 22:27). According to this story, then, there was only one altar for sacrifice before Yahweh, one tabernacle for cultic activities (cf. Lev 17), and this sanctuary was now located at Shiloh.

Whether we understand these allusions to Shiloh as brief interspersions into preexisting narrative material or find in these references to the location a broader and more intentional reworking of Joshua that forms the great conclusion to P's lengthy narrative,[62] Shiloh emerges forthwith in these texts as

---

175–92; Avraham Faust, "The World of P: The Material Realm of Priestly Writings," *Vetus Testamentum* 69 (2019): 173–218.

[62] So, for example, Haran, "Shiloh and Jerusalem," 20–21; Norbert Lohfink, "Die Priesterschrift und Die Geschichte," in *Congress Volume: Göttingen, 1977*, ed. J. Emerton,

one of the most meaningful sites in Israel's early history in Canaan. The story told in Joshua depicts Shiloh as a location of considerable importance, enclosing the central sanctuary of the Israelite tribes and the presence of Yahweh within it.[63] And though the LXX's reading of Shiloh in Josh 24:1 and 24:25 is likely a later reworking and harmonization of what was originally a story located at Shechem (so the MT),[64] the impulse in the LXX to make Shiloh both the religious and the political center of the Israelite tribes is in keeping with the sudden prominence Shiloh attains in the course of the story told in Josh 18–22.

Nevertheless, this positive portrayal of Shiloh is conspicuous given how the site is represented elsewhere in the Hebrew Bible. In the Book of Samuel, which we turn to in Section 2.2.3, Shiloh is depicted as a sanctuary with a troubled priesthood whose hold on the ark is lost, and in Jeremiah and Ps 78 Shiloh represents a location of divine abandonment. Yet in Josh 18–22 no critical remarks are made about the site, no foreshadowing of its demise is offered, and no challenges to its cultic status appear. If we were to possess no other texts beyond Joshua in the Hebrew Bible and approached these writings in their final form, the story of Israel that began in Genesis would find in these concluding moments of the tabernacle's establishment a crowning achievement of the entire narrative, with Yahweh now dwelling with the Israelites in the land promised to them long ago. The events that transpire at Shiloh in Josh 18–22 are, in many ways, the proverbial happy ending. At a time when other, less approving traditions surrounding Shiloh likely existed, why scribes writing many centuries after the location's destruction chose to represent the location in this light is the central question these texts raise.

2.2.2 *The Book of Judges*

Between the numerous references to Shiloh in the Books of Joshua and Samuel, the location also appears briefly in four passages from the Book of Judges. As with Joshua, these allusions to the location are found only in the last chapters of this literary work (Judges 18:31, 21:12, 19, 21). Of these, both Judges 18:31 and 21:12 are primarily anecdotal. The story of Judges 17–18 centers on the household cult of Micah and its eventual transfer to the city of Dan, with the Levitical priest and cultic objects under Micah's care being

---

189–225 (Leiden: Brill, 1978), 198; Joseph Blenkinsopp, "The Structure of P," *Catholic Biblical Quarterly* 38.3 (1976): 275–92; Schley, *Shiloh*, 115–26.

[63] As Schley suggests, "That Shiloh was the site which P associated with the culmination of the settlement in the Promised Land means that the Shilonite cultus held a special status, one above all other sanctuaries, in the priestly tradition." Schley, *Shiloh*, 118.

[64] For a helpful overview of this point, see Knittel, *Heiligtum*, 227–29. Cf. Schley, *Shiloh*, 225; Richard Nelson, *Joshua: A Commentary* (Louisville, KY: Westminster John Knox, 1997), 264.

maintained at the sanctuary of this city, we are told, "as long as the house of God was at Shiloh" (Judges 18:31). Judges 21:12 concludes the troubled story of the slaughter of the inhabitants of Jabesh-Gilead and the kidnapping of young women from the site, four hundred of whom were brought "to the camp at Shiloh" for Benjaminite men to obtain. The final references to Shiloh in Judges occur in a narrative that takes place at the location itself: During a "yearly festival of Yahweh at Shiloh" (Judges 21:19), Benjaminite men abduct "the young women of Shiloh" who had come out to dance during the festival (Judges 21:21).

The time period in which these narratives occur is murky. But what can be drawn out from other references in Judges is that the narrative setting of these stories takes place after that of Joshua (Judges 1:1) and precedes the time of the monarchy (i.e., Judges 18:1), placing these incidents in the Iron I period sometime between ca. 1150 and 1050 BCE. When these stories were composed and brought into the larger narrative complex of Judges is an issue that has been heavily shaped by Martin Noth's assessment that Judges 17–21 was appended to the larger literary work at a later period.[65] For Noth, these chapters in Judges were perhaps composed after Jerusalem's destruction in 586 BCE or, more likely, still later. Even among studies that have found more coherence between Judges 17–21 and earlier chapters of the work, these, too, have argued for later scribal revisions to these chapters.[66] More recently, others have followed suit.[67]

In a manner not far removed from Shiloh's appearance in Joshua, there is some consensus, then, that the references to Shiloh in Judges are located in

---

[65] Martin Noth, *The Deuteronomistic History*, 2nd ed. (Sheffield: JSOT Press, 1981), 77 fn. 2. This point is also made in Martin Noth, "The Background of Judges 17–18," in *Israel's Prophetic Heritage: Essays in Honor of James Muilenburg*, eds. B. W. Anderson and W. Harrelson, 68–85 (London: SCM, 1962).

[66] Timo Veijola, *Das Königtum in der Beurteilung der deuteronomistischen Historiographie: Eine redaktionsgeschichtliche Untersuchung* (Helsinki: Suomalainen Tiedeakatemia, 1977), 27–29. Cf. Kratz, *Composition*, 208–9.

[67] Alberto Soggin's commentary entitles these chapters an "Appendix on Various Themes" and hews closely to the studies of Noth and Veijola in terms of dating. J. Alberto Soggin, *Judges*, trans. J. Bowden, 261–301 (Philadelphia: Westminster, 1981). Robert Boling, following instead F. M. Cross's theory of a double redaction to the Deuteronomistic history, situates the concluding chapters of Judges in the second of these movements during the sixth century BCE. Robert Boling, *Judges* (New York: Doubleday, 1975), 30. More recently, S. Niditch connects these chapters to a third, "humanist voice," that is said to reflect a worldview more at home in the Persian and Hellenistic periods. Susan Niditch, *Judges* (Louisville, KY: Westminster John Knox, 2008), 11–12. Walter Groß's monumental work on Judges finds ten distinct redactional layers within this book, with Judges 17–21 again situated in the post-exilic era (Walter Groß, *Richter* [Freiburg im Breisgau: Herder, 2009]), and the recent comment by Mark Smith and Elizabeth Bloch-Smith terms these chapters an "epilogue" that, though perhaps drawing on Iron Age sources, is postexilic in form. Mark S. Smith and Elizabeth Bloch-Smith, *Judges 1* (Minneapolis: Fortress, 2021), 26–34.

texts that arose many centuries after the settlement had been destroyed. For our purposes, what matters once more is the lengthy temporal gap between the period in which these stories are set (roughly in the early Iron I period) and the era in which they were likely woven into the Book of Judges that we now possess (ca. sixth century BCE or after). The stories that make mention of Shiloh in Judges thus appear to be the work of scribes who wrote down stories about a past that preceded their own era by five hundred years or more.

But what is recounted about Shiloh in these stories is distinct from the vision the Book of Joshua represents. The first reference to Shiloh in Judges 18:31 is already enigmatic.[68] For a story centered on the tribe of Dan and the founding of their city in the far north of Israel, the abrupt notice of the "temple of God" (בית־האלהים) that resided at Shiloh is striking. Here no mention is made of the tabernacle, and if we presume that the Danite cult ended with the site's destruction in the late eighth century BCE by the Assyrians ("until the time the land went into captivity" [Judges 18:30]), then the temple referred to at Shiloh, which is said to have endured as long as the Danite sanctuary (Judges 18:31), would have existed far longer than what is intimated in other biblical writings about the duration of the site and its shrine.[69]

The references to Shiloh in Judges 21 are no less curious. "We do not know the reason," Alberto Soggin observes, for why the abducted young women of Jabesh-Gilead are suddenly brought to Shiloh at the end of this tale (Judges 21:12),[70] where the site is described as a "camp" that resided in "Canaan," though the subsequent story of the kidnapping of Shilonite women perhaps influenced this reference to the settlement before it.[71] But it is the abduction of these Shilonite women for Benjaminite men, the last story told in the Book of Judges (Judges 21:15–24), in which Shiloh features most prominently. For our study, what is significant about this narrative are two details that concern Shiloh, both of which occur in Judges 21:19. The first is the memory of an

---

[68] So Niditch: "The concluding verses of ch. 18 include intriguing and somewhat confusing material." (Niditch, *Judges*, 184). Among the possible readings offered in the Biblica Hebraica Stuttgartensia, for example, בלישה ("while it was intact") is offered for בשלה (with no textual evidence) so as to work around the strange reference to Shiloh at this moment in the narrative.

[69] Already with Budde, however, the possibility is raised that 18:31b is a separate conclusion independent of v. 30. Karl Budde, *Das Buch der Richter* (Freiburg: J. C. B. Mohr, 1897), 123. Knittel contends that the verses should be read together, where the illegitimate character of the Danite sanctuary is juxtaposed with the legitimate sanctuary at Shiloh (Knittel, *Heiligtum*, 194).

[70] On this passage, see Alice Bach, "Rereading the Body Politic: Women and Violence in Judges 21," *Biblical Interpretation* 6.1 (1998): 1–19; Megan Case, "Procuring Virgins, Performing Peace: Reconciliation through the Exchange of Women in Judges 21," *Vetus Testamentum* 70.3 (2020): 396–413.

[71] The reference to the "camp of Shiloh" in this passage also resembles the P language of Joshua 21:2 and 22:23. Soggin, *Judges*, 298.

annual "festival of Yahweh" (חג־יהוה) connected to viticulture that took place within Shiloh's environs. The other is the vivid topographic details as to where Shiloh is located: "north of Bethel, on the east of the highway that goes up from Bethel to Shechem, and south of Lebonah."

This description of Shiloh's location raises the question as to why we are offered this information at such a late moment in both this particular story and the Book of Judges as a whole. As Soggin notes, the details "can hardly be put on the lips of the 'elders of the assembly'"[72] since previous to this gloss the location of Shiloh appears to be well known to the characters involved. But if we follow Susan Niditch's suggestion that this information derived from an older "verbal map," and if we situate the dating of these stories to a period far after the era in which their events occur, then it may be that this editorial gloss was introduced into Judges 21 by later scribes for an audience whose sense of Shiloh's whereabouts and significance was beginning to fade many centuries after it had fallen.[73] In addition to the obscure reference to the camp of Shiloh in "Canaan," (Judges 21:12), these details would have provided a way of calling to mind a more remote past and an ancient route that connected important centers from Israel's early history, underscoring for a later audience of this work that, as Niditch puts it in her observations on this passage, "the roots of Israelite identity are ancient and deep,"[74] reflecting a venerable landscape that still could be traversed and visited if so desired.

2.2.3 *The Book of Samuel*

The densest concentration of references to Shiloh in the Hebrew Bible occurs in the opening chapters of the Book of Samuel (1 Sam 1–4), where the time period portrayed is sometime in the early to mid-eleventh century BCE. When the narrative of Samuel opens, we find a man named Elkanah and his two wives, Peninnah and Hannah, traveling from their home at Ramathaim "to worship and sacrifice to Yahweh of Hosts at Shiloh, where the two sons of Eli, Hophni and Phinehas, were priests of Yahweh" (1 Sam 1:3). It is at Shiloh that Hannah presents herself "before Yahweh" (1 Sam 1:9)[75] while the priest Eli sits at the doorpost of the "temple of Yahweh" (היכל יהוה), and it is at this sanctuary where Hannah vows that her child, if she is able to conceive, will serve as a nazirite until his death. The child born is Samuel (1 Sam 1:20). Once

---

[72] Soggin, *Judges*, 299.
[73] Niditch, *Judges*, 210. So Niditch notes the resonance between this passage and the itinerary preserved in Numbers 21:11–20. For a similar perspective, see Knittel, *Heiligtum*, 198–99; Carolyn Pressler, *Judges, Joshua, Ruth* (Louisville, KY: Westminster John Knox, 2002), 256.
[74] Pressler, *Judges, Joshua, Ruth*, 210.
[75] Here, reading with the LXX "και κατέστη ἐνώπιον κυρίου," the MT omits the phrase due to haplography.

weaned, the boy is brought to the temple of Yahweh (בת־יהוה) at Shiloh and dedicated to the deity (1 Sam 1:24, 28).

After an account of the corruption of the Elide priesthood (1 Sam 2:11–26) and an oracle against the House of Eli (1 Sam 2:27–36), the story returns to Samuel himself. In 1 Sam 3:1–4:1a the call narrative of Samuel unfolds, where the boy hears Yahweh's voice while "lying down in the temple of Yahweh" at Shiloh (1 Sam 3:3). It is in this temple that Samuel receives word of Yahweh's judgment once more on the House of Eli and where, over time, "all Israel from Dan to Beersheba came to know that Samuel was confirmed as a prophet of Yahweh" (1 Sam 3:20). In the concluding passages to this story, we are told that "Yahweh continued to appear at Shiloh when he revealed himself to Samuel" (1 Sam 3:21).

The final references to Shiloh in the Book of Samuel detail the loss of the ark and the fall of the Elide priesthood. After an initial confrontation with the Philistines at the site of Ebenezer, "people are sent to Shiloh" in order to bring out the ark of the covenant and to use it as a war palladium (1 Sam 4:4), accompanied by the priests Hophni and Phinehas. The Israelites are defeated, the ark captured by the Philistines, and the two priests slain. Word of the loss is brought to Shiloh by an unnamed Benjaminite man (1 Sam 4:12), whereupon the elderly Eli dies after hearing the news. Other than brief appearances within the patronyms of later Elide priests (Ahijah [1 Sam 14:3] and Abiathar [1 Kings 2:27]), Shiloh subsequently disappears from the story the Book of Samuel tells.

Of all the references to Shiloh in the Hebrew Bible, the issues surrounding the compositional history of the opening chapters of Samuel and the dating of the textual layers discerned are some the most complex.[76] The significant studies of the Book of Samuel by Walter Dietrich[77] and P. Kyle McCarter,[78] however, represent a prominent cross-section of Germanic and Anglophone scholarship on Samuel that sees 1 Sam 1–7 as an Iron Age collection of texts woven together and composed in the aftermath of the destruction of the northern kingdom of Israel in 722/21 BCE.[79] On this view, the distinctly

---

[76] For a recent, detailed overview of these issues, see Knittel, *Heiligtum*, 60–89.

[77] Walter Dietrich, *Samuel*, Teilband I, 1 Sam 1–12 (Neukirchen Vluyn: Neukirchener Verlagsgesellschaft, 2011), 47–52. Dietrich does see later redactional seams in these chapters, placing the Song of Hannah and the prophecy against the House of Eli in 1 Sam 2, for example, in the post-exilic period as late revisions. The narrative of Samuel's youth (*1:1–28; 2:11a, 18b, 21a, 26; 3:1b–11a, 15–18, 21), however, is thought to be the oldest of this material, the *terminus ad quem* for its composition being no later than 722 BCE. For a detailed breakdown of the redactional layers that Dietrich finds in 1 Sam 1–3, see Ibid., 125.

[78] P. Kyle McCarter, *1 Samuel* (New Haven, CT: Yale University Press, 1980).

[79] For McCarter, 1 Sam 1–7 (omitting the oracle against the House of Eli in 1 Sam 2:27–36 + 3:11–14) is part of a larger "Prophetic History" that developed in northern circles but was written down in the aftermath of the destruction of the northern kingdom of Israel [McCarter, *1 Samuel*, 21–22]. For Dietrich, a "court storyteller" (*Höfische Erzähler*), writing sometime during the reigns of Hezekiah or Mannasseh in the late eighth/early seventh

"northern" traditions surrounding Shiloh and the career of Samuel are thought to have been threaded into a larger narrative complex surrounding the stories of Saul and David once the kingdom of Israel had come to an end. Nevertheless, both Dietrich and McCarter argue that 1 Sam 1–7 is dependent on still earlier sources. McCarter contends, for example, that the Ark Narrative of 1 Sam 4–6 was part of an older narrative tradition, originally composed "before David's defeat of the Philistines reported in II Sam 5:17–25,"[80] which included information on the corruption of the Elide priesthood. The texts of 1 Sam 2:12–17, 22–25, and 1 Sam 4:1b–7:1 are, consequently, derived from sources written sometime in the tenth century BCE.[81] Dietrich is more reticent to place a date on the sources his court storyteller drew on and more willing to consider them as predominantly oral in form, but he, too, writes that an "old, indigenous story from Shiloh"[82] of some antiquity was reworked by later court scribes when developing the story of Samuel's early career.

What these studies detail is that references to Shiloh in the Book of Samuel are some of the oldest in the Hebrew Bible, likely composed within a few centuries after the location had been destroyed.[83] The most prominent feature of Shiloh found in these writings is undoubtedly its sanctuary and the presence of the ark – a place where "all Israel" came to sacrifice according to 1 Sam 2:22 (cf. 1 Sam 2:14). The stories of Hannah, the Elides, Samuel's youth, and the Battle of Ebenezer all orbit around the image of a Shilonite temple found throughout these early narratives. Even more, certain details of this temple are provided, including a nave (היכל), a "lamp of God" (נר־אלהים), doorposts (מזוזת), and chambers in which visitors stayed (LXX: κατάλυμα = לשכה) (1 Sam 1:9, 18; 1 Sam 3:3). How this temple building pertains to the mention of the tabernacle at Shiloh in other biblical writings, especially in Joshua, is a matter of

---

century BCE, is said to have drawn on older sources for both the story of Samuel's youth in 1 Sam 1–3 and the ark narrative of 1 Sam 4–6. Dietrich, *Samuel*, 50–52. For a further study of these chapters, see Julio Barrera, "Textual Criticism and the Composition History of Samuel: Connection between Pericopes in 1 Samuel 1–4," in *Archaeology of the Books of Samuel: The Entangling of the Textual and Literary History*, eds. P. Hugo and A. Schenker, 15–46 (Leiden: Brill, 2010).

[80] Barrera, "Textual Criticism and the Composition History of Samuel," 25.
[81] Regarding 1 Sam 1–15 as a whole, McCarter writes that during the "intermediate stage" of the Book of Samuel's growth, the Prophetic History was one in which "the older sources were systematically reworked to produce a continuous prophetic history of the origins of monarchy in Israel." McCarter, *1 Samuel*, 18.
[82] Dietrich, *Samuel*, 52.
[83] So also, the recent assessment of Knittel, where "Der älteste literarische Zusammnehang," once again believed to have been written sometime after the fall of the northern kingdom of Israel, is thought to be found in "1. Sam 1,1–28*; 2:18–21; 4:1–18*." Knittel, *Heiligtum*, 233. For similar assessments of an Iron IIB or IIC provenance for these writings, see Antony Campbell, *1 Samuel* (Grand Rapids, MI: Eerdmans, 2003), 327–31. For a contrasting opinion, see Kratz, *Composition*, 174–82, who argues that a large collection of texts from 1 Sam 1–7 are later, "(Priestly) expansions" to a pre-existing Deuteronomistic redaction.

longstanding debate. The Mishnah opts to dissolve this tension by suggesting that the Shiloh temple had no roof other than curtains, thus being comprised of both a building and the original tent shrine.[84] But it is more likely that competing memories of a sanctuary at Shiloh informed the biblical writings about it, where the temple building in Judges and Samuel was remembered alongside the tabernacle referred to in Joshua and, elsewhere, in Ps 78.[85] Even within the Book Samuel, however, this tension emerges, with the "House of Yahweh" (1 Sam 1:7, 24) and "Temple of Yahweh" (1 Sam 3:3) at Shiloh standing in contrast to the later claim made by Yahweh to David that the deity had never lived in a temple in a time before (2 Sam 7:6; cf. 2 Sam 6:17).[86]

The fate of Shiloh after the ark's capture in 1 Sam 4 is also somewhat difficult to determine. The Book of Samuel itself makes no mention of what transpired at Shiloh in the aftermath of the Philistine victory at Ebenezer. But, in light of the later references in Ps 78:60 and Jeremiah 26:6, 9, to the abandonment of the site and its ruins, the prevailing sentiment is that Shiloh came to be destroyed subsequent to the battle reported in 1 Sam 4 or sometime soon after.[87] The merit of this view is that it would offer an explanation as to why Shiloh suddenly disappears from the Book of Samuel after playing such a pivotal role in its opening chapters.[88] This is particularly so with regard to the later narratives centered on Samuel and the Elides. Twenty years after the loss of the ark (1 Sam 7:2), for example, Samuel is said to have assembled the Israelites at Mizpah, rather than Shiloh, for a rededication ceremony to Yahweh and to prepare them for battle (1 Sam 7:5–12) and afterward is said to judge at Mizpah, Gilgal, and Bethel (1 Sam 7:15) – with Shiloh never

---

[84] *M. Zeb.* 14.6: "When they came to Shiloh ... [The Tabernacle] there had no roof, but [consisted of] a base of stones with a ceiling of curtains." In another effort to contend with this discrepancy, Haran holds that later Jerusalemite scribes revised features of the tabernacle ("anachronistic touches") to make it conform to the later temple in Jerusalem. Haran, "Shiloh and Jerusalem," 22.

[85] On this point, see 2.3.4, "Ruins and Remembrance: The Competition of Memory."

[86] The one mention of the tabernacle in Samuel (1 Sam 2:22: "They were lying with women who served at the entrance to the Tent of Meeting") is textually suspect, as it is missing from both LXX^B and 4QSam^a. The reference may, then, descend from a much later revision that sought to further indict the Elides.

[87] E.g., Martin Noth, *The History of Ancient Israel*, 2nd ed., trans. P. Ackroyd (New York: Harper and Row, 1959), 96; John Day, "The Destruction of the Shiloh Sanctuary and Jeremiah VII 12, 14," in *Studies in the Historical Books of the Old Testament*, ed. J. Emerton, 87–94 (Leiden: Brill, 1979); Menahem Haran, *Temples and Temple-Service in Ancient Israel: An Inquiry into Biblical Cult Phenomena and the Historical Setting of the Priestly School* (Winona Lake, IN: Eisenbrauns, 1985), 194–204; Mordechai Cogan, *1 Kings* (New York: Doubleday, 2001), 339; Walter Dietrich, *The Early Monarchy in Israel: The Tenth Century B.C.E.*, trans. J. Vette (Atlanta: SBL Press, 2007), 274; Finkelstein, *Forgotten Kingdom*, 49–50; Knittel, *Heiligtum*, 239.

[88] See also Amos 5:5 where Bethel and Gilgal appear prominently in the prophet's denunciation of eighth century BCE cultic centers in Israel, but with no mention of Shiloh. On this point, see the preceding text by Karl Budde, *Die Bücher Samuel* (Tübingen: J. C. B. Mohr, 1902), 30.

featuring in these moments of Samuel's later career. In 1 Sam 22:9, furthermore, we learn that the priest Ahimelech, the son of Ahitub and great-grandson of Eli (1 Sam 14:3), presided at the village of Nob with other Elides who evidently had come to settle at this location, presumably because Shiloh was no more. In time, Abiathar, the sole member of the family to escape Saul's purge with his life, joins David (1 Sam 22:20) and eventually becomes high priest in Jerusalem alongside Zadok (2 Sam 20:25). When later expelled by Solomon from Jerusalem, however, Abiathar does not return to the ancestral site of Shiloh but resides at the village of Anathoth (1 Kings 2:26). It is here, centuries later, that Jeremiah will be born, likely a descendent of this priestly family from Shiloh.

2.2.4 *The Books of Kings, Jeremiah, and Psalm 78*

The final references to Shiloh occur in the later canonical writings of Kings, Jeremiah, and Psalm 78. Each of these works contains more concise allusions to Shiloh than those found in the broader narratives examined above and so can be treated together. The first of these depictions is in the Book of Kings and centers on a prophet named Ahijah the Shilonite. In 1 Kings 11–15 five references to Shiloh are included in the narratives surrounding this prophet, who foretells of the dissolution of Solomon's kingdom and the rise of Jeroboam as the first ruler of Israel. Three of these references to Shiloh are simply gentilics (השילני – 1 Kings 11:29; 12:15; 15:29). But in 1 Kings 14 we are offered details that pertain to the site of Shiloh itself.[89] In this text, Jeroboam sends his wife, disguised, to Shiloh so as to inquire about the fate of their young son who had become ill (1 Kings 14:2). Jeroboam's wife departs and comes to the "house of Ahijah" at Shiloh (1 Kings 14:4), whereupon she receives news from the blind and elderly prophet that the child will soon die and that the House of Jeroboam will fall.

With the reign of Jeroboam, the time period in which these stories are set becomes more precise, transpiring sometime in the last quarter of the tenth century BCE, or the early Iron IIA period. Discussions of the era in which these texts were composed has again been shaped by Noth's theory of the Deuteronomistic History and his argument that Kings is the final book in this larger work, written in the sixth century BCE in the aftermath of Jerusalem's destruction.[90] If we follow Cross' influential modification of Noth's work, a first version of Kings would have been written in the seventh century BCE

---

[89] In the LXX, the entire episode is missing, having been placed instead after 1 Kings 12:24 (LXX 12:24a–z). On the post-Dtr (Deuteronomist) character of this passage, see Cogan, *1 Kings*, 355–56.

[90] Noth, *Deuteronomistic History*, 79. More recently, see the discussion in Baruch Halpern and André Lemaire, "The Composition of Kings," in *The Book of Kings: Sources, Composition, Historiography and Reception*, eds. A. Lemaire and B. Halpern, 123–54 (Leiden: Brill, 2010).

during the reign of Josiah.[91] But, as with Samuel, the sources on which the writers of Kings depended were likely older still, particularly with regard to the numerous prophetic tales that appear throughout this book[92] – including the story of Ahijah and Jeroboam's wife in 1 Kings 14:1–18.[93]

The details we are provided about Shiloh in 1 Kings are brief but significant. Sometime in the late tenth century BCE a prominent prophet who hails from Shiloh delivers one of the most important prophecies in the Book of Kings. The old cultic center thus appears to have retained some of its prior significance according to this story and, it seems, some of its inhabitants.[94] At first, Ahijah is portrayed as supporting Jeroboam and the succession of the northern tribes from Solomon's realm, perhaps in an effort to reclaim Shiloh's former role in the religious life of the region after Abiathar, the last of the Elides, had been expelled from Jerusalem. But later in life the prophet appears to have turned against Jeroboam, a decision that may have reflected the king's choice to establish his cultic centers in the old northern sanctuaries of Bethel and Dan, thus bypassing Shiloh in the process.[95]

Turning to the Book of Jeremiah, the references to Shiloh that it contains are some of the most important for our study of ruins and remembrance, but all of them, save one (Jer 41:5),[96] are derived from a single event told twice (Jer 7:12, 14; 26:6, 9): Jeremiah's Temple Speech, said to have been delivered "at the beginning of the reign of King Jehoiakim" (Jer 26:1), or shortly after 609

---

[91] Frank Moore Cross, *Canaanite Myth and Hebrew Epic: Essays in the History of Religion* (Cambridge, MA: Harvard University Press, 1973), 274–90.

[92] Mordechai Cogan, *1 Kings*, 92–94, 98. For other possible redactions that preceded the Deuteronomistic revisions, see Baruch Halpern and David Vanderhooft, "The Editions of Kings in the 7th–6th Centuries," *Hebrew Union College Annual* 62 (1991): 179–244; and the survey in Marvin Sweeney, *1&2 Kings* (Louisville, KY: Westminster John Knox, 2007), 15–32.

[93] John Gray, *I & II Kings* (London: SCM Press, 1980), 288; Walter Dietrich, *Prophetie und Geschichte: Eine redaktionsgeschichte Untersuchung zum deuteronomistischen Geschichtswerk* (Göttingen: Vandenhoek & Ruprecht, 1972), 112–14; Gary Knoppers, *Two Nations under God: The Deuteronomistic History of Solomon and the Dual Monarchies*, Vol. 2 (Atlanta: Harvard Semitic Monographs, 1993), 94–101. Würthwein and Schley both see the episode as based on an old "memory" sustained by prophetic circles over time. Ernst Würthwein, *Die Bücher der Könige: 1 Könige 1–16* (Göttingen: Vandenhoek & Ruprecht, 1985), 175; Schley, *Shiloh*, 167. McKenzie accepts the possibility of an older legend undergirding 1 Kings 14:1–18 but does not think it is recoverable in its later Dtr reworkings. Steven McKenzie, *The Trouble with Kings: The Composition of the Book of Kings in the Deuteronomistic History* (Leiden: Brill, 1991), 62–63.

[94] Schley, *Shiloh*, 200; Knittel, *Heiligtum*, 119.

[95] On this theory, see Martin Cohen, "The Role of Shilonite Priesthood in the United Monarchy of Ancient Israel," *Hebrew Union College Annual* 36 (1965): 59–98; 92–94; Cogan, *1 Kings*, 383; Mark Leuchter, "Jeroboam the Ephratite," *Journal of Biblical Literature* 125.1 (2006): 51–72.

[96] In Jer 41:5 we are simply told that "eighty men from Shechem, Shiloh, and Samaria" were bringing offerings to the destroyed temple of Yahweh in Jerusalem after the Babylonian conquest, only to be slain by Ishmael shortly after the murder of Gedaliah.

BCE. In the first version of this episode, Yahweh commands Jeremiah's audience to "Go now to my place that was in Shiloh, where I made my name dwell at first, and see what I did to it on account of the wickedness of the people of Israel" (Jer 7:12). Later, Yahweh addresses the Jerusalem temple itself, declaring, "I will do to that house … just what I did to Shiloh" (Jer 7:14). In the second version of this speech, Yahweh again threatens both Jerusalem and its temple by calling to mind Shiloh's past, stating, "I will make this house like Shiloh, and I will make this city a curse for all the nations of the earth" (Jer 26:6). The response of those listening provides insights as to the implications of Jeremiah's prophecy: "Why have you prophesied in the name of the Lord, saying 'This house will be like Shiloh, and this city will be reduced to ruins, without inhabitant?'" (Jer 26:9).

In contrast to the earlier allusions to Shiloh in the Hebrew Bible, these references to the location have a clear *terminus post quem* of 609 BCE by virtue of the notice regarding the date of this speech. Within the compositional history of the Book of Jeremiah, both passages are frequently assigned to what are termed the "prose speeches" of the book, likely written down, or at least reworked, in the period after Jeremiah's life.[97] Of these, Jer 26 appears to have been dependent on Jer 7, with later scribes having developed the initial version of the speech further in the period after Jerusalem's destruction.[98]

What is meaningful about these allusions to Shiloh, accordingly, is that they refer to a location that had been destroyed in a distant past. When Shiloh fell is not stated explicitly in these passages, but the meaning of Jeremiah's invective in Jer 7:12–14 is dependent on the Deuteronomistic idea of Yahweh's name "dwelling" at one particular sanctuary – which, after Solomon's building of the temple, was Jerusalem.[99] If Yahweh's name first dwelled at Shiloh (Jer 7:12), according to these claims, it could have only done so in an era before the tenth century BCE previous to when Solomon built the Jerusalem sanctuary.[100] For

---

[97] Bernhard Duhm, *Das Buch Jeremia* (Tübingen: Mohr, 1907), xvi–xx; Sigmund Mowinckel, *Zur Komposition des Buches Jeremia* (Kristiana: Jacob Dybwad, 1914), 17–45; Robert Carroll, *Jeremiah* (Louisville, KY: Westminster John Knox, 1986), 38–50; Konrad Schmid, "How to Date the Book of Jeremiah: Combining and Modifying Linguistic- and Profile-Based Approaches," *Vetus Testamentum* 68.3 (2018): 444–62; Carolyn Sharpe, *Jeremiah 26–52* (Stuttgart: Kohlhammer, 2021), 23–33. Though for some, such as J. Bright and H. Weippert, these prose speeches may reach back to Jeremiah himself. John Bright, "The Date of the Prose Sermons of Jeremiah," *Journal of Biblical Literature* 70.1 (1951): 15–35; Helga Weippert, *Die Prosareden des Jeremiabuches* (Berlin: De Gruyter, 1973), 1–21.

[98] On the textual relationship between these accounts, see Weippert, *Prosareden*, 30–34; Carroll, *Jeremiah*, 513–16; and Mark Leuchter, *The Polemics of Exile in Jeremiah 26–45* (Cambridge: Cambridge University Press, 2008), 25–38.

[99] See, for example, Deut 12:11; 16:2, 6, 11. On the Jerusalem temple being the place where the name of Yahweh dwelled, see 1 Kings 9:3, 11:36, and 14:21, among others.

[100] On this point, see especially Day, "Destruction of Shiloh," 88–91; Knittel, *Heiligtum*, 130–33. Cf. Carroll, *Jeremiah*, 209–10.

the writers behind the composition of this passage, in other words, Shiloh's downfall was conceived as a pre-Solomonic, pre-tenth century BCE event when the location's "house," or temple (Jer 7:14), appears to have been undone.[101]

That this pre-Solomonic sanctuary fell into ruin is made evident in Jer 26. In this report of Jeremiah's prophecy, Shiloh is likened to a site that is a "curse" to the nations (קלל) and "reduced to ruin, without inhabitant" (תחרב מאין יושב). Both expressions are used to describe ruined locations throughout the Hebrew Bible, including within the Book of Jeremiah itself.[102] But the ruins of Shiloh are also alluded to in Jer 7 more indirectly, where the thrust of the initial report of Jeremiah's oracle is dependent on the audience's awareness of Shiloh's previous fate. The directive to "go to Shiloh" and "see" what had happened to the location, this is to say, presupposes that there was something at this location to view. In Jer 26, it is clear that what could be seen at Shiloh were the ruins that presaged Jerusalem's imminent downfall.

If the Book of Samuel provided few indications of what happened to Shiloh after the loss of the ark, it is these passages from Jeremiah, then, that offer textual support for Shiloh having come to ruin during the era which the Book of Samuel spans. No account is offered in Jeremiah as to how Shiloh came to such an end. But what is apparent is that for four centuries after Shiloh's downfall the memory of its destruction and the physical remains that attested to this event persisted. The continued resonance of this destruction centuries afterward is also apparent in how this memory destabilized any worldview that held to the belief that a sanctuary of Yahweh safeguarded the location where it was built. The memory of Shiloh's past proved otherwise. The attempt to summarily execute Jeremiah after his oracle on Shiloh's ruins (Jer 26:8, 11) demonstrates just how powerful this memory was.

Finally, the fall of Shiloh is also remembered in Ps 78.[103] Within this lengthy poetic narrative devoted to various moments of past deliverance and rebellion,

---

[101] A number of studies – led amiss by the renewed Danish excavations of Khirbet Seilun in 1963 and the contention of the excavators at the time that Shiloh was not destroyed in the Iron I period (Buhl and Holm-Nielsen, *Shiloh*, 34) – argued that the destruction of Shiloh referred to in the Book of Jeremiah was based on a putative Assyrian overthrow of the site in the late eighth century BCE (see, for example, Robert Pearce, "Shiloh and Jer VII 2, 14 & 15," *Vetus Testamentum* 23 [1973]: 105–8; Schley, *Shiloh*, 171–81). Excavations in the 1980s demonstrated that no Assyrian destruction occurred at the site and, as related above, that the site instead was destroyed in the eleventh century BCE.

[102] On קלל, see Jer 44:22; 49:13. On חרב, Jer 7:34; 22:5; 34:22; 44:2, 6, 22, among others.

[103] On the "practices of memory" exercised within this psalm, see Edward Greenstein, "Mixing Memory and Design: Reading Psalm 78," *Prooftexts* 10.2 (1990): 197–218; for another reading that links the psalm to memory, see Rebecca W. P. Hays, "Trauma, Remembrance, and Healing: The Meeting of Wisdom and History in Psalm 78," *Journal for the Study of the Old Testament* 41.2 (2016): 183–204.

we come across the theme of the rejection of Israel (Ps 78:59) and, subsequently, the divine abandonment of Shiloh (Ps 78:60–64):

> He [Yahweh] abandoned his dwelling (משכן) at Shiloh,
> The tent (אהל) where he dwelt among humankind.
> He delivered his power to captivity,
> His glory to the hand of the foe.
> He gave his people to the sword,
> Against his inheritance he was enraged.
> Their young men were devoured by fire,
> Their young women had no marriage song.
> Their priests fell by the sword,
> Their widows made no lamentation.

In addition to the reference to Shiloh's abandonment, the allusions to the captivity of the deity's power[104] in this poem and the death of priests suggest that, as with Jeremiah's prophesy, the events referred to in this psalm are those related to what was recounted in 1 Sam 4. The memory of Shiloh's abandonment in Ps 78, in other words, was understood once more as an event that preceded the time of David, reaching back into an era before monarchic times. But other details in the poem are also noteworthy. As in Joshua, the cultic site at Shiloh is envisioned here as the tent shrine of the tabernacle, distinct from the sanctuary that would come to be "built" later on Mount Zion (Ps 78:69). What is also depicted in the context of Shiloh's abandonment, however, are distinct images of warfare and loss (Ps 78:62–63), making more explicit a connection between the divine desertion of the location and those battles within Shiloh's vicinity that are intimated in the Book of Samuel.[105]

How to date Ps 78 is a matter of longstanding disagreement, resisting, as this poem does, any clear indication of its compositional setting.[106] The value of the poem for our discussion, however, resides in how it offers a further witness to the memory of Shiloh's downfall and how this past was drawn on to support the claim that Jerusalem, Judah, and David had been chosen in its stead ("but he chose the tribe of Judah, Mount Zion which he loves ... he chose his servant David" [Ps 78:68, 70]). Said differently, in Ps 78 we find the fate of Shiloh and Jerusalem once again intertwined but in a manner distinct from Jeremiah's coupling of the two locations. If for Jeremiah the ruins of Shiloh offered a warning to those in Jerusalem that Yahweh could allow for the downfall of a location where the deity resided, in Ps 78 Shiloh's abandonment

---

[104] On this terminology for the ark of the covenant, see, for example, Ps 132:8; 2 Chr 6:41.
[105] See Amos Frisch, "Ephraim and Treachery, Loyalty and (the House) of David: The Meaning of a Structural Parallel in Psalm 78," *Vetus Testamentum* 59.2 (2009): 190–98.
[106] For an incisive overview of the scholarship surrounding the dating of this psalm, see Mark Leuchter, "The Reference to Shiloh in Ps 78," *Hebrew Union College Annual* 77 (2006): 1–31. Cf. Knittel, *Heiligtum*, 168–70; Gili Kugler, "Not Moses, but David: Theology and Politics in Psalm 78," *Scottish Journal of Theology* 73.2 (2020): 126–36.

is recalled rather as evidence that Jerusalem had supplanted it as Yahweh's chosen place. What Shiloh once was, for the poet of this psalm, Jerusalem had become.

2.3 THE HEBREW BIBLE AND SHILOH'S PAST: SUMMARY

For a place dispossessed of its significance relatively early in Israel's history according to the biblical writings, the foregoing discussion illustrates how Shiloh nevertheless appears in a variety of texts written at different times and for different ends. Not only do stories of Shiloh's past feature in narratives that depict Israel's initial settlement in Canaan, but the location also continued to resonate among poems and prophetic admonitions set in later eras. Shiloh is depicted within these writings at a frequency comparable to that of other important highland sites within its vicinity – such as Gilgal, Gibeon, or Mizpah.[107] Yet the portrayal of Shiloh often takes precedence over these sites in biblical storytelling because of the period when the ark and sanctuary of Yahweh were said to have resided at the location. The establishment of the tabernacle at Shiloh helps bring the story of the Book of Joshua and much narrative material before it to a close, while the abandonment of the location in the Book of Samuel commences a new narrative trajectory that will result in David's ascent to the throne in Jerusalem. From this larger sweep of biblical storytelling, Shiloh functions as the literary pivot on which the entire story of Genesis through 2 Kings turns.

When we situate the biblical references to Shiloh within the framework of the site's archaeological remains, what becomes evident, however, is that these texts were written down after the location had been destroyed. In the end, it matters little if we date the composition of particular biblical writings to the tenth or fifth century BCE or even later: The archaeological remains from Khirbet Seilun demonstrate that Shiloh was in ruins throughout these eras. When stories about Shiloh were being composed and revised in antiquity, what was in view at Shiloh were the remnants of Bronze and early Iron Age communities that had vanished long ago.

How to account for such an array of biblical stories told about a location that was in ruins is the question that confronts us. Typically, scholars have sought answers within the biblical writings themselves. Common responses as to why Shiloh appears as it does in the Hebrew Bible, that is, are those wedded to literary and ideological considerations drawn out from these texts. The recent erudite study of Ann-Kathrin Knittel, for example, represents a stream of scholarship that sees in references to Shiloh a "long overdue" series of revisions

---

[107] Shiloh appears 32 times, Gilgal 41, Gibeon 38, and Mizpah 44.

made to older narratives, where allusions to Shiloh were introduced as part of a series of redactions to earlier stories performed by later scribes in order to provide textual connections between the tabernacle's journey through the wilderness in the Pentateuch and the temple's eventual construction in 1 Kings 6–8.[108] From this perspective, the depictions of the pre-monarchical sanctuary at Shiloh that we find in Joshua or Samuel were due "in large part to the literary fashioning" of these images, manufactured by later writers and retrofitted into a more distant past through the scribal revisions introduced.[109] The appearance of Shiloh in these texts was largely determined, consequently, by later scribes who desired to construct a literary bridge of sorts between narrative strains in Exodus through Numbers and the Jerusalem temple's eventual construction by Solomon in the Book of Kings.

Others trace Shiloh's presence in these writings to more explicit ideological convictions. Since the ark is said to have been transferred to Jerusalem in the Book of Samuel (2 Sam 6),[110] references to Shiloh in the biblical corpus have been connected to later Jerusalemite writers who sought to legitimize the cult in Jerusalem by demonstrating continuity with earlier cultic traditions centered at Shiloh. The favorable references to Shiloh and the tabernacle during Israel's entrance into Canaan, and the later corruption of the cult by the Elides, were produced, on this view, in order to bolster Jerusalem's later cultic status by illustrating its direct relationship to a sanctuary once chosen by Yahweh but sullied by a disgraced priesthood. Richard Nelson writes that though an "older tradition" may perhaps have influenced the mention of the Shiloh in Joshua, "an ideological attachment to Shiloh ... would be understandable from a Judahite (and priestly) perspective because Shiloh was viewed as the legitimate forerunner to Jerusalem."[111] Earlier, Menahem Haran had also advocated for a Jerusalemite reshaping of earlier "legends" centered on the tabernacle, including those that located the shrine at Shiloh,[112] and Martin Noth had detected the possible influence of Jerusalemite scribes in the polemical account of the downfall of the House of Eli in 1 Sam 2:12–36.[113] The claims of Ps 78 that Jerusalem had unseated Shiloh as Yahweh's chosen location are further situated within this ideological framework.[114]

---

[108] Knittel, *Heiligtum*, 230. Cf. Knauf, *Josua*, 21.   [109] Knittel, *Heiligtum*, 236.
[110] On the possible historical connections between the Shiloh cult and the later Jerusalem sanctuary, see Otto Eißfeld, "Silo und Jerusalem," in *Volume du Congrès, Strasbourg 1956*, ed. P. De Boer, 138–47 (Leiden: Brill, 1957); Ben Ollenburger, *Zion, City of the Great King: A Theological Symbol of the Jerusalem Cult* (Sheffield: JSOT Press, 1987), 37–41.
[111] Nelson, *Joshua*, 209. For a similar perspective, see Pressler, *Joshua, Judges, Ruth*, 98.
[112] Haran, "Shiloh and Jerusalem," 14–24 (esp. 23–24).
[113] Martin Noth, "Samuel und Silo," *Vetus Testamentum* 13.4 (1963): 390–400; 393–94.
[114] See, for example, Robert Carroll, "Psalm LXXVIII: Vestiges of a Tribal Polemic," *Vetus Testamentum* 21.1 (1971): 33–50; Schley, *Shiloh*, 186–87; Oded Tammuz, "Psalm 78: A Case Study in Redaction as Propaganda," *Catholic Biblical Quarterly* 79:2 (2017): 205–21. For

SHILOH AND THE RUINS OF MEMORY

The value of these studies is without question, drawing out, as they do, the biblical writers' retrospective interest in Shiloh that this study also foregrounds. But what is lacking among these discussions is a more concrete historical response to a fundamental historical question: Why do we find specific references to *Shiloh* within these narratives? Why, in other words, would scribes writing hundreds of years after Shiloh's destruction introduce literary revisions to foreground a site whose significance had waned many centuries before? Why write about a location that appears to have been only sparsely settled when these scribes were active, and perhaps not inhabited at all?

To put a sharper point on it: If references to Shiloh in texts such as Josh 18 or 1 Sam 3, among others, were motivated by purely redactional or ideological interests among later scribes reworking earlier traditions, why not select other locations from Israel's past for their revisions? Gilgal, to cite only one example, would have offered rich redactional opportunities to later writers by virtue of its role as the base of operations for the Israelites on their entry into Canaan (Josh 5–10). Gilgal is portrayed within these texts as a place where rituals of circumcision are carried out and where the Passover is first celebrated in Canaan (Josh 5:2–12), and Samuel later serves as judge from the settlement (1 Sam 7:16), thus offering a myriad of textual connections to later biblical stories. Or why not revise these stories so that the ark and tabernacle were attached more prominently to Bethel, Mt. Ebal, or even Gibeon? Each site held cultic significance at other moments in biblical storytelling and could have been drawn on for similar ideological ends by later Jerusalemite writers who desired to bolster their city's cultic status. Any number of highland locations, in other words, could have been selected by later scribes to provide the literary associations and ideological support that biblical scholars have long contended were behind the allusions to Shiloh in the Hebrew Bible. But for some reason Shiloh was singled out.

To understand why requires an investigation that extends beyond the biblical writings alone. The considerable gap in time between Shiloh's brief florescence in the eleventh century BCE and its prominence within the documents written down hundreds of years later cannot be explained by attending solely to compositional features or ideological tendencies embedded in these accounts. Instead, we need to examine what may have given rise to the "legends" and "lore" about Shiloh's past that scholars believe were preserved about it in antiquity,[115] or how "older traditions" about the location found their way into later texts.[116] The question that remains unresolved is

---

helpful overviews of these perspectives, see again Leuchter, "The Reference to Shiloh," 1–31; Knittel, *Heiligtum*, 168–78.
[115] Haran, "Shiloh and Jerusalem," 23–24; Schley, *Shiloh*, 186. [116] Nelson, *Joshua*, 209.

why biblical scribes chose to portray Shiloh so vividly in their writings when what they would have encountered at the location was a settlement in ruins.

2.3.1 Ruins and Remembrance

My response to these issues is indebted at the outset to Albrecht Alt's famous essay on the Book of Joshua and his theory of *Ortsgebundenheit,* or being "place-bound."[117] What Alt indicates by this term is a phenomenon whereby certain sites in ancient Israel gave rise to local stories that were shaped by visible features within their precincts (*Haftpunkte*).[118] Such locations were often distinguished, Alt contends, by the presence of a sanctuary or some form of cultic space in their environs, attracting pilgrims who visited their sacred enclosures and recounted tales (*Sagen*) about their past until, in time, they were written down. Particular places in ancient Israel anchored accounts about the past in their physical settings, according to Alt's theory, communicating information about their origins to later visitors through the experience of their built and natural environments.[119] At its core, Alt maintains, the narrative of Joshua 1–11 was originally comprised of independent, etiological tales that explained how particular locations came to have the appearance and status that they did, such as we find in the notice regarding the fate of the city of 'Ai: "So Joshua burned down 'Ai [Hebrew: "the ruin"] and made it a perpetual mound of ruin, a desolation until this day" (Josh 8:28).

What is meaningful about Alt's discussion for our study is his sensitivity to how the experience of places contributed to a sense of the past in ancient Israel. There is something about an encounter with meaningful locations, Alt suggests, that shaped how former times were thought about by the biblical writers and the communities from which they descended. In terms of Shiloh, what Alt's theory of *Ortsgebundenheit* encourages are investigations into the "place-bounded" character of the biblical references to it, or how the physical features of the location, dominated by ruins from the MB II and Iron I periods, may have influenced what was recalled about the settlement in antiquity. But rather than situating this relationship emphatically within etiological considerations, as Alt does, my investigation will build on these insights by drawing on wider

---

[117] Albrecht Alt, "Josua," in *Kleine Schriften zur Geschichte des Volkes Israel*, Vol. I, 176–92 (Munich: C. H. Beck, 1953 [1936]), esp. 182–85. Martin Noth would develop this theory further in his *A History of the Pentateuchal Traditions*, trans. B. Anderson (Englewood Cliffs, NJ: Prentice-Hall, 1972 [1948]), esp. 54–62.

[118] Alt, "Josua," 183–87. Alt accents these "echten alten Erzählungen" over against secondary elements of Joshua's narrative that lack etiological interest (183).

[119] Alt emphasizes that for many of these tales the origins of contemporary circumstances were derived from supposed past events, often in an effort to answer the question "why" – why are these features, these stones, these ruins here? Ibid., 182–83.

philosophical and historical discussions of memory and the experience of material remains, a scholarly orientation that emerged largely in the years subsequent to the horrors that would come to pass shortly after the publication of Alt's essay.[120]

It is the pioneering work of Maurice Halbwachs and, in particular, the publication of his *La topographie légendaire des Évangiles en Terre Sainte*,[121] that advanced this connection between memory and place.[122] In that work – the last of Halbwachs' monographs to be published before he perished at Buchenwald weeks before its liberation in 1945 – a series of Christian pilgrimage accounts from the fourth century CE onward are examined in order to investigate the relationship between the locations described in these writings and stories told about them in the New Testament.[123] What Halbwachs details in his study is how certain pilgrimage sites – the Church of the Nativity in

---

[120] On the upsurge in studies devoted to memory after the Shoah, see, for example, the essays in Susannah Radstone and Bill Schwarz, eds., *Memory: Histories, Theories, Debates* (New York: Fordham University Press, 2010), and Jeffrey Olick et al., *The Collective Memory Reader* (New York: Oxford University Press, 2011). For a leading work on this theme, to which many later studies were indebted, including this one, see Lawrence Langer, *Holocaust Testimonies: The Ruins of Memory* (New Haven, CT: Yale University Press, 1991).

[121] Maurice Halbwachs, *La topographie légendaire des Evangiles en Terre sainte: Étude de mémoire collective* (Paris: Presses Universitaires de France, 1941).

[122] For studies on place and memory in the wake of Halbwachs's work, see Gaston Bachelard, *The Poetics of Space*, trans. M. Jolas (Boston: Beacon Press, 1994 [1958]), esp. 8–9; Edward Casey, *Remembering: A Phenomenological Study* (Bloomington: Indiana University Press, 1987), 181–215; Pierre Nora, "Between Memory and History: Les Lieux de Mémoire," *Representations* 26 (1989): 7–24; Simon Schama, *Landscape and Memory* (New York: Vintage Books, 1995); M. Christine Boyer, *The City of Collective Memory: Its Historical Imagery and Architectural Entertainments* (Cambridge, MA: MIT Press, 1996); Jan Assmann, *Das kulturelle Gedächtnis: Schrift, Erinnerung, und politische Identität in frühen Hochkulturen* (München: C. H. Beck, 1997), 34–65; Jeffrey Malpas, *Place and Experience: A Philosophical Topography* (New York: Routledge, 1999), 175–93; Susan Alcock, *Archaeologies of the Greek Past: Landscape, Monuments, and Memories* (Cambridge: Cambridge University Press, 2002); Lynn Meskell, "Memory's Materiality: Ancestral Presence, Commemorative Practice and Disjunctive Locales," in *Archaeologies of Memory*, eds. R. Van Dycke and S. Alcock, 28–55 (Malden, MA: Blackwell, 2003); Yannis Hamilakis and Jo Labanyi, "Introduction: Time, Materiality, and the Work of Memory," *History and Memory* 20.2 (2008): 5–17; Jay Winter, "Sites of Memory," in *Memory: Histories, Theories, Debates*, eds. S. Radstone and B. Schwarz, 312–24 (New York: Fordham University Press, 2010); Gérôme Truc, "Memory of Places and Places of Memory: For a Halbwachsian Socio-Ethnography of Collective Memory," *International Social Sciences Journal* 62 (2011): 147–159; Laurent Olivier, *The Dark Abyss of Time: Archaeology and Memory*, trans. A. Greenspan (London: Rowan and Littlefield, 2011); Dylan Trigg, *The Memory of Place: A Phenomenology of the Uncanny* (Athens: Ohio University Press, 2012); Ömür Harmanşah, *Cities and the Shaping of Memory in the Ancient Near East* (Cambridge: Cambridge University Press, 2013); Bjørnar Olsen and Dóra Pétursdóttir, eds., *Ruin Memories: Materialities, Aesthetics, and the Archaeology of the Recent Past* (London: Routledge, 2014); Daniel Pioske, *David's Jerusalem: Between Memory and History* (New York: Routledge, 2015), 1–62; Daniel Pioske, *Memory in a Time of Prose*, esp. 67–84; Ruth Van Dyke, "Archaeology and Social Memory," *Annual Review of Anthropology* 48 (2019): 207–25.

[123] Halbwachs, *La topographie*, 11–147.

Bethlehem, the Cenacle in Jerusalem – attracted visitors because of the memories connected to their physical remains. To journey to these locations was to participate in a remembered past, Halbwachs argues, precisely because something tangible of it could be experienced in the present. If early Christian figures had perished long ago and events connected to them were of a bygone era, the places connected to them could nevertheless be visited and memories about them experienced once more by those who came later. For Halbwachs, what these pilgrim accounts reveal is that it is places, above all else, that both produce and sustain the memories of a community over time.

But what also comes to light in Halbwachs's study is the tenuous historical connections these locations often had to events and figures from the first century CE. A remembered past and a historical one, Halbwachs observes throughout his work, are distinct modes of retrospection that may generate overlapping claims but also, at moments, distinct or competing ones. More important than the underlying history of these places of memory for those who visited them, consequently, was the commemorative power accorded to these locations in the minds of the faithful.

And indispensable to this power were the physical features found at such sites. For Halbwachs, it was a location's concrete reality that generated shared memories, offering the possibility of having "direct contact" with the past sought by those who visited it.[124] Material remains associated with early Christian occurrences were all the more significant, Halbwachs further contends, for a community whose sense of its origins was obscured by the fact that its early adherents were largely of insignificant backgrounds removed from the more powerful societal structures of their time, and thus left behind few traces of their existence in historical sources from the first or second century CE.[125] Consequently, for those Christians who journeyed to Palestine in order to visit sacred sites from a more distant past, "How could such a memory persist," Halbwachs asks of various early Christian events, "if it had not attached itself to certain points in the terrain?"[126]

In posing this question, Halbwachs returns to his earlier studies on collective memory. In a posthumous publication, *La Mémoire Collective*, Halbwachs explores the relationship between place and remembering in a chapter entitled

---

[124] So Halbwachs writes of such a location: "It is like a tangible witness, a tangible certitude which is added to the others, and which is perhaps more decisive. The past becomes part of the present: we touch it, we have direct contact with it." (C'est comme un témoignage sensible, c'est une certitude sensible qui s'ajoute aux autres, et qui est peut-être plus decisive. Le passé devient en partie le présent: on le touche, on est en contact direct avec lui.) Ibid., 2. In his conclusion, this point is returned to, where Halbwachs observes that it was important that the faithful were assured of "seeing and touching" the places believed to have been connected to the life of Jesus (158).

[125] Ibid., esp. 149–65.   [126] Ibid., 161.

"Collective Memory and Space."[127] Halbwachs theorizes in this discussion what he brings to light in his later investigation of the Holy Land, where the argument is put forward that the very possibility of remembrance depends on our ability to localize our memories among the places that we find meaningful. The reason places are of such consequence for remembering, Halbwachs writes, is that the "material environment" (*milieu materiel*) of a landscape endures over long stretches of time, allowing for the possibility that we might visit and encounter once again those pasts connected to this landscape.[128] Pilgrimage sites were so evocative for Christian travelers because shared recollections are contingent on those material remains that frame and sustain their claims, particularly for a more remote past that we experience only through the memories of others. So Halbwachs remarks,[129]

> Thus, every collective memory unfolds within a spatial framework. As it happens, space is a reality that endures: because our impressions move quickly past, one to the other, and leave nothing behind in our mind, we understand that we are able to recover the past only if it is preserved, in effect, by the material environment that surrounds us.

In Halbwachs' strong thesis, memories shared over time are enabled through the common experience of a material world, a collective past that can be recalled *only* by way of the "material environment that surrounds us." Memories of Jesus' life or the lives of his disciples were maintained over the centuries by various Christian groups, in short, because these memories came to be affixed to distinct places in the southern Levant. A remembered past persisted because the landscape of these memories also endured.

Halbwachs's contribution to our investigation resides in his theory – borne out through his own study of the relationship between ancient texts and material remains – that the physical environs of a landscape are crucial, even necessary, for how a community remembers its shared past. Through the work of Halbwachs, Alt's theory of *Ortsgebundenheit* is thus refined further when we examine how and why places attract the stories that they do about former periods. Beyond the rather vague "sayings" or "traditions" that Alt associates with those pilgrims who visited sacred sites in antiquity, Halbwachs broadens and deepens this discussion by theorizing how a community's memories are dependent on the material frameworks visible at meaningful places.

---

[127] Maurice Halbwachs, *La collective mémoire*, 2nd ed. (Paris: Presses Universitaires de France, 1968), 130–67.
[128] Halbwachs comments further: "Space alone is stable enough to last without growing old or losing any of its parts" (L'espace seul est assez stable pour pouvoir durer sans vieillir ni perdre aucune de ses parties). Halbwachs, *La mémoire collective*, 167.
[129] Ibid., 146.

And it is within this domain of memory that studies of place and the pasts associated with them have been further advanced. Perhaps most significant in this vein is Edward Casey's phenomenological study of remembering, which, much like that of Halbwachs before him, included a chapter devoted to what is termed "Place Memory."[130] In this discussion, Casey draws out what he describes as an "elective affinity" between places and remembering, an attachment – often unbidden and acute – that arises because *"place is selective for memories"* and memories, in turn, *"are selective for place."*[131] The reason for this selectivity is the "stabilizing persistence" of places, as Casey describes it, where the fixed frameworks of a location resist the mutability of time.[132] Drawing on Aristotle's reflections on these themes, Casey accents how places conserve, contain, and reserve the past, all of which contrasts with how time fundamentally disperses it. Through this capacity to oppose, or at least mitigate, the wearing away of time, locations are able to serve as "place-holders" of a remembered past that would otherwise dissolve, these memories being bound to landmarks or buildings or a natural terrain that could be returned to and, when visited again, remembered once more.[133] There is a visibility and expressiveness to place that marks it out along the horizon and invites our recollections to take hold – a power akin, Casey observes, to what the Romans once called the *genius loci* of a place, which elicits an atmosphere of familiarity and intimacy or, when away, nostalgia.[134] An "alert and alive memory connects spontaneously with place,"[135] Casey maintains, and, in the end, cannot be sustained without these sites of remembrance. Every memory we have "takes place" somewhere.

In these writings, what is accented once more are the material frameworks of remembrance. This perspective accords places a certain agency within memory – eliciting, conjuring, shaping our sense of the past by virtue of the physical settings in which our memories coalesce.[136] Paul Ricoeur, in his own reading of Halbwachs and Casey, underscores this feature of remembrance by linking it to memory's "worldliness"[137] (*mondanéité*) or to the fact that one "does not simply remember oneself, seeing, experiencing, learning; rather one recalls the situations in the world in which one has seen, experienced, learned."[138] Memory orients itself by way of inhabiting certain locations, Ricoeur observes,

---

[130] Casey, *Remembering*, 181–215.   [131] Ibid., 214, 189. (italics original)   [132] Ibid., 186.
[133] Ibid., 186, 189.   [134] Ibid., 199–200.   [135] Ibid., 186.
[136] Halbwachs, for his part, will therefore accent the vulnerability of memory to the changing character of places over time. Places endure, and as such provide an essential aid to remembering, but their physical transformations – decay, renovation, wanton destruction – mean that memories of the past will also necessarily adapt to these new landscapes. Halbwachs, *La topographie*, 165.
[137] Paul Ricoeur, *Memory, History, Forgetting*, trans. K. Blamey and D. Pellauer (Chicago: University of Chicago Press, 2004), 36–44.
[138] Ibid., 36.

such that "the 'things' remembered are intrinsically associated with places."[139] But what Ricoeur adds to this discussion is a more robust sense of temporality to these structures of remembrance, or what he terms the "varying degrees of temporal distanciation" that arise through the memories associated with place, where the "magnitude of the interval of time elapsed can itself be perceived, felt," through our encounter with memorable locations.[140] When we come across the remains of a place, we meet again those memories that arose in connection to them, but we also come to recognize that a duration of time, perhaps substantial, has transpired between our present and the past that is recollected.[141] "This moment of awakening," as Ricoeur describes it, our sense of a "world gone by to which these ruins sadly referred,"[142] is an affective one, deepening our impression of the passing of time by our encounter with remnants left behind from previous ages. The "worldliness" of memory often calls us back to former times, some quite distant. "Memory," Aristotle writes in a famous section of his *De Memoria*, is "of the past," but, as he comments further, what is significant about this past is that it is "conditioned by lapse of time."[143]

It is the twin themes of memory's contingency and duration with regard to those places remembered that will matter most for how we understand the pasts associated with Shiloh in the Hebrew Bible.[144] That Shiloh was memorable is evident across these writings.[145] In Jeremiah, the memory of Shiloh's

---

[139] Ibid., 41.   [140] Ibid., 40.   [141] Cf. Halbwachs, *La topographie*, 164–65.

[142] Ibid., 40.

[143] Aristotle, *De memoria et reminiscentia*, 449b 15–25. For English translation, see Aristotle, *The Parva Naturalia*, trans. J. I. Beare (Oxford: Clarendon Press, 1908).

[144] For further reflections on this point from the standpoint of the biblical writings, see Victor Matthews, "Remembered Space in Biblical Narrative," in *Constructions of Space IV: Further Developments in Examining Ancient Israel's Social Space*, ed. M. George, 61–75 (New York: Bloomsbury, 2013). Ancient Greek and Roman writers were also well aware of this relationship, developing an *ars memoire* through their method of *loci* that drew on places to aid in remembering. So Cicero, for example, writes that the "structure of memory, like a wax tablet, employs places and in these gathers together images like letters" (*confectio memoriae tamquam cera locis utitur*). Cicero, *Partitiones oratoriae*, §26 in Cicero, *On the Orator*, trans. H. Rackham, LCL 349 (Cambridge, MA: Harvard University Press, 1942), 330–31. For the classic study of this art of memory through emplacement, see Mary Carruthers, *The Book of Memory: A Study of Memory in Medieval Culture*, 2nd ed. (Cambridge: Cambridge University Press, 2008).

[145] Scholarship on memory and the biblical writings is now vast, but for representative studies from different vantage points, see Mark Smith, *The Memoirs of God: History, Memory, and the Experience of the Divine in Ancient Israel* (Minneapolis: Fortress Press, 2004); Ronald Hendel, *Remembering Abraham: Culture, Memory, and History in the Hebrew Bible* (Oxford: Oxford University Press, 2005); Ian Wilson, *Kingship and Memory in Ancient Judah* (New York: Oxford, 2017); Ian Wilson, "History and Hebrew Bible: Culture, Narrative, and Memory," *Brill Research Perspectives in Biblical Interpretation* 3.2 (2018): 1–69; Daniel Pioske, "Retracing a Remembered Past: Methodological Remarks on Memory, History, and the Hebrew Bible," *Biblical Interpretation* 23.3. (2015): 291–315; Pioske, *Memory in a Time of Prose*; Ehud Ben Zvi, *Social Memory among the Literati of Yehud* (Berlin: De Gruyter, 2019); Johannes Unsok Ro and Diana Edelman, eds., *Collective Memory and Collective Identity: Deuteronomy*

destruction persisted for at least four hundred years and could be recalled to unsettling effect. But the allusions to Shiloh in Joshua, Judges, Samuel, Kings, and Ps 78 further attest to the powerful hold exerted by Shiloh on memories of Israel's earlier past among those who lived centuries after its destruction. Among the "things of old" that "our ancestors recounted to us," the poet of Ps 78 declares (Ps 78:2–3), was the memory of Shiloh's abandonment.

The archaeological record also offers evidence of this connection. Support for Khirbet Seilun being a place of memory is found in the remains left behind from LBA populations who visited the ruins of the MBA settlement, most likely in connection with cultic traditions that endured at the site after it was destroyed.[146] That later populations would do the same after the Iron I community came to an end would be in keeping, then, with activities that had taken place at Shiloh for centuries prior. Certain remains of the site, such as Shiloh's imposing MBA enclosure or buildings from the Iron I period, would have preserved vestiges of Shiloh's former significance in the highlands for those who came across these ruins later. Other debris, including burned-out structures and the wreckage within them, would have reinforced memories of Shiloh's violent end. If the remains of a sanctuary were indeed once present at the site, as the Books of Samuel and Jeremiah suggest, a further possibility is that highland communities continued to return to Shiloh's temple ruins in the time after its destruction, a practice that evidently took place at Jerusalem after its sanctuary was destroyed (Jer 41:4–5). As a "large ruin,"[147] Shiloh would have been a striking feature in the landscape of the highland region, attracting individuals to it in a manner that was likely not far removed from how Mycenae beckoned visitors to its material remains long after its demise.[148]

To this evidence are added the insights of the theorists of place and memory. For what these studies anticipate and clarify is how Shiloh's material remains would have generated and sustained memories about it in antiquity.[149] If we

---

and the Deuteronomistic History in Their Context (Berlin: De Gruyter, 2021); and Aubrey Buster, *Remembering the Story of Israel: Historical Summaries and Memory Formation in Second Temple Judaism* (Cambridge: Cambridge University Press, 2022).

[146] Finkelstein," Summary and Conclusions," 162–63.

[147] Finkelstein, *Forgotten Kingdom*, 49–50.

[148] The ruined walls of Troy, too, have been much discussed as a site of memory for those living in antiquity. See especially Elizabeth Minchin, "Commemoration and Pilgrimage in the Ancient World: Troy and the Stratigraphy of Cultural Memory," *Greece and Rome* 59.1 (2012): 76–89. Cf. Jonas Grethlein, "Memory and Material Objects in the Iliad and Odyssey," *Journal of Hellenic Studies* 128 (2008): 27–51.

[149] For a brief allusion to the link between the ruins of Shiloh and memory, see also Finkelstein, *Forgotten Kingdom*, 49–50. In the final moments of Knittel's monograph, a similar argument is put forward regarding Shiloh (Knittel, *Heiligtum*, 241), where it is observed that "the memory of Shiloh's destruction through the centuries is associated with the visible remains of this destruction" (die Errinerung an die Zerstörung Schilos durch die Jahrhunderte hinweg mit den sichtbaren Resten dieser Zerstörung verband). For a study that features

adopt the perspective of Halbwachs, we can even question if remembering is possible at all absent the places in which our memories become attached, and that it is the persistence of Shiloh's ruins, consequently, that would have been decisive in the persistence of stories told about it long after it had been destroyed. Walking the main north-south road that wound through the highlands and gazing east, individuals in antiquity would have been able to make out the hilltop settlement of Shiloh and the remnants of its large wall and those crumbling structures still visible. The enduring remains of Shiloh made it a meaningful site of memory in the highland region, even more so if embedded among its ruins were those of an earlier Yahweh sanctuary. What theorists of place and memory confer on our investigation is a historically meaningful explanation, then, for why Shiloh appears as it does in the biblical writings.[150]

This argument nevertheless leaves an important question unresolved. For if the biblical portrayals of Shiloh's past were shaped by the location's ruined landscape, as is maintained here, then how, more precisely, did these remains factor into what these scribes recounted? How may their stories have been influenced by the ruins that Shiloh had become? What we are after, in this sense, is understanding how "the physical world and tangible objects prompted and guided the course of memory"[151] manifested within the biblical writings, as Susan Alcock traces among ancient Greek texts, or how Shiloh's ruins may have impressed themselves onto what was recollected about them in these ancient documents. We begin with the phenomenon of remembering what never was.

2.3.2 Ruins and Remembrance: Remembering What Never Was

When viewed through the prism of its archaeological remains, perhaps the most striking feature of Shiloh's representation in the Hebrew Bible is the prominence accorded to it during the LBA. Within the Book of Joshua, Shiloh is depicted as a pivotal location during this era (ca. thirteenth century BCE), a site that is said to have housed the tabernacle and drawn together various tribes for the purposes of land allocation and war (Josh 18–22). If we follow those studies that would situate these allusions to the settlement among the final moments of the Priestly narrative, stories about Shiloh and its cultic center are the culmination of a story begun in Genesis.

---

remembrance in its title, however, the lack of interest in developing this argument beyond the paragraph in which it is raised suggests that theoretical issues surrounding memory are outside the bounds of its concerns.

[150] "[G]o back in time to the furthest point possible for us," Halbwachs asks, and what we find is that our memories "must be well placed in a place" (*doivent bien se replacer en un lieu*). Halbwachs, *La mémoire collective*, 167.

[151] Alcock, *Archaeologies of the Greek Past*, 19.

When we turn to the archaeological record, however, Shiloh appears to have been mostly abandoned at this time. There is little evidence that a community was present at Shiloh during the era when the Book of Joshua unfolds. LBA pottery and bones were recovered from Area D of the settlement, but this assemblage was mostly produced from a single deposit that was likely a *favissa* and, further, the collection descended primarily from a LBA I horizon instead of the later LBA II period that would better coincide with the time period that Joshua relates.[152] It may be, as Finkelstein suggests, that some cultic activity continued in the LBA among the ruins of the MBA site,[153] but there is little material evidence to indicate that Shiloh was rebuilt and occupied during this period, nor are there remains that suggest that those in the highlands regularly came to this location to engage in cultic practices or to hold assemblies for territorial claims and muster for battle.

How to understand Shiloh's prominence in the LBA within the Book of Joshua is a matter of debate, including the arguments above that characterize these references as scribal revisions introduced many centuries later. But when reading these claims alongside Shiloh's archaeological remains, a different historical perspective comes into focus that complements those of a more redactional or ideological bent. That is, another way to explain Shiloh's depiction in the Book of Joshua is that the ruins of the site compelled later storytellers to locate certain accounts about Israel's early past among what were to them already ancient remains.

This premise returns us to Alt's theory of *Ortsgebundenheit*. But rather than attributing the development of such storytelling to predominantly etiological interests, the relationship between place and memory provides an alternative interpretive framework for understanding how these stories about Shiloh and Joshua came to be. On this view, certain memories about the tabernacle or Israel's early moments in Canaan were shaped by later communities who were aware of Shiloh's ruins for generations after its destruction. The remains of Shiloh, on this view, provided a setting in which memories of Israel's earlier past came to be affixed, not unlike the Christian pilgrimage accounts that Halbwachs identifies and their attachments to ruins that were still visible centuries after the first century CE events they associated with them.

An advantage of wedding these references to Shiloh to a mode of remembrance is that it conforms to a widespread feature of collective memory. Indeed, in his *La Togopgraphie*, Halbwachs emphasized this type of collective memory above all others, where the Christian claims Halbwachs examined were found to consistently attach past memories to specific locations that had

---

[152] Finkelstein, "Conclusion," 381–82.   [153] Ibid., 382.

few actual historical connections to what was recalled about them.[154] Rather than remnants of first century CE structures or artifacts, a number of these pilgrim sites were affiliated instead with remains that had often appeared long before or many centuries after Jesus and his early followers were active. The ruins of certain places in Palestine that these later pilgrims visited evoked memories of a past that had never, historically speaking, occurred within their specific environs, such as the Garden Tomb in Jerusalem, which was often venerated by those who journeyed to the city but which predated the time of Jesus by seven centuries or more.[155] Ricoeur, too, draws attention to a similar form of remembrance, one termed an "instrumentalized memory," or what is described as the intentional shaping of a remembered past by those in authority, particularly in the sphere of a "demand for identity."[156] Ricoeur observes how material markers at certain sites – monuments, tombs, venerable structures – could be drawn on to recall events that had no historical associations with these remains but were communicated in order to promote a particular vision of the past by those who desired to reframe it.

In addition to Shiloh's standing in Joshua 18–22, this mode of remembrance can be connected to other instances of biblical storytelling, especially those accounts set in the LBA. It was observed in the previous chapter that a collection of ruined sites that we now date to the EBA and MBA periods are portrayed in the Hebrew Bible as the outcome of one era, essentially that of the thirteenth through twelfth centuries BCE (LBA II/Iron I). These include the famous stories of Jericho's fall in Joshua 6 or 'Ai's destruction in Joshua 8, both of which are said to have been destroyed near the time of Shiloh's founding. In a manner not far removed from the archaeological evidence unearthed at Khirbet Seilun, the remains from Tell es-Sultan (Jericho) and et-Tell ('Ai) indicate that these sites were not inhabited when the biblical stories about them depict their fall. Instead, 'Ai came to ruin a thousand years before, and Jericho's destruction occurred two or three centuries prior.[157]

---

[154] For Halbwachs, these circumstances led to the historical locations of Jesus' life being mostly lost, the sites remembered based on only a faint sense of where certain events actually transpired. The significance of these places of memory were reinforced over the centuries, however, through frequent visits and the claims made about them. Halbwachs, *La topographie*, 149–65. On this point, see now the recent work of Jordan Ryan, *From the Passion to the Church of the Holy Sepulchre: Memories of Jesus in Place, Pilgrimage, and Early Holy Sites over the First Three Centuries* (New York: T&T Clark, 2022).

[155] Halbwachs, *La topographie*, 1. On this point, see especially Truc, "Memory of Places," 151–55.

[156] Ricoeur, *Memory, History, Forgetting*, 80–81. For a similar perspective, see Matthews, "Remembered Space," 67–75.

[157] See again Joseph Callaway, "New Evidence on the Conquest of 'Ai," *Journal of Biblical Literature* 87.3 (1968): 312–20; Joseph Callaway, "Excavating Ai (Et-Tell): 1964–1972," *Biblical Archaeologist* 39.1 (1976): 18–30; Joseph Callaway, "Ai," in *New Encyclopedia of Archaeological Excavations in the Holy Land*, Volume I, 39–45; Lorenzo Nigro, "The Built

Much like Shiloh's past in the Book of Joshua, then, we can posit that individuals writing long after Jericho and 'Ai had been overthrown drew on the visible ruins of these sites to construct certain stories about what once had occurred there.[158] The result were narratives that, archaeologically and historically speaking, remembered a past that never was.[159]

Other sites correspond to this mode of remembrance, including the stories in Joshua that portray events that transpire at Gibeon (Josh 9–10), Yarmuth (Josh 10:3, 5, 23), and Hebron (Josh 10:36–39) – none of which appear to have been inhabited during the era in which the events of the Book of Joshua unfold.[160] But what matters about this collection of stories for our purposes is that it was composed in a later era when the ruins of the sites named within it could be visited. The logic of this storytelling among the ruins is something we can therefore appreciate, written as these narratives were in a world in which the origin of so many ruins in the southern Levant was unknown. As Yigal Levin observes in his study of these accounts, "The author of the conquest narrative used what he knew to be 'facts on the ground': large, destroyed, ancient cities, which 'must' have been destroyed by the incoming Israelites."[161] Living among the ruins of a more distant past whose history was so often unknown, these scribes composed certain stories that produced memories of how these ruins came to be.

Remembering a past that never was is, in fact, a widespread phenomenon in antiquity. At the outset to this chapter, we found Thucydides among the ruins of Mycenae, connecting fifth century BCE remains from the Argive destruction of the site to a legendary ruler who would have lived roughly eight centuries before, with no attempt made by Thucydides to disassociate the ruins

---

Tombs on the Spring Hill and the Palace of the Lords of Jericho ('ḎMR RḤ')in the Middle Bronze Age," in *Exploring the Longue Durée: Essays in Honor of Lawrence E. Stager*, ed. J. D. Schloen, 261–76 (Winona Lake, IN: Eisenbrauns, 2009); Lorenzo Nigro, "Tell es-Sultan 2015: A Pilot Project for Archaeology in Palestine," *Near Eastern Archaeology* 79:1 (2016): 4–17.

[158] On the connection between ruins and this manner of biblical storytelling for the site of 'Ai, see already the early reflections by Martin Noth, "Bethel und 'Ai," *Palästinajahrbuch* 31 (1935): 7–29. This point was also recognized by an early excavator of Jericho, Carl Watzinger, who observed that Jericho would have been a "heap of ruins" (*Trümmerstätte*) when Joshua lived. Carl Watzinger, "Zur Chronologie der Schichten von Jericho," *Zeitschrift der Deutschen Morgenländischen Gesellschaft* 80.2/3 (1926): 131–36; 135.

[159] For a further parallel to this phenomenon, see Smith's study of late Second Temple memories of the Wilderness in Daniel Smith, "On Appeals to an Imperfect Past in a Present Future: Remembering the Israelite Wilderness Generation in the Late Second Temple Period," *Journal for the Study of the Pseudepigrapha* 28.2 (2018): 123–42.

[160] For these sites, see again our discussion in Chapter 1. For a more recent, incisive overview of this phenomenon, see Yigal Levin, "Conquered and Unconquered: Reality and Historiography in the Geography of Joshua," in *The Book of Joshua*, ed. E. Noort, 361–70 (Leuven: Peeters, 2012).

[161] Levin, "Conquered and Unconquered," 169.

of a more remote past from a more recent one. Herodotus, too, participates in this manner of storytelling, where in Book VIII of the *Histories* he recounts the famous episode of the attempted Persian assault on the sanctuary at Delphi, "surely one of the most amazing things ever known" (Hdt. VIII: 37), as Herodotus describes the miraculous deliverance of the shrine. Historically, we now know that no assault was made on the sanctuary by the Persians and that, instead, Delphi was likely sympathetic with the Persian cause.[162] In part, Herodotus' account appears to have been predicated on later informants from Delphi who had little interest in recounting the sanctuary's pro-Persian past decades after Greek victory. But what is significant for this study is that Herodotus also bases his story on the material remains of an avalanche that was said to have stymied the Persian advance, remains that Herodotus claims to have observed himself ("the rocks that fell from Parnassus were yet to be seen in my day" [Hdt. VIII 39]). The writers of the Book of Joshua were not alone, in other words, in remembering through their stories a past that never occurred.[163] Nor were they the only writers in antiquity to connect such memories to the ruins that surrounded them.

2.3.3 Ruins and Remembrance: The Persistence of the Past

Other stories about Shiloh's past nevertheless evince a different dynamic of memory. What the references to Shiloh in the Books of Samuel, Jeremiah, and Ps 78 all have in common is their claim that Shiloh's importance was eclipsed a generation or two before David's ascent to the throne. What is significant about these claims in light of the archaeological evidence from Khirbet Seilun is that the settlement appears to have been destroyed in a violent conflagration around this period. The carbon-14 measurements obtained from grain, seed, and raisin samples from Areas D and C of Stratum V from Shiloh are consistent in this regard, indicating that the location was set ablaze sometime between 1050 and 1000 BCE.[164]

The correspondence between these dates and the biblical stories set in this time period does not demonstrate that the biblical writings refer to this specific eleventh century BCE destruction of Shiloh. It is one of the enigmatic features of Shiloh's past in the Hebrew Bible that no biblical text makes any clear

---

[162] Angus M. Bowie, ed., *Herodotus Histories: Book VIII* (Cambridge: Cambridge University Press, 2007), 125–30.
[163] Other instances of this phenomenon from the Hebrew Bible could be drawn out, such as the numerous allusions to the Philistines and Philistine cities in Genesis (Gen 10; 21; 26), the account of the destruction of Heshbon in Num 21, the wilderness itinerary of Numbers 33 (so the references to Ezion-Geber or Kadesh-Barnea), or the Queen of Sheba's visit to Solomon (1 Kings 10), among others.
[164] Finkelstein and Piasetzky, "Iron I–IIA," 46–47.

reference to how Shiloh was destroyed. In the case of Ps 78 and Jeremiah we come across allusions to Shiloh being abandoned by Yahweh and lying in ruins, but no explicit details are offered as to how the location came to such an end. With the Book of Samuel, Shiloh simply disappears from the narrative after battles with Philistine forces in its vicinity for reasons that are never directly revealed to us. Archaeologically, the eleventh century BCE also appears to have been somewhat volatile in the region around Shiloh,[165] meaning that the location's destruction could have been due to causes that simply go unmentioned in the Hebrew Bible.

But the biblical claims that Shiloh lost its significance long ago are meaningful. Such references indicate that individuals living long after Shiloh's destruction were aware that the location once held some importance in the highlands and that the settlement had come to an end before David's rise to the throne. This knowledge was not a product of the biblical writers being contemporaries to these events. Instead, allusions to Shiloh's loss of status in the Book of Jeremiah were written down four centuries after this era and, if we follow the prevailing view of Judges, the brief allusions to Shiloh's early Iron Age past in Judges 18–21 would have been written from a similar temporal distance. But even the older references to Shiloh in 1 Samuel 1–7, as noted above, were likely composed a few centuries after the location's downfall.

For these stories, the relationship between ruins and remembrance is once again suggestive. But in these instances the capacity of ruined locations such as Shiloh to persist over great lengths of time – perhaps a millennium, according to the archaeological remains –allowed for the possibility of older memories, sometimes vague and obscure, others more resonant, to persist as well among the highland communities where Shiloh once stood.[166] One way to account for allusions to Shiloh's significance in the eleventh century BCE among texts written hundreds of years after it came to ruin, in other words, is that the prominent remains of the site contributed to the perpetuation of more venerable memories recalled about it. The "stabilizing" effect of places on memory, as Casey describes it above, would have contributed to the durability of past remembrances connected to these locations.

Once again, we can retrace this phenomenon of ruins and remembrance elsewhere in the Hebrew Bible. A striking example is the city of Gath (Tell es-Safi). Much like Shiloh, Gath is featured in a variety of biblical books, including Joshua, Kings, Amos, Micah, and, most prominently, the Book of

---

[165] So the abandonment of 'Ai, for example, or the short-lived fortress of Khirbet ed-Dawwara. On the latter, see Israel Finkelstein, "The Excavations at Khirbet ed-Dawwara: An Iron Age Site Northeast of Jerusalem," *Tel Aviv* 17.2 (1990): 163–208; for the wider phenomenon, see again Faust, *Israel's Ethnogenesis*, 116–27.

[166] On this point, see Mark Leuchter, *The Levites and the Boundaries of Israelite Identity* (New York: Oxford University Press, 2017), 70–77.

Samuel.[167] Yet, as with Shiloh, archaeological evidence from the site (Tell es-Safi) demonstrates that Gath is destroyed relatively early in the Iron Age, being brought to an end by the Aramean ruler Hazael sometime in the mid-ninth century BCE.[168] Many of the biblical descriptions we have of Gath as a prominent, eleventh to tenth century BCE city were thus written down after the city had been burned to the ground. The significance of Gath within biblical storytelling was likely an outcome, therefore, of memories about the Philistine center being reinforced over the generations by the large mound of ruins that Gath had become, ruins that were never fully restored or reoccupied during the centuries when the biblical writers were active. Other locations referred to in the Hebrew Bible correspond to this mode of remembrance, such as accounts about early Iron Age incidents that take place at Shechem (Judges 9) or Bethel (Judges 20:18, 26; 21:2), stories that were also composed when the ruins marking these locations were almost assuredly still visible.[169]

The point of drawing attention to this mode of remembrance is not to contend for the historicity of these biblical portrayals. Rather, what is maintained here is the more modest assertion that the ruins of certain locations in ancient Israel contributed to the perpetuation of what can be described as older memories about them, memories whose claims were more reflective of the earlier eras in which these stories were set than the later periods in which they were composed. In a comparative vein, studies of Homer have documented a similar phenomenon.[170] In the Catalogue of Ships in Book II of the *Iliad*

---

[167] Yigal Levin, "Philistine Gath in the Biblical Record," in *Tell es Safi/Gath I: The 1996–2005 Seasons, Part I: Texts,* ed. A. Maeir, 141–52 (Wiesbaden: Harrossowitz Verlag, 2012).

[168] Aren Maeir, "Introduction," in *Tell es Safi/Gath I: The 1996–2005 Seasons, Part I: Texts,* ed. A. Maeir, 1–88 (Wiesbaden: Harrossowitz Verlag, 2012); Aren Maeir, "Memories, Myths, and Megalithics: Reconsidering the Giants of Gath," *Journal of Biblical Literature* 139.4 (2020): 675–90; Pioske, *Memory in a Time of Prose,* 85–133.

[169] Mark Smith and Elizabeth Bloch-Smith comment on Shechem, for example, that an old core of the story in Judges 9 "may have originated during the period of knowledge or memory of the razed site and the Shechem temple ruins, which were visible from the later twelfth through the mid-ninth century." Mark Smith and Elizabeth Bloch-Smith, *Judges 1* (Minneapolis: Fortress, 2021), 20, cf. 657–65. On the preservation of older memories in the bible viewed through the lens of archaeology, see also Amihai Mazar, "Archaeology and the Bible: Reflections on Historical Memory in the Deuteronomistic History," in *Congress Volume, Munich 2013,* ed. C. Maier, 347–69 (Leiden: Brill, 2014); Israel Finkelstein, "What the Biblical Authors Knew about Canaan before and in the Early Days of the Hebrew Kingdoms," *Ugarit-Forschungen* 48 (2017): 173–98. Israel Finkelstein and Thomas Römer, "Early North Israelite 'Memories' of Moab," in *The Formation of the Pentateuch,* eds. J. Gertz et al., 711–27 (Tübingen: Mohr Siebeck, 2016); Pioske, *Memory in a Time of Prose,* 85–133. For arguments that some biblical texts may preserve even Bronze Age memories, see Ron Hendel, *Remembering Abraham,* 45–56; Brendon Benz, "The Destruction of Hazor: Israelite History and the Construction of History in Israel," *Journal for the Study of the Old Testament* 44.2 (2019): 262–78.

[170] For a helpful overview, see Susan Sherratt, "Archaeological Contexts," in *A Companion to Ancient Epic,* ed. J. M. Foley, 119–41 (Malden, MA: Blackwell, 2005), and more recently the

(Hom. *Il.* 2.484–93), for example, there are references to locations that are more at home in the LBA world in which the epic unfolds than in the much later era, at least five centuries hence, when these poems were first written down. In his commentary, Geoffrey Kirk argues that one reason for the persistence of these references is that the ruins of certain sites in the Aegean remained visible over the centuries, thereby bolstering the memories of a Homeric past attached to them.[171] Certain ruined sites, whether in the Peloponnese or the Levant, would have thus acted as "place-holders" of memory in antiquity, to return to Casey's terminology above. The persistence of collapsed structures or dilapidated features of a landscape over great stretches of time, from this perspective, contributed to older memories of the past that persisted with them.

2.3.4 Ruins and Remembrance: The Competition of Memory

What is also apparent about the biblical portrayal of Shiloh's past is what we would understand today as its inconsistencies. Perhaps the most glaring of these variances is the discrepancy between those texts that claim Shiloh housed the tabernacle (Josh 18:1; 19:51; 22:19, 29; Ps 78:60; and indirectly, 2 Sam 7) and those that assert that Shiloh was instead the site of an early Yahweh temple (Judges 18:31; 1 Sam 1–3), none of whose claims can be confirmed or discounted through the archaeological evidence that is currently available. But other deviations obtain, including the account of the loss of the ark from Shiloh in 1 Sam 4:11 and the continued possession of it by the Israelites in 1 Sam 14:18, or the possible allusions to Saul's birth in 1 Sam 1 and his dedication at Shiloh rather than, as the story now relates, Samuel's attachment to the location.[172] Yet even the importance accorded to Shiloh in the pre-monarchic period can be somewhat ambiguous. In Joshua, Shiloh finds prominence as the final resting place of the tabernacle, and in Samuel it is home to the ark and the Elide priesthood; in Judges, however, Shiloh can be something of an afterthought, a place situated "in the land of Canaan" (Judges 21:12), whose young women could be abducted in an agreement forged between the Benjaminites and other Israelite tribes (Judges 21:21). In 1 Kings 14:4, the

---

essays contained in Susan Sherratt and John Bennet, eds., *Archaeology and Homeric Epic* (Oxford: Oxbow, 2017).

[171] G. S. Kirk, *The Iliad: A Commentary*, I (Cambridge: Cambridge University Press, 1985), 238–39. The connection between ruins and the Catalogue of Ships is also underscored in J. K. Anderson, "The Geometric Catalogue of Ships," in *The Ages of Homer: A Tribute to Emily Townsend Vermeule*, eds. J. Carter and S. Morris, 181–92 (Austin: University of Texas Press, 1995).

[172] On the theory that 1 Sam 1 contains elements of a birth legend of Saul interspersed into that of Samuel's, see McCarter, *1 Samuel*, 26–27; 62, 65–66; J. Maxwell Miller and John Hayes, *A History of Ancient Israel and Judah* (Philadelphia: Westminster, 1986), 120–36.

prophet Ahijah, furthermore, is housed at Shiloh in a period after the site, or at least its sanctuary, was thought to have been abandoned or destroyed.

These differing perspectives of Shiloh's past are the result of distinct scribal hands who wove into these narratives divergent claims about the location over time. But this phenomenon can also be helpfully linked to a mode of ruins and remembrance, where a multiplicity of memories came to be attached to Shiloh's remains that resisted a seamless harmonization of what was remembered about the location. Because the ruins of Shiloh endured over the centuries, that is, different groups from distinct periods would have been able to recall the location in ways that were not always consonant. For some, the old ruins of Shiloh conjured memories of the former tabernacle, while, for others, they recalled the site of a Yahweh temple. Some memories claimed that the ark was lost from the location during the Battle of Ebenezer, while others alleged that the ark continued in use by Saul and the Israelites afterward. The Book of Jeremiah and Ps 78 intimate that Shiloh became a ruin before David came to the throne, while 1 Kings remembers a pivotal prophet who resided at the location two generations after David's reign. The point of reference for each of these claims was the site of Shiloh, but as a place of memory the location attracted a heterogeneous collection of stories about it through the centuries. The wreckage present at the site that descended from different centuries in the Bronze and Iron Ages, in this sense, was mirrored by the layered and disorderly pasts recalled about it.

This interplay between variants of memory is, however, a common feature of how a community's recollections develop over time.[173] Because places are so memorable, that is, they attract an accumulation of memories about the past, some of which arise in tension with one another and others of which are suppressed or quelled. Memories of places are not singular or cohesive but often polysemous, reflecting the distinct perspectives of various social groups, which manifest disparate concerns.[174] How one remembers the ruins of Masada or World War I battlefields largely depends on the community of which one is a part and the time period in which their past is recalled, a point as true now as it was in antiquity. That Shiloh and certain features connected with it could be remembered with competing or somewhat divergent claims would conform, therefore, to a widespread feature of remembrance.

---

[173] On this phenomenon, see Ann Rigney, "Plenitude, Scarcity, and the Circulation of Cultural Memory," *Journal of European Studies* 35.1 (2005): 11–28; Astrid Erll, "Travelling Memory," *Parallax* 17.4 (2011): 4–18; Barry Schwartz, "Where There Is Smoke There Is Fire: Memory and History," in *Memory and Identity in Ancient Judaism and Early Christianity: A Conversation with Barry Schwartz*, ed. T. Thatcher, 7–37 (Atlanta: SBL Press, 2014).

[174] For antiquity and the region of the Levant, see, for example, Harmansah, *Cities and the Shaping of Memory*, 15–71; James Osborne, "Counter-Monumentality and the Vulnerability of Memory," *Journal of Social Archaeology* 17.2 (2017): 163–87.

Biblically, scholars have observed this phenomenon elsewhere. Perhaps the most famous instance of competing memories within the Hebrew Bible has to do with discrepancies found between the conquest accounts of Joshua and the opening chapters of Judges, which contend that many sites said to have been overrun by the Israelites were not, in fact, subdued.[175] But other examples can be found, including how memories of Sinai in the Hebrew Bible were "recast" over the centuries, as Mark Smith observes, being revised and altered as new groups contributed different and at times competing stories that came to be attached to this location.[176] More recently, Aren Maeir has also pointed up a similar phenomenon within the broader exodus story, drawing on archaeological evidence to illustrate a "matrix of events, memories, and traditions, emanating from many periods and contexts, in which the Exodus mnemo-narratives were formed."[177] If ruins of locations in the ancient world afforded the possibility for older memories to endure, what was recollected within these remembrances was often an aggregate of claims that came together over time, bound by their associations with specific locations rather than by their conformity with regard to what was remembered about them. As a site of memory, Shiloh could also be a site of contestation: For the psalmist, Shiloh's ruins and the memory of its downfall signaled Jerusalem's rise to preeminence; for Jeremiah, these same ruins and memories warned of Jerusalem's imminent demise.

2.3.5 Ruins and Remembrance: On Forgetting

Lastly, what the archaeological evidence recovered from Khirbet Seilun reveals is how much of Shiloh's past was overlooked within biblical storytelling. Foremost among these absences are any references to the site's MBA existence. The archaeological remains of Shiloh indicate that ca. 1600 BCE the location reached its apogee in terms of infrastructure and public works. In no other era would the community in and around Shiloh have had either the capacity or

---

[175] Ovidiu Creanga, "The Conquest of Memory in the Book of Joshua," in *The Oxford Handbook of Biblical Narrative*, ed. D. Fewell, 168–79 (New York: Oxford, 2016); Koert van Bekkum, "Coexistence as Guilt: Iron I Memories in Judges 1," in *The Ancient Near East in the 12th–10th Centuries BCE: Culture and History*, eds. G. Galil et al., 525–47 (Münster: Ugarit-Verlag, 2012); Nadav Na'aman, "Memories of Canaan in the Old Testament," *Ugarit-Forschungen* 47 (2016): 129–46.

[176] Smith, *The Memoirs of God*, 140–52.

[177] Aren Maeir, "Exodus as a *Mnemo-Narrative*: An Archaeological Perspective," in *Israel's Exodus in Transdisciplinary Perspective: Text, Archaeology, Culture, and Geoscience*, eds. T. Levy et al., 409–18 (New York: Springer, 2015). On the Exodus and the various memories attached to it, see also Nadav Na'aman, "The Exodus Story: Between Historical Memory and Historiographical Composition," *Journal of Ancient Near Eastern Religions* 11 (2011): 39–69.

the will to muster the resources necessary to perform the construction projects that were carried out at the site during this period. Many of the ruins encountered at Shiloh in antiquity, as with those remains visible at Shechem, Jerusalem, or Hebron, were in fact the vestiges of the MBA period and the enclosures that had once surrounded these settlements. But there does not exist a single biblical text that connects Shiloh's ruins to the time when the location flourished in the seventeenth to sixteenth centuries BCE.

One of the more arresting differences between our understanding of Shiloh's history and the biblical writers' representation of the site is that they appear unaware of the location's MBA past. There is no indication in the Hebrew Bible that any of its writers knew of Shiloh's status during these centuries. This unfamiliarity is all the more striking since it is evident that some material remains from this Canaanite center were visible throughout the site in the centuries that followed, from architectural features to fragmented cultic items, whose forms were considerably distinct from those of the later eras in which the biblical writers lived. Such Bronze Age remnants must have seemed rather strange to their later onlookers. But, writing perhaps a thousand years after the MBA location was destroyed, the biblical writers had little knowledge of the community that had developed Shiloh and reconfigured its landscape, nor did the biblical writers express any interest in what may have transpired during this time. Shiloh's past was of consequence insofar as memories about it were connected with the lives of those who came later – a past that began with Israel's entrance into Canaan – and not in a time before.

If the ruins of Shiloh precipitated an interest in the location's past for the biblical writers and their contemporaries, this interest was nevertheless directed toward a limited temporal horizon.[178] It may be that what could be seen of Shiloh's MBA remains were, like those ruins at 'Ai and Jericho, connected by later scribes to stories about Israel's entrance into Canaan under Joshua's command. Or perhaps some found in these ruins the wreckage of Shiloh's existence under the Elides and Samuel before the location's downfall. Unable to date these ruins and lacking written texts that described the location's Bronze Age past, the remains of Shiloh would have been in a certain sense timeless for those who experienced these remains centuries later, existing as vestiges of a world that transpired long ago and which could be connected therefore to any number of memories from different periods. The massive fieldstones that comprised Shiloh's ruined wall could have been the result of Joshua's efforts, or Eli's, or those communities hazily remembered in the Book of Judges. If the remains of a Bronze Age Canaanite temple or cultic space

---

[178] For a further example of a "remarkable case of historical amnesia" within biblical storytelling, see again Na'aman's discussion of the strange absence of references to Egypt in LBA Canaan in Na'aman, "Memories of Canaan," 129–46.

were present at Shiloh,[179] the biblical writers make no mention of them. Or, perhaps, they associated these remains, too, with remembered figures and events of their own Israelite lineage – a lineage that, though perhaps unknown to the biblical writers, was of mostly Canaanite stock.

But even Shiloh's early Iron Age past is inflected only intermittently within the biblical writings. What is remembered about the site most vividly is its sanctuary and downfall, the latter of which is well attested in the archaeological record and the former, perhaps, indirectly so. Yet a glaring absence within the Hebrew Bible is a description of how Shiloh came to be destroyed and what happened in the aftermath. Why we are not told of these events is unknown. It may be that the details related to the destruction of a Yahweh sanctuary or cultic site were intentionally suppressed. Or that such information and specifics about the small community that lived among the ruins of Shiloh in the centuries that followed were of little interest to biblical scribes more invested in Jerusalem's past and its cultic life. But it is just as likely that later biblical scribes writing centuries after the site's eleventh century BCE destruction simply did not know how, exactly, Shiloh had come to such an end. In the Book of Jeremiah, we are given the impression that Shiloh's destruction was familiar to its audience but that the specifics behind its downfall – now hundreds of years later – were less familiar, its destruction essentially attributed to divine causes and not mundane ones.

What this suggests is that the depth of the past that Shiloh's ruins evoked for the biblical writers was narrower and more circumscribed than our historical understanding of these remains. In large measure, what the biblical writers knew about Shiloh's past was information that had been preserved over time through what was remembered about it, a form of knowledge that we know is particularly vulnerable to loss and erasure.[180] But on this point, too, the biblical writings are akin to other texts in antiquity, where certain pasts were remembered only partially and often not at all. A frequent reference found among royal writings from Mesopotamia, for example, is that of "abandoned" (*nadû*) or "ancient" (*labīru*) cities that had come to ruin long before the documents that mention them, the origins of these mounds being often unfamiliar to those rulers and their scribes who make mention of them.[181] In a vivid passage

---

[179] On the cultic remains from MBA Shiloh, see again the summary in Finkelstein, "Conclusion," 372–81.

[180] Ricoeur, *Memory, History, Forgetting*, 26–30, 68–92; Alan Megill, *Historical Knowledge, Historical Error: A Contemporary Guide to Practice* (Chicago: University of Chicago Press, 2007), 17–35.

[181] In the stela of Ashurnasirpal II (879 BCE), for example, it is reported that "I rebuilt the abandoned cities (URU.MEŠ-*ni na-ṭu-te*) which had become ruin mounds" (RIMA 2, A.0.101.30 78), and, later, Esarhaddon (681–669 BCE) writes of temple restorations in which "I renovated what was old, repaired what had fallen into ruin" (*la-ab-ru ú-šiš ma-aq-tu*

SHILOH AND THE RUINS OF MEMORY

from Herodotus, a ruined fortress in a foreign landscape is connected with a campaign of Darius that never occurred, a description of ancient ruins that were "fantastically ascribed" to Darius because knowledge of these remains had fallen out of local memory.[182]

What was remembered about Shiloh in the Hebrew Bible stands in tension, then, with what was forgotten. In reading the biblical references to the location among the ruins unearthed through archaeological excavations at the site, this final theme of loss further demonstrates the dynamics of memory related to Shiloh. How Shiloh's past was remembered in the biblical writings was not singular or consistent but participated in different modes of remembrance that would have been shaped by the experience of Shiloh's remains in the centuries after its fall. For ancient scribes, whose sense of the past would have been so often dependent on the ruins of older locations, the knowledge conveyed through such modes of memory and material remains could not be otherwise. It is the "stability" of material remains at places, Halbwachs writes, "that explain[s] how their memories endure." And yet, at the same time, "this stability is at the mercy of all the material accidents that destroy and transform, bit by bit," those places to which our memories are attached.[183]

§

"For my part," Schliemann writes near the end of his memoirs, "I have always firmly believed in the Trojan War; my full faith in Homer and in the tradition has never been shaken by modern criticism, and to this faith of mine I am indebted for the discovery of Troy and its Treasure."[184] In many ways, Schliemann is a specter that stands at a crossroads traversed in this chapter's study, pitched between the paths of ancient Homeric memories and what is known about antiquity through modern historical and archaeological inquiry. If Schliemann saw these as a singular passageway, few others would after his death.[185] Schliemann's excavations at Mycenae were soon to give way to more rigorous and exacting standards, while those fellow adherents who shared in his Homeric faith would become far less numerous, as the Homeric epics came under ever greater historical scrutiny. However much faith Schliemann placed in the historical authenticity of a Homeric past and however strong his belief that those entombed at Mycenae were Agamemnon and his contemporaries,

---

ak-šir). Riekele Borger, *Die Inschriften Asarhaddons Königs von Assyrien* (Osnabrück: Biblio-Verlag, 1967), 94 (r. 6).

[182] David Asheri, Alan Lloyd, and Aldo Corcella, *A Commentary on Herodotus, Books I–IV*, eds. O. Murray and A. Moreno (Oxford: Oxford University Press, 2007), 662.

[183] Halbwachs, *La topographie*, 164.   [184] Schliemann, *Memoirs*, 250.

[185] Shortly after one last trip to the ruins of Pompeii, Schliemann fell into a coma on Christmas, 1890, dying the next day in a hotel room in Naples. See Sophie Schliemann, ed., *Heinrich Schliemann's Selbstbiographie* (Leipzig: F. A. Brockhaus, 1892), 98–99.

the archaeological evidence unearthed at the location showed this to be a false confession.[186]

If, 135 years later, we are now located firmly on one side of the divide that Schliemann sought to narrow, the biblical writings stand positioned on the other. This is not to deny the rich storytelling about ruins found in these ancient texts. This study has demonstrated that those behind the Hebrew Bible expressed a widespread interest in the pasts associated with places that were in ruins when these writers were active. The many references to Shiloh further this point, where it is evident that, much like us, those who came across the location's remains in antiquity wondered what had occurred at the site previous to when it fell. And in response, they also told stories about a time before these ruins came to be.

But the stories they told are often different from our own. To explain why, this study has turned to theories of memory and ruination. Rather than digging among the ruins of Shiloh to learn about those who lived at the location in times previous, as is our practice, what the biblical writings suggest is that the experience of Shiloh's remains instead elicited a constellation of memories that were recalled about it among different communities at different periods. Some of these memories were likely quite venerable, reaching back centuries to when the location was a place of some standing in the highlands during the early Iron Age period. Others were more recent, created in response to particular questions that arose later about why Shiloh's ruins appeared as they did. When refracted through the prism of the site's archaeological remains, what the biblical stories about Shiloh indicate is that its ruins gave rise to distinct and varied impressions of the past for those who came across them in antiquity, conditioned, above all, by what I term a temporality of remembrance.

For such reasons, the biblical writings often convey little about the historical concerns we bring to these ruins. Details about Shiloh's MBA community who constructed monumental features of the site are absent from the stories the biblical writers tell, as is more explicit information about how Shiloh was destroyed, and by whom, in the eleventh century BCE. Instead, in the Hebrew Bible the story of Shiloh begins with Israel's entrance into Canaan and not in a time before, detailing a site that included a sanctuary, priesthood, and prophetic traditions, which, however troubled, are deeply connected to the times that will follow. Jeremiah can evoke Shiloh's past four hundred years

---

[186] For a penetrating study on the rise of historical critical practices within biblical studies and, further, those resistant to them, see Paul Michael Kurtz, "A Historical, Critical Retrospective on Historical Criticism," in *The New Cambridge Companion to Biblical Interpretation*, eds. I. Boxall and B. C. Gregory, 15–36 (New York: Cambridge University Press, 2022).

after its destruction because this past is still resonant and meaningful, an impression evidently shared by Jeremiah's audience who sought to execute him for it. What was remembered about Shiloh, in short, is what mattered for the present when these pasts were recalled. Shiloh's past is not a historical curiosity in these writings, its ruins an assemblage of remains to be exhumed and examined. Rather, its ruins are a place of memory where the past can be experienced in the here and now. "Go to my place that was at Shiloh," Yahweh commands, "and see" (Jer 7:12).

If Khirbet Seilun's ruins no longer offer this experience to us, it is because we are sensitive to a depth of time and the discontinuities that mark its passing, an impression recent in its emergence, as was argued at length in Chapter 1. In contrast to Schliemann's, it may be, then, that ours is the faith of the fallen, as Yosef Yerushalmi provocatively maintains,[187] we who are unable to "firmly believe" in the pasts conveyed through ancient texts because of the historical commitments to which we are now beholden. Perhaps then we, too, are caught, but in a position distinct from Schliemann's, poised between what Ricoeur terms "the competition between memory and history, between the faithfulness of the one and the truth of the other" that "cannot be resolved on the epistemological plane."[188] For Yerushalmi, the irresolvable tension between the claims of memory and history precipitates a sense of discontentedness, a malaise that leads to speculation about when a "new consciousness" might prevail when history ceases to be our dominant way of knowing the past.[189]

Nevertheless, there is "a privilege," Ricoeur comments, that "cannot be refused" to our modern historical practices. This prerogative resides in the space where the claims of memory encounter the critical faculties of the historian and what Ricoeur describes as "a sense of justice."[190] For though modern criticism and its historical methods could not shake the faith of Schliemann, their potency would take hold in more pressing moments. Decades after Schliemann's death, Himmler, Goebbels, and Göring together visited the ruins of Mycenae, proposing Agamemnon and Mycenean culture more broadly to be the forebears of the Nazi movement.[191] Regarding these attempts to harness the memory of Agamemnon for fascist ends, it was the research of historians and archaeologists that demonstrated these views to be wildly inaccurate and nefarious, the warped workings of warped minds.

---

[187] Yosef Yerushalmi, *Zakhor: Jewish History and Jewish Memory*, 2nd ed. (Seattle: University of Washington Press, 1996), 86; Cf. David Myers and Alexander Kaye, eds., *The Faith of Fallen Jews: Yosef Hayim Yerushalmi and the Writing of Jewish History* (Waltham: Brandeis University Press, 2014).

[188] Ricoeur, *Memory, History, Forgetting*, 498–99. [189] Yerushalmi, *Zakhor*, 103.

[190] "It is along the path of critical history," Ricoeur writes, "that memory encounters the sense of justice." Ricoeur, *Memory, History, Forgetting*, 500.

[191] Gere, *Tomb of Agamemnon*, 132–33.

THREE

THE RUINS OF RACHEL'S TOMB AND THE PRESENCE OF THE PAST

> Three crows flap for the trees
> And settle, creaking the eucalyptus boughs.
> A smell of dead limes quickens in the nose
> The leprosy of empire.
> "Farewell, green fields"
> "Farewell, ye happy groves!"
>
> Marble like Greece, like Faulkner's South in stone,
> Deciduous beauty prospered and is gone.[1]

On May 19, 1798 CE, a force of approximately 35,000 soldiers set sail from the French port of Toulon across the Mediterranean.[2] Among them were over 150 scholars chosen from a broad range of specializations, including engineers, geologists, and artists, who, after the fleet's subjugation of Malta, reached the Egyptian city of Alexandria on July 1 of that year. The task set before these learned professionals was to study and document the Egyptian lands that

---

[1] Derek Walcott, "Ruins of a Great House," in *The Poetry of Derek Walcott 1948–2013*, ed. G. Maxwell, 29–30 (New York: Farrar, Straus and Giroux, 2014 [1953–54]).

[2] On the French invasion, see Henry Laurens, *L'expédition d'Égypte: 1798–1801*, 2nd ed. (Paris: Seuil, 1997), 1–35. See also André Raymond, *Égyptiens et Français au Caire 1798–1801* (Cairo: Institut Français d'Archéologie Orientale, 1998); Stuart Harten, "Rediscovering Ancient Egypt: Bonaparte's Expedition and the Colonial Ideology of the French Revolution," in *Napoleon in Egypt*, ed. I. Bierman, 33–46 (Reading: Ithaca Press, 2003); and Donald Malcolm Reid, *Whose Pharaohs? Archaeology, Museums, and Egyptian National Identity from Napoleon to World War I* (Berkeley: University of California Press, 2002), 31–44.

France would soon occupy, foremost for the construction of a canal through Suez but also to chart Egyptian territories that France sought to control in their colonial battles with the British.

Though France's hold on Egypt would be short-lived with the Capitulation of Alexandria in 1801, one outcome of this invasion was the publication of the twenty-three volume *Description de l'Égypte* written by the scholars who had accompanied Napoleon's regiments.[3] It is in the fifth book of this series that a lengthy entry appears on the "Ruines de Sân," a location that was known to the ancient Greeks and Romans as the city of Tanis, located in the far northeast delta region of the Nile.[4] In the opening to this account, the future founder of the *Société géologique de France*, Louis Cordier, provides a description of the monumental character of the ruins he encountered. From a distance of over twenty kilometers, Cordier writes, the ruins of the site became visible on the horizon, appearing as a "small mountain" set against the low terrain of the delta.[5] What Cordier details from afar was, in fact, one of the largest ruin mounds known in Egypt, a site approaching nearly 2 km² in size (177 ha) and reaching a height of 32 m (ca. 100 feet) above the surrounding plain.

Of the remains Cordier came across in late November of 1798, the most impressive was a "vast square" situated on the summit of the location that was bounded by an imposing mudbrick wall, clearly depicted in Figure 32 composed at the time. Within this enclosure Cordier encountered numerous monumental ruins, including a row of ancient obelisks, an avenue of broken columns, two mutilated statues, and the vestiges of a number of temples, among other debris located on the surface of the site. But what made these ruins particularly meaningful were their connections to the Bible. Cordier observes that the ancient city of Sân was once known as the biblical site of Zoan (Num 13:22) or the Fields of Zoan (Psalm 78:12, 43), a settlement later mentioned also in Isaiah and Ezekiel (Is 19:11; Ezek 30:14), though Jeremiah, who at the end of his life evidently came to live there, Cordier remarks, calls the location Taphanes (Jer 2:14; 43:7–9).[6]

---

[3] Commission des Sciences et Arts d'Égypte, *Description de l'Égypte, ou, Recueil des observations et des recherches qui ont été faites en Égypte pendant l'expédition de l'Armée française*, 23 vols. (Paris: L'Imprimerie impériale, 1809–1828).

[4] Louis Cordier, "Description des Ruines de Sân," in *Description de l'Égypte, ou, Recueil des observations et des recherches qui ont été faites en Égypte pendant l'expédition de l'Armée française*, Tome 5, 99–134 (Paris: De l'Imprimerie impériale, 1809–1828).

[5] Cordier writes, "One sees the ruins of Sân from two to three myriameters [10,000m] away. From any side one approaches them, they appear on the horizon in the form of a small mountain." (On aperçoit les ruines de Sân de deux à trois myriamètres de distance. De quelque côté qu'on les aborde, elles s'annoncent à l'horizon sous la forme d'une petite montagne.) Ibid., 100.

[6] Ibid., 123.

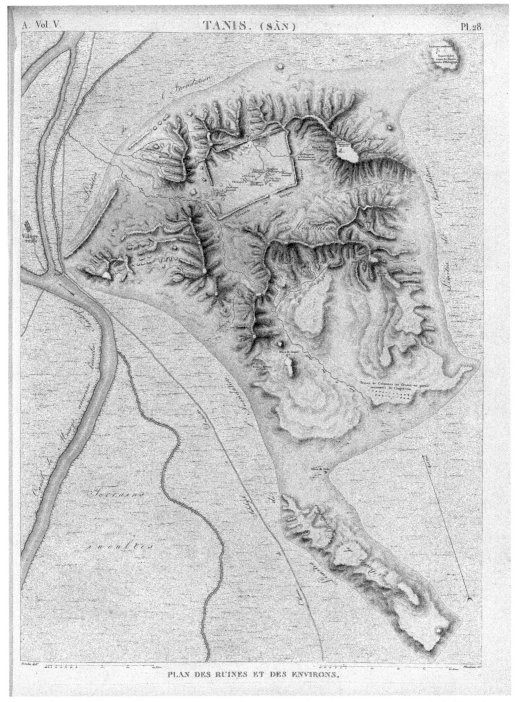

32 Plan of Tanis from *Description de l'Egypte*. Rare Book Division, New York Public Library

But above all it is the exodus story that matters most for how Cordier views these remains. "One can presume," Cordier writes, "that the construction of the great wall of Tanis was one of a number of painful works imposed on the Israelites before their exodus from Egypt."[7] Indeed, Cordier observes that it was among these ruins of Sân that Moses had "managed to wrest from the royal authorities the orders ... for the deliverance of the Jewish people."[8]

For those who came to Tanis after Cordier's visit, the link between its ruins and the exodus story continued. Auguste Mariette, who undertook the first large-scale excavation of the site from 1860 to 1864, recovered a number of artifacts connected to the Hyksos, a foreign people from the Levant who ruled Egypt during the fifteenth Dynasty (ca. 1650–1550 BCE).[9] For readers of Josephus, Mariette among them, Hyksos ruins were of special significance because of their potential connections to the ancient Israelites, a relationship Josephus details in his *Contra Apionem* (1.14–16) from the first century CE. In excerpts taken from Manetho's lost work, the *Aegyptiaca*, Josephus records that the Hyksos had been driven out of Egypt in a more distant past after residing in the region for a number of centuries. The city of Avaris, Josephus writes further, was the last eastern stronghold of this group until, after a failed Egyptian siege of the location, the Hyksos agreed to leave the region peaceably and return to their native Syrian lands. Unable to reach their destination because of various hostilities encountered, the Hyksos settled instead in Judea, Josephus relates, and founded the city of Jerusalem.

To Josephus, Manetho's story held obvious allusions to the plight of the Israelites as found in the late chapters of Genesis and the Book of Exodus. The references to the Hyksos in Manetho's writings were taken, then, as Egyptian accounts of the Israelites who were led out of Egypt by Moses, the Hyksos simply being the Israelites as understood from an Egyptian point of view.[10] When Mariette, 1,800 hundred years later, came across the famous 400 Year Stela honoring the Semitic deity Seth among the ruins of Tanis, as well as a sphinx and other assorted remains connected to Hyksos rulers, it became apparent to him that what had been found was the lost city of Avaris, and, with it, the last bastion of the Israelites before the exodus event occurred.[11]

---

[7] Ibid., 124. [8] Ibid.
[9] Anna-Latifa Mourad, *Rise of the Hyksos: Egypt and the Levant from the Middle Kingdom to the Early Second Intermediate Period* (Oxford: Archeopress, 2015), 215–18.
[10] "These herdsmen [the Hyksos], as they are called, were no other than our ancestors," Josephus remarks, "who were delivered out of Egypt." (οἱ καλούμενοι ποιμένες ἡμέτεροι δὲ πρόγονοι ... ἐκ τῆς Αἰγύπτου ἀπαλλαγέντες.) (*J. Ap.* 1.16).
[11] Auguste Mariette, "Fragments et documents relatifs aux fouilles de San," in *Recueil de Travaux relatifs á la philologie et á l'archéologie égyptiennes et assyriennes*, Vol. 9, 1–20 (Paris: Libraire Emile Bouillon, 1887). Cf. Philippe Brissaud, "Tanis (Tell San el-Hagar)," in *Royal Cities of the Biblical World*, ed. J. Westenholz, 113–49 (Jerusalem: Bible Lands Museum, 1996), 117–20. Two decades later, in February of 1884, a young Flinders Petrie came to Tanis to undertake

33 Ruins of Tanis. B. Strassberger, 1878. Rice University. Public domain

It is Pierre Montet, however, who would shape interpretations of Tanis' ruins for decades to come. After leaving the French excavations at Byblos in modern-day Lebanon, Montet embarked on a new expedition at the Egyptian site in 1929. In addition to Hyksos remains, what also drew Montet's interest was a substantial collection of inscriptions and statuary that were the product of later Ramesside rulers. To Montet, these finds were clear evidence that Tanis was not only the ancient city of Avaris but also that of Pi-Ramesses, the location being renamed, according to Montet, during the nineteenth dynasty when Ramesses II took the throne (ca. thirteenth century BCE).[12] Montet's forceful arguments connecting Tanis with Pi-Ramesses, the biblical city of Rameses referred to throughout the exodus story (e.g., Ex 1:11, 12:37; Num 33:3), found a prominent supporter in the American archaeologist W. F.

---

his first dig, excavating for three seasons and leaving persuaded, with Mariette, that Tanis was indeed the ancient city of Avaris, its monuments littered throughout the site. W. M. Flinders Petrie, *Tanis, Part I: 1883–1884*, 2nd ed. (London: Trübner & Company, 1889), 2, 10–12.

[12] Pierre Montet, "Tanis, Avaris et Pi-Ramsès," *Révue Biblique* 39.1 (1930): 5–28. Cf. Pierre Montet, *Le Drame d'Avaris* (Paris: Paul Geuthner, 1940), 119–25; Brissaud, "Tanis," 130.

Albright, who wrote that Montet's discoveries had made all "objections to the historicity of the Exodus vanish."[13] The eminent British Egyptologist Alan Gardiner, who had previously disputed the identification of Tanis with Pi-Ramesses, published a rare retraction of his views in 1933 in light of the overwhelming evidence. "I have now to confess," Gardiner writes, "that my [previous] identification of Pi-Ram'messe with Pelusium was a mistake."[14] The impressive ruins of Ramesside rulers that were also unearthed at Tanis made the connection to the biblical city of Ramesses and the historical background of the exodus story certain.

Until it wasn't. As archaeological practices were refined and the stratigraphy of Tanis became more apparent, it became evident that Tanis had been founded *de novo* during the waning moments of the Twentieth Dynasty in the early eleventh century BCE, or at least two centuries, if not longer, after a Moses would have lived.[15] Manfred Bietak's careful study of the waterways of the eastern delta and his survey of the region provided further evidence that during the Twentieth Dynasty the Pelusiac branch of the Nile had silted up,[16] leaving the older cities and their harbors in the region defunct. In their place, Tanis was built as the primary port of Lower Egypt and became a new ruling center named Djanet in Egyptian – a city cited as the location from which Wenamun sets sail for Byblos in the famous story that bears his name.[17]

The ruins of Tanis were, in the end, neither those of Pi-Ramesses nor Avaris. Instead, both of these ancient cities were soon located 30km further south with excavations undertaken at Tell el-Dab'a and Qantir in the 1960s

---

[13] W. F. Albright, "Archaeology and the Date of the Hebrew Conquest of Palestine," *Bulletin of the American Schools of Oriental Research* 58 (1938): 10–18. Albright remarks, "Now, however, Montet has obtained conclusive evidence for the identification of these two places ... that Avaris, the Hysksos capital, Raamses, capital of the Nineteenth Dynasty, and Tanis were all successive phases of the same city" (16).

[14] Alan Gardiner, "Tanis and Pi-Ra'messe: A Retraction," *Journal of Egyptian Archaeology* 5 (1933): 122–28.

[15] For objections to Tanis as Pi-Ramesses that would presage later developments, see E. P. Uphill, "Pithom and Raamses: Their Location and Significance," *Journal of Near Eastern Studies* 27.4 (1968): 291–316. For a more recent discussion and overview of the finds from Tanis, see Philippe Brissaud, "Les Principaux résultats des fouilles récentes à Tanis (1987–1997): L'emergence d'une vision nouvelle du site," in *Tanis: travaux récents sur le Tell Sân el-Hagar 1987–1997*, ed. P. Brissaud and C. Zivie-Coche, 13–70 (Paris: Noêsis, 1998). For a discussion of the differing interpretations of the site over the past two centuries, see Philippe Brissaud, Violaine Chauvet, and Isabelle Hairy, "Deux siècles de fouilles à Tanis: Analyse des divers modes d'intervention sur le site," in *Tanis: travaux récents sur le Tell Sân el-Hagar 1987–1997*, ed. P. Brissaud and C. Zivie-Coche, 71–100 (Paris: Noêsis, 1998).

[16] Manfred Bietak, *Tell el-Dab'a II: Der Fundort im Rahmen einer archäologish-geographischen Untersuchung über das ägyptishche Ostdelta* (Vienna: Österreichische Akademie der Wissenschaften, 1975), 215–16.

[17] Miriam Lichtheim, "The Report of Wenamun," in *Ancient Egyptian Literature*, Vol. II, ed. M. Lichtheim, 224–30 (Berkeley: University of California Press, 2006).

and 1970s.[18] The mystery of the lost cities from antiquity had been solved, but not according to the way scholars had long thought it would be decided. Many of the more prominent names in nineteenth- and twentieth-century archaeology, from Petrie to Gardiner to Montet to Albright, had all been mistaken.

Yet the reasons for their errors were not unsound. Undoubtedly, the desire to demonstrate the historical character of the biblical exodus story shaped the interpretations of Tanis that were put forward. But a more significant factor in these assessments were the ruins of Tanis themselves. As all excavators of Tanis recognized, what had been unearthed among the debris of the site were monuments, inscriptions, and building materials that had explicit connections to rulers from times previous to the eleventh century BCE. E. P. Uphill comments, for example, that Montet's discoveries[19]

> have added many examples of the work of Ramessess II to the long list of those already found here [Tanis] by earlier diggers such as Mariette and Petrie, and the accumulation of archaeological material seemed to be overwhelmingly in favor of his identification when he first set out his views ... With so many monuments dated to the Ramesside period and such a wealth of evidence to attest to the work of Ramesses II at Tanis, it is not surprising that many scholars have accepted it as Per Ramesses as Montet has done.

To excavate at Tanis was to encounter ruins left behind from dynasties that long preceded that of the Third Intermediate Period, including some descending from Middle Kingdom rulers who had reigned a thousand years before Tanis was built.

How such remains were found at a location that did not exist when these buildings and monuments were constructed, it is now known, is that they were brought to Tanis from elsewhere. Rulers of the Twenty-First and Twenty-Second Dynasties, active during an era when their power was diminished and when resources for developing a new harbor were scarce, reused what they could of older building remains that were transported along waterways from more venerable Egyptian cities located nearby, above all from the former ruling center of Pi-Ramesses.[20]

The result was that Tanis arose as a monumental anachronism on the delta plain, its massive constructions consisting of items derived from different sites

---

[18] Bietak, *Tell el-Dab'a II*, 213–20; Manfred Bietak, "Avaris and Piramesse: Archaeological Exploration in the Eastern Nile Delta," *Proceedings of the British Academy* 65 (1979): 225–90.

[19] Uphill, "Pithom and Raamses," 304, 306.

[20] Uphill, "Pithom and Raamses," 307; Bietak, *Tell el-Dab'a II*, 213–15; John Van Seters, *The Hyksos: A New Investigation* (New Haven, CT: Yale University Press, 1966), 128–31. For this broader phenomenon, see especially Barbara Magen, *Steineme Palimpseste: Zur Wiederverwendung von Statuen durch Ramses II und seine Nachfolger* (Wiesbaden: Harrassowitz Verlag, 2011).

34 Great Sphinx (twenty-sixth century BCE) found at Tanis, with inscriptions from Twelfth, Nineteenth, and Twenty-Second Dynasty rulers. Louvre, Paris. Christian Décamps, photograph. © 2010 Musée du Louvre. https://collections.louvre.fr/ark:/53355/cl010010062

and many centuries in time, repurposed and superimposed in such a way that the new buildings of the capital appeared as if they were also somehow ancient. Modern interpretations of Tanis' ruins foundered, then, on historical considerations of time and space, where premises based on an orderly, sequential chronology of the site's ruins and their associated assemblages were defied by the location's ancient engineers. The builders of Tanis had long ago undermined these assumptions, blurring the lines between past and present in how their structures were composed, obscuring the provenance of their materials by salvaging them from elsewhere and leaving no record of the locations from which they had been retrieved or when they had been taken, often not even removing the names of older rulers and previous sites inscribed on the components they reworked. The attempt to recover Tanis' history came undone among its ruins. It was a city where past and present were one.

§

Tanis was not the only location from antiquity where remains from the past prevailed among more recent landscapes. In this chapter, I examine how the biblical writings also refer to ruins that continued to resonate into the present. This phenomenon is perhaps best captured in the phrase "to this day" (עד היום הזה/עד היום), which came to be affixed to certain ruins of import within these texts – an expression used alongside other references to index the presence of older artifacts among the settings in which particular biblical stories took place.[21] The title of this chapter is taken from one of these moments, where, in Gen 35:20, we read that after Rachel's postpartum death, "Jacob set up a pillar over her tomb; it is the pillar of Rachel's tomb to this day" (הוא מצבת קברת רחל עד היום).

This brief notice concerning Rachel's tomb is exemplary for the following discussion because of how it refers to a past incident that endured into the storyteller's present by way of its material remains. Though Rachel died in a former age, the pillar that marks her internment still exists, we are told, "to this day," offering the possibility of experiencing something that survived from a past otherwise lost long ago. The distance between past and present is made somewhat less so through an encounter with materials that have survived, according to this account, where the possibility of coming into contact with former occurrences or individuals is enabled by the ruins that have been left behind. It is Rachel herself, the Book of Jeremiah relates, who is heard weeping many centuries after her death, her maternal laments echoing throughout the region where her tomb was found (Jer 31:15).[22] This was a present haunted by its past, harrowed by figures bound to the ruins that remained.

The intent of Chapter 3 is to examine this experience of ruins within biblical storytelling. To begin, this study considers how the biblical writers lived in a world where ruins frequently impinged on present ways of life, affecting the practices and affairs of those who came across older remains at later periods. The focus of Section 3.1 is consequently on the afterlife of ruins and their associated artifacts, including those remains that were handled by later populations or avoided by them, or that continued to compel responses to their features long after their initial dissolution. In this discussion, four themes are drawn out from this assemblage of archaeological evidence: ruins associated with the dead (mortuary remains), the displaced (squatter populations), the

---

[21] On this phrase, see Brevard Childs, "A Study of the Formula 'Until this Day,'" *Journal of Biblical Literature* 82 (1963): 279–92; Jeffrey Geoghegan, "'Until this Day' and the Preexilic Redaction of the Deuteronomistic History," *Journal of Biblical Literature* 122.2 (2003): 201–27; Jeffrey Geoghegan, *The Time, Place, and Purpose of the Deuteronomistic History: The Evidence of "Until this Day"* (Providence, RI: Brown Judaic Studies, 2006).

[22] "A cry is heard in Ramah, wailing, bitter weeping, Rachel weeping for her children." Jer 31:15a.

gods (cultic remains), and the empires (sites of destruction, foreign monuments). During the eras in which the biblical writings came to be, I argue, ruins such as these brought individuals of the southern Levant into contact with pasts that continued to linger into their contemporary settings.

After this archaeological study, we turn to the biblical writings and examine a series of texts where specific ruins are identified for their visibility and meaningfulness within the speaker's present. What is of interest about these accounts is the sense of contemporaneity that ruins register, signified by the speaker's interruption into the story being told so as to affirm the presence of certain ruins in the here and now. Most frequently, such parentheticals are rendered through the use of deictic expressions within these accounts (i.e., there, today, etc.). But what makes these passages peculiar is how the anonymity of the storyteller leaves the speaker's present undisclosed, producing a narrative effect whereby its moment of utterance is unmoored from any identifiable situation, and thus unattached to any specific historical horizon. The enduring presence of the past visible in the ruins that populated the lands of the southern Levant comes to be mirrored, consequently, by narrative descriptions of ruins whose presence is also unremitting.

This sense of presence will nevertheless be met by questions the historian cannot countermand. Already in the brief report of Rachel's tomb, certain historical issues arise, where information regarding whose "day" is referred to in this notice and how much time has passed between its utterance and Rachel's death are not conveyed by the speaker. How to situate either Rachel's tomb or the account of it in time is therefore uncertain, made so by a story that exhibits little interest in matters of historical chronology or periodization. These questions only become more acute with the realization that, as one continues reading, Rachel's tomb is found at not one location in the biblical corpus, but two: the first, we are told, is found at the village of Ephrath, near Bethlehem (Gen 35:19 and 48:7); the second site, at Zelzah, is located in the vicinity of Ramah nearly twenty-five kilometers to the north (1 Sam 10:2; Jer 31:15). Not only are considerations pertaining to the passing of time obscured within these references, then, but those tied to place are as well.

How to account for these features of ruins and biblical storytelling is connected in Section 3.2 to more recent theoretical reflections on what has been termed the phenomenon of presence and its affinities with material remains.[23] This impression of time, as Ethan Kleinberg describes it, is rooted

---

[23] Ewa Domanska, "The Material Presence of the Past," *History and Theory* 45 (2006): 337–48; Hans Ulrich Gumbrecht, *The Production of Presence: What Meaning Cannot Convey* (Stanford, CA: Stanford University Press, 2004); Hans Ulrich Gumbrecht, "Presence Achieved in Language," *History and Theory* 45 (2006): 317–27; Eelco Runia, "Presence," *History and Theory* 45 (2006): 1–29; Frank Ankersmit, *Sublime Historical Experience* (Stanford, CA: Stanford University Press, 2005); Ethan Kleinberg, "Prologue," in *Presence: Philosophy,*

in an appreciation of how "the past is literally with us in the present" through "our unmediated access to actual things that we can feel and touch and that bring us into contact with the past."[24] What is emphasized in these discussions is how previous eras continue to occupy the present by way of their fragments and deposits, being "protuberances, so to say, of the past in the present"[25] that affect how we perceive our contemporary settings and our place within them. What matters about ruins, on this view, is not what they disclose about the past but how they shape present affairs, their remains exhibiting a temporality of proximity rather than of distance.

The threads that bind this chapter's theme of presence to the study of memory in Chapter 2 are therefore apparent. In Halbwachs's discussion of early Christian pilgrimage sites, as noted in Chapter 2, for example, the argument was put forward that it was the tangibility of material remains in the present that permitted the past to be recollected by those who encountered them, that "*Le passé deviant en partie le present: on le touche, on est en contact direct avec lui,*" as Halbwachs characterizes this experience.[26] It is our present intuition of things past, Augustine had similarly argued fifteen hundred years before, that is intimately bound to what we remember, the past otherwise being lost to the relentless attritions of oblivion.[27] If Chapter 2 examined this relationship between past and present through the lens of retrospection, of how the experience of ruins in antiquity gave rise to stories of what had once occurred among their remains, this study moves to the other side of the looking glass, so to speak, and examines how older ruins also affected the beliefs and practices of the present.

3.1 AN ARCHAEOLOGY OF PRESENCE: THE DEAD, THE DISPLACED, THE GODS, THE EMPIRES

It was not only the large ruin mounds of ancient cities viewed from afar, of toppled buildings and fortifications that appeared on the horizon, that

---

History, and Cultural Theory for the Twenty-First Century, eds. R. Ghosh and E. Kleinberg, 1–7 (Ithaca, NY: Cornell University Press, 2013); Dariusz Gafijczuk, "Dwelling Within: The Inhabited Ruins of History," *History and Theory* 52 (2013): 149–70. On this turn toward presence in historical theory, see the perceptive comments in Gabrielle Spiegel, "The Limits of Empiricism: The Utility of Theory in Historical Thought and Writing," *The Medieval History Journal* 22.1 (2018): 1–22; 16–20.

[24] Kleinberg, "Prologue," 1.   [25] Ankersmit, *Sublime Historical Experience*, 115.
[26] Maurice Halbwachs, *La Topographie légendaire des Évangiles en Terre sainte: Étude de mémoire collective* (Paris: Presses Universitaires de France, 1941), 2. (italics original)
[27] "These three things do somehow exist in the soul, and I do not perceive them anywhere else: for the present of things past is memory." (Sunt enim haec in anima tria quaedam, et alibi ea non video praesans de praeteritis memoria.) Augustine, *Confessions: Books 9–13*, ed. C. Hammond, Loeb 27 (Cambridge, MA: Harvard University Press, 2016), Book 11: 20, 231.

individuals from the southern Levant would have encountered in the first millennium BCE. What also featured in their surroundings were remains with which later populations actively involved themselves, including older artifacts found in public precincts, outside the walls of these sites, on hilltops and in ravines, or on pathways that cut through the region. As the story of Rachel's tomb suggests, some of the most meaningful were those ruins connected to the dead.

3.1.1 *The Dead*

For the vast majority of those who died in the lands of the southern Levant in antiquity, few traces remain. Many were placed in simple pit inhumations that have left behind little evidence of their burials. But in the coastal plain and Shephelah region a distinct type of burial practice emerged that would, in time, be used in the highlands, particularly during the course of the late Iron Age period (eighth through early sixth centuries BCE) in the territory of Judah.[28] Derived from earlier forms of cave burials, these "bench tombs," as they are termed, were created by being hewn out of the soft limestone rock or chalk found in the region's hills, typically situated outside the walls of a settlement along the slopes and cliffs of the surrounding terrain. Jerusalem, for example, where the largest number of these tombs has been excavated, was bounded by at least three of these extramural cemeteries in antiquity to its west (Hinnom Valley), north (Saint-Étienne and adjacent areas), and east (Silwan).[29]

What made these tombs distinctive were the stone benches on which the dead were placed to decompose. To access such burial chambers, an individual would typically come to a *dromos*, or entrance shaft, proceed through a carved doorway, and then descend steps to a room around 5m^2 in size.

---

[28] For the important archaeological treatment of these tombs, see Elizabeth Bloch-Smith, *Judahite Burial Practices and Beliefs about the Dead* (Sheffield: JSOT Press, 1992), 41–52, 110–12, 135–39. See also Avraham Faust and Shlomo Bunimovitz, "The Judahite Rock-Cut Tomb: Family Response at a Time of Change," *Israel Exploration Journal* 58 (2008): 150–70; Alexander Fantalkin, "The Appearance of Rock-Cut Bench Tombs in Iron Age Judah as a Reflection of State Formation," in *Bene Israel: Studies in the Archaeology of Israel and the Levant during the Bronze and Iron Ages in Honour of Israel Finkelstein*, eds. A. Fantalkin and A. Yasur-Landau, 17–44 (Leiden: Brill, 2008); James Osborne, "Secondary and Mortuary Practice and the Bench Tomb: Structure and Practice in Iron Age Judah," *Journal of Near Eastern Studies* 70.1 (2011): 33–53; Avraham Faust and Haya Katz, "Tel 'Eton Cemetery: An Introduction," *Hebrew Bible and Ancient Israel* 5 (2016): 171–86; and Matthew Suriano, *A History of Death in the Hebrew Bible* (New York: Oxford University Press, 2018), 56–97.

[29] Gabriel Barkay, "Excavations at Ketef Hinnom in Jerusalem," in *Ancient Jerusalem Revealed*, ed. H. Geva, 84–106 (Jerusalem: Israel Exploration Society, 1994); Gabriel Barkay, Amos Kloner, and Amihai Mazar, "The Northern Necropolis of Jerusalem during the First Temple Period," in *Ancient Jerusalem Revealed*, ed. H. Geva, 119–27 (Jerusalem: Israel Exploration Society, 1994); David Ussishkin, *The Village of Silwan: The Necropolis from the Period of the Judean Kingdom* (Jerusalem: Israel Exploration Society, 1993).

35 Garden Tomb (eighth–seventh centuries BCE), Jerusalem. Creative Commons CC0 1.0 universal public domain

Once inside, an individual encountered "waist-high benches arranged around the perimeter of the room,"[30] though more elaborate and larger tombs could also contain loculi that extended out from the central chamber in various directions. Situated on the stone benches would be the deceased, "reposed, extended on their backs, with their heads on stone pillows or headrests when provided."[31]

For those who lived in the highlands during this era, the terrain familiar to them would have thus been marked by openings of caves cut out of the hills and valleys that surrounded their settlements. Among the more highly wrought, the façade of such tombs could be stylized with decorative elements, and in a few instances from Silwan funerary inscriptions were placed on the exteriors of these chambers near the doorways.[32] Within the undisturbed caves

---

[30] Elizabeth Bloch-Smith, "The Cult of the Dead in Judah: Interpreting the Material Remains," *Journal of Biblical Literature* 111.2 (1992): 213–24; 217; Elizabeth Bloch-Smith, *Judahite Burial Practices*, 41–52.

[31] Bloch-Smith, "Cult of the Dead," 217.

[32] Bloch-Smith, *Judahite Burial Practices*, 43, 103–4, 204, 209. For further discussion of these inscriptions, see Suriano, *History of Death*, 98–127. Elsewhere, inscriptions were found within the spaces of tombs. For Khirbet Beit Lei, see Joseph Naveh, "Old Hebrew Inscriptions in a Burial Cave," *Israel Exploration Journal* 13 (1963): 74–92; on Khirbet el-Qom, see William Dever, "Iron Age Epigraphic Material from the Area of Khirbet el-Kom," *Hebrew Union College Annual* 40/41 (1969–1970): 139–204.

that have been investigated, it is evident that these tombs were typically multigenerational, housing the remains of a family across decades and even centuries. To make room for the newly deceased over the years, the older, desiccated bones were removed from the benches where they lay and placed in a common repository during a secondary burial – some of the pits located beneath the benches and others found in more recessed areas within the chamber.[33]

But two features of these tombs matter most for our discussion. The first is that the hollows carved out of the rock were frequently patterned on the general layout of domestic homes, suggesting that these tombs were in some sense conceived as "houses" for the dead.[34] Much like the standard pillared or four-room homes in the region, rock-cut tombs were fashioned to have an internal, rectangular space with benches hewn out of the rock on the periphery, mirroring where rooms were commonly located in houses of the period in their placement off a central corridor. The addition of niches for lamps, gabled ceilings, right-angled cornices, and carved pillars to support the ceilings would have only added to this impression of domestic space, each feature mimicking architectural styles of typical households from the period.[35] The result of this common design was that the dead could be visited within locations carved to resemble a dwelling that reflected those familiar to the living, where deceased ancestors could be cared for and communed with. The placement of these cemeteries in the landscapes just outside of towns and villages thus had the effect of positioning the households of the living "within the collective presence of the dead," their homes situated adjacent to clusters of other "homes" in which their deceased ancestors resided and with whom they could have contact.[36]

The second feature of these tombs is that they were provisioned.[37] The dead themselves were wrapped in cloth, as is attested by the remains of toggle pins and fibulae, and some were adorned with jewelry, amulets, or other tokens connected to their lives. Once a body was laid on a bench, various items – many of which were dedicated to food and drink – were then placed next to the body. Jugs, juglets, bowls, plates, and cooking pots have all been recovered from these tombs[38] – some perhaps used by the living but others carefully positioned at the corpse's head and feet in ways that suggest these objects were meant to nourish the deceased in a postmortem existence.[39] To these items of

---

[33] Osborne, "Secondary Mortuary Practice," 35–43.
[34] Bloch-Smith, *Judahite Burial Practices*, 43–44; Faust and Bunimovitz, "Judahite Rock-Cut Tomb," 152–62; Osborne, "Secondary Mortuary Practice," 47–53; Suriano, *History of Death*, 93–98.
[35] Bloch-Smith, *Judahite Burial Practices*, 41–43.   [36] Suriano, *History of Death*, 91.
[37] Bloch-Smith, *Judahite Burial Practices*, 63–108.   [38] Ibid., 72–81.
[39] Bloch-Smith, "Cult of the Dead," 218; Osborne, "Secondary Mortuary Practices," 42–43; Suriano, *History of Death*, 48–51.

consumption, lamps were also frequently situated next to the dead, likely for use, once again, in the time after death. Once the body was fully decomposed, both bones and associated objects were then placed in a repository together, creating an assemblage of artifacts that would accrue within these chambers over time.[40]

Significant about these mortuary remains for our study is their relationship to the living. Rock-cut tombs were fashioned for the express purpose of being visited, built for families to gather together, to confer with the deceased, and to tend to their bodies through various ritual practices.[41] Bench tombs were burial spaces created as much for the living as for the dead, on this view, with their mortuary spaces fraught with symbolic meanings where connections with departed ancestors were maintained across generations. If the Book of Isaiah condemns practices associated with the consultation of the dead, of "ghosts and familiar spirits" who are sought "on behalf of the living" (Is 8:19), such proscriptions likely reflect what was in fact a rather commonplace feature of life in the highlands, attesting to Iron Age practices in which families sought communion with those who had passed away.

But more was experienced in these tombs than the bodies of the deceased. In addition to the corpses laid out on their stone beds, those who entered into these chambers were surrounded by older material remains throughout, items connected to deceased ancestors that were stacked in repositories or still situated around the body.[42] What was experienced in these spaces, therefore, was a past very much still present, made so by the artifacts strewn throughout the ruined homes of the deceased. Arrayed within these chambers were decomposing bodies, bones of the older dead, broken and intact pottery, tools, jewelry, and other objects associated with past lives, all of which created a setting that would have resembled, in the end, what was often left behind within the decaying homes of a town or village that had come to ruin.[43]

---

[40] Osborne, "Secondary Mortuary Practices," 40–41.

[41] Bloch-Smith, *Judahite Burial Practices*, 122–26; Bloch-Smith, "Cult of the Dead," 213–24; Osborne, "Secondary Mortuary Practice," 33–53; Suriano, *History of Death*, 39–55.

[42] In a tomb from Ketef Hinnom, nearly one hundred bodies were found with 263 complete vessels, in addition to an impressive collection of artifacts attached to the dead. Amihai Mazar, *Archaeology of the Land of the Bible: 10,000–586 BCE* (New York: Doubleday, 1990), 525–26.

[43] This would have been particularly so among ruins that were brought about violently. Human remains have been recovered from a number of such sites, typically buried under the debris of collapsed structures. Examples include those recovered from Lachish's LBA destruction (Patricia Smith, "Skeletal Remains from Level VI," in *The Renewed Archaeological Excavations at Lachish [1973–1994]*, ed. D. Ussishkin, 2504–7 [Tel Aviv: Yass Publications, 2004]), or the early Iron Age evidence from Megiddo (Yossi Nagar, "Human Skeletal Remains," in *Megiddo IV: The 1998–2002 Seasons*, eds. I. Finkelstein, D. Ussishkin, and B. Halpern, 471–72 [Tel Aviv: Yass Publications, 2006]) and Gath (Aren Maeir, "Introduction," in *Tell es-Safi-Gath I: The 1996–2005 Seasons, Part I: Texts*, ed. A Maeir, 43–49 [Wiesbaden: Harrassowitz Verlag, 2012]), or the remains of a female inhabitant of Ashkelon from Babylon's destruction

When Ezekiel portrays the dead of Tyre descending to the ancient ruins of the underworld – "I will make you dwell in the land below, as ruins from of old, with those that go down to the Pit" (Ezek 26:20) – the connection between death and ruination that existed within the rock-cut tombs of Iron Age Judah is crystallized in prophetic speech.

The care of such tombs would have been a common feature of life in the highlands. These spaces of death and ruin were frequented by families during the latter centuries of the Iron Age, with many chambers – after the discontinuation of this burial type in the time after Jerusalem's fall – also reused in later centuries or assailed by thieves. Among these forms, a number of examples also took on a more monumental appearance. The most impressive of these tombs were located on the slopes of the Kidron Valley to the east of Jerusalem in what is now the village of Silwan.[44] Though modeled on the general layout of the bench tomb, the architecture of these tombs was made distinctive by being much grander, positioned above-ground, and built for single or double interment instead of the multigenerational use of tombs that were typical in the region.[45] The "Tomb of Pharaoh's Daughter," still visible today, is a famous example of such monoliths, though its original appearance in antiquity would have been marked by a pyramidal superstructure that crowned the chamber and by an inscription near the entryway that has been mostly chipped away by later Byzantine monks who came to live in the enclosure. Four such monolithic tombs have been located in this area of Silwan among a total of fifty graves,[46] though the necropolis almost assuredly contained more in antiquity, these lost over time through intensive quarrying activity in the area and other damage throughout the millennia.

Nevertheless, what remains of the Silwan cemetery offers a glimpse of how the landscape to the east of Jerusalem once appeared during the late Iron Age and after. In what was likely a necropolis for Judeans of high status,[47] monumental tombs arose along the Kidron valley slopes in the ninth through early sixth centuries BCE, differentiated from other tombs of the period by being

---

of the location in the late seventh century BCE (Patricia Smith, "Human Remains from the Babylonian Destruction of 604 B.C.," in *Ashkelon I: Introduction and Overview [1985–2006]*, eds. L. Stager, J. D. Schloen, and D. Master, 533–36 [Winona Lake, IN: Eisenbrauns, 2008]). At Tel Rehov, the Assyrians apparently did not burn down the site after its conquest but instead left the homes to slowly deteriorate over time. The decapitated skeleton of a woman found in an abandoned house, however, suggests that some, at least, were massacred and not buried after the settlement's downfall. See Amihai Mazar and Shmuel Ahituv, "Tel Rehov in the Assyrian Period: Squatters, Burials, and a Hebrew Seal," in *The Fire Signals of Lachish: Studies in the Archaeology and History of Israel in the Late Bronze Age, Iron Age, and Persian Period in Honor of David Ussishkin*, 265–80 (Winona Lake, IN: Eisenbrauns, 2011), 266–67.

[44] Ussishkin, *The Village of Silwan*; David Ussishkin, "The Necropolis from the Time of the Kingdom of Judah at Silwan, Jerusalem," *Biblical Archaeologist* 33 (1970): 33–46.

[45] Ussishkin, *Village of Silwan*, 257–85.   [46] Ibid., 266–67.   [47] Ibid., 328–31.

36 Tomb of Pharaoh's Daughter (ca. ninth–seventh centuries BCE), Jerusalem. Public domain

cut out of the cliffs to stand alone, their stylized features modeled on what were likely Egyptian and Phoenician antecedents.[48] If these monoliths, absent the repositories of contemporary bench tombs and intended for only one or two bodies, did not participate in the multigenerational mortuary practices found elsewhere in the region, they were, however, fashioned in order to convey an impression of permanence and continuity, though now in terms of an individual rather than the kinship ties of a collective. These monumental tombs, too, then, would haunt the landscape of Jerusalem over the centuries, their forms displayed prominently across from the city's temple, attesting to an affluence and power of late Iron Age Jerusalemite citizens that would not be rivaled until the Hasmonean period four centuries later when, suddenly, monumental tombs appear once more.[49]

---

[48] Ussishkin, "The Necropolis," 45–46; Bloch-Smith, *Judahite Burial Practices*, 188.
[49] Andrea Berlin, "Power and Its Afterlife: Tombs in Hellenistic Palestine," *Near Eastern Archaeology* 65.2 (2002): 138–48.

3.1.2 The Displaced

The presence of older remains also touched the lives of the displaced. As discussed in Chapter 1, the long history of ruination in the southern Levant left a landscape marked by numerous fallen settlements, their old fortifications and structures often visible on the mounds that had accumulated over time. Many sites remained abandoned across the centuries, eventually becoming overgrown or used for agriculture. But other ruins came to be inhabited by those who had been uprooted. What we find in the archaeological record, that is, are indications that transient populations – many of whom were likely survivors of conflicts – chose to live within the remains of what had been left behind after the destruction of a site, determining to use what they could to subsist. In such instances, the older remains of a settlement came to be reused, sheltering the displaced or being interlaced with new materials so as to reconstruct segments of what had been lost.

The remains of those who came to live in ruined settlements have been recovered within a number of excavations. Often identified as squatter settlements, the traces these individuals left behind are faint, muted by the abject conditions in which such groups often lived and the few material resources at their disposal. When a squatter phase is located within the stratigraphy of a site, it is typically distressed, exhibiting few imported remains or diversity of foodstuffs, elite wares, or prestige items. The sporadic removal of destruction debris within an area, ostensibly for domestic space, and the appearance of floor surfaces without associated architectural features typically mark where these residents would have lived, among other indicators such as beaten earth floors, pits, scattered ovens, and flimsy partition walls.[50] These briefer phases of occupation are usually couched between the more impressive remains of older and newer strata of a settlement or simply positioned above the final destruction layer of a site. The impression conveyed through this material is of individuals who settled among ruined structures that were not fully rebuilt, huddled within the remains

---

[50] For a general orientation toward archaeological evidence of squatter remains, see the discussions in James Hardin, *Lahav II: Households and the Use of Domestic Space at Iron II Tell Halif: An Archaeology of Destruction* (Winona Lake, IN: Eisenbrauns, 2010), 41, 93–113; Nimrod Marom and Sharon Zuckerman, "Applying On-Site Analysis of Faunal Assemblages from Domestic Contexts: A Case Study from the Lower City of Hazor," in *Household Archaeology in Ancient Israel and Beyond*, eds. A. Yasur-Landau, J. Ebeling, and L. Mazow, 37–54 (Leiden: Brill, 2011), 43–45; Mazar and Ahituv, "Tel Rehov in the Assyrian Period," 265–80; Aaron Burke, "The Decline of Egyptian Empire, Refugees, and Social Change in the Southern Levant, ca. 1200–1000 BCE," in *The Archaeology of Forced Migration: Conflict-Induced Movement and the Collapse of the 13th c. BCE Eastern Mediterranean*, ed. J. Driessen, 229–49 (Louvain: Presses Universitaires de Louvain, 2018), 243–48. Eli Itkin's study appeared just before this work went to press, with its discussion touching on many of the sites discussed below. Eli Itkin, "Post-Destruction Squatter Phases in the Iron IIB–IIC Southern Levant," *Bulletin of the American Schools of Overseas Research* 388 (2022): 51–72.

of former homes and living among makeshift spaces within the walls or portion of walls that were still standing, surviving by "using available materials, scavenging, and practicing poor agriculture nearby."[51]

When evidence of the reoccupation of ruined settlements is found, it is often located within the larger structures of a location, such as its former palaces or temples, whose more monumental remains could be used for shelter. With the fall of Middle Bronze Age (MBA) Lachish, for example, a large building in Area P, likely a palatial residence, was occupied by squatters "in and above the ruined edifice" after it had been destroyed by fire – the old structure being occupied, it appears, for some time.[52] Following the collapse of the expansive Late Bronze Age (LBA) city at Hazor, an impoverished Iron I community came to live among the older ruins in the acropolis, digging pits throughout the abandoned upper city and constructing poor dwellings that "utilized the walls of the ruined Canaanite structures for their own purposes," in what the excavators term a temporary campsite.[53] At Tell es-Saidiyeh, across the Jordan, an impressive public building of Egyptian design was destroyed in the LBA, after which two rooms of the fallen structure housed new residents sometime in the century before the site was rebuilt.[54] And among the Iron I ruins of Beth-Shemesh, furthermore, a short-lived phase (Level 5) included a squatter settlement built above the impressive "Patrician house" that had recently been destroyed.[55]

But of more relevance to the biblical writings would be the squatter communities that arose at various locations after the Assyrian and Babylonian invasions of the region. At both Beth-Shean and Tel Rehov, for example, which came to an end during the campaign of Tiglath-Pileser III in 732 BCE, some refugees returned to the sites after their downfall. At Beth-Shean, a squatter's population arose just east of the ruins of a large building after the settlement had been put to fire in area P-6 of the site, likely using the walls as a buttress for their shelters.[56] At Tel Rehov, located a few kilometers south, excavators once more recovered remains of those who had returned after the

---

[51] Avraham Faust, *Judah in the Neo-Babylonian Period: The Archaeology of Desolation* (Atlanta: Society of Biblical Literature, 2012), 240.

[52] David Ussishkin, *The Renewed Archaeological Excavations at Lachish (1973–1994)*, ed. D. Ussishkin (Tel Aviv: Tel Aviv University, 2004), 188.

[53] Doron Ben-Ami and Amnon Ben-Tor, "The Iron Age (Stratum "XII/XI"): Stratigraphy and Pottery," in *Hazor VI: The 1990–2009 Excavations: The Iron Age*, eds. A. Ben-Tor, D. Ben-Ami, and D. Sandhaus, 7–25 (Jerusalem: Israel Exploration Society, 2012).

[54] Jonathan Tubb, "Tell es-Sa'idiyeh," in *New Encyclopedia of Archaeological Excavations in the Holy Land*, Volume IV, ed. E. Stern, 1295–1300 (Jerusalem: Israel Exploration Society, 1993), 1298.

[55] Shlomo Bunimovitz and Zvi Lederman, "Beth-Shemesh," in *New Encyclopedia of Archaeological Excavations in the Holy Land*, Volume V, 1644–48; 1645.

[56] Amihai Mazar, "Tel Beth-Shan: History and Archaeology," in *One God – One Cult – One Nation: Archaeological and Biblical Perspectives*, eds. R. Kratz and H. Spieckermann, 239–72 (Berlin: De Gruyter, 2010), 266.

Assyrians overran the settlement. Atop the collapsed city wall, floor surfaces, loom weights, and pottery indicate that individuals carried out their lives along the toppled fortifications of the abandoned city.[57] And much like the Iron I community at Hazor, which occupied the LBA remains of the acropolis, three centuries later a "few survivors" returned to the eighth century BCE city after it fell once more, this time at the hands of the Assyrians, leaving behind "flimsy walls, pits, and the remains of a paved courtyard," which these individuals had constructed among Hazor's remains.[58]

A similar situation is found among the ruins of Judah after the Babylonian advance. At Timnah, a sizable late Iron Age settlement was burned down in the closing moments of the seventh century BCE. Following the destruction, an agricultural installation was built atop the remains, suggesting to its excavators that "a few farmers lived in the ruined town" after its demise.[59] The Iron Age fortress of Khirbet Abu et-Twein, just southeast of Bethlehem, also housed survivors of the Babylonian campaign who came to live in the large, abandoned building and likely farmed in its surroundings.[60] Traces of squatter remains have also been recovered from Jerusalem's ruins, where above the debris of the late Iron Age Ashlar Building, for example, a beaten earth floor and two tabuns from the post-destruction phase of the location suggest that survivors lived and cooked here in the open-air rubble of the former capital.[61]

For those who withstood the various calamities that came to pass in the southern Levant during the Iron Age, some, then, returned to the ruins of what had been destroyed or abandoned. How many came back is difficult to determine. In light of the poor quality of the remains connected to them, what traces these denizens of ruins left behind is probably only a fragment of what was a more substantial number of inhabitants who came to the remains of

---

[57] Mazar and Ahituv, "Tel Rehov in the Assyrian Period," 267.
[58] Amnon Ben-Tor, *Hazor: Canaanite Metropolis, Israelite City* (Jerusalem: Israel Exploration Society, 2016), 167; Débora Sandhaus, "Hazor in the Ninth and Eighth Centuries BCE," *Near Eastern Archaeology* 76.2 (2013): 110–17; 117.
[59] Amihai Mazar and Nava Panitz-Cohen, *Timnah (Tel Batash) II: The Finds from the First Millennium BCE* (Jerusalem: Hebrew University Press, 2001), 282.
[60] Faust, *Judah in the Neo-Babylonian Period*, 237–40. A fortress on the French Hill just north of Jerusalem also bore signs of activity after its destruction, including the deposit of a Persian-period coin, suggesting to its excavators that the item "was lost by a person who may have resided nearby and was engaged in scavenging or collecting activities from the ruined fortress." Gabriel Barkay, Alexander Fantalkin, and Oren Tal, "A Late Iron Age Fortress North of Jerusalem," *Bulletin of the American Schools of Oriental Research* 328 (2002): 68.
[61] Alon De Groot and Hannah Bernick-Greenberg, *Excavations at the City of David, 1978–1985, Directed by Yigal Shiloh, Volume VIIA: Area E: Stratigraphy and Architecture* (Jerusalem: Hebrew University of Jerusalem, 2012), 176. See also the reuse of a large building on the western slope of Iron Age Jerusalem after it was destroyed in Yiftah Shalev, Nitsam Shalom, Efrat Bocher, and Yuval Gadot, "New Evidence on the Location and Nature of Iron Age, Persian and Early Hellenistic Period Jerusalem," *Tel Aviv* 47.2 (2020): 149–72; 167.

former settlements, some to what was left of their homes. Others were simply seeking refuge in the ruined settlements that had endured.[62] As Avraham Faust observes, "It is more than likely that in every city there were squatters who lived amid the ruins," even if the remnants we have of them are faint.[63]

What is significant about these squatter remains for our study is how they attest to lives in antiquity adapted to and shaped by the older ruins that had endured in their surroundings, repurposed, in these instances, to offer refuge to those displaced after social and demographic collapse. For those who lived during these centuries, the biblical writers among them, it would have been common, it appears, to come across ruined sites and find individuals housed among the older remains, often living through subsistence farming in areas adjacent to these ruins. Ezekiel's prophecy (Ezek 33:24–27) against the "inhabitants of ruins" (ישבי החרבות) in Judah after the Babylonian campaign or Isaiah's oracle that Babylon would one day become so desolate that not even flocks would graze among its remains (Is 13:20) are indicative, then, of a world in which ruins were commonly sought for refuge or sustenance. Much like the continued presence of the dead, the presence of displaced individuals occupying older ruins of a site would have been a defining feature of the terrain, with some residing within fallen settlements like those at Hazor, Lachish, or Jerusalem that were once of considerable size and splendor.

But the power of older ruins to shape life in the present is also attested by instances where they were intentionally avoided. At Aphek, an impressive two-story palace (Palace VI) came to ruin at the end of the LBA sometime in the thirteenth century BCE.[64] In the aftermath of its destruction, the site was eventually resettled in the Iron I period, with the construction of homes built around the former palace, whose ruins, as attested by a retaining wall built to contain them, were still visible at the time.[65] Yet, rather than drawing on these palatial remains and rebuilding at the summit of the site, the new residents of Aphek instead "consciously and conspicuously avoided locating their dwellings above them,"[66] with the new domestic structures constructed in areas that carefully abutted the former palace.

A similar phenomenon is found at Hazor. After the destruction of the LBA city, "the still visible remains" of its downfall, both in the upper and lower city,

---

[62] Faust writes of those who survived the Babylonian campaigns that the "remaining population probably clung to deserted and destroyed forts (e.g., Kh. Abu et-Twein), where security from bandits ... was probably better." Faust, *Judah in the Neo-Babylonian Period*, 235.
[63] Ibid., 240.
[64] Yuval Gadot, "The Late Bronze Egyptian Estate at Aphek," *Tel Aviv* 37 (2010): 48–66.
[65] Yuval Gadot, "Iron Age (Strata XII–X6)," in *Aphek-Antipatris II: The Remains of the Acropolis*, 88–108 (Tel Aviv: Emery and Claire Yass Publications, 2009), 88.
[66] Gadot, "Iron Age," 88.

survived into the subsequent Iron I period in the centuries after.[67] As at Aphek, the new residents of the site consciously avoided building atop certain ruins of the older acropolis, where the remains of the Ceremonial Building (Building 7050) – perhaps the finest temple of the LBA in the all the southern Levant – were deliberately circumvented by the new inhabitants.[68]

Why later individuals refrained from building on the older ruins at Aphek and Hazor is unknown. Drawing on parallels from Aegean contexts,[69] Sharon Zuckerman posits cultic significance to this activity, in which early Iron Age occupants at Hazor, such as those at Knossos or Troy, may have engaged in ritual practices among the older, Bronze Age ruins from centuries before.[70] Relatedly, the decision to leave in place the ruins of Palace VI at Aphek or the Ceremonial Building at Hazor may have been driven by additional political or commemorative considerations, whether in reverence to more ancient forebears who built in ways the Iron I communities at these locations could not or as a testament to the former conquests of these locations by groups with whom later residents were aligned. Yet in the absence of written references to these activities, the specific motivations that informed them are obscure. That these ruins were willfully avoided by later inhabitants is, however, clear. At Hazor, the remains of the Ceremonial Building were not disturbed until Tiglath-Pileser III's conquest of the site in 732 BCE, meaning that its ruins were maintained and remained visible for an extraordinary five hundred years after its LBA destruction.[71]

3.1.3 The Gods

The ruins of the gods also endured.[72] Many remains of past cultic practices were of only modest dimensions, such as figurines or smaller cult objects

---

[67] Sharon Zuckerman, "Ruin Cults at Iron Age I Hazor," in *The Fire Signals of Lachish: Studies in the Archaeology and History of Israel in the Late Bronze Age, Iron Age, and Persian Period in Honor of David Ussishkin*, eds. I. Finkelstein and N. Na'aman, 387–94 (Winona Lake, IN: Eisenbrauns, 2011), 392.

[68] Ben-Ami and Ben Tor, "The Iron Age," 7–15; Zuckerman, "Ruin Cults," 392–93. At Megiddo, a monolith was situated on the ruins of a prominent temple after its destruction in the Iron I period, again marking and preserving the location where a sanctuary had once stood. See Assaf Kleiman et al., "Cult Activity at Megiddo in the Iron Age: New Evidence and a Long-Term Perspective," *Zeitschrift des Deutschen Palästina-Vereins* 133 (2017): 24–52; 26.

[69] Mieke Prent, "Glories of the Past in the Past: Ritual Activities at Palatial Ruins in Early Iron Age Crete," in *Archaeologies of Memory*, eds. R. Van Dyke and S. Alcock, 81–103 (Malden, MA: Blackwell, 2003); Sarah Morris, "Troy between Bronze and Iron Ages: Myth, Cult and Memory in a Sacred Landscape," in *Epos: Reconsidering Greek Epic and Aegean Bronze Age Archaeology*, 59–68 (Liège: Aegaeum, 2007).

[70] Zuckerman, "Ruin Cults," 389–93.   [71] Ben-Tor, *Hazor: Canaanite Metropolis*, 168–69.

[72] For broader surveys on the archaeological data surrounding cultic practices and developments, see John Holladay, "Religion in Israel and Judah under the Monarchy: An

(incense stands, small altars, model shrines) that have been unearthed at a large number of sites.[73] Other relics were located in private homes or found in the recesses of rooms within larger buildings,[74] their contents often lost and buried away when a site was destroyed or rebuilt.[75] But other materials from past religious practices in the southern Levant would have been more lasting and apparent.

Prominent among them were temples. During the Bronze Age, temples were constructed at nearly all the settlements that arose in the southern Levant.[76] The grandest of these forms were the *migdal* temples of the MBA, such as the ones constructed at Megiddo, Shechem, Hazor, or Pella. These sanctuaries were defined by their thick walls, symmetrical layout, and position on elevated mounds or platforms, rising high above the surrounding terrain.[77] Due to their monumental features, these temples continued in use for centuries. Those located at Shechem and Megiddo appear to have been maintained into the Iron I period – or some six centuries after they were first

---

Explicitly Archaeological Approach," in *Ancient Israelite Religion: Essays in Honor of Frank Moore Cross*, eds. P. Miller et al., 249–99 (Philadelphia: Fortress, 1987); Beth Alpert Nakhai, *Archaeology and the Religions of Canaan and Israel* (Boston: American Schools of Oriental Research, 2001); Ziony Zevit, *The Religions of Ancient Israel: A Synthesis of Parallactic Approaches* (London: Continuum, 2001); William Dever, *Did God Have a Wife? Archaeology and Folk Religion in Ancient Israel* (Grand Rapids, MI: Eerdmans, 2005); Richard Hess, *Israelite Religions: An Archaeological and Biblical Survey* (Grand Rapids, MI: Baker, 2007).

[73] For Bronze Age remains, see James Pritchard, *Palestinian Figurines in Relation to Certain Goddesses Known through Literature* (New Haven, CT: American Oriental Society, 1943); Othmar Keel and Christoph Uehlinger, *Gods, Goddesses, and Images of God in Ancient Israel*, trans. T. Trapp (Edinburgh: T&T Clark, 1998), 19–108; Alpert Nakhai, *Archaeology*, 90–99, 140–48. On later Judean pillar figurines, see Raz Kletter, *The Judean Pillar Figurines and the Archaeology of Asherah* (Oxford: Tempus Reparatum, 1996); Erin Darby, *Interpreting Judean Pillar Figurines: Gender and Empire in Judean Apotropaic Ritual* (Tübingen: Mohr Siebeck, 2014). For other cult objects, see the fine overview in Zevit, *Religions*, 298–349.

[74] Among the households excavated from Stratum II at Tel Beer-Sheba (late eighth century BCE), for example, ca. 150 zoomorphic figures, forty-seven female figurines, and seventeen small altars were unearthed, attesting to the widespread practices associated with these items in the home. See Lily Singer-Avitz, "Household Activities at Tel Beersheba," in *Household Archaeology in Ancient Israel and Beyond*, eds. A. Yasur-Landau et al., 275–302 (Leiden: Brill, 2011).

[75] See, for example, the discussion of "cult room 49" at Lachish stratum V or the "cult corner 2081" from Iron Age Megiddo in Zevit, *Religions*, 213–17, 219–25; Alpert Nakhai, *Religions*, 178–79.

[76] Amihai Mazar, "Temples of the Middle and Late Bronze Age and the Iron Age," in *The Architecture of Ancient Israel from the Prehistoric to the Persian Period*, eds. A. Kempinski and H. Katzenstein, 161–89 (Jerusalem: Israel Exploration Society, 1992); Alpert Nakhai, *Archaeology*, 119–60; Hess, *Israelite Religions*, 125–40; Avraham Faust, "Israelite Temples: Where Was Israelite Cult Not Practiced and Why," *Religions* 10 (2019): 1–26; 4–6; Stephen Bourke, "The Six Canaanite Temples of *Tabaqat Fahil*. Excavating Pella's 'Fortress' Temple (1994–2009)," in *Temple Building and Temple Cult: Architecture and Cultic Paraphernalia of Temples in the Levant (2.–1. Mill. B.C.E.)*, ed. J. Kamlah, 159–202 (Wiesbaden: Harrassowitz Verlag, 2012).

[77] Mazar, "Temples," 164–66; Alpert Nakhai, *Archaeology*, 101–8.

37 Seated deity figurines, Late Bronze Age. Hazor. Fabien Gatti, photograph. Creative Commons Attribution-Share Alike 4.0 international license

founded – and at Pella a new Iron II sanctuary was built directly on the massive Bronze Age ruins of its predecessor.[78] The remains of other Bronze Age

---

[78] Alpert Nakhai, 101–4; Assaf Kleiman et al., "Cult Activity at Megiddo," 24–52; Lawrence Stager, "The Shechem Temple Where Abimelech Massacred a Thousand," *Biblical Archaeology Review* 29 (2003): 26–35; Ido Koch, "Southern Levantine Temples during the Iron Age II: Towards a Multivocal Narrative," *Ancient Judaism* 8 (2020): 325–44.

38 Monumental remains of Pella Temple, looking east. Ben Churcher, photograph. Creative Commons Attribution 3.0 unported license

temples also persisted. At Beth-Shean, a series of LBA sanctuaries were constructed atop one another until, in the Iron I period, a new temple (northern temple) was built that incorporated older Egyptian monuments in its courtyard and within the temple building itself, thereby linking the present Canaanite community with the cultic life of the site's past.[79] Three successive temples were also built at the regional cult center of Tell Kittan during the MBA and LBA eras until, after the site's destruction at the close of the LBA, the remains of the large sanctuary were abandoned and stood exposed for well over a thousand years.[80] Ruins of former temples would have also been encountered outside of larger centers, such as the isolated sanctuary situated near a main road to the Carmel region at Tel Mevorakh,[81] along the Mediterranean coast, or even in more rural settings among the remains of smaller Bronze Age villages.[82]

[79] Amihai Mazar, "Tel Beth-Shean: History and Archaeology," 247–62.
[80] Emmanuel Eisenberg, "Tel Kitan," in *New Encyclopedia of Archaeological Excavations in the Holy Land*, Volume III: 878–81; 881; Emmanuel Eisenberg, "The Temples at Tell Kittan," *Biblical Archaeology* 40.2 (1977): 77–81.
[81] Ephraim Stern, *Tel Mevorakh*, Vol. II, 4–39 (Jerusalem: Hebrew University Press, 1984).
[82] Faust, "Israelite Temples," 5–6.

It is evident, then, that the ruins of older Bronze Age sanctuaries would have persisted throughout the region during the first millennium BCE. At certain sites, new Iron Age sanctuaries would be constructed atop or near the remains of more venerable sanctuaries, likely in an effort to sustain the sacred character of these precincts.[83] But at many settlements during this era, no new temples emerged, leaving the ruins of former Bronze Age sanctuaries as visible features of the terrain. Only Arad, Dan, and the recently unearthed structure at Tel Moza have produced finds connected to Iron Age temple buildings in the southern Levant,[84] though Jerusalem's sanctuary is inaccessible to archaeologists, and the temple at Bethel, which features prominently in the Hebrew Bible, has not been found. Yet, as Faust observes, what is striking about our current evidence is that "temples are practically missing in the archaeological record of Iron Age II Israel and Judah. There was no 'city temple,' 'village temple,' or 'neighborhood temple' in those polities, and there were no regional cultic centers spread across the landscape."[85] In contrast to the Bronze Age, then, cultic life in the Iron Age and Persian period was no longer defined by the widespread construction of large temple buildings and their associated rituals and cultic objects. It is the ruins of the Iron Age Jerusalem sanctuary, therefore, that would have mattered most in the period after its destruction by the Babylonians (ca. 586 BCE). In the Book of Jeremiah, we find mourners traveling to the ruins of this temple from the north (Jer 41:5), and in Haggai those tasked with reconstructing the sanctuary years later are surrounded by remains that offer a reminder of the temple's former monumentality, which its new builders cannot match (Hag 2:3).

In addition to the ruins of older sanctuaries that would have dotted the landscape of the southern Levant were the remains of sacred precincts. An early Iron Age example is that of the "Bull Site," located on a summit in the Samaria hills between the towns of Dothan and Tirzah.[86] Named after a bull statuette 12cm high and 17cm in length found among its ruins, the site was defined by an elliptical wall of boulders that enclosed an open-air cultic space, inside which was found a standing stone (*massebah*) and associated remains from what

---

[83] Koch, "Southern Levantine Temples," 329–32; Kleiman, "Cultic Activity at Megiddo," 24–52; Zuckerman, "Ruin Cults," 387–94.

[84] Ze'ev Herzog, "The Fortress Mound at Tel Arad: An Interim Report," *Tel Aviv* 29 (2002): 3–109; 49–72; Shua Kisilevitz, "The Iron IIA Judahite Temple at Tel Moza," *TA* 42 (2015): 147–64. The sacred precinct at Dan may be the remains of a temple or, as the initial excavator contended, an open-air sanctuary. See Avraham Biran, *Biblical Dan* (Jerusalem: Israel Exploration Society, 1994), 159–233.

[85] Faust, "Israelite Temples," 12–13. So also Mazar: "Whereas finds from the Late Bronze Age are abundant, only a small number of sacred structures from the Iron Age II (tenth–sixth centuries B.C.) have been uncovered in Israel." Mazar, "Temples," 183.

[86] Amihai Mazar, "The 'Bull Site': An Iron Age I Open Cult Place," *Bulletin of the American Schools of Oriental Research* 247 (1982): 27–42; Zevit, *Religions*, 176–80.

39 Mount Ebal complex, Iron I. Bukvoed, photograph. Creative Commons Attribution 4.0 international license

was likely its use as an altar.[87] The cultic activities that took place at the site were nevertheless short-lived, as the location was abandoned not long after its construction in the Iron I period and never rebuilt.

A further Iron I hilltop complex was discovered on Mt. Ebal.[88] Though an understanding of this structure is more ambiguous because of its uniqueness in the region, the remains were interpreted by its excavator as an altar, a possibility that has been debated because of its divergence from other altar forms found elsewhere in its vicinity.

Nevertheless, a broader cultic interpretation of the site is supported by its location on an isolated hilltop, removed from settlements or agricultural land, and the abundance of faunal remains and ash found within its enclosures.[89] The Bull Site and Mt. Ebal structure would, then, provide evidence of open-

---

[87] Mazar, "Bull Site," 32–36.
[88] Adam Zertal, "An Early Iron Age Cultic Site on Mt. Ebal: Excavation Seasons 1982–1987," *Tel Aviv* 13–14 (1986–1987): 105–65. For a more recent discussion, see Baruch Halpern, "Touch of Ebal: Tesselated Identity in the Historical Frontier of Iron I," in *Biblical and Ancient Near Eastern Studies in Honor of P. Kyle McCarter, Jr.*, eds. C. Rollston, S. Garfein, and N. Walls, 535–74 (Atlanta: SBL Press, 2022).
[89] For arguments that support the cultic nature of the site, see Elizabeth Bloch-Smith and Beth Alpert Nakhai, "A Landscape Comes to Life: The Iron Age I," *Near Eastern Archaeology* 62.2 (1999): 62–127; 76–77; Zevit, *Religions*, 196–201.

40 Arad Sanctuary with standing stone (background) and incense stands (foreground). Ian Scott, photograph. Creative Commons Attribution-Share Alike 2.0 generic license

air, Iron I hilltop sites whose cultic ruins endured in the highlands long after these locations were abandoned.

The cultic landscape of the southern Levant was also marked by the appearance of prominent standing stones, or *massebot*, which were typically defined by their wide base, rounded top, and flattened face when positioned upright. The use of such stones in cultic contexts stretches back for millennia in the Levant into the Neolithic period,[90] but their forms continued to be

---

[90] Elizabeth Bloch-Smith, "Will the Real Massebot Please Stand Up: Cases of Real and Mistakenly Identified Standing Stones in Ancient Israel," in *Text, Artifact, and Image: Revealing Ancient Israelite Religion*, eds. G. Beckman and T. Lewis, 64–79 (Providence, RI: Brown University Press, 2006); Zevit, *Religions*, 256; Alpert Nakhai, *Religions*, 82.

produced at a number of Bronze and Iron Age sites. Many were associated with temples.

At Hazor, a MBA cultic precinct was filled with dozens of standing stones, typically found in pairs and facing west, which were situated among widespread faunal remains that attest to the area's cultic function,[91] and similar stones were recovered from MBA temples at Megiddo and Tell Kittan, among others.[92] At the Iron Age temple of Arad, a finely dressed standing stone was found in the recessed niche of the structure, or *debir*.[93] And a large basalt standing stone was also found among the Iron I remains at Hazor in a cultic precinct from Area A, including offering tables placed in front of it, and further *massebot* were located in a cult place in Area B, extending the long tradition of these sacred objects from the city's earlier Bronze Age past.[94] Other examples were found outside of temple precincts. The monumental standing stones from MBA Gezer were positioned prominently along a north-south axis at an elevated location at the site absent larger structural remains,[95] and the Bull Site, as noted above, was constructed around a standing stone on a hilltop shrine set apart from any known settlement. At Dan, furthermore, five *massebot* were located near the site's southern gate entrance, erected there sometime in the ninth through eighth centuries BCE.[96]

The construction of standing stones dwindles by the eighth century BCE and comes to an end, as a number of Iron Age cultic practices do, with the destruction of Jerusalem and the surrounding Judahite kingdom in 586 BCE.[97] What later communities thought about these older Bronze and Iron Age remains in their environment, of standing stones and statuettes of deities, the ruins of ancient temples and abandoned sacred precincts, is difficult to surmise. The biblical prohibitions against a number of practices associated with remains such as these, including specific bans on figurines and sacred pillars, and injunctions against worship on open-air hilltop precincts or at temples outside Jerusalem (e.g., Lev 19:4, 26:1; Deut 7:25, 12:2, 27:15; 2 Kings 23:5), suggest that these cultic features and their attendant rituals had been rather widespread

---

[91] Doron Ben-Ami, "Mysterious Standing Stones," *Biblical Archaeology Review* 32.2 (2006): 38–45; Sharon Zuckerman, "The Temples of Canaanite Hazor," in *Temple Buildings and Temple Cult*, ed. J. Kamla, 99–125 (Wiesbaden: Harrassowitz Verlag, 2012).

[92] G. Ernest Wright, *Shechem: The Biography of a Biblical City* (New York: McGraw-Hill, 1965), 82–86; Eisenberg, "The Temples at Tel Kitan," 77–81.

[93] Herzog, "Arad," 57–67.

[94] Doron Ben-Ami, "Early Iron Age Cult Places – New Evidence from Tel Hazor," *Tel Aviv* 33.2 (2006): 121–33.

[95] William Dever, "The Middle Bronze Age 'High Place' at Gezer," *Bulletin of the American Schools of Oriental Research* 371 (2014): 17–57.

[96] Biran, *Biblical Dan*, 244–45.

[97] Elizabeth Bloch-Smith, "Massebot Standing for Yhwh: The Fall of a Yhwistic Cult Symbol," in *Worship, Women, and War: Essays in Honor of Susan Niditch*, eds. J. Collins, T. M. Lemos, and S. Olyan, 99–116 (Providence, RI: Brown Judaic Studies, 2015), 112.

and persistent. The continued presence of material remains wedded to past religious practices, carried out for centuries among residents of the southern Levant, would have likely made it difficult for any efforts at reform or the introduction of new cultic mandates to take hold, as Jeremiah's (e.g. Jer 7:17–26, 44:15–19) or Ezekiel's (e.g. Ezek 8:7–18, 14:1–5) grievances, set at the very end of the Iron Age, intimate. If the ruins of the gods persisted across time, so also, it appears, did many cultic practices affiliated with them.

3.1.4 *The Empires*

Lastly, the landscape that the biblical writers knew also bore the longstanding marks of imperial involvement. The earliest forms were those linked to Egypt's control of the region in the LBA. Beginning with Thutmose III (ca. 1479–1425 BCE), Egypt began to extend its authority eastward into Canaan through the establishment of permanent bases in the region.[98] The coastal settlement of Tell el-Ajjul and the inland site of Beth-Shean both provide evidence of Egyptian infrastructure and other material remains from this period,[99] and by the Nineteenth Dynasty (ca. thirteenth century BCE) the Egyptian presence in Canaan was strengthened across a number of additional locations. At Jaffa, an impressive Egyptian fortress and monumental gateway can be attributed to this era, attesting to its role as a dominant Egyptian harbor of its time,[100] and at Lachish the Fosse Temple, rebuilt under Egyptian influence in the LBA II period, continued to exhibit a preponderance of Egyptian cultic wares in its sanctuary for centuries.[101] A large building interpreted as an Egyptian governor's residence was unearthed at the site of Tel Sera' from a thirteenth century BCE context,[102] joining Egyptian administrative buildings that have been unearthed from this time at Tel el-Hesi,[103] Aphek (Palace

---

[98] For an overview of the material remains from the Egyptian presence in the Levant, see the seminal work by Ellen Fowles Morris, *The Architecture of Imperialism: Military Bases and the Evolution of Foreign Policy in Egypt's New Kingdom* (Leiden: Brill, 2005). For a more recent discussion see Felix Höflmayer, "Egypt's 'Empire' in the Southern Levant during the Early 18th Dynasty," in *Policies of Exchange: Political Systems and Modes of Interaction in the Aegean and the Near East in the 2nd Millennium B.C.E.*, eds. B. Eder and R. Pruszinszky, 191–206 (Vienna: Austrian Academy of Science, 2015).

[99] Morris, *Architecture of Imperialism*, 271–72, 305–10.

[100] Aaron Burke, "Early Jaffa: From the Bronze Age to the Persian Period," in *The History and Archaeology of Jaffa*, Vol. 1, 63–78 (Los Angeles: Cotsen Institute of Archaeology Press, 2011), 69–70.

[101] Ido Koch, "Revisiting the Fosse Temple at Tel Lachish," *Journal of Ancient Near Eastern Religions* 17 (2017): 64–75.

[102] Eliezer Oren, "Tel Sera'" in *New Encyclopedia of Archaeological Excavations in the Holy Land*, Volume IV: 1329–35; 1331.

[103] Eliezer Oren, "'Governors' Residences' in Canaan under the New Kingdom: A Case Study of Egyptian Administration," *Journal of the Society for the Study of Egyptian Antiquities* 14 (1984): 37–56; 46–47.

41 Replica of Stela of Seti I, Beth-Shean. Ian Scott, photograph. Wikimedia Commons. Creative Commons Attribution-Share Alike 2.0 generic license

VI),[104] and Tel Mor,[105] among others.[106] The Egyptian outpost at Beth-Shean is completely redesigned in the thirteenth century BCE, furthermore, with the

---

[104] Yuval Gadot, "The Late Bronze Egyptian Estate at Aphek," *Tel Aviv* 37 (2010): 48–66.
[105] Moshe Dothan, "Tel Mor," *New Encyclopedia of Archaeological Excavations in the Holy Land*, Volume III: 1072–74; 1073.
[106] For an overview, see Morris, *Architecture of Imperialism*, 504–610.

construction of new temples, administrative buildings, and a residential quarter, much of which likely took place under the auspices of Seti I, who left behind two royal stelae at the site marking his achievements.[107] Later, his successor, Ramesses II, would do the same, erecting a stela at Beth-Shean celebrating a military campaign in the region.[108]

What materials remained of Egypt's presence in Canaan after its withdrawal in the twelfth century BCE is only known through the fragmentary traces found at a handful of locations. But Beth-Shean provides a striking instance of the intentional preservation of older artifacts connected to an earlier Egyptian past. In the courtyard of the Double Temple complex, dated to the later Iron I period (ca. eleventh through tenth centuries BCE), residents of the site carefully situated the two stelae of Seti I, the stela of Ramesses II, and a statue of Ramesses III near the entrance to the sanctuary.[109] This "monuments courtyard," as its excavator terms it, would join the preserved ruins of the Egyptian estate at Aphek, both locations preserving remains of an Egyptian past that were public and visible for centuries.

Yet more pervasive than these monumental ruins were the smaller items that bore the lasting imprint of Egyptian motifs and stylistic elements. As Othmar Keel and Christoph Uehlinger demonstrate in their extensive study of this assemblage, finds from the LBA, particularly in regions from Megiddo southward, show the dominant influence of Egyptian forms that would continue well into the Iron Age.[110] Scarabs, terra-cotta figurines, ivories, faience objects, cylinder seals, pendants, and ceramics all attest to Egypt's prominence in the southern Levant during this period and its strong influence on Canaanite practices and culture.[111]

If it is difficult to determine the historical character of the numerous biblical references to the presence of Egyptians in the era after Egypt's LBA withdrawal – from the names of Eli's sons (1 Sam 1:3) and David's court scribe (2 Sam 8:16–18//2 Sam 20:23–26), to Solomon's marriage to an Egyptian princess (1 Kings 3:1) – these allusions nevertheless reflect something of the lasting

---

[107] Amihai Mazar, "The Egyptian Garrison Town at Beth-Shean," in *Egypt, Canaan and Israel: History, Imperialism, Ideology and Literature*, eds. S. Bar, D. Kahn, and J. Shirley, 155–89 (Leiden: Brill, 2011), 159–61.

[108] Ibid., 162.

[109] Amihai Mazar, "The Beth-Shean Valley and Its Vicinity in the 10th Century BCE," *Jerusalem Journal of Archaeology* 1 (2021): 241–71; 247–48.

[110] Othmar Keel and Christoph Uehlinger, *Gods, Goddesses, and Images of God in Ancient Israel*, 49–108. For Iron Age influence, see 114–19, 265–80, 350–53.

[111] On the ceramic repertoire from key settlements, see the conclusion and summary to Mario Martin, *Egyptian-Type Pottery in the Late Bronze Age Southern Levant* (Vienna: Verlag der Österreichische Akademie der Wissenschaften, 2011), 243–53, 273–74.

presence of Egypt in the region, preserved in the material remains of LBA buildings, monuments, and small items that Egypt left behind.[112]

But more imposing than Egyptian remains were the ruins that arose from later Assyrian and Babylonian invasions. Most conspicuous of these were the many destroyed settlements these empires produced during their campaigns – many not rebuilt for centuries and some not at all. Tel Kinrot in the Galilee region,[113] Tel Jokneam in the Jezreel Valley,[114] Shechem in the highlands,[115] and Tel Eton and Khirbet el Qom[116] in the Shephelah are representative of the wide-scale Assyrian destruction of sites across the southern Levant in the late eighth century BCE that were left in ruins for many centuries.[117] In Zvi Gal's survey of the lower Galilee region, once a prosperous area of the kingdom of Israel, the lands are described as "significantly deserted" after the Assyrian destructions, with many of their settlements not reoccupied for hundreds of years.[118] A similar picture emerges in the early sixth century BCE when Judah was invaded by Babylon, where the Babylonian army "deliberately destroyed, burned, and robbed all the settlements they occupied," most of which were left in their fallen state and not rebuilt.[119] Arad,[120] Hebron,[121] Gezer,[122] and Jerusalem[123] were all destroyed, with none reaching their previous Iron Age

---

[112] On the meager evidence of political and cultural contact between Egypt and the southern Levant in the eleventh through early tenth centuries BCE, see Bernd Schipper, *Israel und Ägypten in der Königszeit: Die kulturellen Kontakte von Salomo bis zum Fall Jerusalems* (Göttingen: Vandenhoeck & Ruprecht, 1999), 31–35.

[113] Volkmar Fritz, "Chinnereth, Tell," in *New Encyclopedia of Archaeological Excavations in the Holy Land*, Volume V: 1684–86; 1685.

[114] Amnon Ben-Tor, "Jokneam," in *New Encyclopedia of Archaeological Excavations in the Holy Land*, Volume III: 805–11; 807.

[115] Arye Bornstein, "Shechem," in *The Oxford Encyclopedia of Bible and Archaeology*, Vol. 2, ed. D. Master, 354 (New York: Oxford University Press, 2013).

[116] Shlomo Bunimovitz and Zvi Lederman, "The Final Destruction of Beth-Shemesh and the *Pax Assyriaca* in the Judean Shephelah," *Tel Aviv* 30.1 (2003): 3–26.

[117] For an extensive overview of demographic and settlement history of the region under Assyrian control, see Avraham Faust, *The Neo-Assyrian Empire in the Southwest: Imperial Domination and Its Consequences* (New York: Oxford University Press, 2021), 73–115.

[118] Zvi Gal, *Lower Galilee during the Iron Age*, trans. M. Josephy (Winona Lake, IN: Eisenbrauns, 1992), 108.

[119] Ephraim Stern, *Archaeology of the Land of the Bible*, Vol. II (New Haven, CT: Yale University Press, 2001), 350; Faust, *Judah in the Neo-Babylonian Period*, 188–94.

[120] Herzog, "Arad," 101–2.

[121] Jeffrey Chadwick, "Discovering Hebron: The City of the Patriarchs Slowly Yields Its Secrets," *Biblical Archaeology Review* 31.5 (2005): 24–33; David Ben-Shlomo, "New Evidence of Iron Age II Fortifications at Tel Hebron," in *The Last Century in the History of Judah: The Seventh Century BCE in Archaeological, Historical, and Biblical Perspectives*, eds. F. Capek and O. Lipschits, 63–88 (Atlanta: SBL Press, 2019).

[122] William Dever and Joe Seger, "A Brief Summary of the Stratigraphy and Cultural History of Gezer," in *Gezer VI: The Objects from Phases I and II (1964–74)*, eds. J. Seger, W. Dever, and S. Gitin, 8–17 (Winona Lake, IN: Eisenbrauns, 2014), 16.

[123] Oded Lipschits, *The Fall and Rise of Jerusalem: Judah under Babylonian Rule* (Winona Lake, IN: Eisenbrauns, 2005), 68–96.

size and population for at least four hundred years after. The total area of settlements in Judah, as Oded Lipschits details in his study, declines by a remarkable 70 percent after the Babylonian invasion, signaling demographic and social collapse. What remained for those who lived in the region during the Persian and early Hellenistic eras (ca. 515–175 BCE), consequently, was a rather ghostly landscape, a terrain where the ruins of numerous cities and towns enclosed remains of populations that had mostly vanished.

At a few conquered sites, what would have been visible were the remains of Assyrian and Babylonian administrative buildings erected to oversee the regions they had once controlled. Remnants of an impressive structure from Megiddo, which functioned as an Assyrian administrative outpost, provide evidence of a large Assyrian palatial complex in the northern area of the city,[124] and the sites of Ashdod and Tel Jemmeh, located to the southwest along the Mediterranean coast, were also regional centers occupied by Assyrian forces during their engagement with Egypt.[125] At Mizpah, which functioned as the Babylonian provincial center after Jerusalem's destruction, the town was redesigned under Babylonian influence, including at its northern end the construction of a large building modeled on Babylonian forms,[126] and the ornate building at Ramat Rahel, just south of Jerusalem, also appears to have been commandeered by the Babylonians and continued in use after Judah's fall.[127]

In addition to these monumental buildings, a number of royal monuments dotted the landscape of the southern Levant, commemorating its conquest in ways the Egyptians had introduced before in the LBA. In his annals, Shalmaneser III describes two royal stelae he had constructed, one near the border of northern Israel "at the gateway to Tyre" and another on Mt. Lebanon near Damascus, and Tiglath Pileser III writes of a royal monument he left at Gaza and one further south at the Brook of Egypt, most likely near the site of Tell Jemmeh.[128]

---

[124] Alexander Joffe, Eric Cline, and Oded Lipschitz, "Area H," in *Megiddo III*, Vol. 1, eds. I. Finkelstein, D. Ussishkin, and B. Halpern, 153–60 (Tel Aviv: Emery and Claire Yass Publications, 2000).

[125] David Ben-Shlomo, "Tell Jemmeh, Philistia and the Neo Assyrian Empire during the Late Iron Age," *Levant* 46.1 (2014): 58–88.

[126] For a vivid, detailed description of the changes that took place at Mizpah under the Babylonians, see Jeffrey Zorn, "Jeremiah at Mizpah of Benjamin (Tell en-Nasbeh): The Archaeological Setting," in *The Book of Jeremiah: Composition, Reception, and Interpretation*, eds. J. Lundbom, C. A. Evans, and B. Anderson, 69–92 (Leiden: Brill, 2018).

[127] Oded Lipschits, "Shedding New Light on the Dark Years of the 'Exilic Period': New Studies, Further Elucidation, and Some Questions Regarding the Archaeology of Judah as an 'Empty Land,'" in *Interpreting Exile: Displacement and Deportation in Biblical and Modern Contexts*, eds. B. Kelle, F. Ames, and J. Wright, 57–90 (Atlanta: SBL Press, 2011), 59–61.

[128] For a detailed study of the peripheral royal monuments erected by Assyrian kings, see Ann Shafer, "The Carving of an Empire: Neo-Assyrian Monuments on the Periphery" (Ph.D.

42 Image of Assyrian royal monument (right) with stone carvers (left). Balawat Gates relief, ca. 858–824 BCE. BM 124662. ©Trustees of the British Museum

The ruins that the Assyrian and Babylonian empires left behind were therefore considerable and lasting. Never before had the lands of the southern Levant experienced such devastation through imperial hostilities, nor would they again until the Jewish-Roman wars of the first through second centuries CE, some six hundred years later. Perhaps the most meaningful artifact that attests to the aftermath of this ruined terrain is the Hebrew Bible itself. Among the many works set in these centuries of Assyrian and Babylonian aggression, from Isaiah to Ezekiel to the final chapters of Kings and the poems of Lamentations, references to ruins are frequent. Hezekiah's petition for deliverance from the "kings of Assyria who have ruined all the nations and their lands" (Is 37:18) or Jeremiah's warning that Babylon will make Judah "a ruin and a waste" (Jer 25:11) attest to experiences of ruins that these Mesopotamian empires had wrought or would soon create. In the Book of Lamentations, the ruined ramparts and broken walls of Jerusalem cry out (Lam 2: 8) in lament in the aftermath of the city's destruction.

But the biblical silence that takes hold in the years after Jerusalem's fall is also suggestive of the presence exerted by these ruins. After Gedaliah's assassination in Mizpah around 583 BCE, we are offered few details about what transpired in the region until, roughly seventy years later, a community comes together to rebuild the temple. Even then, more substantial stories about this era emerge

diss., Harvard University, 1998). For a discussion of these specific southern Levantine monuments, see 201–3, 247–49.

only during the period of Ezra and Nehemiah (450 BCE), meaning that well over a century is effectively passed over in silence. During this period of pronounced ruination, little is recorded in the biblical writings of life in the former territories of Israel and Judah, the bleak landscape of the defeated kingdoms precipitating a wordlessness about conditions in the region that would last for generations.

3.1.5 Summary: An Archaeology of Presence

During the centuries in which the biblical writings were produced, the past persisted into the present through an array of material forms. What the archaeological evidence demonstrates are frequent encounters with older ruins and their associated artifacts when the biblical writers were active, from visitations with the dead to scenes of squatter populations living among settlements destroyed or long abandoned. Indeed, experiences of more venerable remains extend far beyond what can be examined here. At a number of locations in the southern Levant, the ruins of older buildings and fortifications were reused in more recent constructions, obviating the need for the expensive and labor-intensive practices of quarrying stone and procuring other materials necessary to assemble homes and larger enclosures. When the monumental Stepped Stone Structure in Jerusalem fell out of use, to cite one instance, parts of it were implemented for the foundations of new homes built in this eastern precinct of the city, including the House of Ahiel and House of the Bullae positioned directly on it sometime in the Iron II period.[129] At Hazor, finely wrought basalt orthostats of the Bronze Age, previously used in monumental buildings of the period, were recut for mundane building material and used in the construction of Iron Age homes and in the city's fortifications.[130] Within both Gath and Hebron, as noted in Chapter 1, elements of Bronze Age fortifications continued in use well into the Iron Age, and, at Shiloh, as discussed in Chapter 2, Iron I inhabitants built structures into and atop the older MBA wall of the site. The large administrative building at Ramat Rahel was renovated during the Persian period and continued in use for centuries after,[131] as did the massive Iron Age wall that encircled Mizpah when it

---

[129] For an Iron IIA date of these homes, see Jane Cahill, "Jerusalem at the Time of the Monarchy: The Archaeological Evidence," in *Jerusalem in Bible and Archaeology: The First Temple Period*, eds. A. Vaughn and A. Killebrew, 13–80 (Atlanta: Society of Biblical Literature, 2003), 58; for a later Iron IIC date, see Yigal Shiloh, *Excavations in the City of David, I: 1978–1982* (Jerusalem: Hebrew University Press, 1984), 28–29.

[130] Shlomit Bechar, "Abuse, Reuse, Recycle: The Use of Basalt Orthostats at Hazor in the Bronze and Iron Ages," *Oxford Journal of Archaeology* 40.1 (2021): 65–86.

[131] Oded Lipschits, Yuval Gadot, Benjamine Arubas, and Manfred Oeming, *What Are the Stones Whispering? Ramat Rahel: 3,000 Years of Forgotten History* (Winona Lake, IN: Eisenbrauns, 2017), 98–116.

became the administrative center of the Babylonian province after Jerusalem's destruction.[132]

In our world of incredibly high consumption and dross, it can be difficult to grasp how frequent and necessary was the reuse of older materials in "pre- or non-industrial economies that generate little surplus and cannot afford waste."[133] But for those who lived in the southern Levant, as elsewhere in antiquity, what was in ruin was often woven into what was newly contrived.[134] In a manner that would be disquieting to the logic of our late capitalist moment, older remains pervaded the built environments of the lands of this region, often adopted, reworked, and drawn on for life in the present.

Encounters with ruins during these eras were therefore more than passive engagements. Archaeologically, the evidence we possess indicates that inhabitants of the southern Levant were deeply involved with and affected by older remains.[135] This impact is apparent in how ruins continued to be implemented and inhabited across time, sheltering survivors, aiding in cultic rituals, some shielded against further disturbance, others resonant simply in the devastation and loss they represented. Those of these eras did not simply live among the ruins that surrounded them. They actively made recourse to these remains in how they approached their present circumstances and advanced their contemporary interests.

3.2 THE HEBREW BIBLE AND THE PRESENCE OF THE PAST

But once more we have no evidence of individuals digging among these ruins to learn about those who had lived there before. This in spite of many instances examined above where residents of the southern Levant interacted with older material remains. To these examples can added ritual objects

---

[132] Zorn, "Jeremiah at Mizpah," 75–77.
[133] Dale Kinney, "Introduction," in *Reuse Value: Spolia and Appropriation in Art and Architecture from Constantine to Sherrie Levine*, eds. R. Brilliant and D. Kinney, 1–12 (New York: Routledge, 2011), 2.
[134] See, for example, Seymour Gitin, "Bronze Age Egyptian-Type Stone Stands from a Late Iron Age IIC Context at Tel Miqne-Ekron," *Eretz-Israel* 33 (2018): 83–90; Ömür Harmanşah, "Upright Stones and Building Narratives: Formation of a Shared Architectural Practice in the Ancient Near East," in *Ancient Near Eastern Art in Context: Studies in Ancient Near Eastern Art in Context: Studies in Honor of Irene Winter*, eds. J. Cheng and M. Feldman, 69–99 (Leiden: Brill, 2007); Virginia Hermann, "Appropriation and Emulation in the Earliest Sculptures from Zincirli (Iron Age Sam'al)," *American Journal of Archaeology* 121.2 (2017): 237–74.
[135] On this point, see similar arguments about archaeological evidence that pertains to engagements with older remains in Roman Anatolia in Felipe Rojas, *The Pasts of Roman Anatolia: Interpreters, Traces, Horizons* (Cambridge: Cambridge University Press, 2019), 30–60.

deposited in *favissae* beneath the ground (e.g., Lachish),[136] older sanctuaries intentionally and carefully buried away (e.g., Hazor),[137] and the ruins of palaces built over (e.g., Megiddo).[138] Nevertheless, there is no indication that anyone reversed these acts to surface and investigate what had been concealed. By the Iron Age, the southern Levant had witnessed the rise and fall of settlements for over two thousand years previous, with EBA ruins still visible (e.g., Tel Jarmuth, Tel Arad) from millennia before, in addition to an assemblage of already ancient ceramics, figurines, scarabs, and other artifacts that would have been apparent across the landscape.[139] Remnants of the past were manifest throughout the terrain, but we have no indication that anyone sought out older objects or buildings to exhume and examine the pasts connected to them.

Nor do the biblical writings suggest otherwise. Even the claims of a Nabonidus or other Neo-Babylonian rulers who aimed at locating antiquities beneath more ancient buildings, as discussed in Chapter 1, find no parallel in the Hebrew Bible. When renovations are made to the temple during the reign of Joash (2 Kings 12) or when it is later rebuilt in the Persian period (Ezra 3–6), we find few references to older relics from previous ages that must have been encountered. In the brief moments when older items do appear in these texts, such as in the account of Hezekiah's cultic reforms, such artifacts are said to have been singled out for destruction and not, as with us, studied and preserved. Thus Hezekiah "broke into pieces the bronze snake that Moses had made" (2 Kings 18:4), a cultic item from the temple that, according to biblical chronology, would have been at least five centuries old when it was demolished.

But what the biblical writings do convey is a familiarity with other material remains that continued to hold significance in the present. The clearest indication of this awareness is the expression "to this day" that occurs nearly one hundred times across different biblical books, from Genesis to Chronicles.[140] Widespread and varied in its references, this saying can be attached to very different phenomena, including geographic designations ("so that place is called Gilgal to this day" [Josh 5:9]) or political realities ("Israel has been in rebellion against the House of David to this day" [1

---

[136] David Ussishkin, "Area P: The Level VI Temple," in *The Renewed Archaeological Excavations at Lachish (1973–1994)*, ed. D. Ussishkin, 215–81 (Tel Aviv: Emery and Claire Yass, 2004), 249–57.

[137] Zuckerman, "Temples of Canaanite Hazor," 14–15.

[138] Gunnar Lehmann and Ann Killebrew, "Palace 6000 at Megiddo in Context: Iron Age Central Hall Tetra-Partite Residencies and the *Bit-Hilani* Building Tradition in the Levant," *Bulletin of the American Schools of Oriental Research* 369 (2010): 13–33.

[139] See again Keel and Uehlinger, *Gods, Goddesses, and Images of God*, 19–108.

[140] The phrase עד היום הזה occurs eighty-four times, with עד היום occurring in another seven instances.

Kings 12:19]). Yet frequently, this phrase is connected to older artifacts and the ruins of specific locations. The large stones that sealed the burial cave of five Canaanite kings at Makkedah remain standing "to this very day" (Josh 10:27), the narrator reports, as does the rock on which the ark once rested in its deliverance from the Philistines, located in the "field of Joshua of Beth Shemesh" (1 Sam 6:18).

Since antiquity, scholars have seized on this expression for an understanding of when certain biblical books or passages were composed.[141] The temporal distance implied in this terminology between an event and its continued visibility sometime later led to discussions about the non-contemporaneity of biblical documents with what was reported within them, studies that, in the modern period, led to dates being applied to the composition of these writings that were situated in eras after the affairs they report.[142] For some scholars, such as in the studies of Brevard Childs and Richard Nelson, the diffuse attestation of this terminology indicated that it was used by multiple individuals who employed it as a stock expression in different literary works across time, inserted as a gloss when older features or practices were still distinguishable.[143] Others viewed the expression as more restricted in agency and scope, anchored to a late Iron Age context and derived from only a few, or perhaps one hand, often in conjunction with a larger literary project connected to Deuteronomistic language and concerns.[144]

But more important for our purposes is what this language suggests about the temporal attributes of the ruins described. Above all, the saying "to this day" has to do with a sense of proximity. By attaching this phrase to references set back in time, what the speaker of these parentheticals indexes is the present reality of past affairs that were visible in their material remains, effectively situating phenomena from previous events, or at least the possible experience of them, into the period of the speaker's present.[145] So in the Book of Judges

---

[141] For an overview of the history of scholarship on this phrase, see Jeffrey Geoghegan, *Time, Place, and Purpose*, 9–41.

[142] Spinoza, for example, argues against Mosaic authorship of the Torah on the basis of this phrase, among other considerations. Benedict De Spinoza, *Theological-Political Treatise*, ed. J. Israel, trans. M. Silverthorne and J. Israel (Cambridge: Cambridge University Press, 2007), VIII: 3, 121.

[143] Brevard Childs, "A Study of the Formula, 'Until this Day,'" *Journal of Biblical Literature* 82.3 (1963): 279–92; Richard Nelson, *The Double Redaction of the Deuteronomistic History* (Sheffield: JSOT Press, 1981), 23–25.

[144] On the late Iron Age provenance of this expression in the Book of Kings, see already Abraham Kuenen, *Historisch-kritische Einleitung in die Bücher des alten Testaments*, Band 1 (Leipzig: Otto Schulze, 1892), 90–91; and Julius Wellhausen, *Die Composition des Hexateuchs und der historischen Bücher des alten Testaments*, 3rd ed. (Berlin: De Gruyter, 1899), 298–99. In contrast to Childs's theory of multiple authorship, an argument for a single writer and time period for this expression is found in the more recent work of Geoghegan, *Time, Place, and Purpose*, 141–52.

[145] From a comparative angle, see the rich study of οὗτος in Egbert Bakker, "Homeric ΟΥΤΟΣ and the Poetics of Deixis," *Classical Philology* 94.1 (1999): 1–19.

we read, "Then Gideon built an altar there to Yahweh and called it 'Yahweh is peace.' *To this day it is still* (עד היום הזה עודנו) at Ophrah, which belongs to the Abiezrites" (Judges 6:24). Through the use of such deictic expressions, something of the past comes to occupy the present in this report, narrowing the distance between when certain stories once took place and the era of the speaker through statements regarding the *hic et nunc* of what remains. There is an immediacy to 'Ai's conquest because *to this day* the ruins from this event are still perceptible, its desolation (שממה) still available to be visited and seen (Josh 8:28), as are the stones placed on the body of the city's executed king, raised at the entrance of the city gate (Josh 8:29). Though the speaker of these glosses is at some remove from the period when 'Ai was razed and its ruler hung, the phrase עד היום הזה attests to the continued presence of what happened long ago. Crucially, something of the past itself, of the material remains of previous occurrences mundane or divine, is encountered in the present through the speaker's insistence that certain traces have persisted "to this day."

The redactional history of this phrase further underscores its appeal to proximity. In light of its appearance across a number of separate biblical books and its affiliation with Deuteronomistic language and concerns, the expression "to this day" was likely not original to the older stories told that now include it.[146] Instead, this saying was layered into independent, older accounts at a later time in order to draw attention to the existence of particular phenomena referred to in more venerable tales.[147] Through such parentheticals, the settings of older stories were reframed by linking them to the present. If the twelve stones set up in the Jordan River were erected in a more distant past, witnessing to where the ark was once held while the Israelites crossed its embankments (Josh 4:1–9), they nevertheless persist as a visible reminder of divine deliverance "to this day" for those who still visit this crossing of the waterway. The ruins of a Baal temple in Samaria, turned into a latrine by Jehu in generations prior, can be seen "to this day," preserving the remnants of the apostasies once committed there (2 Kings 10:27). The boulders of Achan's burial mound can be located in the Valley of Achor "to this day," once more drawing attention to past moments of infidelity and perdition that endured (Josh 7:26). The rhetorical strategy employed in these later glosses is thus exercised to give the impression of contemporaneity, drawing attention to a

---

[146] See, for example, Richard Nelson, *Joshua: A Commentary* (Louisville, KY: Westminster John Knox, 1997), 10; Mordechai Cogan and Hayim Tadmor, *II Kings* (New York: Doubleday, 1988), 36, 96, 193–94. For overviews of the expression's redactional history, see again Childs, "Until this Day," 284–90, and the lengthy redactional survey in Geoghegan, *Time, Place, Purpose*, 66–95.

[147] The interjection of this formula, Childs observes, serves as "an archaeological note that expresses the extension in time of a past phenomenon into the present." Childs, "Until this Day," 282.

past that informs current practices and communal identity by way of the ruins that remain.[148] Or, as Egbert Bakker writes of the similar use of temporal deixis in Homeric epic, such language foregrounds a "past that is alive thanks to the power of words that can reveal its presence."[149]

But, rather than Homer, more frequent recourse has been made by scholars to Herodotus for comparative studies of this expression. The reason for doing so stems from language in the *Histories* that finds a close resemblance to the "to this day" of biblical narrative, voiced in the formula of "to/until my time" (ἐς ἐμέ, ἐπ ἐμεῦ, μέχρις ἐμέο) that is used in conjunction with older phenomena still current when Herodotus was active.[150] In Book II of the *Histories*, for example, Herodotus reports that two wooden statues dedicated at the Heraion of Samos by the Egyptian ruler Amasis (Pharaoh Ahmose II) "were *still* standing in the great temple behind the doors *in my time*" (ἔτι καὶ τὸ μέχρι ἐμεῦ [Hdt. 2.182]), or roughly a century after Amasis would have sent his gift. As is so often the case with Herodotus, information about the past taken from others is judged in this account as to its validity, here by way of empirical evidence that can be drawn on to support certain claims. In this instance, older reports about Amasis' diplomatic relations with Greek polities are reliable because Herodotus himself claims to have seen the statues of the Egyptian ruler still standing during his travels. What Herodotus offers his audience in these moments is the language of testimony and demonstration, as Rosalind Thomas observes, in the service of persuasion.[151] One can trust elements of Herodotus' story because he claims to have witnessed what he relates.

Perhaps, as Childs concludes, something similar is at work in the biblical usage of "to this day."[152] Underpinning this expression would be a desire for authentication, articulated to confirm the reliability of older stories through the speaker's testimony that physical remnants of this past can still be encountered. But a key difference between Herodotus' statements and those of the biblical narrator is the use of the first-person voice. Certain phenomena persist

---

[148] "Specifically," Geoghegan writes in a similar vein, the author "takes the opportunity afforded him by the interruption of his source to insert additional material reflecting his own historical circumstances and religio-political perspective." Geoghegan, *Time, Place, Purpose*, 144.

[149] Bakkert, "Poetics of Deixis," 17.

[150] In Herodotus, this phrase occurs twenty-one times. For a trenchant discussion of its usage in conjunction with material remains, see Karen Bassi, *Traces of the Past: Classics between History & Archaeology* (Ann Arbor: University of Michigan Press, 2016), 106–43. Later Greek writers emulated this phrase, especially Pausanias. On this usage, see Christian Habicht, *Pausanias' Guide to Ancient Greece* (Berkeley: University of California Press, 1986), 176–80.

[151] Rosalind Thomas, *Herodotus in Context: Ethnography, Science, and the Art of Persuasion* (Cambridge: Cambridge University Press, 2000), 168–212.

[152] "We can conclude," Childs writes, "that the biblical formula ... is a formula of personal testimony added to, and confirming, a received tradition." Childs, "Until this Day," 292. For a similar conclusion, see Geoghegan, *Time, Place, Purpose*, 143–44.

until "my" time, as Herodotus puts it, centering this experience decidedly within the specific era that Herodotus occupies (i.e., the fifth century BCE). In contrast, the biblical language of "to this day" cannot be linked to any identifiable speaking subject or their time period, obscuring a central feature of deixis itself: namely, to provide information regarding the particular situation and perspective a speaker inhabits.[153] What is so distinctive about the biblical phrase "to this day" is that it belongs to no one we can name, and therefore to no specific day we can identify.[154]

Rather than the language of personal testimony, then, the proximity evoked through the biblical "to this day" is something set apart from what Herodotus and later Greek writers claim. Unable to identify the biblical writers by name or location, what results from this anonymity is a duration of time attached to "this day" that cannot be delimited by any point of reference. Jeffrey Geoghegan's cogent arguments that the speaker of these glosses resided predominantly in a late Iron Age world are significant, from this perspective, not necessarily in what they conclude but rather in the lengths to which a scholar must go for these arguments to be won.[155] At the very outset of his work, Herodotus explicitly names the narrator of his account (himself) and from where he descends (Halicarnassus). But only through careful historical scrutiny of subtle clues can we theorize the possible location and time in which the speaker or speakers of the biblical phrase may reside, so hidden are they from view. The jarring effect of this anonymity is that the deictic "this day" resists being linked to any explicit temporal horizon. "This day" can therefore designate any present moment when this expression is uttered, even our own. The pillar that Absalom fashioned "is called 'The Monument of Absalom' to this day" (2 Sam 18:18) – to the day that is this one: today.

Of course, we are aware that these are ancient writings composed long ago, and, though there is a Monument of Absalom that stands outside of Jerusalem today, historically speaking it is a product of the first century CE and not the

---

[153] From this perspective, such parentheticals draw near to the domain of what A. Banfield terms "represented speech and thought." By this expression, Banfield distinguishes between "another moment behind the PRESENT moment of the act of utterance – the moment represented by NOW and which is realized grammatically by the present time adverbs. This is the moment of the act of consciousness, the moment in which the SELF is thinking, the moment of the *cogito*." This NOW, Banfield further remarks, is "the reference point of the present and future time deictics." Ann Banfield, *Unspeakable Sentences: Narration and Representation in the Language of Fiction*, 2nd ed. (New York: Routledge, 2015), 99.

[154] It may be that the problem of deixis raised here is a consequence of an aboriginal performative context to these stories, where the storyteller once represented the missing clues of deixis bodily, relating to an audience who were present when a story was recounted. But absent this storyteller, the time and place of deixis become suspended in written narrative prose.

[155] Geoghegan, *Time, Place, Purpose*, 66–95.

tenth century BCE.[156] But if we were to bracket our historical perspectives and take this expression at face value, what it registers is an experience of material remains held in common, where "this day" is the present one. There is a pronounced sense of presence in this language about ruins, in other words, a presence that envelops the time of the audience and that of the speaker with the remains of incidents that are otherwise past. The time exemplified in "to this day" is resolutely now, its references existing at this time and not another, coincident with the speaker and those who are the audience of what is spoken. It may be that we were not at Jericho when Elisha purified a poisoned spring, but something of this prophetic act performed long ago can still be experienced "to this day" by drinking from the water (2 Kings 2:22), connecting us bodily to a past that, apart from this experience, has long since vanished.

In light of the archaeological evidence retraced above, what is striking about this language of presence and ruination is how it reflects the visible material remains that existed when these texts were composed. As with Herodotus, we cannot know exactly what the speakers of these expressions saw and whether they were indeed familiar with what is portrayed. The ruins of 'Ai are still visible today, but most of the references associated with this expression – the Temple of Baal, Gideon's altar – have not been identified. But what the language of "to this day" signifies more broadly is an awareness of a landscape where past individuals and events could still be experienced in the present through the debris left behind. Archaeological evidence suggests that this awareness was awakened by a lived reality, an embeddedness in a terrain where encounters with ruins and the stories connected to them were frequent.

In such passages, ruins have more to do with the present than the past for the speaker who refers to them. There is little in these remarks that resembles Herodotus' reflections on the reliability of older λόγοι and the evidence that artifacts afford, such as when Herodotus labels certain Egyptian stories "nonsense" (φλυηρέοντες) because Herodotus claims to have examined the monuments mentioned by his informants and has come to different conclusions about their past (Hdt. 2.131). Nor do these observations prompt considerations of how ruins corresponded to different ways of life in former times, as when Pausanias, passing by an old palace in Sparta during his travels, comments on how the building was once purchased through the commodities of oxen since no coinage had yet been developed in the city at the time of its sale (Paus. 3.12.3). Rather, what matters about ruins in these biblical texts is that they continue to exist into the here and now. Or, to put it differently, what is meaningful about ruins are the attachments they provide with previous eras, how their physical remains disclose a past that can still somehow be

---

[156] Rachel Hachlili, *Jewish Funerary Customs, Practices and Rites in the Second Temple Period* (Leiden: Brill, 2005), 30–34.

experienced in the present. The temporality of ruins referred to in these passages is residual and durative, arresting the typical flow of time that distances former moments from the present.[157] Rachel's death long ago can still be experienced in the ruins that remain, her presence felt in the sounds of weeping and the sense of stone.

But this experience of presence and material remains within the Hebrew Bible is more pervasive than what these parentheticals alone would suggest. In addition, there are a number of other biblical references to tangible phenomena that are depicted as visible and lasting, akin to what Karen Bassi terms "protoarchaeological" narratives within ancient Greek writings that foreground specific material objects in their accounts of the past.[158] Already in the opening chapters of Genesis, for example, Noah and Abraham build altars (מצבח) (Gen 8:20, 12:7–8, 13:18), as do Jacob (Gen 33:20, 35:1–7) and Moses after them (Ex 17:15, 24:4), frequently in conjunction with theophanies that occur at specific locations that would have been familiar to later audiences: "Then God said to Jacob, 'Arise, go up to Bethel and settle there, and fashion there an altar to God [ועשה שם מזבח לאל], who appeared to you when you were fleeing your brother Esau'" (Gen 35:1).[159] Later, Joshua builds an altar to Yahweh on Mt. Ebal when the Israelites enter Canaan (Josh 8:30), followed by altars constructed by Samuel at his hometown of Ramah (1 Sam 7:17) and Saul somewhere in the fields of Ephraim after battle with Philistine forces (1 Sam 14:35). When Transjordanian tribes build an altar of "great size and appearance" near the Jordan River (Josh 22:10), war is avoided only when its builders explain that it was not meant to rival the altar established at Shiloh but instead serves only as a "witness" of solidarity and loyalty to Yahweh (Josh 22:27–28). References to the building of altars are, in fact, ubiquitous in the biblical storytelling.[160] Nearly all major figures in biblical narrative, from David (2 Sam 24:21) to Elijah (1 Kings 18:30) to even Joshua and Zerubabbel in the Persian period (Ezra 3:2), engage in the construction of altars at some point in

---

[157] From this perspective, the temporal (adverbial) deixis in these accounts performs an effect similar to the first- and second-person voice of Deuteronomy, where events in the past are recast into the audience's present: "It was not with our ancestors that Yahweh made this covenant, *but with us, with all of us who are alive here today*" (Deut 5:3). As Banfield notes, "The similarity in the behavior of deictic adverbs and first and second person pronouns should be obvious; indeed, the latter are usually classed with deictics because they also are referred to the speech act for interpretation." Banfield, *Unspeakable Sentences*, 27.

[158] Bassi, *Traces of the Past*, 2.

[159] As Chavel notes, "Nothing conveys the permanence of an altar, its resistance to decomposition, as the largest, dressed stones that give it its smooth, weather-resistant, unfazed surface, which by extension, intimates the longevity of the deity present at the altar, served by it, and therefore in need of it to last." Simeon Chavel, "A Kingdom of Priests and Its Earthen Altars in Exodus 19–24," *Vetus Testamentum* 65 (2015): 169–222; 181.

[160] Elizabeth LaRocca-Pitts, *"Of Wood and Stone": The Significance of Israelite Cultic Items in the Bible and Its Early Interpreters* (Winona Lake, IN: Eisenbrauns, 2001), 230–49.

their lives.[161] What these stories intimate, accordingly, are narrative worlds where old altars are scattered throughout, some in more remote settings of hilltops and pathways, others within settlements themselves.

To these items can be added the frequent biblical descriptions of stone pillars (מצבה).[162] In certain stories, these pillars represent divine presence.[163] When Jacob awakens from a dream theophany, for example, "He took the stone that he had put under his head and set it up for a pillar and poured oil on the top of it" – an act done to signify that "Yahweh is in this place" (Gen 28:18, 16). Like altars, biblical references to sacred pillars are widespread, including Isaiah's prophecy that one day a pillar to Yahweh will be stationed on the border to the land of Egypt (Is 19:19) and Hosea's association of sacred pillars with other cultic items used for the worship of Yahweh that had been suspended (Hosea 3:4). But elsewhere, pillars are associated with older Canaanite practices that are proscribed, including the burning of a "pillar of Baal" in Samaria (2 Kings 10:26). When the Israelites come into the land of Canaan, Yahweh instructs the people to "smash their [residents of Canaan] pillars" (Deut 7:5), echoing the charge in Ex 23:24 to "utterly destroy and completely demolish" the pillars of the residents of Canaan. Later, the apostasies committed in Israel and Judah are connected explicitly to the continued use of sacred pillars into the final days of these kingdoms, suggesting that the attempt to outlaw these sacred objects met limited success (1 Kings 14:23; 2 Kings 27:10).

Standing stones also appear elsewhere in biblical storytelling, representing entities other than deities. In Ex 24:4, Moses sets up twelve pillars, "corresponding to the twelve tribes of Israel," in a covenant ceremony at the base of Sinai, and it may be, as Elizabeth Bloch-Smith observes, that the twelve stones established by Joshua on the Jordan River perform a similar representational function for the Israelite tribes (Josh 4:5).[164] In addition to collectives, individuals are also wedded to what these pillars embody, including Rachel and the pillar connected to Absalom, the latter constructed because the prince had "no son to keep my remembrance" (2 Sam 18:18).[165] The equivalence between the description of Absalom's pillar (מצבה) and its status as a monument (יד) in this verse suggests that the further monuments set up by Saul at Mt. Carmel (1 Sam 15:12) and David somewhere near "the River" (2 Sam 8:3) may also have been understood as pillars of some type, perhaps reflecting the shapes of

---

[161] Wolfgang Zwickel, "Die Altarbaunotizen im Alten Testament," *Biblica* 73.4 (1992): 533–46; 545.
[162] LaRocca-Pitts, *"Of Wood and Stone,"* 205–28.
[163] Bloch-Smith, "Massebot Standing for Yhwh," 106–10. [164] Ibid., 110.
[165] For a comparative analysis of Absalom's monument in the context of Phoenician and Aramaic practices, see Matthew Suriano, "Remembering Absalom's Death in 2 Samuel 18–19: History, Memory, and Inscription," *Hebrew Bible and Ancient Israel* 7.2 (2018): 172–200.

stelae erected by Egyptian and Assyrian rulers that were known to these writers. The impression left behind from these accounts is once more a terrain dotted with older remnants of these installations, found "in a variety of different settings," Elizabeth LaRocca-Pitts comments, "performing a multitude of functions, and representing traditions which could be sanctioned or condemned depending on the point of view of the author who mentions them."[166]

To these references can be added many other objects that appear in the biblical writings. Some are cultic in nature, such as the *asherim*, or sacred wooden items, that are roundly condemned in these texts, or the worship at high places that is also, in time, prohibited.[167] Other references include older features of the landscape that are less attested but meaningful. The extended narrative devoted to Abraham's purchase of the burial cave from Ephron the Hittite, for example, "in the field of Machpelah, facing Mamre, that is, Hebron" (Gen 23:1–20) provides a detailed description of where the mortuary chamber is located and how it came into the possession of Abraham long ago. In Judges 3:19, Ehud turns back "at the carved stones" (פסילים) of Gilgal on his way to assassinate Eglon, a peculiar reference that perhaps indicates sacred statuary of some kind located at the outskirts of the site, and in Josh 24:26, Joshua sets up a "large stone" under the oak tree of Shechem as a "witness" for the covenant enacted there. In an episode where ruins feature prominently, Josiah spots a gravestone (ציון) among old tombs situated in the hills of Bethel. After being made aware of the prophet who had been interred there three centuries before and what had once been prophesied, the king safeguards the bones from being desecrated (2 Kings 23:17)[168] – an act that preserves the old gravestone alongside those other references to tombs and roadside markers referred to in Ezekiel (Ezek 39:15) and Jeremiah (Jer 31:21).[169]

There is a sense of presence in these portrayals of ruined spaces and artifacts, too, if less explicit than what the speaker of "to this day" describes. For what these stories represent are narrative worlds configured through familiar objects set in familiar terrains, offering accounts of the past that nevertheless have deep affiliations with landscapes that we know, archaeologically, would have been

---

[166] LaRocca-Pitts, 227.

[167] For an overview of these references, see again the extensive and incisive discussion in ibid., 127–204.

[168] On the relationship between past and present in this story, see Victor Matthews, "Josiah at Bethel and the 'Monument' to the Unnamed Prophet from Judah," *Biblical Theology Bulletin* 50.4 (2020): 200–6.

[169] Following the LXX σημεῖα, Jer 48:9 may also refer to grave markers, in place of MT "salt:" "Set up gravestones [MT: salt] for Moab, for they will surely fall; her cities will be desolate with no inhabitants in them."

recognizable to later audiences. Perhaps an Amorite named Abraham once constructed an altar of some type at EBA Hebron. But for writings first composed over a thousand years later, what is more significant about the biblical portrayal of Abraham's actions is how such artifacts were commonplace well into the Iron Age and after, fashioned at a location that retained its regional importance into these much later periods. By populating their stories with objects and spaces that were still part of their audiences' surroundings, these narratives of distant times became more proximate, more intimate to the experiences of those who lived in later contexts. The "qualities of a life-world" portrayed in such accounts, as Rita Felski writes of this mimetic act expressed in literature, of "texts that draw us into imagined yet referentially salient worlds," offered stories about the past that could resonate with experiences of those who came after.[170] When audiences in antiquity entered into the narratives of an Abraham or a David that the biblical writers devised, the references to familiar landscapes within them suggested that these past worlds were still their own, drawing near to their own lived experiences and settings.

From this vantage point, it is not an accident of discovery that older objects referred to in biblical narrative retain connections with what archaeologists have unearthed in the lands of the southern Levant. Refracted within biblical stories about the past were images of present landscapes and the practices shaped by them, of terrains that we know were dotted with material remains that these narratives also represent. The point of drawing attention to these associations is not a positivistic but a phenomenological one, focalized so as to better understand the experiences that informed how past incidents and individuals were portrayed at moments in the biblical corpus. When examining the biblical writings through this lens, it is a sense of presence that once more prevails: Joshua builds an altar like those that were still visible throughout the highlands when these writings were composed; Jacob erects a pillar of stone as inhabitants of the Levant had done for millennia when representing divine encounters; Saul sets up a monument in a manner that resembles actions undertaken by Egyptian and Neo-Assyrian rulers for centuries in the eastern Mediterranean region. The passing of time intimated through these references is of a duration in which much is held in common, and much stays the same.

The material presence of the past drawn out through archaeological research encounters in these narratives a presence evoked through storytelling. Through such accounts, the biblical writers reinforced points of affiliation with a past that would under other conditions have been lost, an affiliation captured in references to familiar artifacts embedded in the landscape or in phrases that expressly identified ruins that continued to exist in the here and

---

[170] Rita Felski, *The Uses of Literature* (Malden, MA: Blackwell, 2008), 89, 104.

now. Much as the physical existence of ruins offered possible attachments with previous incidents and individuals, so too, then, did narratives that represented a more distant past in ways that retained meaningful associations with the present.

3.2.1 Ruins and the Phenomenology of Presence

But such impressions of ruins are not the biblical writers' alone. In a growing body of historical theory, scholars have turned to potential affiliations discerned between material remains and what has been termed the phenomenon of presence.[171] A touchstone for these discussions is Georg Simmel's essay on ruination, discussed in the Introduction, in which it is claimed that material remains convey a presence that is perceived directly (*unmittelbar anschauliche Gegenwart*) and unencumbered by other associations.[172] This sense of immediacy is brought about by the physical encounter with older material forms, Simmel writes, in which "the ruin creates the present form of past life, not according to the contents or remnants of that life, but according to its past as such."[173] In the ruin we experience something of the past itself, Simmel contends, described as an "extreme intensification and fulfillment"[174] of a former reality that is summoned through our contact with what has been left behind. "In this fragment we hold in our hand," Simmel remarks, "we preside in spirit over the entire timespan since its inception, the past with its destinies and transformations gathered into this instant of a present."[175] In keeping with those biblical texts examined above, for Simmel ruins were more than repositories of a static, inanimate past, but were apertures for previous lives to enter into our present, occasioning an "unlimited impressionability" (*unbegrenzte Beeindruckbarkeit*)[176] for those who experienced them. In this telling, ruins are dynamic and allusive, "seizing" the onlooker and placing them into a state where past and present "coalesce into a unified form."[177]

The experience of presence expressed in Simmel's essay has been at the center of a number of more recent studies. Perhaps the most rigorous treatment of this phenomenon stems from Frank Ankersmit, who, in a series of monographs and essays, has argued for the necessity of the experiential for historical thought and practice, a proposal deeply wedded to what Ankersmit also characterizes as a sense of presence. To further articulate what this

---

[171] So Ahlskog begins his recent study with the remark, "'Presence' is arguably the most discussed notion in contemporary philosophy of history." Jonas Ahlskog, "R. G. Collingwood and the Presence of the Past," *Journal of the Philosophy of History* 11 (2017): 289–305; 289.
[172] Georg Simmel, "Die Ruine," in *Philosophische Kultur: Gesammelte Essais* (Leipzig: Kröner, 1919), 125–33; 132.
[173] Ibid., 132.   [174] Ibid.   [175] Ibid.   [176] Ibid., 133.   [177] Ibid.

phenomenon portends, Ankersmit turns to the work of a contemporary of Simmel, the Dutch historian Johan Huizinga. In his reflections on the conditions that make historical inquiry possible, Huizinga writes of the importance of having some "contact" with former periods. Huizinga remarks that this experience "can be provoked by a line from a chronicle, by an engraving, a few sounds from an old song," which arouse a feeling or "sensation" in which the distance between a past object and one's own subjectivity is diminished.[178] What compels us to investigate the past, and thus what enables historical thought to unfold, Huizinga contends, is that we feel its presence first – a sensation provoked by the remains of past ages that we are able to experience today.

This sensation of presence, which Huizinga can describe as a moment of "ekstasis" and a "response" to a call,[179] is one that Ankersmit terms a "sublime historical experience," or a feeling in which "the past and the present are momentarily united in a way that is familiar to us in the experience of déjà vu."[180] For Ankersmit, as with Huizinga before him,[181] what often elicits this experience are objects or landscapes in which "the past *itself* has been preserved through all these centuries," such as when Bachhofen entered into an Etruscan burial chamber to study its remains, Ankersmit writes, or when Herder gazed on an old city scene when considering former ways of life.[182] This feeling of the presence of the past, which Ankersmit attributes to an aura (*Hauch*) or atmosphere that envelops an individual, is produced by "objects that are given to us here and now, such as paintings, burial chambers, pieces of furniture, and so on."[183] The presence that we feel in such encounters, the aura of the past that comes to surround us, is an outcome of how "the past can properly be said to be present in the artifacts that it has left us."[184] "Indeed," Ankersmit comments, "these objects are like travelers through time … always bearing in themselves the signs of their origin."[185]

There is, then, an ontological density to the presence described by Ankersmit.[186] It is the past itself, as Ankersmit repeatedly asserts, and not some

---

[178] Johan Huizinga, "De taak der cultuurgeschiedenis," in *Verzamelde Werken*, Vol. 7 (Haarlem: H. D. Tjeenk Willink, 1950), 72. Quoted in Ankersmit, *Sublime Historical Experience*, 120–21.
[179] Huizinga, "De taak der cultuurgeschiedenis," 72.
[180] Ankersmit, *Sublime Historical Experience*, 132.
[181] Huizinga, for his part, envisions a museum curated with simple everyday objects from the past, its sole purpose being the eliciting of various historical sensations that Huizinga believes is necessary for historical thought to unfold.
[182] Ankersmit, *Sublime Historical Experience*, 115. (italics original) [183] Ibid., 115.
[184] Ibid. [185] Ibid.
[186] Ankersmit writes, "Now, sublime historical experience is closer to moods and feelings than to knowledge; like them it is ontological rather than epistemological, and sublime experience is to be defined in terms of what you are rather than in terms of what you know, what knowledge you have." Ibid., 225.

semblance or likeness of it, that one feels in these moments of sublime experience, perceived as a reality that rushes in and overwhelms the individual on whom it descends. This awareness is predominantly visceral and precognitive, Ankersmit comments, registered as a response to an impression of something that affects us bodily.[187] In these moments, it is "as if the temporal trajectory between past and present, instead of separating the two, has become the locus of their encounter," a trajectory that "pulls the faces of past and present together in a short but ecstatic kiss."[188] The alienation that may arise when investigating the past is consequently recast in these moments as a feeling of intimacy. "Think," Ankersmit remarks, "of the embrace of Romeo and Juliet."[189]

The presence of the past found in Simmel's description of the ruin meets, in these passages from Ankersmit, an eros of touch and desire. What is significant for Ankersmit about the experience of presence is not its cognitive or epistemological dimensions, but rather, following Huizinga, its ecstatic potentialities, or the capacity of the reality of the past to break into the present in ways that are felt long before they can be communicated through the historian's research. This feeling, Ankersmit observes, resembles "the moment of enrapture and of being carried away by the intensity of experience."[190] When it occurs, "there is only the past itself," revealing to the individual "its quasi noumenal nakedness with an unusual directness and immediacy."[191] There is something palpable about this presence, productive of a tactile reality that is available to the senses, something that is to be felt and perceived. So Ankersmit underscores the Aristotelian conception of experience to understand this encounter over against later Cartesian models of rationality and empiricism:[192]

> [For] the Aristotle of *De Anima* experience and knowledge are the result of a union, interaction, or even outright identification of the subject and the object of knowledge. The subject may be said to possess (experiential) knowledge of the object if the subject succeeds in achieving a formal (that is, not a material) similarity to the object. One may think here of how our hands may come to "know" the form of an object by following its forms and thus by imitating these forms. Knowledge is, hence, a matter of the subject's being "formed" by the object and of a process in which the object leaves its indelible traces in or on the subject. This conception of knowledge is, obviously, captured far better by what we

---

[187] This affective nature of presence is also emphasized by Runia: "Floating through the here and now, this presence of the past also makes me *feel* things, *think* things, and *do* things," some that "are at odds with who I think I am." Eelco Runia, "Spots of Time," *History and Theory* 45.3 (2006): 305–16; 316.
[188] Ankersmit, *Sublime Historical Experience*, 121. [189] Ibid., 130. [190] Ibid., 121.
[191] Ibid., 125. [192] Ibid., 19. Cf. 29, 124, 130–31, 248.

associate with the sense of touch than with the sense of sight ... In this tradition experience articulates itself in how we are *formed* by it.

The presence of the past is, on this view, an affective and embodied encounter, a product of an "interaction" that takes hold of a subject and imprints itself on the senses, often by way of the physical remains that reveal it. "Think again of feeling the form of a vase that we hold in our hands," Ankersmit writes of this encounter,[193] where it is the sensation of physical contact that once more predominates. "We experience reality in the sense of touch – for love is something that you do with your fingers, your mouth, and so on, isn't it?"[194]

Ankersmit's writings return us to questions of temporality and ruination that the biblical writings also evoke. Significant about material remains within this theoretical framework is how they arouse a sensation of the past in the here and now, of a presence mediated bodily through the physical traces that endure. What this sense of presence conveys is an aura or an atmosphere of moods and feelings, an experience that beckons the individual, in Huizinga's language, to cast about in the remains of former periods. Among these theorists, there is a "coalescence" or "union" of the past and present in such moments of encounter, a perception of a "present form of past life" as Simmel describes it. Here, phenomenology prevails over epistemology, sensuality over abstract reflection. The presence of the past is something we feel before we rationalize it, drawing near to us in a manner that, only afterward, compels our attempts to grasp it in thought.

For our purposes, what these studies provide is an alternative vantage point to what is often proposed for why the biblical writers refer to the ruins that they do. To Childs, for example, the reason the biblical writers allude to the continued existence of certain ruins "to this day" is to "confirm" older traditions, and, like their Greek contemporaries, "to validate some aspect of the tradition which can still be verified in [their] own time."[195] Geoghegan largely concurs with Childs's perspective, connecting it to a "similar historical impulse" and manner of "historical appeal" found elsewhere in texts imprinted with Deuteronomistic language and concerns.[196] From the perspective held by these scholars, the biblical writers refer to ruins for purposes that resemble the efforts of many archaeologists and biblical scholars today. For those in antiquity, on this view, ruins are significant because they hold the potential to demonstrate the historical validity of past claims communicated in older stories.

But what the theorists of presence provide is a different framework for understanding why the biblical writings speak of ruins in ways that foreground

---

[193] Ibid., 131. [194] Ibid. [195] Childs, "Until this Day," 292, 291.
[196] Geoghegan, *Time, Place, Purpose*, 143–44.

their visibility and meaningfulness in the present. Rather than a desire to verify past incidents conveyed in older accounts, a key reason for drawing attention to certain remains is that the pasts attached to them continued to be experienced into the later eras in which stories about them were written down. By describing a landscape marked by the physical remains of past incidents, the biblical writers indexed the continuing presence of a past otherwise lost, offering the possibility of having some contact – to Rachel's life, to 'Ai's conquest, to where the ark once stood – with former individuals and occurrences. In a world absent our forms of representation, our museums, archives, libraries, or sites of heritage, the possibility of drawing near to former periods is instead maintained in these accounts by way of references to certain ruins that still were present, still available to be visited and observed. Archaeological evidence further supports these theoretical insights, demonstrating that the landscapes the biblical writers knew were ones where remains from previous centuries were not only familiar but actively engaged and managed for life in the present. Ruins were sites of possible encounters with pasts that endured, whether they were experienced in the tangible landscapes in which these accounts were written or in the stories themselves that were told.

The advantage of this turn toward a theory of presence, then, is that it provides an analytic more attuned to the archaeological and biblical evidence we possess. For Iron Age Judahites drawn to the bench tombs of the recently deceased or the communities at Aphek and Hazor, who intentionally avoided the ruined precincts that were located within their settlements, a theory that accents an embodied, auratic sense of presence provides a richer historical understanding of what would have predominated in these practices, as it does for those Egyptian and Assyrian rulers who erected monuments at places to which they would never return, asserting their presence even though they would be bodily absent from these locations forevermore. Similarly, when we read of the mourners traveling to the Jerusalem temple after its destruction (Jer 41:5) or of the divine mandate forbidding the rebuilding of settlements burned down because of their apostasy (Deut 13:16), it is once more an awareness of the presence of the past that appears more paramount for an understanding of these activities than a quest for the historical verification of prior affairs.

§

"With Napoleon's occupation of Egypt," Edward Said writes, "processes were set in motion between East and West that still dominate our contemporary cultural and political perspectives."[197] The aftermath of the French invasion at the cusp of the nineteenth century CE continued to be felt into the present,

---

[197] Edward Said, *Orientalism* (New York: Vintage, 1978), 42.

Said observes, its means of domination and exploitation, "both antihuman and persistent,"[198] preserved in the reification of cultural attitudes and institutions still with us, including in the realm of politics where colonial mindsets have not been easily disenthralled. The imposing monument to this subordination was the *Description de l'Égypte*, Said comments, "that great collective appropriation of one country by another,"[199] where in its preface J. B. Joseph Fourier writes of redeeming a people "plunged into barbarism" through the efforts of the French savants who studied these lands.[200] By means as aggressive as any military assault, the *Description,* Said contends, was produced "to feel oneself as a European in command, almost at will, of Oriental history, time, and geography" and to "dignify all the knowledge collected during colonial occupation with the title 'contribution to modern learning.'"[201]

The presence of the past is felt acutely in these remarks.[202] But this sense of presence departs from Ankersmit's descriptions of desire where the inbreaking of the past is greeted as a lover, long awaited and fully embraced. For Said, the continuing presence of a colonial past was harrowing rather than redemptive, bearing the lingering effects of subjugation in a manner that, in many ways, has deeper connections to the world the biblical writers knew and their own experiences of foreign subjection.[203] The language of longing expressed in Ankersmit's work is complicated in these passages from Said by a presence stamped instead with impressions of suffering and alarm, unwanted but unrelenting.

Historians, too, have expressed their discomfort with theories of presence. How a sublime experience of the past actually ensues, Gabrielle Spiegel remarks, "is somewhat unclear, at least to those of us who have yet to partake of it,"[204] and charges of quasi-religious undercurrents – of a "mystical, mythical and arguably not even historical" sensibility[205] – to Ankersmit's theory have been leveled, if roundly denied.[206] Yet as Spiegel observes, what could be diminished in this approach is a sensitivity toward the otherness of the past, in which the acute differences that separate past and present are muted, even

---

[198] Ibid., 44. [199] Ibid., 84. [200] Quoted in Ibid., 85. [201] Ibid., 86.
[202] Writing of the Orientalist project, Said comments that its "scope, as much as its institutions and all-pervasive influence, lasts up to the present." Ibid., 44.
[203] See, for example, Shawn Aster, *Reflections of Empire in Isaiah 1–39: Responses to Assyrian Ideology* (Atlanta: SBL Press, 2017); Mario Liverani, *Assyria: The Imperial Mission*, trans. Andrea Trameri and Jonathan Valk (Winona Lake, IN: Eisenbrauns, 2017); Jessie DeGrado, "Authoring Empire: Intellectual Engagement with the Neo-Assyrian Empire in the Bible" (Ph.D. diss., University of Chicago, 2018).
[204] Spiegel, "Limits of Empiricism," 16.
[205] Peter Icke, *Frank Ankersmit's Lost Historical Cause: A Journey from Language to Experience* (New York: Routledge, 2011), 6.
[206] Ankersmit, anticipating these charges, responds to certain features of these issues in *Sublime Historical Experience*, 115, 121–23.

intentionally so.[207] In the attempt to solicit the past and be enraptured by it in the here and now, the bounds that divide the two can be dissolved, its critics argue, producing historical claims that are simply the current experiences and inclinations of the historian who makes them.[208] If an awareness of the "temporalization of history" and its concomitant perception of the discontinuities that mark the passing of time structures modern historical thought, to return once more to Koselleck's work,[209] then how the feeling of presence informs this mode of inquiry is uncertain.[210] The momentary "union" of past and present that is claimed in the feeling of sublime experience would threaten to produce histories riddled with anachronisms, in which the historian's subjectivity would become so intertwined with the past represented as to be indistinguishable from it.

But such concerns were not those of the biblical writers.[211] Rather, the biblical writings anticipate recent theories of presence, I argue, by repeatedly drawing attention to how past realities persist into the present by way of their material remains. Through the anonymous parentheticals of "to this day" and depictions of ruins that were part of familiar landscapes to later audiences, the distance between past and present in biblical storytelling was often narrowed. Herodotus and Pausanias will at moments clarify when they come across certain ruins and how they came to be identified, thereby locating themselves and the ruins they detail in time. But not the scribes behind the Hebrew Bible.

---

[207] Spiegel, "Limits of Empiricism," 16; Anton Froeyman, "Frank Ankersmit and Eelco Runia: The Presence and the Otherness of the Past," *Rethinking History* 16.3 (2012): 393–414; 406–13.

[208] In other words, theories of presence can lead to the old charge of "presentism" in historical research. On this discussion, see Elizabeth Clark, *History, Theory, Text: Historians and the Linguistic Turn* (Cambridge, MA: Harvard University Press, 2004), 19–22, 107–12, 119–21; François Hartog, *Regimes of Historicity: Presentism and Experiences of Time* (New York: Columbia: 2015), 107–19; 193–204.

[209] Reinhart Koselleck, *Futures Past: On the Semantics of Historical Time*, trans. K. Tribe (New York: Columbia University Press, 2004), 11, 40, 137–42.

[210] If Altdorfer's painting of the *Alexanderschlacht* is meaningful for Koselleck because of how within it "the past and the present were enclosed in one historical plane," evoking a sense of "timelessness" (Koselleck, *Futures Past*, 10), a theory of presence appears to draw near to these premodern sensibilities. Ankersmit, for his part, does not deflect this possibility: His project "can be seen both as a moving beyond historism and *as a comeback to what antedated historism.*" Ankersmit, *Sublime Historical Experience*, 14. (my italics)

[211] Nor are they Ankersmit's. The histories of Burckhardt or Michelet are classics, Ankersmit asserts, precisely because of their subjective interests and Romantic longings, and not in spite of them. Rather, the danger is the reverse: "Does not historical experience aim at the union of subject and object, of present and past, whereas professionalized historical writing stakes everything on pulling them apart as much as possible?" Ankersmit, *Sublime Historical Experience*, 170. It is, then, the professional discipline of history itself that should cause concern: "We should be more aware of the historical world we lost when revolutionizing historical writing with its professionalization than we have been up to now." Ibid., 173.

Absent such information, difficulties arise for modern historians who study the biblical writings. Certain biblical references, such as those that allude to Rachel's Tomb, situate these remains at different geographic locations in the Hebrew Bible,[212] while other descriptions, such as the ruins of 'Ai, refer to a destruction that we know, archaeologically, did not occur when these texts suggest they did.[213] The interest in ruins that these writings undeniably express is something that departs, then, from what typically informs how historians approach ruins today.

Rather than exhibiting curiosity regarding the evidence material remains afford about times past, impressions of ruins in the biblical passages examined in this study draw nearer, I contend, to a temporality of presence, or to a past that is experienced as something immediate and lasting through the vestiges that remain. In contrast to our assessment of ruins that are suggestive of a past at odds with the present – that is, older architectural forms that fall out of fashion, ritual spaces to strange gods no longer worshipped – the biblical writings repeatedly foreground remains that are instead contemporary and recognizable to the practices of later communities. In the Book of Genesis, Jacob does not enter into the migdal temple at Shechem to worship Canaanite deities, as we would expect Bronze Age contemporaries might, but instead fashions altars that were familiar to audiences located centuries in the future. Instead of drawing on Egyptian amulets or participating in cultic innovations spurred by contact with Egyptian culture, as manifested prominently at LBA Lachish and its Fosse Temple,[214] Moses, though situated in this era of Egyptian influence in the biblical writings, instead establishes pillars at the base of Sinai in a display still recognizable to those who lived in later contexts. In these narrative worlds, the cadence of time slows through the depiction of certain spaces and artifacts, tempered by way of references in which the symmetries in lived experience take precedence over the discontinuities that, on the basis of the archaeological evidence, we might think should prevail. That individuals did not dig among the ruins in ancient Israel and Judah to learn about the communities who preceded them is, therefore, consistent with a sense of presence that ruins evoke in these writings. There is little impetus to dig when the past is believed to cohere so closely with experiences of life in the present.

The theme of presence examined in this chapter finds some semblance, then, with the study of memory[215] in Chapter 2. In both, a different

---

[212] On this dilemma, see Benjamin Cox and Susan Ackerman, "Rachel's Tomb," *Journal of Biblical Literature* 128.1 (2009): 135–48.

[213] On 'Ai, see again the discussion in Chapter 2.

[214] Ido Koch, "Religion at Lachish under Egyptian Colonialism," *Die Welt des Orients* 49.2 (2019): 161–82.

[215] This point is made explicit by Casey: "Places possess us – in perception, as in memory – by their radiant visibility insinuating themselves into our lives, seizing and surrounding us, even

relationship to ruins and time emerges apart from our current practices of excavation and historical study. Among the experiences of ruins drawn out from the Hebrew Bible in these studies, we find a present that is deeply connected with a past, a connection reinforced by remains that suggest abiding symmetries between past and present. If the transitional period of the *Sattelzeit* (ca. 1750–1850 CE) is, for Koselleck, defined by an overwhelming sense of acceleration that fractures present experiences from those of the past, as discussed in Chapter 1, the biblical writings often represent this relationship in a manner that is the reverse, where ruins are manifestations of continuity rather than rupture.

It may be that what is sacrificed in these sibling experiences of memory and presence is a more robust historical understanding of former ways of life. The staggering gains made in what we know of antiquity through historical modes of inquiry cannot be denied, a research program whose successes have been spurred by a curiosity about the differences that separate our age from those that came before.[216] Historical knowledge is often built on a sense of distance, this is to say, and not contemporaneity.[217] Through these research methods our current knowledge of the ancient landscapes and practices, languages and lifeways of those behind the biblical writings surpasses that of any of our predecessors, being far more precise and detailed, in fact, than what even the biblical writers knew of their own dialects, geography, and past.

Nevertheless, Said's coupling of "all the knowledge collected" with the processes of "colonial occupation" is directed at this work, too, and especially the research of those of us who study the lands of the Levant in ways that cannot be easily disentangled from what once compelled the *Description de l'Égypte*.[218] A similar protest is voiced in the work of Dipesh Chakrabarty: "Insofar as the academic discourse of history – that is, 'history' as a discourse produced at the institutional site of the university – is concerned, 'Europe' remains the sovereign, theoretical subject of all histories, including ones we call

---

taking us over as we sink into their presence." Edward Casey, *Remembering: A Phenomenological Study*, 2nd ed. (Bloomington: Indiana University Press, 2000), 200.

[216] Peter Fritzsche, *Stranded in the Present: Modern Time and the Melancholy of History* (Cambridge, MA: Harvard University Press, 2004), 104.

[217] On this theme, see especially its discussion in Mark Salber Phillips, *On Historical Distance* (New Haven, CT: Yale University Press, 2013), esp. 1–24, 115–39.

[218] On this point, see also Frederick Cooper, *Colonialism in Question: Theory, Knowledge, History* (Berkeley: University of California Press, 2005); Margarita Díaz-Andreu, *A World History of Nineteenth-Century Archaeology: Nationalism, Colonialism, and the Past* (Oxford: Oxford University Press, 2007); Michael Dietler, *Archaeologies of Colonialism: Consumption, Entanglement, and Violence in Ancient Mediterranean France* (Berkeley: University of California Press, 2010); Lea Ypi, "Commerce and Colonialism in Kant's Philosophy of History," in *Kant and Colonialism: Historical and Critical Perspectives*, eds. K. Flikschuh and L. Ypi, 99–126 (Oxford: Oxford University Press, 2014).

'Indian,' 'Chinese,' 'Kenyan,' and so on."[219] How to come to terms with a "politics of despair" experienced by those not part of the European project is not addressed. But what is appealed for is "a history that deliberately makes visible, within the very structure of its narrative forms, its own repressive strategies and practices."[220]

---

[219] Dipesh Chakrabarty, "Postcoloniality and the Artifice of History: Who Speaks for 'Indian' Pasts?" *Representations* 37 (1992): 1–26; 1. For a sympathetic and detailed overview of Chakrabarty's work on this theme, see Suman Seth, "The Politics of Despair and the Calling of History," *History and Theory* 56.2 (2017): 241–57.

[220] Chakrabarty, "Postcoloniality," 23.

FOUR

JERUSALEM AND THE RUINS OF TOMORROW

> There, as here, ruin opens
> the tomb, the temple; enter,
> there as here, there are no doors:
>
> the shrine lies open to the sky,
> the rain falls, here, there
> sand drifts; eternity endures:
>
> ruin everywhere, yet as the fallen roof
> leaves the sealed room
> open to the air,
>
> so, through our desolation,
> thoughts stir, inspiration stalks us
> through gloom.[1]

On December 14, 1783, Constantin-François de Chasseboeuf arrived in the city of Aleppo.[2] Following a year of travel in Egypt, Volney – as Constantine-François had come to be known[3] – would spend the next six weeks

---

[1] Hilda Doolittle (H. D.), "The Walls Do Not Fall," in *Trilogy*, 1–60 (New York: New Directions, 1998 [1942]), 1.
[2] For the seminal treatment of Volney's life and travels, see Jean Gaulmier, *L'idéologue Volney, 1757–1820: contribution à l'histoire de l'orientalisme en France* (Geneva: Slatkine, 1980). For a reconstruction of Volney's travels in Syria and Palestine in 1784–1785, see 68–80.
[3] M. Constantine-François Volney, *Voyage en Syrie et en Égypte, pendant les anneés 1783, 1784, et 1785*, Vol. 2 (Paris: Volland, 1787), 138–40. "Volney" was a name taken in honor of Voltaire

chronicling life in the busy Syrian entrepôt, its pistachio orchards and markets of spun cotton making it one of the most beautiful cities, he comments, in all of the Ottoman Empire. After his stay in the merchant city, the Frenchman departed for the coast, shadowing the sea and journeying south until he reached the sites of Tripoli, Beirut, and, finally, Tyre, where he paused for a number of days to reflect on the ancient settlement's remains.[4] Volney then turned inland, crossing through to Tiberias and north to Baalbek and Damascus, before finally descending through Palestine and appearing in Jerusalem sometime in October of 1784.[5] There he remained for approximately a month, recording preparations made for pilgrims who were soon to celebrate the holiday season. The numbers of those traveling to Jerusalem had nevertheless diminished over the years, Volney remarks, especially from Western European lands, where religious piety was steadily declining.[6]

After his time in Jerusalem and regions further south, Volney returned to Acre in early 1785 to set sail across the Mediterranean. Back in Paris, Volney's account of his travels, entitled *Voyage en Syrie et en Égypte*, won a number of admirers when it was published two years later. Among them were Napoleon, who consulted the work during the French invasion of the region in the decade to come, and Volney's close friend Thomas Jefferson, who reviewed the volume warmly and with whom Volney would later stay at Monticello before being expelled by the Adams administration on suspicion of espionage.[7]

But it would be a second work based on Volney's travels that would become his most famous. This book, entitled *The Ruins* (*Les Ruines*),[8] is a volume set apart from the travel report offered in the *Voyage*, made distinct by its contemplative tone and philosophical interests announced in the subtitle, a *méditation sur les révolutions des empires*. Published four years after the *Voyage* and two years following the French Revolution that Volney would help lead as a deputy of the National Assembly, the theme was timely and the book widely

---

who had recently passed away, the name a contraction of Voltaire and Voltaire's famous residence at Ferney.

[4] On the extended discussion of Tyre's ruins, including reflections on their relationship to biblical history, see Ibid., 200–4.

[5] Ibid., 279–80.

[6] Volney writes approvingly that "le zèle des Européens se refroidissant de jour en jour." However, Christians from the East remained enthralled with pilgrimage, Volney observes with some antipathy, much like their Muslim counterparts. Ibid., 284.

[7] Gaulmier, *L'idéologue Volney*, 243–60. Cf. Robert Irwin, "Volney's Meditations on Ruins and Empires," in *Scholarship between Europe and the Levant: Essays in Honour of Alastair Hamilton*, eds. J. Loop and J. Kraye, 299–317 (Leiden: Brill, 2020), 306–8; Gerhard Katschnig, "The Supportive Voice in the Midst of Solitude and Melancholy: Volney's Genie des Tombeaux et des Ruines," *History of European Ideas* 47:6 (2021): 958–73.

[8] M. Constantine-François Volney, *Les Ruines, ou Méditation sur les Révolutions des Empires* (Paris: Desenne, 1791).

read.[9] Percy Shelley would compose a number of poems under its influence, including "Ozymandias" (1818), as would Friedrich Hölderlin, who set his "Lebensalter" (1804) among the remains that Volney describes.[10] In *Frankenstein*, Mary Shelley – whose father, William Godwin, would translate *Les Ruines* into English – has the creature overhear *Les Ruines* read aloud when hidden in the hovel it occupies.[11]

Volney begins *Les Ruines* in the vocative. In a prayer addressed to "solitary ruins, holy tombs, silent walls," an unnamed supplicant opens the work by voicing the sentiments and weighty thoughts that have arisen when visiting the sacred remains of an unidentified ancient site.[12] Soon we learn that the opening prayer is spoken among the remains of Palmyra, an ancient city situated a three-day journey into the formidable Syrian desert from the site of Homs. In a detailed description of the ruined location, Volney writes of the "astonishing" architecture preserved from antiquity, Palmyra's "avenues of columns" stretching out across the horizon and its ground covered in an assemblage of "cornices, capitals, shafts, entablatures, and pilasters" made of gleaming white marble – their exquisite craftsmanship still apparent even in their current dilapidated forms.[13]

Wandering among the ruins of the ancient city, Volney approaches a large temple dedicated to the sun and comes across locals living within its crumbling remains. Moved by the hospitality of these squatters and the grandeur of what surrounds him, Volney decides to stay at Palmyra for a number of days to contemplate the meaning of what he has encountered. One evening he strays into a valley of tombs and settles on a ruined column as day turns to dusk. Suddenly, he is overwhelmed by a reverie that wanes into despair. The great ruins of Palmyra offer a vision of the future, Volney counsels us, conveying the transitory existence and inevitable end of even the greatest of empires.[14]

While Volney is lost in thought, a phantom in flowing robes suddenly emerges from the graves. Over the course of a lengthy speech, the spirit chastens Volney's resignation, announcing what these ruins actually foretell:

---

[9] Thompson observes that even in England Volney's *Ruins* – a "profounder and more imaginative book" than Paine's *Age of Reason* – was widely circulated and influential, in part, because of the cheap pocketbook form in which it was published, remaining "in the libraries of many artisans in the 19th century." E. P. Thompson, *The Making of the English Working Class* (New York: Vintage, 1966), 98–99. For a helpful study of the reception of Volney's work, see also Minchul Kim, "Volney and the French Revolution," *Journal of the History of Ideas* 79.2 (2018): 221–42.

[10] "Ihr Städte des Euphraths! Ihr Gassen von Palmyra! Ihr Säulenwälder in der Ebne der Wüste, Was seid Ihr?" Friedrich Hölderlin, "Lebensalter," in *Hyperion and Selected Poems*, ed. E. Santner, 190–91 (New York: Continuum, 1990 [1804]), 190. On Volney's influence, see Irwin, "Volney's Meditations," 314–15.

[11] Mary Shelley, *Frankenstein: Or the Modern Prometheus* (London: Penguin Books, 1992 [1818]), 115–16.

[12] Volney, *Les Ruines*, 1.   [13] Ibid., 7.   [14] Ibid., 9.

43 Fallen capital among ruins, Palmyra, ca. 1860s–1920s. The New York Public Library. Photography Collection, Miriam and Ira D. Wallach Division of Art, Prints and Photographs

44 Temple of Baal Shamin, Palmyra, ca. 1920. Library of Congress. Matson Photograph Collection. Public domain

Empires fall, not according to fate or time but by way of the political decisions of their people. The banks of the Seine do not have to come to the same end as the deserts of Palmyra.[15] France's future can be otherwise.

The famous account of Palmyra in *Les Ruines* is all the more remarkable given that Volney never actually visited the site.[16] In his travels through Syria in 1784, the French nobleman ventured no further inland than Baalbek and Damascus, having afterward turned south as he traveled through Palestine. The detailed description of Palmyra's remains, the effect these ruins registered on his thoughts and his interactions with local populations, were, in the end, a fable contrived back home in Paris.

But the ploy was a successful one. The acclaim Volney's work received rested, in part, on audiences who were already familiar with Palmyra's remains. Knowledge of the location had been publicized previously through the accounts of those who had been to the site, foremost among them the British antiquarians Robert Wood and James Dawkins, whose book *The Ruins of Palmyra* captured the imagination of a considerable readership when it appeared in 1753.[17] By the time of the appearance of *Les Ruines* three decades later, the remains of Palmyra were part of a familiar landscape, its terrain a prominent feature of the *Ruinenlust* that was sweeping across Europe at the time.[18] The first publication of Herculaneum's ruins would appear four years after Wood's work on Palmyra – made ever more popular by Johann Winckelmann's *Letter*, which publicized some of the most stunning finds from the buried city in 1764[19] – and a spate of popular books soon emerged with drawings of the ruins of Pompeii and Rome, including the famous renderings of Giovanni Battista Piranesi.[20] When Volney imagines himself among the ruins of Palmyra, it is a dreamscape realized through an array of ruined depictions published in the eighteenth century CE for audiences who had come to be captivated by their forms.

---

[15] See the speech of *Le Fontôme*, ibid., 16–23.

[16] Gaulmier, *L'ideologue Volney*, 75; Irwin, "Volney's Meditations," 312.

[17] Robert Wood, *The Ruins of Palmyra, Otherwise Tedmor in the Desart* (London: Robert Wood, 1753). Volney was well acquainted with Wood's work, quoting from it extensively in the *Voyage*. Volney, *Voyage en Syrie et en Égypte*, 256–60.

[18] On this phenomenon in eighteenth and nineteenth century Europe, see especially Reinhard Zimmerman, *Künstlichen Ruinen: Studien zu ihrer Bedeutung und Form* (Wiesbaden: Reichert, 1989); Andrew Siegmund, *Die romantische Ruine im Landschaftsgarten: Ein Beitrag zum Verhältnis der Romantik zu Barock und Klassik* (Würzburg: Königshausen & Neumann, 2006); and Nicholas Halmi, "Ruins Without a Past," *Essays in Romanticism* 18 (2011): 7–27.

[19] Johann Winckelmann, *Letter and Report on the Discoveries at Herculaneum*, trans. C. Mattusch (Los Angeles: Getty Publications, 2011 [1764]).

[20] On Piranesi, see John Pinto, *Speaking Ruins: Piranesi, Architects, and Antiquity in Eighteenth Century Rome* (Ann Arbor: University of Michigan Press, 2012); Heather Hyde Minor, *Piranesi's Lost Words* (University Park: Pennsylvania State University Press, 2015).

But like many of Volney's contemporaries, what matters about Palmyra in *Les Ruines* is something other than its ancient past. The history of previous eras does vividly come to mind when contemplating the city's remains, Volney writes, where memories of distant ages and the empires that once controlled these lands flood his thoughts.[21] But nowhere in the meditation will Volney connect this history to specific material remains in Palmyra or elsewhere, and there is little interest expressed in this work in studying the site's remains to learn about those who populated it in antiquity. Palmyra's ruins are more exemplary than they are evidential in Volney's writings, representing the great theme found in this work of the deprivation that royalty and religion occasion, the debris of old palaces and temples cited for the social ills they represent. Nor would the site be excavated anytime soon. Though much of its remains were already exposed, thus proving far easier to examine than those ancient settlements still heavily populated or more deeply buried, Palmyra would not be excavated for another century until, in 1902, the German archaeologist Otto Puchstein led the first archaeological expedition to the site.[22] What Palmyra's ruins revealed about the history of the great merchant city in antiquity is a question that Volney and his counterparts do not pursue.

Rather, the ruins of Palmyra are meaningful for what they disclose about a time yet to come. The reverie that takes hold of Volney while reposed in the valley of tombs is a vision that appears so that lessons for the future might be drawn. The marble fragments of Palmyra serve as a warning, a sign of what one day could befall "the Seine, the Thames, or the Zuyder sea."[23] Palmyra is a portent of possible futures, augured for audiences living in an age of revolution. "Who knows," Volney remarks, "if a voyager such as myself will not one day sit on the mute ruins" of certain European landscapes "and weep alone over the ashes of their inhabitants and the memory of their greatness?"[24] Contemplating this thought of the future, Volney stands petrified: "And I remained motionless, absorbed in a deep melancholy."[25]

§

Immobility in the face of future ruin was not Volney's alone. Well over two thousand years before, in a clearing located somewhere outside the city of Nippur, modern Iraq, the Jerusalemite priest Ezekiel is found lying motionless on his side in the book that bears his name. There, tied down by cords, Ezekiel is positioned before a drawing he has inscribed on a mud brick that depicts

---

[21] Volney, *Les Ruines*, 9–10.
[22] Theodor Wiegend, ed., *Palmyra: Ergebnisse der Expeditionen von 1902 und 1917* (Berlin: H. Keller, 1932).
[23] Volney, *Les Ruines*, 15.   [24] Ibid., 15.
[25] "Et je demeurai immobile, absorbé dans une mélancholie profonde." Ibid., 16.

Jerusalem under heavy attack, surrounded by siege forces that Ezekiel had previously fashioned (Ezek 4:1–8). For over a year Ezekiel gazes at this scene while on his left side until, in another vision, he is commanded to continue on for another forty days from his right.[26] With its violent images of siege works and battering rams, the camp of enemy forces encompassing the city and ramps leading over its walls, Jerusalem's grim downfall is portrayed vividly before a political prisoner now in exile over a thousand kilometers from home. But the scene Ezekiel views is not of the narrative's present. According to the chronology provided to us, Jerusalem still stood in Judah as the central city of the region, as it had for a thousand years. What Ezekiel watches unfold is a conquest that has not yet been realized.

Ezekiel's prophecy of Jerusalem's approaching demise is nevertheless in keeping with a prevailing tendency in the writings of the Hebrew Bible to connect the experience of ruins with a time that lies ahead. Though an encounter with material remains gives rise to impressions of the past and present in the biblical writings, as Chapters 2 and 3 have sought to demonstrate, many references to ruins in the Hebrew Bible are occupied with a time yet to come. What one frequently finds in biblical passages that refer to ruins, consequently, is what can be termed a prospective temporality, in which material remains are named in order to provoke reflection on events that are drawing near, exhibiting an interest in the future rather than a concern with what transpired long ago.

The possibility of looming ruination is expressed in a broad swath of biblical writings, the bulk of which are found in the prophetic corpus where admonitions resound with threats of ruins close at hand. A number of these passages are the result of *vaticinium ex eventu*, foretelling moments of destruction after they had already transpired through scribal redactions and consequent revisions to older traditions. In 1 Kings 9:6–9, to cite a clear instance of this phenomenon, Yahweh's address to King Solomon is abruptly interrupted by the deity's brief speech to all Israel, interspersed with Deuteronomistic language and the warning (1 Kings 9:8b) that one day "this temple will become a heap of ruins; everyone passing by it will be appalled and will hiss and will say 'for what reason has Yahweh done such a thing?'" Though this narrative is set in the mid-tenth century BCE, Yahweh's comments are roundly recognized as the

---

[26] Zimmerli observes the uneasy juxtaposition of the portrayal of Jerusalem's siege with Ezekiel's sudden role in this passage as one who bears the guilt of the house of Israel and the house of Judah by being bound, suggesting that originally these were two separate sign-acts. But as the narrative stands now, including the reference to Jerusalem's siege in 4:7a, the overall impression of this story is that of Ezekiel lying immobilized before the scene of Jerusalem under attack. Walter Zimmerli, *Ezekiel 1: A Commentary on the Book of the Prophet Ezekiel, Chapters 1–24*, trans. R. Clements (Philadelphia: Fortress Press, 1979), 163–68.

product of post-586 BCE writers who give voice to the temple's eventual fate at the very beginning of its founding.[27]

But more significant for this study is the underlying temporality expressed in texts that refer to ruins, marked, as they often are, by the language of premonition. In Jeremiah, the audience is urged to flee into fortified settlements before "a destroyer of nations" descends into Judah, turning the kingdom's cities into ruins (Jer 4:5–8), and in the Book of Isaiah an oracle directed at the nobility of Jerusalem foresees a time drawing near when animals will graze among the ruins of a city no longer inhabited (Is 5:17). But it is in Ezekiel – a work permeated with graphic descriptions of destruction that will shortly come to pass[28] – that future ruins are rendered most vividly, a doom to be brought on those "wherever you live" (Ezek 6:6), no matter the attempt to forestall or evade the approaching calamity. And many other prophetic texts foresee the same, from Amos (7:9) to Micah (5:10) to Zephaniah (1:15), to the ruins of the Day of Yahweh foretold in Joel (1:17). Throughout these writings we read of events voiced in the imperfect, announcing destructions that have not yet taken place, according to these works, but which are nevertheless close at hand.

In Sections 4.1–3, we examine this prospective temporality associated with ruins in the biblical writings. To do so, this chapter focuses chiefly on the city of Jerusalem. If a preponderance of biblical references to ruins looks to the future, the location most often identified with impending catastrophe is the city said to have been conquered by David (2 Sam 5:6–9//1 Chr 11:4–9) and templed by Solomon (1 Kings 6–8//2 Chr 3–4), and which existed as the royal center of this royal line for four centuries (ca. early tenth century BCE to early sixth century BCE). Significant about texts that have Jerusalem's ruins in view, consequently, is how they run counter to Jerusalem's status in the Iron Age, an era during which the city averted the widespread destructions that affected many locations in the southern Levant. To all appearances, the future of the city was secure.

A collection of prophetic texts declared otherwise. Within these writings, Jerusalem's past has little bearing on its future. Older ruins in the region – whether those of Gath (Amos 6:2) or Shiloh (Jer 26:6) – can feature in certain oracles. But even these allusions to the past are decidedly about the time to

---

[27] On the dating of this passage in the Persian period and its Deuteronomistic background, see, for example, the extended and recent discussion in Ernst Axel Knauf, *1 Könige 1–14* (Freiburg: Herder, 2016), 287–96. As noted in Chapter 1, a number of textual witnesses preserve "exalted" (עליון) in place of "ruins" (עיין) in this passage, though the context of this speech makes "ruins" a much more likely reading. On this point, see again Mordechai Cogan, *1 Kings* (New York: Doubleday, 2001), 296.

[28] See, for example, the references to future ruination in Ezek 5:14; 6:6; 12:20; 25:13; 26:4, 12, 20; 29:9–10; 30:7; 32:15; 33:28; and 35:4.

come, cited in order to unsettle contemporary audiences and to warn of what the future holds for those locations still standing (i.e., Samaria, Jerusalem). Much like Volney's meditation on Palmyra, when these writings refer to ruins they perceive material remains as harbingers of possible futures to come.

That ruins disclose something about the time ahead, however, stands in opposition to how ruins are understood historically today, predisposed, as historians and archaeologists are, to think of material remains in terms of what they convey about the lived experiences of ancient populations who once inhabited these locations. The tension between our contemporary emphasis on the historicity of ruins and the biblical accent placed on their futurity is a theme that runs throughout Chapter 4. To account for these divergent temporalities, we turn first in Section 4.1 to the ruins of Jerusalem that have been excavated over the past two centuries and the evidence unearthed of the location's Babylonian destruction. Sections 4.2–4 then examine a series of biblical texts that refer to this downfall and its significance. Prominent among the meanings put forward of Jerusalem's demise, I argue, is the contingency of time and ruination on the agency of the deity Yahweh, who, according to these writings, is ultimately the author of the ruins that come to pass. But what this perspective on divine ruination affords, I contend further, is the possibility of envisioning another future, an age to come when ruins are reconstituted and devastated locations restored. This view of the future is crowned by the stunning oracles found in the Books of Ezekiel and Isaiah, in which the ravaged landscape of Jerusalem, desiccated and empty of life, is prophesied to one day become "like the Garden of Eden" (Ezek 36:35; cf. Is 51:3).

In Section 4.5, the divide apparent between this prospective sense of ruination and one that privileges considerations of a historical past is pursued further through the writings of Walter Benjamin. In his own response to the "ruins upon ruins" that have accumulated across the ages, Benjamin, too, advances a vision that looks to the future and the possibility of a different order to come.[29] If the ancient prophetic writings ascribe this new aeon to the coming interventions of Yahweh, Benjamin will instead attribute its occurrence to what he labels a "messianic" power.[30] Opposed to those who desired to preserve the status quo of the present, including historians named as complicit in their support of contemporary political arrangements, Benjamin, like Hebrew prophets long before, I argue, advocates for the disruption and ultimate overthrow of the present age, ushering in a future when the ruins of the past will be ruins no more.

---

[29] Walter Benjamin, "Theses on the Philosophy of History," in *Illuminations: Essays and Reflection*, ed. H. Arendt, 253–64 (New York: Mariner, 2019 [1968]).
[30] Ibid., 254–55, 263–64.

The final moments of this study return full circle to the work of Reinhart Koselleck and his reading of Altdorfer's painting *Alexanderschlacht*, which was explored in Chapter 1. When we revisit this essay and the portrait it describes, what comes into view are impressions of time that share a certain kinship with themes taken up in Chapter 4 regarding the prophetic writings and the messianic temporality developed by Benjamin. This kinship comes to fullest expression in Koselleck's provocative argument, which provides the culmination of this four-chapter investigation, that modern historical thought is born when a belief in the eschaton, in the Last Judgment and the imminent ruin of this world, is finally abandoned.[31]

4.1 JERUSALEM, 586 BCE: THE DOWNFALL

Why it happened receives different responses in the Hebrew Bible.[32] For certain scribes behind the Book of Kings, it was principally the misdeeds of King Manasseh (ca. 687–643 BCE), especially in matters of the Jerusalemite cult, that led to a divine enmity from which Jerusalem could not recover (2 Kings 21:1–17; 23:26–27; 24:3). The Book of Jeremiah places blame on the moral depravity of the general population (e.g., Jer 5:1–17; 7:16–34; 8:4–17) and its leaders (e.g., Jer 14:13–18; 21:11–14; 22:11–30), with Jerusalem enclosing a populace in which "there is nothing but oppression within her" (Jer 6:6). Ezekiel looks on at the city from afar and finds manifest religious and ethical contaminants that have polluted the location (Ezek 5:11; 8:6–17), its toxicity necessitating Yahweh to vacate the temple and destroy its population, save those marked by a divine figure in linen cloth who walks silently through the city before the onslaught begins (Ezek 9:1–11). Other voices will attribute Jerusalem's downfall to false prophets and priests (Lam 4:13–14) or to the iniquities perpetrated against Yahweh by recent forebears (Ps 79:8).

That it happened is clear. In the summer of 586 BCE, after a siege said to have lasted eighteen months, Babylonian forces finally broke through Jerusalem's walls and, a month later, set the city aflame (2 Kings 25:1–21//Jer 52:1–16).[33]

---

[31] Reinhart Koselleck, *Futures Past: On the Semantics of Historical Time*, trans. K. Tribe (New York: Columbia University Press, 2004), 11–17.

[32] For an incisive study of the distinct and varied literary representations of Jerusalem's fall in the Hebrew Bible, see Cathleen Chopra-McGowan, "Representing the Destruction of Jerusalem: Literary Artistry and the Shaping of Memory in 2 Kings 25, Lamentations, and Ezekiel" (Ph.D. diss., University of Chicago, 2019). For how these responses contemplated different facets of divine agency and the question of the theodicy, see also the recent work of Dalit Rom-Shiloni, *Voices from the Ruins: Theodicy and the Fall of Jerusalem in the Hebrew Bible* (Grand Rapids, MI: Eerdmans, 2021).

[33] For the classic study of the various chronological difficulties involved in the dating of Jerusalem's destruction, see Abraham Malamat, "The Last Kings of Judah and the Fall of Jerusalem: An Historical–Chronological Study," *Israel Exploration Journal* 18.3 (1968): 137–56.

Though the archaeology of Jerusalem is mired in difficulties related to topography, politics, and the continued occupancy of the city today,[34] the Babylonian destruction of the location has left behind distinct remains in a number of excavated areas of the ancient settlement. To gain a sharper sense of what occurred during the summer of the Babylonian conquest, we can begin in the oldest settled district of Jerusalem and at its least elevated, more southern end with Yigal Shiloh's excavations in Area E (Figure 45) in the City of David. In the extensive, 1400 m² sector of this area, evidence for the sacking of Stratum 10 (Iron IIC) appears in a number of structures but perhaps most impressively in the central room of the finely wrought Ashlar House, where charred remains and collapsed stones from its walls attest to a "violent destruction."[35]

A number of the destroyed buildings in Area E, furthermore, were situated near or adjacent to the Iron Age city wall of the location (W219), a fortification line traced for nearly 90 m and found to vary in size between 3–5 m in thickness. This enclosure, initially composed in the Middle Bronze Age (MBA) period and reinforced in the late Iron Age, finally went out of use once the city fell to Babylon.[36]

Further north, in Shiloh's Area G, the remains of the Babylonian destruction are more evident still. There, three structures – the House of Ahiel, the Burnt Room, and the House of the Bullae – each attest to being destroyed by fire, with the charred wooden beams of the collapsed buildings being preserved in situ.[37] In the Burnt Room remains were recovered of finely wrought wooden furniture, imported from the north and inlaid with ivory, and over fifty bullae left behind from incinerated scrolls were found in a thick layer of ash in the House of the Bullae.[38] The "scores" of bronze and iron arrowheads located in the debris of Area G are likely the residue of hostilities, furthermore, that led to the overthrow of these buildings.[39]

Cf. the reconstruction of Jerusalem's fall in Mordechai Cogan and Hayim Tadmor, *II Kings* (New York: Doubleday, 1988), 320–24. For a more recent discussion, see Oded Lipschits, *The Fall and Rise of Jerusalem: Judah under Babylonian Rule* (Winona Lake, IN: Eisenbrauns, 2005), 68–96.

[34] On the difficulties of excavating Jerusalem, see the early observations of Kathleen Kenyon, *Jerusalem: Excavating 3000 Years of History* (New York: McGraw-Hill, 1967), 51–52, there devoted to ancient building materials used in Jerusalem and the challenges in discerning stratigraphic sequences, particularly given Roman engineering practices and challenges resulting from erosion on the slopes of the hilly site.

[35] Alon De Groot and Hannah Bernick-Greenberg, *Excavations at the City of David 1978–1985 Directed by Yigal Shiloh, Volume VIIA: Area E: Stratigraphy and Architecture* (Jerusalem: Hebrew University Press, 2012), 25, 164.

[36] Ibid., 45–48, 158–59.

[37] Yigal Shiloh, *Excavations at the City of David, I: Interim Report of the First Five Seasons* (Jerusalem: Hebrew University Press, 1984), 18–19.

[38] Ibid., 19.   [39] Ibid.

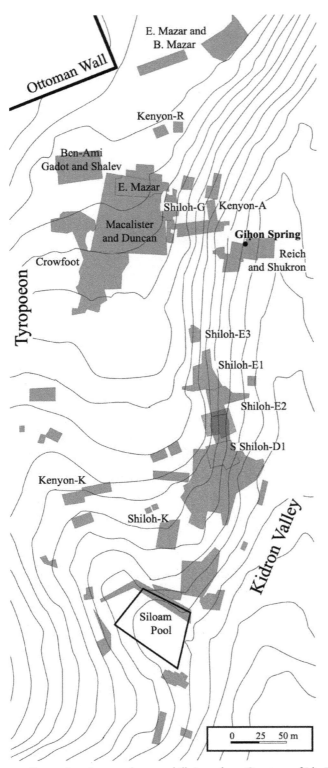

45 Excavation sites, southeastern hill, Jerusalem. Courtesy of Ido Koch. Used by permission

When we depart from Shiloh's excavations and turn to other areas of the ancient city, a similar picture emerges. Abutting Shiloh's Area G to the north, Kathleen Kenyon's Area A revealed two further buildings in Trench I that were destroyed in the Babylonian assault,[40] and in Square XXIV a large building with thick walls contained 128 loom weights in the fallen structure (Building VII), indicating that it may have been involved in large-scale textile production before it was burned down.[41] To this area of well-crafted, multi-story buildings, which Margreet Steiner interprets as a district for artisans and traders,[42] can be added the remains excavated by Benjamin Mazar and Eilat Mazar to the north in the Ophel area near the Temple Mount. An impressive building in Area C – likely a public building of some kind – also provided evidence of an "intense conflagration" in the final Iron Age stratum of the structure.[43]

In moving from the eastern reaches of the Iron Age city westward, we arrive at the ongoing excavations being carried out in the Givati Parking Lot. Of interest for our purposes is the recent appearance of an impressive, elite building (Building 100), again built of ashlar masonry, decorated with proto-aeolic capitals, and containing a collection of elegant ivory panels, most likely the remains of lavish furniture once used in the building.[44] This multi-story building was destroyed during an intense fire in this section of the city that exceeded 500 degrees Celsius and which left over 2m of ashen debris within it.[45] Further west, in the Jewish Quarter excavations, there, too, evidence emerges in Area W of the Babylonian advance. Perhaps most prominently, a massive defensive tower that was part of the fortification system in this area of the city contained a charred destruction layer, including, once more, arrowheads recovered from the assault.[46]

---

[40] Margreet Steiner, *Excavations by Kathleen M. Kenyon in Jerusalem 1961–1967*, Vol. III: *The Settlement in the Bronze and Iron Ages* (London: Sheffield, 2001), 81–85.

[41] Ibid., 100–1.   [42] Ibid., 54, 106.

[43] Eilat Mazar and Benjamin Mazar, *Excavations in the South of the Temple Mount: The Ophel of Biblical Jerusalem* (Jerusalem: Hebrew University Press, 1989), 21, 59.

[44] Doron Ben-Ami and Yana Tchekhanovets, "A New Fragment of Proto-Aeolic Capital from Jerusalem," *Tel Aviv* 42 (2015): 67–71; Yiftah Shalev, Nitsan Shalom, Efrat Bocher, and Yuval Gadot, "New Evidence on the Location and Nature of Iron Age, Persian and Early Hellenistic Period Jerusalem," *Tel Aviv* 47.2 (2020): 149–72; Reli Avisar et al., "'Jerusalem Ivories': Iron Age Decorated Ivory Panels from Building 100, Giv'ati Parking Lot Excavations, and Their Cultural Setting," *Antiqot* 106 (2022): 57–74.

[45] Yoav Vaknin et al., "The Earth's Magnetic Field in Jerusalem during the Babylonian Destruction: A Unique Reference for Field Behavior and an Anchor for Archaeomagnetic Dating," *PLoS ONE* 15.8 (2020): e0237029.

[46] Hillel Geva, ed., *Jewish Quarter Excavations in the Old City of Jerusalem. Volume I: Architecture and Stratigraphy: Areas A, W, and X–2. Final Report* (Jerusalem: Israel Exploration Society, 2000), 134, 155–58.

46 Late Iron Age broad wall, Jewish Quarter, Jerusalem. Author photograph

Among the late Iron Age layers reached by archaeologists in Jerusalem, something of how the location would have appeared in the aftermath of the Babylonian conquest thus comes into focus. If we approached the city from the east and viewed it from across the Kidron Valley, the smoldering ruins of large swaths of the location would have been apparent. In areas as dispersed as the eastern and western reaches of the City of David, the Ophel, and the Mishneh (Jewish Quarter), current evidence indicates that a number of buildings had been destroyed by an intense fire at this time. Many of these structures, furthermore, from the Ashlar House of Area E, the House of the

Bullae in Area G, the large public building recovered in the Ophel, and the ornate Building 100 of the Givati Parking Lot, were of an impressive size and design, either functioning as homes of wealthy individuals or used as public structures for important political and social groups. Considering that the most impressive palatial and temple buildings were presumably situated on the Temple Mount where excavations cannot occur, we can assume that a similar scene of destruction would be present there. When one draws nearer to the destroyed city, segments of the toppled wall and arrowheads found near this fortification system attest to how the location was taken by force.[47] If the biblical description of the Babylonian siege in the Book of Kings reflects something of the historical circumstances surrounding this moment, the debris of siege walls (2 Kings 25:1) and other remains from the lengthy Babylonian encampment (2 Kings 25:1, 3) would have been scattered around the former capital in the years and decades afterward.[48]

Because Jerusalem has been destroyed and rebuilt a number of times since its Babylonian conquest long ago, we are only offered glimpses of what occurred in 586 BCE through the excavations that are viable in the modern city today. Whether the entire city was burned to the ground or only the more wealthy and prominent neighborhoods is an open question.[49] A number of excavated structures do not offer direct evidence of destruction, though, as noted above, a number of buildings do in widespread areas of the site. In her early excavations, Kenyon suggested that only parts of the city were destroyed,[50] an argument further advanced by Gabriel Barkay in light of his archaeological work among Iron Age tombs in Jerusalem that suggested continued occupation of the settlement.[51] But since the publication of these studies it has become increasingly apparent that Jerusalem's destruction was more widespread than could be initially surmised in decades previous, both in the western

---

[47] See again, for example, Steiner, *Excavations by Kathleen M. Kenyon*, 92; Shiloh, *Excavations at the City of David, I*, 19, Plate 33; Geva, *Jewish Quarter Excavations*, 155–58; and H. J. Franken and Margreet Steiner, *Excavations in Jerusalem, 1961–1967, II: The Iron Age Extramural Quarter on the South-East Hill* (Oxford: Oxford University Press, 1990), 56–57.

[48] For a detailed study of the siege works left behind by the Assyrians at Lachish, for example, see David Ussishkin, "Area R and the Assyrian Siege," in *The Renewed Archaeological Excavations at Lachish (1973–1994)*, Vol. II, ed. D. Ussishkin, 695–767 (Tel Aviv: Emery and Clare Yass Publications, 2004).

[49] For a recent overview of the evidence for Jerusalem's Babylonian destruction and an instructive comparison with the total destruction of Ashkelon by the Babylonians in 604 BCE, see Nitsan Shalom, Yiftah Shalev, and Ortal Chalaf, "How Is a City Destroyed? New Archaeological Data of the Babylonian Campaign to Jerusalem," in *New Studies in the Archaeology of Jerusalem and Its Region*, Vol. XIII, 229–48 (Jerusalem: Israel Antiquities Authority, 2019 [Hebrew]).

[50] Kenyon, *Jerusalem: Excavating 3000 Years*, 105–11.

[51] Gabriel Barkay, "Excavations at Ketef Hinnom in Jerusalem," in *Ancient Jerusalem Revealed*, ed. H. Geva, 85–106 (Jerusalem: Israel Exploration Society, 1994).

sector of the City of David currently being excavated, for example, and through ongoing archaeological work in eastern areas of the settlement.[52] The traces of further destruction unearthed more recently do not demonstrate that the entire city was set aflame, but they do indicate that many buildings, particularly those of a more prominent size and status, were burned down.

But what is also conspicuous is the relative absence of luxury goods, prestige items, or, even more, human remains recovered from the late Iron Age stratum of the city. To explain the dearth of such finds, it appears that the conquest of the city by the Babylonians was rather orderly once the walls were breached.[53] After the surviving inhabitants surrendered, Jerusalem was likely systematically emptied and its most valuable goods pillaged, as the Book of Kings suggests (2 Kings 25:8). Once these items had been plundered and certain sections of the fortifications rendered useless (2 Kings 25:10), a number of the larger and more impressive buildings were lit on fire (2 Kings 25:9). In light of the wooden beams used within the frames of a number of structures in the city and other combustible materials found within them, this fire would have spread quickly throughout the settlement.

Left behind was a city in ruins. From the temple mount area where the palace and sanctuary once stood, down through the City of David, and into the expansive western quarter termed the Mishneh by the biblical writers (2 Kings 22:14), the burned-out structures of Iron Age Jerusalem would have predominated across the landscape of the city. A similar scene plays out amid excavations carried out in Jerusalem's environs. A ring of fortresses, it appears, once guarded the late Iron Age capital, until this fortification system was laid waste during the Babylonian incursion, either in 597 BCE when the Babylonian army first advanced on the city or, a decade later, when Jerusalem itself was finally destroyed.[54] Larger farms and villages that surrounded Jerusalem were also devastated at this time.[55] In Oded Lipschits's study of survey data, he observes an 83.5 percent decline in settlements in and around Jerusalem after the Babylonian campaigns.[56] Within 3km of the city, the loss was nearly 90 percent.[57] Yet as Lipschits observes, these figures are drawn from a few centuries after Jerusalem's destruction. Nearer to the

---

[52] Filip Vukosavovic, Ortal Chalaf, and Joe Uziel, "'And You Counted the Houses of Jerusalem and Pulled Houses down to Fortify the Wall' (Isaiah 22:10): The Fortifications of Iron Age II Jerusalem in Light of New Discoveries in the City of David," in *New Studies in the Archaeology of Jerusalem and Its Region*, Vol. XIV, eds. Y. Zelinger et al., 1–38 (Jerusalem: Israel Antiquities Authority, 2021).

[53] Steiner observes, "It seems the inhabitants had already left when these houses [Kenyon's excavation] were set on fire. Not one skeleton was found in the debris of the buildings. They apparently took their valuables with them." Steiner, *Excavations by Kathleen Kenyon*, Vol. III, 108–9.

[54] Gabriel Barkay, Alexander Fantalkin, and Oren Tal, "A Late Iron Age Fortress North of Jerusalem," *Bulletin of the American Schools of Oriental Research* 328 (2002): 49–71.

[55] Lipschits, *The Fall and Rise of Jerusalem*, 367.   [56] Ibid., 217.   [57] Ibid.

JERUSALEM AND THE RUINS OF TOMORROW

Babylonian conquest, in other words, the decline in population and settled area was almost assuredly higher than even these remarkable figures suggest.[58]

Archaeologically, there are few indications of recovery in the centuries after Jerusalem's fall. Lipschits describes the "inferior building techniques, the shabby quality of the pottery ... and the need to reuse existing resources such as building stones and metals" as indicative of the finds unearthed from the centuries of Persian rule (i.e., sixth through fourth centuries BCE).[59] For those who remained in the devastated region after the Babylonian advance, some survivors, it seems, came to Jerusalem and lived among the ruins. The elegant late Iron Age building burned down in the Givati Parking Lot area, for example, was partially cleared and reused, its inhabitants residing in what was left standing of the old building.[60] In Kenyon's Area A/XVIII, H. J. Franken contends that a monumental building located just above this excavation site was "restored during or after the exile, or people squatted in the ruins."[61] And Alon De Groot and Hannah Bernick-Greenberg similarly write of the possibility that the Ashlar House, the most impressive late Iron Age structure located in Area E, was reoccupied in the Persian period for those who lived in its remains.[62] There a new beaten-earth floor was placed above what remained of the Iron Age surface, and two tabuns associated with this layer may be remnants left behind from individuals who cooked their food in the open air amid the rubble. On both the western and eastern flanks of the City of David, then, and most probably in between, we can imagine swaths of this area of the post-Iron Age city being populated by some individuals who came to live among what remained of the larger homes of the site. Both Jeremiah (40:7–12) and Ezekiel (33:23–33) appear to refer to such a situation in the aftermath of Jerusalem's collapse, in which survivors of the Babylonian campaign return to the city and become "denizens of ruins" (Ezek 33:23).

As time wore on, Jerusalem's appearance continued to reflect its former Babylonian destruction. To the north, the humble temple rebuilt sometime around 515 BCE would have been positioned above a small community of perhaps a thousand residents, a population whose homes would have been scattered among the remains of what had once been the flourishing capital.[63]

---

[58] Ibid., 218. A similar conclusion is drawn by Faust in a study of the rural sector of Jerusalem's environs. Avraham Faust, *Judah in the Neo-Babylonian Period: The Archaeology of Desolation* (Atlanta: SBL Press, 2012), 39–46.

[59] Oded Lipschits, "Persian-Period Judah: A New Perspective," in *Texts, Contexts, and Readings in Postexilic Literature*, ed. L. Jonker, 187–212 (Tübingen: Mohr Siebeck, 2011), 208.

[60] Shalev et al., "New Evidence," 160–61.

[61] H. J. Franken, *A History of Potters and Pottery in Ancient Jerusalem: Excavations by K. M. Kenyon in Jerusalem 1961–1967* (London: Equinox, 2005), 98.

[62] De Groot and Bernick-Greenberg, *Excavations at the City of David*, 176.

[63] For different population estimates of Persian-period Jerusalem, ranging from 400 to 1,200 individuals, see Israel Finkelstein, "Jerusalem in the Persian (and Early Hellenistic) Period and

To the west, the Mishneh area of the Western Hill remained mostly abandoned, left in its dilapidated state for centuries.[64] To the east, areas near and beyond the old Iron Age wall in the City of David appear to have been given over to agriculture, with the community there consolidating westward to a more restricted neighborhood atop the hill on which it was situated.[65] Surrounding the city, deserted agricultural properties and crumbling fortresses would have appeared alongside more recent estates erected in cooperation with Persian authorities. If Jerusalem's walls were restored during this era, as the Book of Nehemiah claims (Neh 6:15), evidence for these fortifications is sparse.[66] It may be that some repairs to segments of the old Iron Age wall occurred over time or, otherwise, rather makeshift fortifications were erected in the fifth century BCE, being replaced once the city began to recover in the Hasmonean era with the construction of a more substantial fortification system.[67]

The image of Jerusalem that appears to us through its archaeological remains, then, is of a city that continued to be in a state of disrepair for generations. Walking among even the more affluent and elevated precincts of the Iron Age capital in the centuries after its fall, one would have come across the charred remains of once-imposing structures and of populations living alongside and, at times, within the ruins of what was left standing. When the Book of Haggai reports the distressed conditions afflicting those who had returned to Jerusalem in the late sixth century BCE (Hag 1:6; 2:3), or when, nearly a hundred years later, the Book of Nehemiah reports its namesake riding out in the evening to inspect the extensive ruins of the city's fortifications (Neh 2:13–16), these literary references reflect something of what the archaeological evidence recovered from this era also imparts. After the Babylonian conquest, the ruins of Jerusalem were both visible and lasting, a testament to Babylon's policy of ensuring that the city would remain devastated for generations to come.[68]

---

the Wall of Nehemiah," *Journal for the Study of the Old Testament* 32 (2008): 501–20; 506–7; Oded Lipschits, "Persian Period Finds from Jerusalem: Facts and Interpretations," *Journal of Hebrew Scriptures* 9: Article 2 (2009): 1–20.

[64] Geva, *Jewish Quarter Excavations*, 24, 106–7.

[65] De Groot and Bernick-Greenberg, *Excavations in the City of David*, 177.

[66] Finkelstein, "Jerusalem in the Persian (and Early Hellenistic) Period," 501–20; David Ussishkin, "The Borders and De Facto Size of Jerusalem in the Persian Period," in *Judah and Judeans in the Persian Period*, eds. O. Lipschits and M. Oeming, 147–66 (Winona Lake, In: Eisenbrauns, 2006); Margreet Steiner, "The Persian Period Wall of Jerusalem," in *The Fire Signals of Lachish: Studies in the Archaeology and History of Israel in the Late Bronze, Iron Age and Persian Period in Honor of David Ussishkin*, eds. I. Finkelstein and N. Na'aman (Winona Lake, IN: Eisenbrauns, 2011), 307–17.

[67] For an extensive overview of possible Persian-period fortifications in Jerusalem, see Kenneth Ristau, *Reconstructing Jerusalem: Persian Period Prophetic Perspectives* (Winona Lake, IN: Eisenbrauns, 2016), 39–66.

[68] For a summary of Babylonian policy, see Lipschits, *The Fall and Rise of Jerusalem*, 369; Faust, *Judah in the Neo-Babylonian Period*, 188–94.

4.2 "I WILL MAKE YOU A RUIN AND A DISGRACE" (EZEK 5:14): YAHWEH, BEARER OF RUIN

For those who lived in Jerusalem before the time of its fall, the possibility of ruin was belied by a past that demonstrated the location's uncommon capacity to withstand it. Archaeologically, what is distinct about the location is the absence of clear destruction strata during the volatile millennium that transpired from the MBA until Jerusalem's conquest by the Babylonians (ca. 1850–586 BCE).[69] Of the sites in the southern Levant that reached back for centuries into the Bronze Age period – Hazor, Megiddo, Shechem, and Lachish, among others – Jerusalem is conspicuous for exhibiting few indications that it was destroyed during this timeframe. Thutmose III's invasions of Canaan in the fifteenth century BCE,[70] the rival rulers and outlaws threatening the settlement during Abdi-Heba's command of the site in the Amarna period (fourteenth century BCE),[71] the tumultuous events surrounding Egypt's withdrawal from the region during the course of the twelfth century BCE,[72] Sheshonq I's foray into the highlands in the tenth century,[73] Hazael's southern campaign from Damascus in the ninth century,[74] and, above all, the Assyrian invasions of the eighth century BCE[75] – all left behind widespread ruin across the terrain of the southern Levant. None resulted in the overthrow of Jerusalem.

Historically, this propensity to avoid destruction can in some measure be connected to larger powers having little incentive to expend valuable resources to conquer a modest highland site that harbored few assets and was positioned some distance away from major trade routes, rivers, or bodies of water.[76] But within the biblical writings, Jerusalem's survival over the centuries gave rise to

---

[69] For a summary overview, see Katharina Galor and Hanswulf Bloedhorn, *The Archaeology of Jerusalem: From the Origins to the Ottomans* (New Haven, CT: Yale University Press, 2013), 18–54.

[70] Donald Redford, *The Wars in Syria and Palestine of Thutmose III* (Leiden: Brill, 2003), esp. toponym lists and sites of destruction on pp 43–56; Aaron Burke, "Canaan under Siege: The History and Archaeology of Egypt's War in Canaan during the Early Eighteenth Dynasty," in *Studies on War in the Ancient Near East: Collected Essays on Military History*, ed. J. Vidal, 43–66 (Münster: Ugarit-Verlag, 2010).

[71] See *EA* 285–90 in William Moran, *The Amarna Letters* (Baltimore: Johns Hopkins University Press, 1992), 325–34.

[72] Raphael Greenberg, *The Archaeology of the Bronze Age Levant: From Urban Origins to the Demise of City-States, 3700–1000 BCE* (Cambridge: Cambridge University Press, 2019), 341–48.

[73] Bernd Schipper, *Israel und Ägypten in der Königszeit: Die kulturellen Kontakte von Salomo bis zum Fall Jerusalems* (Göttingen: Vandenhoeck & Ruprecht, 1999), 117–32.

[74] Shuichi Hasegawa, *Aram and Israel during the Jehuite Dynasty* (Berlin: De Gruyter, 2012).

[75] Avraham Faust, *The Neo-Assyrian Empire in the Southwest: Imperial Domination and Its Consequences* (New York: Oxford University Press, 2021), 73–138.

[76] On this point, see the classic essay on the unusual rise of Jerusalem by Albrecht Alt, "Jerusalems Aufstieg," *Zeitschrift der Deutschen Morgenländischen Gesellschaft* 79 (1925): 2–19.

a collection of beliefs grounded in the conviction that the city's resilience should be attributed instead to the patron deity that protected it. These texts are commonly identified as the "Zion traditions."[77]

The belief that a city's patron deity defended it from potential enemies was widespread in the ancient Near East.[78] Such convictions stretched back for thousands of years in the region, appearing already in texts from the late third millennium BCE.[79] In one of the more poignant passages from *The Lamentation over the Destruction of Sumer and Ur* (ca. 2000 BCE), the goddess Ningal, for example, pleads on behalf of the city she oversees so that it might escape the destructive designs of other deities: "'May the city not be destroyed!,' I said indeed to them, 'May Ur not be destroyed!,' I said indeed to them" (COS 1.166: ll. 147–48). Later, in a number of prayers from the first millennium BCE, the deity Marduk is given the epithet "the trust of Babylon" (*tuklat bābili*), so named because of the security Marduk provided against Babylon's enemies.[80]

For those in Jerusalem, the city was secured by Yahweh. This belief was likely given further impetus, as elsewhere in the ancient Near East,[81] when the

---

[77] For discussion, see John Hayes, "The Tradition of Zion's Inviolability," *Journal of Biblical Literature* 82.4 (1963): 419–26; J. J. M. Roberts, "The Davidic Origin of the Zion Tradition," *Journal of Biblical Literature* 92 (1973), 329–44; J. J. M. Roberts, "Zion in the Theology of the Davidic-Solomonic Empire," in *Studies in the Period of David and Solomon and Other Essays*, ed. T. Ishida, 93–108 (Tokyo: Yamakaw-Shuppansha, 1982); J. J. M. Roberts, "Yahweh's Foundation in Zion (Is 28:16)," *Journal of Biblical Literature* 106 (1987): 27–45; Jon Levenson, *Sinai and Zion: An Entry into the Jewish Bible* (Minneapolis: Winston, 1985); Ben Ollenburger, *Zion, City of the Great King: A Theological Symbol of the Jerusalem Cult* (Sheffield: JSOT Press, 1987); F. W. Dobbs-Allsopp, "R(az/ais)ing Zion in Lamentations 2," in *David and Zion: Biblical Studies in Honor of J. J. M. Roberts*, 21–68 (Winona Lake, IN: Eisenbrauns, 2004); Jepp Dekker, *Zion's Rock-Solid Foundations: An Exegetical Study of the Zion Text in Isaiah 28:16* (Leiden: Brill, 2007), esp. 283–317; and Antti Laato, *The Origin of the Israelite Zion Theology* (London: T&T Clark, 2018).

[78] See, for example, Moshe Weinfeld, "Zion and Jerusalem as Religious and Political Capital: Ideology and Utopia," in *The Poet and the Historian: Essays in Literary and Historical Biblical Criticism*, ed. R. Friedman, 93–115 (Chico, CA: Scholars Press, 1983); Otto Eißfeldt, *Baal Zaphon, Zeus Kasios und der Durchzug der Israeliten durchs Meer* (Halle: Niemeyer, 1932), 15–21; Richard Clifford, *The Cosmic Mountain in Canaan and the Old Testament* (Cambridge, MA: Harvard University Press, 1972), esp. 131–59; Laato, *The Origin of the Israelite Zion Theology*, 99–188.

[79] For early instances of this theme from the city of Akkad and the Sargonids, see J. J. M. Roberts, *The Earliest Semitic Pantheon: A Study of Semitic Deities Attested in Mesopotamia before Ur III* (Baltimore: Johns Hopkins University Press, 1972), 147, 153. See also Ake Sjöberg and E. Bergmann, *The Collection of the Sumerian Temple Hymns* (Locust Valley, NY: J. J. Augustin, 1969). In TH 5:63–64, for example, we read of Ninurta's temple at Nippur: "Arm of Battle, heroic(?) meddu-weapon, carrier of the quiver, valiant brickwork that endures, your foundation is eternal!" (20).

[80] For discussion and texts, see Takayoshi Oshima, *Babylonian Prayers to Marduk* (Tübingen: Mohr Siebeck, 2011), 121–22, 33, and epithets listed on 450.

[81] On this point, see the summaries in Victor Hurowitz, *I Have Built You an Exalted House: Temple Building in the Bible in Light of Mesopotamian and North-West Semitic Writings* (Sheffield:

temple for this deity was constructed and the local dynasty claimed a divine mandate to rule.[82] Several psalms attest to the conviction that Yahweh, now enthroned on Mount Zion as its divine king, would protect the location where the deity dwelled. In Ps 48:3b–6, for example, we read:

> Mount Zion at the far end of the north, the city of the Great King!
> God is within its citadels, he has made himself known as a fortress,
> For look! The kings have assembled, they press onward together,
> They looked and were thus astounded, they were terrified, they fled.

And again in Ps 76:3–4, 6:

> His [Yahweh's] abode has been established in Salem, his dwelling in Zion,
> There he shattered the flashing arrows, the shield, the sword, the weapons of war.
> The stouthearted were stripped of their spoil, they sank into sleep,
> None of the warriors were able to lift a hand.

Expressed within these Zion poems, among others (e.g., Pss 46, 84, 132), is the presumption that Jerusalem was protected by Yahweh, its site chosen as the deity's dwelling and rendered unconquerable from its enemies.[83] "This is my resting place forever," Yahweh declares in Ps 132, "here I will reside, for I have desired it" (Ps 132:14). In the conclusion to Ps 48, the physical ramparts and towers of Jerusalem's defenses could even be taken as the physical presence of God: "Count its towers, set your heart on its ramparts... that you may tell the next generation that this *is* God, our God forever and ever" (Ps 48:13–15). Within such lines, traditions of Zion's inviolability are pressed ever further, giving rise to the claim that the city of Jerusalem itself represented the physical presence of the deity who guarded it. To experience the fortifications of the royal city, to walk along its walls and to take in its towers, was to have contact with the divine being who dwelled there. Jerusalem was therefore the "joy of all the earth" (Ps 48:3), the psalmist declares, the city of peace whose tranquility was guaranteed by the deity who lived within it.

To suggest that Jerusalem's future was one of ruin repudiated such claims. Broadcasting ruin in this Iron Age context would have conflicted with the previous centuries in which the city stood, a location that had somehow escaped the events that brought so many other locations in Jerusalem's vicinity to an end. Such pronouncements were impious, even treasonous. Impugned with assertions of coming destruction were contemporary beliefs in Yahweh's

---

Sheffield Academic Press, 1992), 311–21; and Michael Hundley, *Gods in Dwellings: Temples and Divine Presence in the Ancient Near East* (Atlanta: SBL Press, 2013), 363–72.

[82] Gerhard von Rad, "Die Stadt auf dem Berge," *Evangelische Theologie* 9 (1948/1949): 439–47; Martin Noth, "Jerusalem und die israelitische Tradition," *Oudtestamentische Studiën* 8 (1950): 28–46; Roberts, "The Davidic Origin," 329–44; and Laato, *Origin*, 276–82.

[83] Hayes, "The Tradition of Zion's Inviolability," 423.

presence within Jerusalem and commitment to protect it, as well as the enduring legacy of the House of David, which, according to other traditions, was promised to rule from Jerusalem forevermore by this deity (2 Sam 7:13, 16; Ps 132:10–18).[84] Powerful political and religious ideas were wedded to a belief in Jerusalem's indestructibility. As the poet sang, "God is in the midst of our city, *it will never be shaken*" (Ps 46:6). To question this belief was to question the political and theological claims bound to it.

The earliest texts that oppose this perspective appear in the Book of Micah.[85] In a denunciation of the political and religious leaders of his time, Micah of Moresheth announced that "Zion will be a plowed field, Jerusalem will become ruins, and the mount of the temple a wooded height" (Micah 3:12). Historically, these words are commonly understood as the pinnacle and great conclusion to the eighth century BCE prophet's work,[86] voiced after the Assyrian conquest of Samaria (ca. 721 BCE) and near the time of the Assyrian siege of Jerusalem (701 BCE).[87] In this unsettled moment in the Levant, the widespread destructions wrought by the Assyrian army in the region were perceived by Micah as a sign of Jerusalem's impending end, an end brought about by leaders – rulers, priests, and prophets – who had built "Zion with blood, Jerusalem with wrongdoing" (Micah 3:10), cannibalizing the people and selling their influence for a price (Micah 3:2–3, 5–10). As the Assyrians had conquered the royal center of Israel because of its corrupted ruling class, soon a similar fate awaited the capital of Judah. When Micah visualizes the ruins of Samaria (Micah 1:6) or the settlements in the Shephelah that had been overrun

---

[84] Roberts, "Zion in Theology," 105–8.

[85] Amos' oracle directed at the downfall of the "strongholds of Jerusalem" (Amos 2:5) would precede Micah's prophesy by decades, but the overarching Deuteronomistic language of the passage and its structural differences from the other oracles against the nations in Amos 2 have led a preponderance of scholars to date this text to a post-586 BCE context. For a recent summary of issues surrounding the dating of this oracle, see Göran Eidevall, *Amos: A New Translation with Introduction and Commentary* (New Haven, CT: Yale University Press, 2017), 110–12. For earlier comments, see Hans Walter Wolff, *Amos' geistige Heimat* (Neukirchen-Vluyn: Neukirchener Verlag, 1964), 24 fn 3; Jörg Jeremias, *The Book of Amos: A Commentary*, trans. D. W. Scot (Louisville, KY: Westminster John Knox, 1995), 44.

[86] See already the programmatic remarks on Micah *1–3 in Bernhard Stade, "Bemerkungen über das Buch Micha," *Zeitschrift für die alttestamentliche Wissenschaft* 1 (1881): 161–72. For further comments on the compositional history of this passage, see Hans Walter Wolff, *Dodekapropheton 4: Micha* (Neukirchen-Vluyn: Neukirchener Verlag, 1982), xxi–xxii, xxxvi–xxxvii, 78–87; Jörg Jeremias, *Die Propheten Joel, Obadja, Jona, Micha* (Göttingen: Vandenhoek & Ruprecht, 2007), 116–18. For the broader historical context of this passage, see Delbert Hillers, *Micah: A Commentary on the Book of the Prophet Micah* (Philadelphia: Fortress, 1984), 4–8, 48.

[87] For a recent, extended discussion of issues surrounding the dating of this passage close to the events of 701 BCE, see Kristin Weingart, "Wie Samaria so auch Jerusalem: Umfang und Pragmatik einer frühen Micha-Komposition," *Vetus Testamentum* 69 (2019): 460–80.

(Micah 1:9–16), he sees something of what awaits Jerusalem in the time ahead (Micah 1:5). Ruins in the present are a sign of ruins to come, a future already set in motion (Micah 1:3), decided even for those convinced otherwise that "Surely Yahweh is in our midst, no harm can come upon us!" (Micah 3:11b).

Micah's claims of coming destruction disputed older beliefs wedded to Jerusalem's standing, opposed particularly by those in the city, as Micah's oracle suggests, whose authority was buttressed by Zion postulates. Aside from the quotation of these authorities in Micah 3:11, some resistance to Micah's vision may also be discerned in his contemporary, Isaiah, who similarly draws on earlier traditions about Zion's unassailable character but for different ends.[88] In contrast to Micah, passages within Isaiah are more aligned with the regnant belief expressed in the Zion psalms that Jerusalem would be safeguarded against destruction. In response to Assyrian aggression, Yahweh declares in Isaiah 14, for example, that "I will break the Assyrian in my land, and on my mountains trample him underfoot" (Is 14:25), and, earlier, we read that "when Yahweh has finished all his work on Mount Zion and on Jerusalem, he will punish the arrogant boasting of the King of Assyria" (Is 10:12; cf. Is 17:12–14). Though, like Micah, Isaiah decries similar failings on the part of Jerusalem's leadership (e.g., Is 1:21–26; 5:8–10), and though Yahweh is also portrayed as acting against them, Isaiah cannot bring himself to imagine Jerusalem as a ruined city where oxen furrow. When all seems lost, Isaiah sees the divine warrior fighting on behalf of the city (Is 29:5–6):

> But the multitude of your foes shall be like small dust,
> And the multitude of tyrants like flying chaff.
> And in an instant, suddenly,
> You will be visited by Yahweh of the Armies
> With thunder and earthquake and great noise,
> With whirlwind and tempest, and the flame of a devouring fire.

Micah's word of inevitable ruin ran counter to the views of many, it would thus appear, especially for those such as Isaiah "with close contacts to the royal court."[89]

Historically, it is Isaiah's vision of Jerusalem and not Micah's that would prevail. The Assyrian siege of Jerusalem in 701 BCE was suddenly lifted, and the city spared[90] – an event that would have provided powerful backing for

---

[88] Hayes, "Zion's Inviolability," 424–26; J. J. M. Roberts, *First Isaiah* (Minneapolis: Fortress, 2015), 4–6; Ollenburger, *Zion, City of the Great King*, 119–21; 149.

[89] Roberts, *First Isaiah*, 4. So also Hayes: "Micah, a younger contemporary of Isaiah, and the later prophet Jeremiah, both harshly denounce the people's confidence in the security and inviolability of Zion (Micah 3: 9–12; Jer 7:13–15, 26:4–6). In this regard their break with the older traditions *is much more radical*." Hayes, "Zion's Inviolability," 425 fn. 34. (italics mine)

[90] For an overview, see the essays in Isaac Kalimi and Seth Richardson, eds., *Sennacherib at the Gates of Jerusalem: Story, History and Historiography* (Leiden: Brill, 2014).

those Zion beliefs that underscored the city's exceptional stature.[91] Nevertheless, it is Micah's words that would have an afterlife in the era that followed. In the only instance in the Hebrew Bible of an older prophetic saying quoted explicitly in a later prophetic book, Micah's prophecy about Jerusalem's ruin comes to be voiced by certain "elders of the land" when, in a story set nearly a hundred years after Micah's activity, Jeremiah is abruptly put on trial by leaders of the city for announcing that Jerusalem's future was one of destruction (Jer 26:7–11):

> Some of the elders of the land arose and said to all the people assembled, "Micah of Moresheth, who prophesied during the days of King Hezekiah of Judah, said to all the people of Judah, 'Thus says Yahweh of Hosts: Zion will be a plowed field, Jerusalem will become ruins, and the mount of the temple a wooded height.' Did King Hezekiah of Judah and all Judah put him to death? Did he [Hezekiah] not fear Yahweh and entreat Yahweh? And did not Yahweh relent about the catastrophe he had spoken against them?"
>
> (Jer 26:17–19)

In this scene, the memory of Micah is drawn on to safeguard Jeremiah's life. The old prophesy of Jerusalem's ruin calls to mind a previous time when such unwelcome words against the city were not only tolerated but, according to the elders, were received by the former King Hezekiah in a manner that led him to repentance. Here, too, we find a critique of Jerusalem's religious authorities and King Jehoiakim in the Book of Jeremiah, leaders of Jerusalem who act as foils and rebuff the prophet's words (e.g. Jer 27–29; 36) and, in contrast to Hezekiah, shun any notion of atonement.[92] The subsequent episode about the fate of the prophet Uriah ben Shemaiah (Jer 26:20–24) further drives home the point. Executed by King Jehoiakim for speaking out against Jerusalem near the time of Jeremiah's arrest, the brief narrative not only conveys how close Jeremiah was to death, according to the storyteller, but also indicates that at this moment prophesies of Jerusalem's impending ruin would

---

[91] So also Wildberger: "But the fact that Jerusalem did not suffer destruction at that point is amazing enough, in and of itself, being seen even by Isaiah's contemporaries as a 'miracle' of God; this was taken as evidence that proved the validity of the prophet's message." Hans Wildberger, *Isaiah 13–27*, trans. T. Trapp (Minneapolis: Fortress, 1997), 86. For further reflections on the strengthening of Zion traditions after Sennacherib's siege, see Othmar Keel, *Die Geschichte Jerusalems und die Entstehung des Monotheismus*, Vol. 2 (Göttingen: Vandenhoeck & Ruprecht, 2007), 728–54.

[92] Frank-Lothar Hossfeld and Ivo Meyer, "Der Prophet vor dem Tribunal: Auslegungsversuch von Jer. 26," *Zeitschrift für die alttestamentliche Wissenschaft* 86 (1974): 30–50; Mark Leuchter, *The Polemics of Exile in Jeremiah 26–45* (Cambridge: Cambridge University Press, 2008), 30–33; Carolyn Sharp, *Jeremiah 26–52* (Stuttgart: Kohlhammer, 2021), 94–98.

be met with violence rather than contrition.[93] Beliefs about Jerusalem's divine status were not to be questioned.[94]

The quotation of Micah in the Book of Jeremiah further underscores how disruptive the idea of Jerusalem's future destruction could be. The force of such sayings once more presumes Iron Age convictions about Jerusalem's indestructible character, now challenged by prophets from outside the royal center – Micah of Moresheth, Jeremiah of Anathoth – who insist that the city's patron deity could turn against it, Yahweh being a bearer of ruin rather than Jerusalem's defender. Perhaps most troubling about these warnings of impending ruin was the idea that the future lay unresolved in spite of older Zion beliefs that argued for continued security. "Do not trust in these deceptive words," Jeremiah announces in his famous proclamation from the gate of the Jerusalem sanctuary, "the temple of Yahweh, the temple of Yahweh, the temple of Yahweh" (Jer 7:4). The assumption that the temple and its deity will save Jerusalem, expressed in many Zion hymns, is a "lie" (Jer 7:8). Ruin is at hand (7:14).

The past allied with the opponents of Micah and Jeremiah. Their claim was that the future would not. Above all, this impression of time and ruination was a product of a particular understanding of Yahweh, whose agency could not be reduced to precedence. Even Isaiah, the great champion of Zion, broke with other Zion traditions by wedding the future to the conditional: "*If* you do not stand firm in faith, you will not stand firm at all," the prophet counsels King Ahaz (Is 7:9).[95] But within the more radical sayings attributed to Micah and

---

[93] So Brueggemann: "The charges are lodged: he 'prophesied against this city' (v. 11) ... This city is supposed to be immune to such criticism. Clearly the legitimacy of the city required keeping such a harsh critique unspoken ... In this chapter the opponents of the demanding word of God do not dispute the claim of authority. They do not seem to care if it is a word from God, for the defense of their way of life overrides any such theological question. They perceive, rightly, that the word of the prophet constitutes a significant threat to their ideological claims and therefore to their political power." Walter Brueggemann, *A Commentary on Jeremiah: Exile and Homecoming* (Grand Rapids, MI: Eerdmans, 1998), 234–35.

[94] On this point, see Roland de Vaux, "Jerusalem and the Prophets," in *Interpreting the Prophetic Tradition*, ed. H. Orlinsky, 277–300 (New York: Ktav, 1969).

[95] From a comparative perspective, the conditional also appears across a swath of roughly contemporaneous Neo-Assyrian documents that refer to ruins, particularly within the language of treaties. In the earliest of these still extant (c. 825 BCE), made between Šamši-Adad V of Assyria and Marduk-zakir-šumi of Babylon, the god Adad is called on to turn a ruler's land into ruins ([KUR]-*su a*-n[a DU$_6$]) *if* the pact between the two leaders is breached, among other curses levied (see Simo Parpola and Kazuko Watanabe, eds., *Neo-Assyrian Treaties and Loyalty Oaths*, SAA 2 [Helsinki: Helsinki University, 1988], 5 [r 15]). Later, during the reign of Aššur-nerari V (754–745 BCE), an agreement is enacted between the Assyrian ruler and Mati'il of Arpad whereby, if the latter should prove unfaithful, a series of curses are threatened against him, including the imprecation that "Ashur turn your cities into mounds, your house into ruins [URU.MEŠ-*ka ana* DUL.ME É-*ka ana ḫar-ba-ti lu-tir*]" (ibid., 12, V:6–7). A similar expression is found in the curse section of Stele I of the Sefire Inscription,

Jeremiah the conditional, too, finally collapses beneath the weight of a present whose actions set in motion a future that cannot be turned back. In oracles directed at the rulers of Jerusalem, the city is fated to be a ruined site "without inhabitant," Jeremiah proclaims, brought about by "destroyers" who have been consecrated by Yahweh (Jer 22:6–7). The possibility that Jerusalem might avoid this future if some action were taken, as expressed in Isaiah and articulated just previously in Jeremiah (Jer 22:4–5), has now vanished.[96] Yahweh will "make Jerusalem a heap of ruins (גלים)" (Jer 9:10), it is announced elsewhere, a future over which the speaker of the poem already weeps (Jer 9:9).[97]

The heightened sense of future ruination in Jeremiah – more dramatic and encompassing than what is found in Micah's earlier oracle – would only be matched by the biblical writings within the Book of Ezekiel. If Micah's vision of Jerusalem in ruins arose amid a time of Assyrian devastation, the world of Jeremiah and Ezekiel, too, was beset by ruins or the threat thereof, but in this moment under Babylonian imperial duress. The wholesale destruction of Ashkelon by the Babylonians in 604 BCE would have made clear to those in the Judahite capital that Babylon was now the dominant power in the southern Levant, a point expressed explicitly in an oracle in the Book of Jeremiah (Jer 47:5–7).[98] Even before this campaign Jeremiah would name Nebuchadnezzar the "servant of Yahweh" who would bring "everlasting ruin" on the region (Jer 25:1–14).[99] But when the Babylonian army returned to Judah to suppress King Jehoiakim's rebellion in December of 598 BCE and obtained the city's surrender three months later, their direct rule over

---

an Aramaic text from the eighth century BCE, in which Bar-Ga'yah of KTK calls upon the gods to curse the same Mati'il of Arpad if he were to breach the treaty, including the prospect of turning Arpad into a ruin mound (ותהוי ארפד תל) (Joseph Fitzmyer, *The Aramaic Inscriptions of Sefire*, rev. ed. [Roma: Editrice Pontificio Istituto Biblico, 1995], 44–45 [A:32]). With such language, then, we come across a correlation between ruins and divine power similar to that found in the Hebrew Bible: The possibility of destruction hinged on acts of disobedience or rebellion.

[96] On reflexes of the conditional in Jeremiah, see also the perceptive comments in Sharp, *Jeremiah 26–52*, 94–95.

[97] The identity of the speaker is ambiguous, with the MT preserving the *lectio difficilior* first-person "I will lift up [אשא] weeping and wailing" over against the imperative in the Old Greek. The speaker may be Jeremiah or, more provocatively, Yahweh. For discussion and argument that it is the latter, see William Holladay, *Jeremiah 1: A Commentary on the Book of the Prophet Jeremiah, Chapters 1–25* (Minneapolis: Fortress, 1989), 303–5.

[98] For a description of the destruction and its remains, see Lawrence Stager, Daniel Master, and David Schloen, *Ashkelon 3: The Seventh Century B.C.* (Winona Lake, IN: Eisenbrauns, 2011), esp. 3–12, 737–40. That Jerusalem was made subjugate to Babylon at this time is intimated in Jer 36:9 when a fast is proclaimed in late 604 BCE near the moment when Ashkelon is destroyed.

[99] This oracle is dated to 605 BCE and comes after the decisive Babylonian defeat of the Egyptians at the battle of Carchemish. On the use of this epithet in Jeremiah, see Klaas Smelik, "My Servant Nebuchadnezzar," *Vetus Testamentum* 64.1 (2014): 109–34.

Jerusalem was complete.[100] Among the approximately ten thousand Judahites deported to Babylonia in the spring of 597 BCE was the priest Ezekiel.[101] Jeremiah would remain in the city, a witness to Jerusalem's destruction a decade later (Jer 39:1–14).

That ruins would feature so prominently in the sayings attributed to these two prophets cannot be disconnected, then, from the ruins that would have enveloped their lives at the turn of the sixth century BCE. Like Micah before them, ruins wrought by an imperial, Mesopotamian force in the wider Levant were experienced as signs of Jerusalem's future destruction. Neither prophet could envision a time ahead without scenes of the city overrun and devastated. In a lurid description of Jerusalem's future in the early oracles of the Book of Ezekiel, the prophet recounts grisly scenes of filicidal and patricidal cannibalism performed beneath the gaze of a deity who has no pity, performed as the city comes to ruin: "Surely parents shall eat their children in your midst, and children shall eat their parents," Yahweh states, "moreover I will turn you into a ruin and reproach among the nations that surround you" (Ezek 5:10a, 14).[102] The future siege of Jerusalem that Ezekiel is forced to view when lying immobilized (Ezek 4:1–3) is now concluded in this vision – Jerusalem's population starved and on the precipice of destruction. If other prophets were able to foresee survivors of such calamities and offer a semblance of hope to their audiences (e.g., Is 10:20–22; Amos 5:15; Zeph 3:12–13), in these texts there is "utter annihilation."[103]

Within Ezekiel, too, then, older Zion traditions have not been qualified by the conditional. Instead, they have been inverted.[104] Rather than assurances of divine protection found in the Zion traditions (e.g. Ps 48:3; Is 29:7), Yahweh now vows to those in Jerusalem that "I am against you, I myself!" (Ezek

---

[100] For the Babylonian description of this event, see Chronicle 5, ll. 11–13, in A. K. Grayson, *Assyrian and Babylonian Chronicles* (Locust Valley, NY: J. J. Augustin, 1975), 102.

[101] Zimmerli, *Ezekiel 1*, 9–16; Moshe Greenberg, *Ezekiel 1–20* (Garden City, NY: Doubleday, 1983), 12–17.

[102] Here, Ezekiel draws on language found in Leviticus 26:27–33, where disobedience to covenant obligations is to be met with cannibalism and ruin. For the wider ancient Near Eastern context of this language, see Delbert Hillers, *Treaty-Curses and the Old Testament Prophets* (Rome: Pontifical Biblical Institute, 1964), 62–63. On the tangible, embodied character of Ezekiel's ethical vision, see especially Corrine Carvalho, "Ezekiel's Tangible Ethics: Physicality in the Moral Rhetoric of Ezekiel," in *The Oxford Handbook of Ezekiel*, ed. C. Carvalho (Oxford: Oxford University Press, 2020).

[103] Walter Eichrodt, *Ezekiel: A Commentary*, trans. C. Quiz (Philadelphia: Westminster Press, 1970), 89.

[104] On the influence of the Zion traditions on the Book of Ezekiel, see Levenson, *Sinai and Zion*, 115–19, 128–31. On Ezekiel's contestation of older Zion beliefs, see William Tooman, "Ezekiel's Radical Challenge to Inviolability," *Zeitschrift für die alttestamentliche Wissenschaft* 121.4 (2009): 498–514.

5:8).[105] If the divine warrior stationed in Jerusalem once provoked overwhelming dismay in the city's enemies (Pss 46:6, 76:6–7), the surrounding nations will now look on the location as a "warning and a horror," appalled by the site's decaying corpses. The city chosen by Yahweh to dwell within for all time (Is 8:18; Ps 132:13) is, in Ezekiel, finally handed over to divine beings who systematically execute Jerusalem's population: "Pass through the city," Yahweh commands, "and kill; your eye shall not spare, and you shall show no pity" (Ezek 9:5). After the massacre, Jerusalem is set aflame from coals taken from the temple so as to purify it (Ezek 10:2). With the destruction of the city commenced, Yahweh departs the sanctuary in a chariot, Ezekiel's final sight of the deity being Yahweh borne aloft to the Mount of Olives, halting momentarily while the city burns before the vision dissolves (Ezek 11:23).[106]

Unfolding during a time of Babylonian dominance, these visions nevertheless depict Yahweh as the sole agent of the city's destruction. In Ezekiel's extended description of Jerusalem's downfall (Ezek 7:1–11:25), Babylon, in fact, receives no mention, an omission all the more remarkable given that Ezekiel was living in Babylonian lands when the vision transpired, relocated there by way of Babylonian military intervention. Yet for Ezekiel the overthrow of Jerusalem would not be Babylon's doing, but Yahweh's. "Basically, the enemy was God," Moshe Greenberg observes of these passages, "the Babylonian army was but a later projection of his celestial executioners."[107] In Jeremiah, the idea is much the same. Nebuchadnezzar descends into the Levant only because Yahweh has sent him: "I am bringing evil from the north, and a great destruction ... to make your land desolate, your cities ruins" (Jer 4:6).

In these texts, the ruins to come are the result of the deity who brings them about. A central theme found throughout these prophetic works is the ascription of ruins solely to divine machinations.[108] In a striking passage from Isaiah

---

[105] As Dobbs-Allsopp observes for Lamentations 2, this discourse in Ezekiel similarly "enacts one of the boldest theological innovations of the exile, the figuration of Yahweh as enemy." Dobbs-Allsopp, "R(az/ais)ing Zion," 23.

[106] The image is not Ezekiel's alone. In a nearly contemporaneous account from the Mesopotamian city of Harran, the deity Sîn also becomes angry with the city and abandons his temple, flying to heaven instead: "Sîn, king of all gods, became angry with his city and his temple, and went up to heaven and the city and the people in it became desolate." *Ancient Near Eastern Texts,³* 560.

[107] Greenberg, *Ezekiel 1–20*, 202–3. Similar imagery of the divine warrior assaulting Jerusalem appears, once more, in Lamentations. On this imagery, see the discussion throughout Dobbs-Allsopp, "R(az/ais)ing Zion," 22–50.

[108] This discourse can be contrasted with Greek historians who rarely link ruins with divine works, with Thucydides (fifth century BCE), Strabo (first century BCE), and Pausanias (second century CE), for example, not associating the many ruins they describe in their writings with the gods. In royal inscriptions from Mesopotamia, rulers often speak of ruins in the context of turning a location into one through military assault, but seldom is a deity acknowledged for this achievement. In the Nimrud Prism of Sargon II (722–705 BCE), to cite a roughly contemporaneous instance to the biblical texts examined here, a series of

that speaks to this theme, Yahweh addresses Sennacherib, King of Assyria, and announces, "I planned from days of old what now I bring to pass, that you will make fortified cities crash into heaps of ruin" (גלים נצים; Is 37:26 [//2 Kgs 19:25]).[109] Similarly, in a famous speech to Cyrus the Great of Persia, Yahweh declares that doors of bronze will be torn down and iron bars cut through in advance of Cyrus' forces – divine acts performed on behalf of the Persian ruler who "does not know me" (Is 45:4). In Zephaniah, Yahweh undertakes acts of ruination without any intermediary, claiming that "I have cut off the nations; their battlements are devastated, I have made their streets ruins, so that no one walks in them" (Zeph 3:6), and in Isaiah 25 the poet celebrates the power of Yahweh to make a nameless location "a heap of rubble (גל), the fortified city ruins (מפלה)" so devastated that it "will not be rebuilt for all time" (לעלם לא יבנה) (Is 25:2). In Ps 89, acts of divine ruination are directed even toward the House of David's holdings: "You have broken through his walls," the poet writes of Yahweh, "you have laid his strongholds in ruins" (מחתה)(Ps 89:41).

The reversal of older Zion beliefs in the Books of Micah, Jeremiah, and Ezekiel are in keeping with this broader perspective of divine agency, pivoting on the conviction that the divine warrior who had once chosen Jerusalem to defend could also decide against it.[110] The oracles of ruin found in these works did not annul the Zion traditions, on this view, but were enabled by them, the language of Zion repurposed in these prophetic texts so as to be turned against the location in which these traditions had been sustained over the centuries. The future of Zion was recast in these visions, accordingly, from expectations of continued security (i.e., Ps 46:6) to an unsettled sensibility that arose in response to the actions of those bound to the deity who oversaw their affairs.

---

exploits is mentioned, including the turning of fifteen strongholds and their towns "into ruins (ti-la-niš u-še-me) (C. J. Gadd, "Inscribed Prisms of Sargon II from Nimrud," *Iraq* 16.2 [1954]: 173–201; 186 [vi: 59]), and a similar claim is made later by Sennacherib (704–681 BCE), who "destroyed, burned with fire, and heaped into ruins (aš-pu-ka ti-la-niš)" a number of towns in a military campaign directed at a Babylonian-Elamite coalition formed against him" (A. K. Grayson, "The Walter Art Gallery Sennacherib Inscription," *Archiv für Orientforschung* 20 [1963]: 83–96; 90). Yet for reasons likely related to genre – that is, royal inscriptions – nowhere among these Assyrian texts is there an allusion to a deity who is credited for the ruins a ruler's own armies had wrought. But what these instances reveal is that the language of ruination applied to Yahweh in the biblical writings is frequently drawn from the broader discourse of ancient Near Eastern royal ideology.

[109] What is striking about this statement, in light of the citation above, is how it mimics the language used by Assyrian rulers, who "heap up" (šapāku) ruins with some frequency (see CAD Š, Part 1, Vol. 17, 421 [9b]). Yahweh addresses Sennacherib, in other words, in language that echoes Assyrian royal ideology.

[110] This sense of reversal is captured prominently in Ps 89. After announcing that David's "line will be forever, and his throne before me like the sun, like the moon it will be established forever, an enduring witness in the skies," (Ps 89:37–38), the very next verse responds "But now you have spurned, you have rejected him; you are full of wrath against your anointed" (Ps 89:39).

Perhaps the most resonant image of this unresolved sense of time and ruination is found in Jeremiah's oracle of the potter (Jer 18:7–10):

> At a certain moment I may declare concerning a nation or a kingdom, that I will pluck up and break down and destroy it, but if that nation, concerning which I have spoken, turns from its evil, I will change my mind about the disaster that I intended to bring on it. And at another moment I may declare concerning a nation or a kingdom that I will build and plant it, but if it does evil in my sight, not listening to my voice, then I will change my mind about the good that I had intended to do to it.

In this scene the contingency of the future is laid bare, the time ahead ever vulnerable to collapse and restructuring. "The future is no simple continuation of the present," Abraham Heschel comments in his reading of this text, but rather what is to come may "overturn the seeming solidity" of current affairs.[111]

If Jerusalem had survived the Assyrian siege of 701 BCE and weathered the Babylonian campaigns into the southern Levant in 604, 601, and 597 BCE, in these prophetic writings such events provided few assurances for what lay ahead. Nor did these moments of deliverance demonstrate, as they did to others, the salience of old beliefs bound to Jerusalem's indestructibility. Rather, the ruins that appeared in increasing numbers in territories adjacent to Jerusalem during this age were interpreted as a presentiment of more ruins to come, signs not of Jerusalem's safekeeping but of the city's own impending downfall. Opposition to this perspective is preserved in a number of biblical texts where beliefs in the unassailability of Jerusalem are manifest. The prophetic writings examined here nevertheless refuted these ideas of time and place, underscoring instead the agency of Yahweh, the ultimate bearer of ruin, who could bring about a future at odds with the present. In perhaps the most totalizing and haunting of such visions of reversal, Jeremiah watches not just Jerusalem but all of creation come undone:

> I looked on the earth, and lo, it was waste and void;
> And to the heavens, and they had not light . . .
> I looked, and lo, there was no one at all,
> And all the birds of the air had fled.
> I looked, and lo, the fertile land was a desert,
> And all its cities were laid in ruins,
> Before Yahweh, before the fury of his anger.
> (Jer 4:23, 26)

In these lines, the opening words of Genesis are rescinded,[112] creation is overturned, and the future is conceptualized as a wholly ruined landscape, its

---

[111] Abraham Heschel, *The Prophets* (New York: Harper and Row, 1962), 221.
[112] Michael Fishbane, "Jeremiah iv 23–26 and Job iii 3–13: A Recovered Use of the Creation Pattern," *Vetus Testamentum* 21 (1971): 151–67.

demolished cities (נתץ) abandoned, their precincts without life, "Before Yahweh, before the fury of his anger."

4.3 "I WILL RAISE UP THEIR RUINS" (IS 44:26): YAHWEH, RESTORER OF RUIN

The Babylonian destruction of Jerusalem was extensive, its effect total. Once conquered, the location appears to have been abandoned for upwards of fifty years.[113] The absence of settlement activity at the site may have been an outcome of Babylonian policy that prohibited rebuilding efforts in a bid to prevent Jerusalem from fomenting future uprisings, though severe demographic decline and social fragmentation after the Babylonian campaign would have contributed to the dearth of undertakings in the former city. The destruction of Jerusalem also led to widespread collapse across the small kingdom it had once overseen. A prominent line of southern fortresses in the Negev region would be overwhelmed during this period, and locations in the Shephelah that had been rebuilt after the Assyrian invasion in the century before, such as the impressive settlements at Lachish and Timnah, were also destroyed.[114] Other sites to the south and east of Jerusalem, such as Hebron, Jericho, and En-Gedi, were either brought down at this time or abandoned in the decades after the Babylonian incursion.[115] For those who remained in the territory of Judah in the aftermath of Babylon's invasion, the ruins of recent destructions would have predominated across the landscapes familiar to them.

After Jerusalem's destruction, the political center of the former kingdom shifted north to the city of Mizpah (Tell en-Nasbeh), where the Babylonians appear to have revamped the city and retrofitted its fortification system.[116] Some squatters returned to the ruins of Jerusalem, and certain biblical texts

---

[113] Lipschits, *Fall and Rise of Jerusalem*, 215–18; Oded Lipschits, "Jerusalem between Two Periods of Greatness: The Size and Status of the City in the Babylonian, Persian, and Early Hellenistic Periods," in *Judah between East and West: The Transition from Persian to Greek Rule (ca. 400–200 BCE)*, eds. L. L. Grabbe and O. Lipschits, 163–75 (London: Bloomsbury, 2011), 167.

[114] David Ussishkin, "A Synopsis of the Stratigraphical, Chronological, and Historical Issues," in *The Renewed Excavations at Lachish (1973–1994)*, Vol. I, Part I, ed. D. Ussishkin, 50–119 (Tel Aviv: Emery and Claire Yass Publications, 2004), 90–92; Amihai Mazar and Nava Panitz-Cohen, *Timnah (Tel Batash) II: The Finds from the First Millennium BCE* (Jerusalem: Hebrew University, 2001), 281–83.

[115] For a summary of destruction and abandonment in this region, see Faust, *Judah in the Neo-Babylonian Period*, 21–32.

[116] Jeffrey Zorn, "Tell en Nasbeh: A Re-Evaluation of the Architecture and Stratigraphy of the Early Bronze Age, Iron Age, and Later Periods" (Ph.D. diss., University of California, Berkeley, 1993), 163–185; Jeffrey Zorn, "Jeremiah at Mizpah of Benjamin (Tell en-Nasbeh): The Archaeological Setting," in *The Book of Jeremiah: Composition, Reception, and Interpretation*, eds. J. Lundbom, C. A. Evans, and B. Anderson, 69–92 (Leiden: Brill, 2018).

suggest that individuals made their way to the site to engage in sporadic rituals connected to the destroyed temple (i.e., Jer 41:5). But, overall, Jerusalem remained a deserted, burned-out site for decades, lifeless and run down, the city's remains left exposed to the elements. In Lamentations, the roads to Zion mourn because there are no longer pilgrims who make their way to the city for its festivals (Lam 1:4) – these travelers replaced instead by those who now pass by the ruins of the city and "hiss and wag their heads" at what the location had become (Lam 2:15).

Jerusalem would not recover for centuries. If leaders of the Persian Empire permitted Jerusalem to be resettled sometime after 539 BCE, they nevertheless continued the Babylonian policy of preventing Cis- and Transjordanian urban centers from returning to their Iron Age forms.[117] Lipschits observes that even at the height of resettlement activity in Jerusalem during the Persian period, the city's size and population were approximately 15 percent of what they had been on the eve of their Babylonian destruction.[118] Over four-fifths of the former capital, in other words, remained uninhabited until the Hasmonean period four hundred years later. During these centuries some of the city's Iron Age materials and infrastructure may have been reused for the building of homes as time wore on.[119] Other areas of the city, such as the eastern slope of the City of David, were given over to agrarian pursuits.[120] Still other precincts, including the expansive Western Hill, were left in their ruined state.[121] Those who resided at the location during this era seem to have occupied a thin strip of homes in the City of David that ran south of the temple, forming a modest village composed of a population who were likely engaged primarily in the maintenance of the temple and the agricultural lands that supported it.[122] To date, there is yet to emerge a single building in Jerusalem that can be situated archaeologically within this era.[123]

---

[117] Lipschits, *The Fall and Rise of Jerusalem*, 214–16; Lipschits, "Jerusalem between Two Periods," 168.

[118] Lipschits, "Jerusalem between Two Periods," 167. So also Ristau writes of the location that the majority of its population "lived on rural estates, farmsteads, and tenements rather than in the city." Ristau, *Reconstructing Jerusalem*, 75.

[119] De Groot and Bernick-Greenberg, *Excavations at the City of David 1978–1985, Volume VIIA: Area E*, 21–22.

[120] Ibid., 177–79.

[121] Hillel Geva, "Summary and Discussion of Findings from Areas A, W, and X–2," in *Jewish Quarter Excavations in the Old City of Jerusalem Conducted by Nahman Avigad 1969–1982, Vol. 2: The Finds from Areas A, W, and X–2: The Final Report*, ed. H. Geva, 501–52 (Jerusalem: Israel Exploration Society, 2003), 524–26.

[122] Finkelstein, "Jerusalem in the Persian (and Early Hellenistic) Period," 504–7; Lipschits, "Persian Period Finds from Jerusalem," 10–11; Lipschits, "Jerusalem between Two Periods," 169–73.

[123] For an overview, see again Lipschits, "Persian Period Finds," 2–20; Finkelstein, "Jerusalem in the Persian (and Early Hellenistic) Period," 504–7. As noted above, evidence for the reuse of older Iron Age structures, such as the Ashlar House of Shiloh's Area E and Building 100 of

What these residents of Jerusalem thought about the impoverished, ruined city they inhabited is difficult to know, in part because few biblical texts speak directly to the conditions of the location during these centuries. If brief references in the Book of Haggai offer some insights into life at the end of the sixth century BCE, hardships seem to have prevailed ("You have sown much, and harvested little . . . you clothe yourselves, but no one is warm" [Hag 1:6]). In the opening chapters of the Book of Ezra – set just after this period – the older generation who remembered what the city once was before it fell begin to weep when they witness the new, middling temple's foundation laid, "so that the people could not distinguish the sound of the joyful shout from the sound of the people's weeping" (Ezra 3:13). Elsewhere, indications of the desperation and trauma experienced during this era appear in certain poems, such as when the psalmist questions Yahweh as to how long Jerusalem must remain in ruins (Ps 79:1–5) or, relatedly, when in Isaiah the poet voices a bitter complaint against the silence of Yahweh in response to life in a city where "all our pleasant places have become ruins" (Is 64:11). In Psalm 74, the speaker beckons Yahweh, the divine "king of old" (Ps 74:12), to "direct your steps to the enduring ruins" now located on Mount Zion so that the deity might take in the rubble that remains (Ps 74:3).

These textual glimpses into life in the ruined post-Iron Age settlement correspond to what we can discern about Jerusalem's status during the centuries of Persian and early Hellenistic rule (ca. 515–167 BCE). Those who resided within the former royal center occupied a location that was substantially diminished from its late Iron Age form. Remnants of Jerusalem's previous size and affluence would have been evident across the settlement. Monumental ruins were ostensibly located throughout the temple mount, as the psalmist observes, and the site's toppled fortifications and burned-out buildings would have provided a persistent reminder of both Jerusalem's former status and its ultimate destruction. Historically, what is arresting about these circumstances is that they did not last a generation or two but prevailed across a considerable expanse of time. The period in which Jerusalem remained a small settlement embedded among the older ruins of a once expansive city extended for a longer duration (ca. 586–167 BCE) than the era in which it had served as the royal center of an Iron Age kingdom (ca. 1000–586 BCE).

The biblical references to the ruined character of Jerusalem are in keeping, then, with what archaeologists have revealed about the fallen landscape that the city had become. What is unanticipated, however, are texts that describe Jerusalem on the very precipice of restoration, foreseeing a future when the ruins of the city would be restored. Many of these references appear in the later

---

the Givati Parking Lot excavation, does exist, as do a few floors and retaining walls for terracing. The vast majority of finds, however, are ceramic wares, especially from fills.

portions of the Books of Isaiah, Jeremiah, and Ezekiel, widely understood as post-exilic writings that address communities who arose after Jerusalem's destruction. In the Book of Jeremiah, for example, "a voice of joy and a voice of gladness" will ring out once more, Yahweh declares, echoing throughout "the ruined streets of Jerusalem" that are currently without inhabitants (Jer 33:10–11).[124] Oracles located in the "Book of Consolation" in Jeremiah (Jer 30–33) are centered on this theme, pieced together after the fall of Jerusalem in order to offer a vision of the future in which the city would one day be renewed, when there would be "hope for the future," as Jer 31:17 puts it.[125]

In Second and Third Isaiah, similar claims appear. Isaiah 61:4 calls on the "mourners of Zion" to "rebuild the old ruins" of Jerusalem and "raise up the former devastations," ushering in a new age of growth and rebirth at the settlement (Is 61:11). Another poem from Isaiah commands Zion to "lift up your eyes all around and see" the coming restoration, a future when the "ruins and desolate places, your land of destruction – indeed now it will be crowded because of the residents" (Is 49:18–19).[126] So promising is the time ahead that the "ruins of Jerusalem" are summoned to "break forth into songs of joy" (Is 52:9), echoing the jubilant songs sung at creation by the heavenly luminaries in the Book of Job (Job 38:7). Later, the theme of joy once more appears when Yahweh declares, "I shall create Jerusalem as a joy" (Is 65:18), a somewhat jarring statement given the depressed conditions of the city at the time when the poem was composed. Yet the connection between the current ruins of Jerusalem and a new creation that is approaching is interspersed throughout these poems, whether in Jeremiah (Jer 33:12–13) or Isaiah (51:3).[127] In the Book of Ezekiel, this connection is emboldened further still with the claim that the ruins of Jerusalem will one day resemble Eden: "And they will say," Yahweh announces, "This land that was devastated has become like the Garden of Eden; the ruined, despoiled, and destroyed towns are now inhabited" (Ezek 36:35).

In a time of ruin, the future of Jerusalem is envisioned otherwise in these later prophetic writings.[128] Once more, this prospective sense of time is bound

---

[124] Sharp similarly observes the "surprising proleptic note of promise" within a poem that begins with a "grim" description of Jerusalem's fall in Jer 33. Sharp, *Jeremiah 26–52*, 208.

[125] For a succinct discussion, see Alexander Rofé, "The Arrangement of the Book of Jeremiah," *Zeitschrift fur die Alttestamentliche Wissenschaft* 101.3 (1989): 390–98. For a more expansive treatment, see Siegfried Herrmann, *Jeremia: Der Prophet und das Buch* (Darmstadt: Wissenschaftliche Buchgesellschaft, 1990), 146–82; Jack Lundbom, *Jeremiah 21–36* (New York: Doubleday, 2004), 368–76.

[126] As Westermann notes of the ruined city at the time, "What a demand the prophet makes of his hearers! There is absolutely nothing to be seen." Claus Westermann, *Isaiah 50–66: A Commentary*, trans. D. M. G. Stalker (Philadelphia: Westminster Press, 1969), 220.

[127] On this point, see Jon Levenson, *Creation and the Persistence of Evil* (Princeton, NJ: Princeton University Press, 1994), 89–90.

[128] On this point, see also the concluding remarks in Ristau, *Reconstructing Jerusalem*, 188–95.

to ideas of divine agency and the reversal of fortunes.[129] But if Yahweh is consistently identified as the author of Jerusalem's ruin in other prophetic passages, within these writings the deity is described as the one who now restores what has fallen. In Isaiah 44:26, Yahweh vows to Jerusalem and the cities of Judah that "I will raise up their ruins" (חרבותיה אקומם). In Jeremiah, the first-person voice once more appears: "I will restore (כי אשיב)," Yahweh declares, "the fortunes of the land as at first" (Jer 33:11). And in Ezekiel, the divine restoration of ruins is put forward as a witness of Yahweh's power to the surrounding peoples: "Then the nations that remain around you shall know that I, Yahweh, have rebuilt the ruined places (אני יהוה בניתי הנהרסות)" (Ezek 36:36). Later in Isaiah (Is 51:3), we are offered an extended description of this divine activity, once more adorned with the image of Eden:

> For Yahweh will comfort Zion,
> He will comfort all her ruins,
> And he will make her wilderness like Eden,
> And her desert plains like the Garden of Yahweh;
> Joy and gladness will be found in her,
> Thanksgiving and the sound of song.

In these passages, the Great King of Jerusalem, so named throughout the Zion traditions, returns to the city and its lands in order to rebuild. "I will raise up the booth of David that is fallen," Yahweh declares in a poem from Amos written after Jerusalem's destruction,[130] "I will repair the breaches in its wall, I will raise up its ruins, and I will rebuild it as in the days of old" (Amos 9:11).

In contrast to images of Yahweh as the bearer of ruin, throughout these passages the deity is described as the builder of what has fallen. No ruler or political leader is credited with the recovery that is to come in these texts – an absence all the more conspicuous given that royal writings from the period frequently draw attention to a ruler's capacity to rebuild what had been formerly in ruins.[131] But in these passages, it is Yahweh who is envisioned as

---

[129] Once more, Dobbs-Allsopp's incisive reading of the Zion traditions in Lamentations is instructive in this vein, where the "razing" of Zion in these poems gives way to the "raising" of Zion "into vocality" through language that performatively and imaginatively reconstitutes the location. Dobbs-Allsopp, "R(az/aising) Zion," 50. In the prophetic passages examined here, what is distinct is that the physical rebuilding of Jerusalem's ruins is principally in view, a restoration that is vocalized through these writings but also, according to the poets, realized as something tangible.

[130] Hans Walter Wolff, *Dodekapropheton 2: Joel und Amos* (Neukirchen-Vluyn: Neukirchener Verlag, 1969), 406; Jörg Jeremias, *The Book of Amos: A Commentary*, trans. D. Stott (Louisville, KY: Westminster John Knox, 1998), 160–70.

[131] If Yahweh's capacity to turn locations into ruins draws near to ancient Near Eastern royal discourse, so also does the language of rebuilding. In the one occurrence of עי apart from the biblical writings in West Semitic, Mesha of Dibon (ninth century BCE) claims, for example, to have rebuilt the city of Bezer "because it was in ruins" (*ky 'yn* [KAI 181:27]). Similarly, Yaḥimilk (tenth century BCE), King of Byblos, claims to have "restored all the ruins" (*ḥwy*

the divine ruler of Jerusalem who returns to the site in order to revitalize it – a king responsive to the psalmist's plea that Zion's ruler walk among the ruins of the location and overturn its state of affairs (Ps 74:3).

A belief in the future renewal of Jerusalem was spurred, then, by similar convictions of divine agency that had prevailed in earlier accounts of Jerusalem's impending demise. The deity who had formerly chosen to bring ruin about could also, in these passages, decide to revitalize what had been lost. In the era after Jerusalem's fall, the contingency of time and ruination on the will of Yahweh thus provided the foundation of something new: hope for the future.[132] This theme is announced explicitly in Jer 31:17 in Yahweh's declaration that "there is hope for your future" and appears again in Jer 29:11: "For I, I know the plans I have planned for you," Yahweh announces, "plans for your well-being and not evil, to give you a hopeful future."[133] The coming reversal of present circumstances, once directed at Zion adherents who thought their city indestructible, is an expectation drawn on by later communities to countenance the possibility that the ruined city of Jerusalem would one day be ruins no more. "The city shall be rebuilt on its ruin mound (תלה)," Yahweh vows in Jeremiah, "and the citadel on its rightful site" (Jer 30:18). Elsewhere, the psalmist affirms this promise: "For God will save Zion and rebuild the cities of Judah" (Ps 69:35).

When this restoration would take place is not disclosed. The impression these writings convey is of an event that is soon approaching, ever near. When we return to the centuries of the Persian and early Hellenistic period, what becomes evident, however, is that these claims would long go unfulfilled. A modest temple is rebuilt. A small community comes to be resettled at the location. Certain fortifications may have been repaired. But our current archaeological picture of Jerusalem during this era is that of a site still awaiting the great reclamation promised in these writings. When the location finally begins to recover under the Hasmoneans (ca. 167–37 BCE), the era of recovery is, nevertheless, short-lived. Jerusalem again comes to ruin during the First Jewish-Roman War (66–73 CE), though the loftiest towers of the city's

---

kl mplt) of the structures referred to in his building inscription (KAI 4:3). The Book of Nehemiah's attribution of rebuilding to the work's namesake would be in keeping, then, with this broader ideology. For other instances of this ideological discourse among West Semitic inscriptions and their significance for a ruler's authority, see Douglas Green, *"I Undertook Great Works": The Ideology of Domestic Achievements in West Semitic Royal Inscriptions* (Tübingen: Mohr Siebeck, 2010).

[132] On this theme, see also the poem of Lamentations 3, following on the images of ruination in Lam 1–2, where two stanzas in the middle of the poem hinge on an idea of hope "that is not facile, easy to come to, but one borne out of pain." F. W. Dobbs-Allsopp, *Lamentations* (Louisville, KY: Westminster John Knox, 2002), 116–19.

[133] The absence of the beginning of this verse in the LXX is a clear instance of haplography, a point supported by its preservation in OG^L, the Vulgate, and other witnesses.

ramparts are preserved by the Roman army, Josephus tells us, so as to "signify what kind of city it was," (σημαίνωσιν οἵας πόλεως) before they destroyed it (*B.J.* 7.1.1).

4.4 THE PROPHETIC WRITINGS AND RUINS: SUMMARY

It is within the prophetic writings and, above all, in the lengthy works of Isaiah, Jeremiah, and Ezekiel, that the densest concentration of references to ruins in the Hebrew Bible appears. If locations such as Memphis (Jer 46:18), Babylon (Jer 51:37), Damascus (Is 17:1), and Tyre (Ezek 26:4, 12) – among other foreign sites – are named as sites of ruin or on the precipice of destruction, the bulk of passages that refer to ruins do so with the city of Jerusalem in view. Both in the admonitions that Jerusalem would soon come undone and the later avowals that the ruined city would be rebuilt, the language of ruination found within these writings is centered on the place where, according to the Zion traditions, Yahweh chose to dwell forevermore (Ps 132:14).

In these texts, ruins foretell something of a time to come. Never are ruins cited in these writings to reflect on occurrences from former times, and nowhere do we come across interest in what older remains reveal about the lives of those who left them behind from generations previous. Instead, ruins are invoked in order to exhort, bidding audiences to be prepared for a time drawing near when present circumstances will be overturned and the fate of Jerusalem recast. The language of ruination expressed in these works is charged by a sense of urgency, communicated to forewarn of impending calamity or, once Jerusalem is destroyed, to arouse hope among a population whose experiences within the tattered remains of the fallen city may have offered little of it.

Ruins, in sum, presage a future distinct and disconnected from what is experienced in the present. Historically, this conviction crystalized in response to claims made about Zion that emerged in Iron Age Jerusalem, a city that, for over a thousand years, had never been destroyed. Opposed to the confidence placed in Jerusalem's continued standing, certain prophetic voices arose that challenged such sentiments by accenting the agency of the deity who was believed to oversee the city's affairs. The time approaching is consistently bound to the will of Yahweh in these prophetic texts – the deity's designs for the future predicated on the current conduct of Jerusalem's population rather than assurances inferred from the past. Both in their critiques of an ideology that promoted Jerusalem's inviolability and in later visions regarding Yahweh's return to Zion to restore what has been destroyed, ruins are a sign of a future that is open and undetermined. "I am doing something new," Yahweh announces to a community in ruin, "now it appears – can you not perceive it?" (Is 43:19b). In these writings, the time to come is liable at any moment to the sudden appearance of the "king of old" (Ps 72:12), who could countermand the present, bearing either destruction or renewal.

4.5 THE ANGEL OF HISTORY: WALTER BENJAMIN, RUINS, AND THE MESSIANIC

In a letter written from Paris on May 20, 1935, Walter Benjamin contemplates a journey to Jerusalem he will never take.[134] "What I wish for myself now," Benjamin writes, "would be to work in the library for a number of months and then be able to travel to Jerusalem after bringing my research to a more or less definitive conclusion in October or November." It was a consideration the letter's addressee, Gershom Scholem, was accustomed to receiving. Scholem had worked to arrange Benjamin's move to Jerusalem since the early 1920s, and, as late as February of 1939, Scholem still attempted to see his immigration through in spite of Benjamin's reluctance.[135] Instead, on September 26, 1940, after fleeing from Vichy officials and the Gestapo, Benjamin would die at the Hotel de Francia in Portbou, Spain, of a self-inflicted morphine overdose after receiving word that his transit visa had been rejected and he was to be returned across the border to France.

It was "as though he had drifted out of the nineteenth century and into the twentieth," Hannah Arendt writes of her friend, "the way one is driven onto the coast of a strange land."[136] Accustomed to personal failure and financial collapse,[137] exiled in 1933 with Nazi power ascendant, and acutely sensitive to a world "in which nothing remained unchanged but the clouds,"[138] this visitor "to a strange land," perhaps unsurprisingly, produced in the writings composed months before his death just prior to Germany's invasion of France in May of 1940 one of the most resonant images of ruination in the twentieth century. Appearing in Thesis IX of his "Theses on the Philosophy of History," Benjamin cites lines from a poem by Scholem, "Gruss vom Angelus," and then comments on the Paul Klee painting, "Angelus Novus" (1920), writing,[139]

---

[134] Gershom Scholem and Theodor Adorno, eds., *The Correspondence of Walter Benjamin, 1910–1940*, trans. M. Jacobson and E. Jacobson (Chicago: University of Chicago Press, 1994), 483.
[135] Ibid., 594.
[136] Hannah Arendt, "Walter Benjamin, 1892–1940," in *Illuminations: Essays and Reflection*, ed. H. Arendt, trans. H. Zohn, 1–55 (New York: Schocken, 1968), 19.
[137] Ibid., 16–18; Scholem and Adorno, *Correspondence*, 220–21.
[138] Walter Benjamin, "The Storyteller," in *Illuminations*, ed. H. Arendt, 83–110 (New York: Mariner, 2019 [1968]), 84.
[139] Walter Benjamin, "Theses on the Philosophy of History," in *Illuminations*, ed. H. Arendt, 253–64 (New York: Mariner, 2019 [1968]), 257–58.

> His eyes are staring, his mouth is open, his wings are spread. This is how one pictures the angel of history. His face is turned toward the past. Where we perceive a chain of events, he sees one single catastrophe which keeps heaping ruins on ruins (*Trümmer auf Trümmer häuft*) and hurls it in front of his feet. The angel would like to stay, awaken the dead, and make whole what has been smashed. But a storm is blowing from Paradise; it has got caught in his wings with such violence that the angel can no longer close them. This storm irresistibly propels him into the future to which his back is turned, while the pile of debris before him grows skyward. This storm is what we call progress.

Ruin upon ruin, Benjamin writes, the angel of history looks on at the debris left behind from peoples who had come before, their remains ascending skyward as the spirit is propelled into the future. If Kant had optimistically connected the European Enlightenment with the time of "progress" (*Fortschritt*),[140] to Benjamin the idea of progress was rather a violent storm that thrusts the heavenly being over the ruins that modernity did not thwart but only furthered.[141]

It is in this description of history and ruination that Benjamin's writings begin to intersect with themes expressed earlier in the prophetic corpus of the Hebrew Bible, above all in a future menaced by ruins close at hand. Throughout the "Theses," in fact, Benjamin's concern is with a time that lies ahead and the inability of his contemporaries to think beyond or other than the current state of affairs. Symptomatic of this failure for Benjamin was the work of historians who had preceded him. In part, the issue with the scholars who had come before, such as Leopold von Ranke and Fustel de Coulanges, whom Benjamin names, was their "indolence of heart" (*Trägheit des Herzens*).[142] Advocates of impartiality and a detachment from the present in the histories they produced, both historians, Benjamin contends, masked contemporary

---

[140] So, for example, we find in Kant's Ninth Proposition in "Idea for a Universal History": "For such a plan opens up the comforting prospect of a future in which we are shown from afar how the human race eventually works its way upward to a situation in which all germs implanted by nature are developed fully, and in which man's destiny can be fulfilled on earth." Immanuel Kant, "Idea for a Universal History with a Cosmopolitan Purpose," in *Political Writings*, 2nd ed., ed. H. Reiss, trans. H. B. Nisbet, 41–53 (Cambridge: Cambridge University Press, 1991), 52–53. On this point and the broader connection to the experience of history, see Christian Meier and Reinhart Koselleck "Fortschritt," in *Geschichtliche Grundbegriffe. Historisches Lexikon zur politisch-sozialen Sprache in Deutschland*, Vol. 2, eds. R. Koselleck, W. Conze, and O. Brunner, 351–423 (Stuttgart: Klett Cotta, 1975).

[141] "Das, was wir den Fortschritt nennen, ist *dieser* Sturm." Walter Benjamin, "Über den Begriff der Geschichte," in *Gesammelte Schriften*, I–2, 693–704 (Frankfurt: Suhrkamp, 1980), 698 (italics original). For further reflection on the theme of ruins and modernity, see the fine collection of essays in Julia Hell and Andreas Schöle, eds., *Ruins of Modernity* (Durham, NC: Duke University Press, 2010), and, further, Julia Hell, *The Conquest of Ruins: The Third Reich and the Fall of Rome* (Chicago: University of Chicago Press, 2019).

[142] Benjamin, "Über den Begriff," 696.

47 Paul Klee, *Angelus Novus*, 1920 CE. Wikimedia Commons. Public domain

interests, often political, that motivated their work.[143] As a result, these ennobled figures represented a crisis in thought that stands out "more clearly if one asks with whom the adherents of historicism actually empathize." The answer, Benjamin writes, "is inevitable: with the victor."[144]

But this failure of sympathy was compounded by a failure of vision. Problematic about the histories written was the "homogenous, empty time," as Benjamin describes it, within which historical narratives were so often

---

[143] Ibid., 696.   [144] Benjamin, "Theses," 256.

sequenced.[145] This impression of how time unfolds — linearly, successively, singularly, without end — was a product of time being perceived everywhere as uniform and sequential, a perspective that positioned all of human history on a common trajectory, which was, as a consequence, emptied of its potentialities to be something other than what it was (Thesis XIII).[146] Measured and mapped out by fastidious historians who "muster a mass of data" (Thesis XVII) to draw out "causal connections" (Thesis A) in order to explain why history has advanced as it has,[147] the present state of affairs was the necessary outcome of what had preceded it, according to these scholars, their sense of history being something that was inevitable and unalterable. The disorderly and unsettled associations between past and present, and therefore the future, Benjamin contends, were thus flattened into a teleology of mere consecutiveness.[148] The future was simply an extension of the present in this historicist rendering of time, situated on a shared continuum from which it flows, we the passive agents bound to its clockwork progression.[149]

Opposed to this temporality is what Benjamin labels the "messianic."[150] Throughout his "Theses," what is essential to a messianic order of time is its

---

[145] Ibid., 261–63. Benjamin's concept of "homogeneous, empty time" is cited across a number of influential studies, including Anderson's *Imagined Communities*, which connects this experience of time to the rise of the modern nation state (Benedict Anderson, *Imagined Communities: Reflections on the Origin and Spread of Nationalism*, rev. ed. [London: Verso, 2006], 23–33, 204–5) and in a number of essays by Giorgio Agamben, including "Time and History: Critique of the Instant and the Continuum," in *Infancy and History: Essays on the Destruction of Experience*, trans. L. Heron, 89–106 (London: Verso, 1993). Its origins, however, can be traced to H. Bergson. See, for example, Henri Bergson, *Time and Free Will: An Essay on the Immediate Data of Consciousness*, trans. P. L. Pogson (New York: Cosimo, 2008 [1910]), esp. 88–106.

[146] Benjamin, "Theses," 260–61. For such reasons, Benjamin writes, history more often than not becomes a "tool" of the victors.

[147] Ibid., 262–63.

[148] Benjamin, "Theses," 262. Agamben writes in his penetrating reading of this theme, "The modern concept of time is a secularization of rectilinear, irreversible Christian time, albeit sundered from any notion of end and emptied of any other meaning but that of a structure process in terms of before and after." Agamben, "Time and History," 96.

[149] Ibid., 260–61. Benjamin observes that revolutionaries in Paris fired on the city's clocks from different directions, refusing to be controlled by the order of time imposed on them by the authorities. Ibid., 262.

[150] "There is likely no theme more over-exposed and over-theorized in Benjamin's work," R. Gibbs observes, "than the messianic." Robert Gibbs, "Messianic Epistemology: Thesis XV," in *Walter Benjamin and History*, ed. A. Benjamin, 197–214 (London: Continuum, 2005), 197. The literature on this theme is, as such, vast, including generative readings of Benjamin's concept in the works of Arendt, Derrida, and Agamben, among others. For seminal treatments of this concept within the larger framework of Benjamin's work, and influential for this study, see Irving Wohlfarth, "On the Messianic Structure of Walter Benjamin's Last Reflections," *Glyph* 3 (1978): 148–212; Rolf Tiedemann, "Historical Materialism or Political Messianism? An Interpretation of the Theses 'On the Concept of History,'" *The Philosophical Forum* 15.1–2 (1983–1984): 71–104; Rebecca Comay, "Benjamin's Endgame," in *Walter Benjamin's Philosophy: Destruction and Experience*, eds.

capacity to arrest and "blast apart" (*herauszusprengen*) the continuum on which time is presumed to advance (Theses XIV, XVI, XVII).[151] As Rebecca Comay puts it succinctly in her reading of this messianic theme, "The clock must be stopped."[152] What the messianic forestalls for Benjamin is a sense of time as continuous and invariable, an impression that was instrumentalized in the modern era and artificially imposed on our daily affairs. Where once time was made meaningful through the recurrence of holidays and festivals embedded in sacred calendars, "of which not the slightest trace has been apparent in Europe in the past hundred years," the temporality we now embrace is empty of the meanings it held before (Thesis XV), Benjamin contends, our time a time that continues on as it always has, and always will.[153]

Where Benjamin's reflections converge with the prophetic writings, then, is in their shared critique of a temporal outlook that presumes the future to be an extension of what came before, determined largely by what has already been experienced. Jerusalem will never fall because it never has, the opponents of the prophets once argued (Micah 3:11); new technological developments will always and only benefit society, Benjamin has its supporters proclaim (Thesis XI), creating a future whose fate is bound ever more closely to what is produced and controlled in the present. If Yahweh disrupts this temporal perspective in the prophetic corpus by breaking into time and ushering in a new state of affairs, in Benjamin's "Theses" it is a messianic power that does much the same, producing what Benjamin terms a "standstill" to the temporal order that prevails.[154] In this structure of suspended time, Benjamin writes in Thesis XVII, one "recognizes the sign of a messianic standstill of happenings (*Zeichen einer messianischen Stillstellung des Geschehens*), or, said differently, a revolutionary chance in the fight for the oppressed past."[155] Lulled into a conformism of thought (Thesis VI) and apathy of action (Thesis XII) by our sense that current affairs must advance in a certain direction,[156] the messianic

---

A. Benjamin and P. Osborne, 251–91 (Manchester: Clinamen, 1994); and Werner Hamacher, "'Now': Walter Benjamin on Historical Time," in *Walter Benjamin and History*, ed. A. Benjamin, 38–68 (London: Continuum, 2005).

[151] Benjamin, "Theses," 261–63. [152] Comay, "Benjamin's Endgame," 262–63.

[153] Benjamin, "Theses," 261–62. In his essay on Baudelaire, Benjamin writes similarly that, "The man who loses his capacity for experiencing feels as though he is dropped from the calendar. The big-city dweller knows this feeling on Sundays." Walter Benjamin, "On Some Motifs in Baudelaire," in *Illuminations: Essays and Reflection*, ed. H. Arendt, 155–200 (New York: Mariner, 2019), 184–85.

[154] Benjamin, "Theses," 262. On the significance of Benjamin's notion of the standstill, see especially Rolf Tiedemann, "Dialectics at a Standstill," in *The Arcades Project*, trans. H. Eiland and K. McLaughlin, 929–46 (Cambridge, MA: Harvard University Press, 1999). Cf. Comay, "Benjamin's Endgame," 272–73.

[155] Benjamin, "Über den Begriff," 703.

[156] In Convolute N of the *Arcades Project*, Benjamin offers the biting comment on the historical practices that arose in the nineteenth century: "The history that showed things 'as they really were' was the strongest narcotic of the century." Benjamin, *Arcades Project*, 463.

dispels this perception of a continuum in order to destabilize it, revealing instead a configuration "pregnant with tensions" – a time in which experiences, past and present, draw together in a constellation to detonate into a future that was previously unforeseen.[157] The future is "radically unthinkable," Comay writes of this framework, "because unassimilable to what is on hand" – a time that is intrusive, "radically new,"[158] and other than the progression we assume. The angel of history is propelled backward in Benjamin's vision, Comay observes, catching "not even a glimpse of the future to which his back is turned."[159] He, too, awaits a pause (*verweilen*) in the trajectory in which he is caught, for only then what has been ruined might be restored (*das Zerschlagene zusammenfügen*).[160]

Echoing the claims of the prophetic writings from long before, the future within this messianic vision of time is therefore marked by possibility rather than inevitability. "There is a secret agreement between past generations and the present one," Benjamin writes in Thesis II, "[o]ur coming was expected on earth." What has been accorded to us by those previous who anticipated our arrival, Benjamin continues, is "a *weak* messianic power, a power to which the past has a claim."[161] The residual power that courses through time resides in the aspirations of those who were subjugated in the past, their desires reduced or defeated in previous lifetimes, but whose hopes for the future persist into ours. The past endures and spirals into the present through the survival of the dreams of the vanquished, Benjamin argues, conferring a messianic power on us to achieve a future that those previous could not.[162] "Nothing that has ever happened should be regarded as lost for history," Thesis III declares.[163] In the messianic standing of time, the "chance" is opened up for the "oppressed past" to be liberated. It is an opportunity, Werner Hamacher writes in his reading of this theme, "to correct the miss, to do the undone, to regain the wasted and actualize the has-been-possible."[164]

The messianic is a "weak" power, however, neither fated nor assured. Bound up with its appearance is the prospect that it can be missed. "There is

---

[157] "Thus, to Robespierre," Benjamin writes, "ancient Rome was a past charged with the time of the now (*Jetztzeit*) which he blasted out of the continuum of history." Ibid., 262.

[158] Comay, "Benjamin's Endgame," 265–66. So also Gibbs: "The messianic, however, is a name for a not-yet, a future that exceeds the present, that interrupts it and our own expectations for a future." Gibbs, "Messianic Epistemology," 197.

[159] Comay," Benjamin's Endgame," 272.   [160] Benjamin, "Über den Begriff," 697.

[161] Benjamin, "Theses," 254. (italics original)

[162] Hamacher comments: "What is said here is that we are first of all and primarily the ones that were expected by the missed possibilities of the past. Only *qua* expected have we been given 'a *weak* messianic power' ... This messianic power is the intentional correlate of the claim that calls upon us from the missed possibilities of the past, not to miss them a second time but to perceive them in every sense: cognizingly (*sic*) to seize and to actualize them." Hamacher, "'Now': Walter Benjamin on Historical Time," 41.

[163] Benjamin, "Theses," 254.

[164] Hamacher, "'Now': Walter Benjamin on Historical Time," 41.

a messianic power," Hamacher comments, "only where it can fail."[165] The past "flits by," Benjamin remarks in this vein, flashing up in an "instant" when it may be recognized and, afterward, is "never seen again" (Thesis V).[166] We do not know when this *rendez-vous mystérieux*, as Benjamin describes it, will occur. Its arrival cannot be prepared for in advance but only recognized when it suddenly comes into view. Benjamin, a close reader of Kafka,[167] likely knew well the famous aphorism of the latter: "The Messiah will come only when he is no longer necessary, he will come only on that day after his arrival; he will come, not on the last day, but on the day after."[168] The power at work within messianic time is not ours to command, from this perspective, but remains something "secret" (*geheim*) that is granted (*mitgeben*) to us, an experience we cannot foresee or determine. Much like the workings of Yawheh depicted within the prophetic writings, the messianic is beyond our capacity to control. Benjamin thus concludes his reflections with a final thesis centered, once more, on the time ahead: "We know that the Jews were prohibited from investigating the future," it is observed, a prohibition that removed the soothsayers of old from their positions of influence. He continues: "This does not mean, however, that for the Jews the future was a homogeneous, empty time. For in it, every second was the small gate through which the Messiah might enter" (Thesis B).[169]

Written among the ruins of a world come undone, Benjamin's "Theses" draw near to a number of convictions expressed in the prophetic writings, bringing their sense of ruination and time into sharper focus. In both, images of ruin are a defining theme. At the very center of Benjamin's discussion is the Angel of History, who is forced to gaze at the ruins that have accumulated over the ages (Thesis IX), a figure that acts as the fulcrum around which the other expositions on history turn. And it is the occurrence of ruins, present or those to come, that so often animates the admonitions the prophetic writings put forward to their contemporaries in antiquity. A discourse of ruination is found across these writings, this is to say, to all appearances an outcome of shared experiences pertaining to loss and devastation.

But it is the impression of time associated with ruins that matters most for our discussion. For Benjamin, like the prophetic writings long before, the experience of ruin compels reflections on the time ahead, oriented toward a

---

[165] Ibid., 44.   [166] Benjamin, "Theses," 255.
[167] See, for example, Walter Benjamin, "Franz Kafka: On the 10th Anniversary of His Death," in *Illuminations*, ed. H. Arendt, 111–40 (New York: Mariner, 2019 [1968]).
[168] Franz Kafka, "The Coming of the Messiah," in *The Basic Kafka* (New York: Washington Square Press, 1979), 182.
[169] "Den Juden wurde die Zukunft aber darum doch nicht zur homogenen und leeren Zeit. Denn in ihr war jede Sekunde die kleine Pforte, durch die der Messias treten konnte." Benjamin, "Über den Begriff," 704.

future finally sundered from the "one single catastrophe" the angel views while driven from paradise. Though devoted to the concept (*Begriff*) of history, there is little interest in the past as such expressed in the "Theses." Benjamin resists at the outset both the famous dictum that historians recover the past "as it really was" (Thesis VI) and, later, the task of "establishing a causal connection between various moments in history" (Thesis A) so as to explain how the present came to be.[170] Rather, what the ruins of history compel is an investigation into the past desires of the defeated, spurred on in this research by a weak messianic power that drives the historian to recover such lost aspirations in an effort to "fan the spark of hope" for a better future to come (Thesis VI).

Benjamin's reflections on the messianic thus resonate with injunctions of the prophetic writings that had previously warned of calcified beliefs fixed on the past and bent toward those in power. Ancestral to Benjamin's writings, this is to say, are the prophetic critiques of contemporaries unable, or unwilling, to contemplate a future apart from their present circumstances. These biblical objections are most apparent in the denunciation of Zion traditions that presumed Jerusalem's past standing would simply continue on. As the Book of Jeremiah bluntly puts it, such sentiments were a "lie" (Jer 7:8), contrived by leading authorities to vacate the demands made by Yahweh for life together. Common to these writings, consequently, is the sentiment that the assumed continuity between past, present, and future be dispelled so that the ruins at hand be more fully recognized.

It is the idea of a messianic power, however, whose genealogy reaches most deeply into the biblical writings. To be sure, no explicit messianic figure or movement is mentioned among the references to ruins examined in the prophetic texts this chapter has discussed. What influence the Hebrew Bible had on Benjamin's late writings is, furthermore, uncertain.[171] Citations of specific biblical texts are not found within the "Theses." Messianic ideas were worked out among a number of key Jewish thinkers in the early twentieth century, moreover, from Kafka to Rosenzweig to Scholem – the latter discussing messianic themes at length with Benjamin during their years of friendship.[172]

---

[170] Ibid., 263.

[171] For Benjamin's misgivings about the possibility of reading the Bible under the alienating effects of modernity, see especially Brian Britt, "The Romantic Roots of the Debate on the Buber-Rosenzweig Bible," *Prooftexts* 20.3 (2000): 262–89. Cf. Brian Britt, *Walter Benjamin and the Bible* (London: Continuum, 1996). For Agamben's famous thesis, however, that Benjamin's concept of the messianic was influenced by the Pauline writings of the New Testament, see Giorgio Agamben, *The Time That Remains: A Commentary on the Letter to the Romans*, trans. P. Dailey (Stanford, CA: Stanford University Press, 2005), esp. 138–45.

[172] On these conversations, see Peter Fenves, *The Messianic Reduction: Walter Benjamin and the Shape of Time* (Stanford, CA: Stanford University Press, 2011), 103–24. For Scholem's views, see his classic *The Messianic Idea in Judaism* (New York: Schocken, 1972).

Nevertheless, in their claims about the agency of Yahweh, the divine king who intervenes in history to bring about a different future, early antecedents of later messianic thought, including those expressed in Benjamin's "Theses," were forged in the prophetic corpus. In these texts, Yahweh is envisioned as a deity who may at any moment undo present forms (e.g., Jer 18:7; Is 43:19), bringing about ruination or restoration in response to the conduct of the populace that this deity oversees. In the misshapen and diminutive theological vision that Benjamin announces in Thesis I,[173] this future and its demands are now wedded to a messianic power whose coming may appear at any second. In both collections of writings there is a sense of desperation.[174] In both, imminent ruin is felt to be close at hand.

But, in both, this prospective sense of time also gives rise to a future envisioned apart from such remains. In the first mention of the messianic that occurs in the "Theses," Benjamin writes that the "past carries with it a temporal index through which it refers to redemption" (Thesis II).[175] Much like the biblical writings that relate ruins to a future restoration, in Benjamin it is the wreckage of the past that bears within it the possibility of a redemption to come (Thesis IX), or what Geoffrey Hartman terms "a defeated potentiality of retroactive force"[176] that compels later generations to alter the current course of human affairs and attend to what has been lost. If the prophetic writings on the agency of Yahweh are ancestral to Benjamin's reflections on time, so too, then, can it be argued that Benjamin's idea of a messianic redemption is predicated, however obliquely, on the ancient premise that the "king of old" would one day return to Zion to restore its remains. Elsewhere in Benjamin's writings, there appears a passage that would even be at home in

---

[173] Benjamin, "Theses," 253.

[174] In the Book of Jeremiah, for example, we read: "My anguish, my anguish! I writhe in pain! Oh, the walls of my heart! My heart is beating wildly; I cannot keep silent; for I hear the sound of the trumpet, the alarm of war" (Jer 4:19). Benjamin, for his part, writes in Thesis VIII that "The tradition of the oppressed teaches us that the 'state of exception' [formulated by the Nazi government to authorize its measures] in which we live is not the exception but the rule." Benjamin, "Theses," 257. So also R. Wolin writes of Benjamin, "As the nightmare of German fascism threatened to efface all remnants of tradition from the face of the earth, his task became more urgent and his tone all the more exhortatory – culminating in the apocalyptic pitch of the 'Geschichtsphilosophische Thesen.'" Richard Wolin, *Walter Benjamin: An Aesthetic of Redemption* (Berkeley: University of California Press, 1994), 262.

[175] Benjamin, "Über den Begriff," 693. A similar theme opens the *Confessions*: "Narrow is the dwelling of my soul; expand it that You may enter in. It is in ruins, restore it." Augustine, *Confessions*, ed. R. S. Pine-Coffin; New York: Penguin, 1961), Book I: 5 (24). On the overlapping sense of temporality and restoration within Benjamin and Augustine, see Stéphane Mosès, "The Theological-Political Model of History in the Thought of Walter Benjamin," *History and Memory* 1.2 (1989): 5–33.

[176] Geoffrey Hartman, *Criticism in the Wilderness: The Study of Literature Today*, 2nd ed. (New Haven, CT: Yale University Press, 2007), 77. (italics original)

Jeremiah's Book of Consolation: "Only for the sake of the hopeless ones have we been given hope."[177]

§

Once more we accompany Jeremiah to the potter's house located somewhere on the outskirts of Jerusalem. For a millennium, if not longer, the city has stood above the Gihon spring and between the Kidron and Tyropoeon Valleys, watered and defended by the location's natural terrain. Now, in Jeremiah's day, it has reached a size and affluence it had never known before. Within the potter's home we watch as a vessel is made and remade on the turning stone, the wet clay collapsing and rising again at the potter's will. "At any moment," the voice of Yahweh calls out to Jeremiah (Jer 18:7, 9), the present state of affairs may be undone like the potter's ware, and Jerusalem, even at its height, may come to ruin. If there is a central theme that can be drawn out from this chapter's study of the prophetic discourse on ruination, it would be this claim of a future susceptible to transformation "at any moment," the status quo suddenly upended so that a different era may dawn. At any moment ruin may be at hand. At any moment, the king of old may return to restore what has been lost.

In his "Theses on the Philosophy of History," Walter Benjamin provides a more recent consideration of ruination and time that also foregrounds this sense of radical imminence. The ruins that the Angel of History views demand the arrival of a new dispensation for Benjamin, one that shatters our modern sense of the empty, homogeneous time that continues on as it always has, and always must. "The fact that 'things keep going on like this' is the catastrophe," Comay observes of Benjamin's writings,[178] a present state of affairs that can only be countermanded by what Benjamin describes as the arrival of a messianic power capable of halting the ruins that modernity has wrought. If the idea of "at any moment" animates the temporality of ruination in the prophetic writings, for Benjamin the anticipatory character of messianic time, then, is much the same: for the Jews "every second" of the future, Benjamin writes, is "the small gate through which the Messiah might enter."[179]

The divide between this prospective sense of ruination and the pastmindedness that guides historians and archaeologists today is apparent, the latter invested in events from antiquity and not possible events to come.[180] Such an

---

[177] This line is the concluding sentence to Benjamin's essay on Goethe's *Elective Affinities*, in which the "mystery of hope" is drawn out and elaborated on. Walter Benjamin, *Selected Writings: Volume I, 1913–1926*, eds. M. Bullock and M. Jennings (Cambridge: Belknap, 1996), 356. The phrase is also quoted in Hannah Arendt, "Walter Benjamin, 1892–1940," 17.

[178] Comay, "Benjamin's Endgame," 262.   [179] Benjamin, "Über den Begriff," 704.

[180] I am indebted to Paul Kurtz for the expression of pastmindedness. For his own study of the rise of modern historical thought and the influence of the prophetic works of the Hebrew Bible on it, see now Paul Michael Kurtz, "Is Kant among the Prophets? Hebrew Prophecy

observation returns us once more to Koselleck's reading of Altdorfer's *Alexanderschlacht* (1529 CE) discussed in Chapter 1. For Koselleck, the significance of Altdorfer's painting was twofold. Earlier, we traced the first of these implications when it was observed that Altdorfer had represented the ancient Battle of Issus as if it were also a contemporaneous event, rendering combatants and images of war as if they occupied the early sixteenth century CE world that Altdorfer knew. Differences between fourth century BCE customs and practices and those that arose two thousand years later were often elided in Altdorfer's portrait, accordingly, enclosing a past and present within what Koselleck describes as "a common historical plane."[181] For such reasons, Altdorfer's painting was riddled with what we today would perceive as anachronisms and historically mistaken representations. But such inaccuracies were of little interest to Altdorfer's audience or to those who viewed the painting in the generations that followed. Not until Friedrich Schlegel's commentary on the *Alexanderschlacht* three hundred years later, Koselleck writes, is there a sense that the ideas of time expressed within the portrait were a product of a different, former age that could no longer be sustained.[182]

But what was not touched on in that discussion is what Koselleck describes as the painting's "eschatological status."[183] In the depiction of Alexander's defeat of Darius, what is also represented, Koselleck comments, is the end of an age. Koselleck writes:

> This battle, in which the Persian army was destined for defeat, was no ordinary one; rather, it was one of the few events between the beginning of the world and its end that also prefigured the fall of the Holy Roman Empire. Analogous events were expected to occur with the coming of the End of the World. Altdorfer's image had, in other words, an eschatological status. The *Alexanderschlacht* was timeless as the prelude, figure, or archetype of the final struggle between Christ and Antichrist; those participating in it were contemporaries of those who lived in expectation of the Last Judgment.

In the course of Koselleck's essay, he meticulously draws out how this "expectation" of the Last Judgment in Altdorfer's work, so apparent, too, in Luther's contemporaneous writings, slowly gives way and diminishes in the generations that followed. The first cracks appear in the writings of the French historian Jean Bodin (late sixteenth century CE), who resists any specific eschatological horizon to how he conceives of the scope of human history, instead considering this span of time to be a matter of natural and cosmological

and German Historical Thought, 1880–1920," *Journal of Central European History* 54.1 (2021): 34–60.
[181] Reinhart Koselleck, *Futures Past*, 10. [182] Ibid., 10. [183] Ibid., 11.

calculation that may not culminate for another fifty millennia.[184] A century later Baruch Spinoza denounces visionary experiences and ridicules those who consider prophetic experiences of the future to be authentic. When Voltaire, a century later still, mocks prophetic prognostication, it "is simply the scorn," Koselleck comments, "of the victor."[185]

The way was thus prepared for Maximilien Robespierre's famous speech at the Revolutionary Constitution in 1793. In it, Robespierre announces that "the time has come to call upon each to realize his own destiny," a destiny guided by the "progress of human reason" rather than outmoded ideas of a future contingent on divine will.[186] The break with previous experiences of time was now complete. "Instead of the anticipated millennium" of a messianic return and Last Judgment, Koselleck observes, "a new and different temporal perspective had opened up."[187] In this opening, a discipline of history would be born that was severed from previous centuries of eschatological expectations, its eye now fixed on the past rather than considerations that could impinge on the time ahead. Since then, "one has lived in modernity and has been conscious of doing so."[188] The refutation of eschatology became a *sine qua non* of contemporary historical thought.

If "modernity represents the conditions of archaeology," as Julian Thomas argues in a monograph devoted to this theme,[189] then such conditions would demand, following Koselleck, that ruins be emptied of the future-oriented meanings that the biblical writings so often convey. Gained from our disavowal of this perspective and our turn to the historicity of material remains are prodigious insights into life in antiquity, whether among those who experienced Jerusalem's fall in the early sixth century BCE, as examined in this chapter's study, or those who lived elsewhere and at different times.

But in Robespierre's invocation of progress, something of the image of Benjamin's Angel of History appears before us once more, "his eyes staring, his mouth open." Like Ezekiel bound before the image of Jerusalem's impending destruction, the angel is unable to halt the wreckage to come. "The angel would like to stay, awaken the dead, and make whole what has been ruined," Benjamin writes.[190] But the angel cannot arrest the ruins that continue to mount, being propelled onward instead by a violent storm that blows from

---

[184] Ibid., 15–16.　[185] Ibid., 17.　[186] Quoted in Ibid., 12.
[187] Ibid., 17.　[188] Ibid.
[189] Thomas comments further, "By that I mean that archaeology as we presently practice it is intimately connected with the modern experience, and indeed amounts to a distillation of a modern sensibility." Julian Thomas, *Archaeology and Modernity* (London: Routledge, 2004), 2.
[190] Benjamin, "Theses," 257.

paradise, a storm that "we call progress." Earlier, some decades before, Benjamin had foreshadowed this theme, writing in a fragmentary text that it was not historians or historical knowledge, but "only the Messiah himself [who] consummates all history, in the sense that he alone redeems, completes, creates."[191]

---

[191] Walter Benjamin, "Theologico-Political Fragment," in *Reflections: Essays, Aphorisms, Autobiographical Writings*, ed. P. Demetz, trans. E. Jephcott, 312–13 (New York: Schocken, 1986), 312.

CONCLUSION

> In Breughel's Icarus, for instance: how everything turns away
> Quite leisurely from the disaster; the ploughman may
> Have heard the splash, the forsaken cry,
> But for him it was not an important failure; the sun shone
> As it had to on the white legs disappearing into the green
> Water, and the expensive delicate ship that must have seen
> Something amazing, a boy falling out of the sky,
> Had somewhere to get to and sailed calmly on.[1]

On October 12, 1935, the digging began. Shovel to soil, three trenches 6m wide and 50–70 m in length began to emerge at separate areas of Tell el-Mutesellim, Palestine, known in antiquity as the city of Megiddo. For the previous ten years the Oriental Institute of the University of Chicago had sought to expose each stratum of the massive mound in its entirety, a gargantuan project that, even with Rockefeller funds, was abandoned for reasons of time and money in order to descend more rapidly through the many layers of the ancient site.[2] Nearly one hundred years later, visitors to Megiddo today can still make out where the Oriental Institute commenced their work in that late

---

[1] W. H. Auden, "Musée des Beaux Arts" in *Poems: Volume 1 – 1927–1939*, ed. E. Mendelson, 338 (Princeton, NJ: Princeton University Press, 2022).

[2] For a discussion of this new approach to the site, see Gordon Loud, *Megiddo II* (Chicago: University of Chicago Press, 1948), 1–5. For a lively account of the University of Chicago's excavation at Megiddo, see Eric Cline, *Digging up Armageddon: The Search for the Lost City of Solomon* (Princeton, NJ: Princeton University Press, 2020).

48 Aerial view of Tel Megiddo, with north to the left of the image. Avramgr, photograph. Creative Commons Attribution-Share Alike 4.0 international license

autumn, including the eastern Area BB of the site where a substantial chunk of the mound is now missing.

In his excavation report published after the World War II, Gordon Loud, the former field director at Megiddo, writes that the decision to dig trenches met with almost immediate success. In Area AA, located on the northern edge of the tel, the team came down on the remains of a Late Bronze Age (LBA) palace and city gate, the former containing an impressive courtyard and a room with an intricate shell-paved floor, in addition to a gold and ivory hoard buried in another palatial chamber.[3] Area BB proved more significant still. There, workers uncovered the corner of a large building that, in time, would be known as Temple 2048, a monumental structure with massive walls constructed around a central sacred space.[4] Loud comments in his description of the building that the temple bore a striking resemblance to a sanctuary found at Shechem just a decade before, and indeed both would later be identified among the famous Bronze Age "migdal," or tower temples, that would also be uncovered at Hazor and Pella.[5]

---

[3] Loud, *Megiddo II*, 16–33. Cf. David Ussishkin, "The Destruction of Megiddo at the End of the Late Bronze Age and Its Historical Significance," *Tel Aviv* 22 (1995): 240–67.

[4] Loud, *Megiddo II*, 102–5.

[5] Ibid., 104. On these buildings, see Amihai Mazar, "Temples of the Middle and Late Bronze Ages and the Iron Age," in *The Architecture of Ancient Israel: From the Prehistoric to the Persian Periods*, eds. A. Kempinski and R. Reich, 161–87 (Jerusalem: Israel Exploration Society,

What Loud did not know during that first season of digging is what lay beneath the sanctuary. As excavations continued in Area BB and new strata appeared from more ancient periods, it became apparent that Temple 2048 was built above the ruins of forerunners. Among them were three "megaron" temples of the Intermediate Bronze Age (IBA) (ca. 2400–2000 BCE), an impressive round altar of the Early Bronze Age (EBA) III era (ca. 2800–2400 BCE) built directly on the highest point of the city, and, finally, the "Great Temple" of the EBA I period (ca. 3500–3000 BCE) – a sanctuary that remains one of the largest and most impressive structures ever recovered from this era in the entire Levant.[6] In the end, Temple 2048 was simply the last in a long line of sacred buildings located in this precinct of the settlement. When Loud did finally reach bedrock, furthermore, remains from the Neolithic period suggest that those who came to Megiddo also engaged in cultic practices within these spaces (Area BB) – a location situated on the most elevated section of the original hill on which Megiddo was built and which may have functioned as a pilgrimage site already during this early timeframe.[7] What it was about Megiddo that attracted such intensive religious activity is not known. But the decision to construct temple atop temple at this specific place for thousands of years indicates something of the location's enduring sacredness in antiquity.

Nor did Loud know the fate of Temple 2048. As later excavations would reveal in the decades to come, this sanctuary continued in use for a lengthy duration, persisting into the waning moments of the Iron I period.[8] In light of its likely founding in the Middle Bronze Age (MBA), the sanctuary would have stood in Area BB for perhaps eight centuries (ca. 1700 BCE–950 BCE), serving as the primary temple of the city throughout much of the second millennium BCE. When Megiddo was destroyed and the temple with it in the tenth century BCE, a single monolith situated above the burnt ruins of the sanctuary suggests that some memory of the structure may have also continued into the era after its destruction.[9] Such evidence would connect with Hazor,

---

1992). On the dating of this temple to the MB II period, see Claire Epstein, "An Interpretation of the Megiddo Sacred Area during Middle Bronze II," *Israel Exploration Journal* 15 (1965): 204–21.

[6] On these sanctuaries and sacred spaces, see David Ussishkin, "The Sacred Area of Early Bronze Age Megiddo: History and Interpretation," *Bulletin of the American Schools of Oriental Research* 373 (2015): 69–104; Matthew Adams, Israel Finkelstein, and David Ussishkin, "The Great Temple of Early Bronze I Megiddo," *American Journal of Archaeology* 118 (2014): 285–305.

[7] Ussishkin, "Sacred Area," 71, 73.

[8] Epstein, "An Interpretation of the Megiddo Sacred Area," 204–22; Assaf Kleiman et al., "Cult Activity at Megiddo in the Iron Age: New Evidence and a Long-Term Perspective," *Zeitschrift des Deutschen Palästina-Vereins* 133 (2017): 24–52.

[9] Kleiman et al. write, "In Square H/4 a single stone monolith, which resembles a *massebah*, was erected directly on top of the pile of collapsed and burnt bricks." Kleiman et al., "Cult Activity," 26.

49 Area BB, Megiddo, with Early Bronze Age round altar to the left and remains of Bronze Age temples in the foreground. Author photography

among other places in the eastern Mediterranean world, for communities that marked or safeguarded the remains of sacred locations from ages past, seemingly aware of what had once existed above the rubble.[10]

For generations of those who lived within Megiddo's vicinity, the towering Temple 2048 would have represented the heart of the city's sacred landscape. But the centuries in which this temple stood still pale in comparison to the much lengthier timeframe when Area BB drew individuals to it. If we situate Temple 2048 among its predecessors, Area BB appears to have served as a cultic precinct for what may have been three thousand years of nearly continuous activity. For millennia, those who resided in the western Jezreel Valley came to this location to perform rituals and build sanctuaries, and they did so

---

[10] On Hazor, see Sharon Zuckerman, "Ruin Cults at Iron Age I Hazor," in *The Fire Signals of Lachish: Studies in the Archaeology and History of Israel in the Late Bronze Age, Iron Age, and Persian Period in Honor of David Ussishkin*, eds. I. Finkelstein and N. Na'aman, 387–94 (Winona Lake, IN: Eisenbrauns, 2011). In a comparative vein, see Joseph Maran, "The Presence of the Past: Ruin Mounds and Social Memory in Bronze and Early Iron Age Israel and Greece," in *Nomads of the Mediterranean: Trade and Contact in the Bronze and Iron Ages: Studies in Honour of Michael Artzy*, eds. A. Gilboa and A. Yasur-Landau, 177–98 (Leiden: Brill, 2020).

CONCLUSION 257

for a period of time far longer than the history of either Islam or Christianity. But Loud did not come to Megiddo to worship. He came to dig.

§

In turning to the concluding thoughts of this study, the excavations at Megiddo are meaningful for how they demonstrate the divide that has been examined throughout this work. We now know that the ancient inhabitants of Megiddo encountered older ruins in their surroundings from at least the late fourth millennium through the first.[11] A number of these remains, such as the Great Temple of the EBA I period or the later Temple 2048, would have been monumental in form, attesting to the remarkable achievements of inhabitants who lived long ago. The remnants of intricate city gates and thick defensive walls, palaces, and other elite residences would have also been apparent. Yet as new communities built atop the ruins of those who preceded them and the city rose higher and higher over the centuries, there is no evidence that anyone at Megiddo attempted to unearth and study what was located beneath, nor is there any written text from antiquity that expresses a subterranean interest in the lives of those who occupied the site previously. Some older materials were reused for renovations and new buildings to come. Certain structures continued in use for centuries. The vestiges of former sacred spaces may have been commemorated by those who came later. But for over three thousand years the residents of Megiddo built above the remains of earlier settlements rather than digging down into what lay below.

Until 1903 CE, when the first archaeological efforts at Megiddo began.[12] And well over a century later, excavations continue at the site[13] – a practice so commonplace to our time that we rarely pause to ask how it is that it came to be. But why the ancient inhabitants of Megiddo, among others explored in this study, did not dig more extensively to learn about those who had preceded them – and why, at the turn of the twentieth century CE, we suddenly did – is the question that has been at the heart of this investigation.

On the surface, the most straightforward response is that we dig because we can. Experts trained in archaeological fieldwork and housed in universities continue to refine what and how we excavate, working within an academic discipline that emerged late, however, appearing only in the early decades of

---

[11] The settlement was finally abandoned sometime during the Persian Period (ca. 515–330 BCE). See Robert Lamon and Geoffrey Shipton, *Megiddo I* (Chicago: University of Chicago Press, 1939), 88–91.
[12] These were the work of the American Gottlieb Schumacher on behalf of the Deutscher Palästina-Verein. Gottlieb Schumacher, *Tell el-Mutesellim*, Vol. I (Leipzig: R. Haupt, 1908).
[13] See now Israel Finkelstein and Mario A. S. Martin, eds., *Megiddo VI: The 2010–2014 Seasons* (Tel Aviv: Sonia and Marco Nadler Institute of Archaeology, 2022).

the twentieth century CE.[14] In tandem with the rise of this new professional guild can be added economic resources that are marshalled today to study a wide collection of ancient settlements in ways not true of earlier efforts when digs were funded predominantly by the personal fortunes of specific individuals and guided by their personal interests. Furthermore, technological advancements have revamped how excavations unfold, not simply in terms of automation but also through the use of ground penetrating radar (GPR), carbon-14 dating, light detection and ranging (LiDAR) remote sensing, 3D printing, and the use of programming for modeling and inventory. Much like the builders of modern cities themselves, we possess the ability to perform astonishing feats of research and engineering to exhume ancient locations at a scale those in antiquity could never have dreamed of, much less have realized.[15]

But more than capacity is needed to explain this divide. Though new advancements have transformed how we excavate, the possibility of unearthing ruins and studying their remains is not a prerogative limited to our age. Indeed, throughout the previous studies certain figures have appeared that complicate a perspective that would see more recent responses to ruination as those uniquely available to us. The Babylonian ruler Nabonidus goes to great lengths in the sixth century BCE to recover artifacts from more distant predecessors, drawing on the resources of a sizable empire to obtain venerable items and restore old buildings through means that could have been used to excavate larger tracts of land and examine what was underground. In the eighteenth century CE, Volney travels throughout Egypt and the Levant to explore ruined sites found in these landscapes, producing widely read works that could have urged more systematic excavations. And Leonard Barkan, too – mentioned at the very beginning of this study – asked why it was that Roman citizens of the fifteenth century CE, residing in a city with "an enormous industry of intellect, aesthetics, politics, and economy ... should *not* give rise to the professional enterprise of archaeology" when their encounters with older material remains were so frequent.[16] What these examples,

---

[14] "During the years from 1860 to 1914," R. Boast writes in this vein, "there simply were no professional archaeologists ... As it was for John Evans in the last four decades of the nineteenth century, or for his son Arthur Evans at the beginning of the twentieth, many would consider it unfortunate or even unthinkable for someone to simply make their living at archaeology." Robin Boast, "The Formative Century, 1860–1960," in *The Oxford Handbook of Archaeology*, ed. C. Gosden, 47–70 (Oxford: Oxford University Press, 2009), 48.

[15] On this point, see Lewis Mumford, *The City in History: Its Origins, Its Transformations, Its Prospects* (New York: Harcourt Brace Jovanovich, 1961), 410–578; Fernand Braudel, *Civilization and Capitalism: 15th–18th Century, Volume III*, trans. S. Reynolds (Berkeley: University of California Press, 1992), 175–276; Joel Kotkin, *The City: A Global History* (New York: Modern Library, 2005), 111–60.

[16] Leonard Barkan, *Unearthing the Past: Archaeology and Aesthetics in the Making of Renaissance Culture* (New Haven, CT: Yale University Press, 1999), 18–19. (italics original)

among others, demonstrate, is that the prospect of disinterring ruins and learning about those who left them behind preceded our era and did not need to await its advent.

For such reasons, this book has looked beyond these developments for reasons why encounters with ruins have compelled different responses across the ages. Following Barkan's insights, among others,[17] I have argued that more is at work than changing material conditions alone. In addition, the impressions ruins leave on us are the result of certain presuppositions we harbor about their meanings, what Barkan terms the mentalities that take hold in response to ruination within a given period,[18] or what Peter Fritzsche, in his own study of ruins, describes as a "field" through which material remains come to be apprehended.[19] How we experience ruins, in short, is a product of the era we happen to occupy and the shared convictions that inform it. Or, as Fritzsche puts it, though the ruins have not changed across the centuries, the way we see them has.[20]

To explain why we excavate locations such as Megiddo when those before us did not requires us, then, to account for these changing perspectives and the prevailing ideas about ruination that gave rise to them. Such an explanation, this book has argued, cannot be made without taking into consideration impressions of time that ruins convey to their onlookers. Above all, I have maintained, ruins have to do with time, and it is in the distillation of temporal experience through an encounter with older material remains that distinct attitudes toward them become apparent. Said differently, ruins focalize issues of temporality by virtue of their capacity to endure, being at once vestiges of the past and features of the present that call into question the relationship between the two.

What scholars of the Hebrew Bible can contribute to this larger discussion are studies of how ruins and time were experienced by those in antiquity,

---

[17] Stewart, too, underscores that how we make sense of ruins is indebted to certain assumptions we hold about them ("As we respond to ruins," she writes, "we transform materiality into ideas, learning something about the value of human making."). And, as her rich study makes abundantly clear, these meanings are historically situated, finding distinct expressions across time and among diverse regions. Susan Stewart, *The Ruins Lesson: Meaning and Material in Western History* (Chicago: University of Chicago Press, 2020), 2. On this point, see also Alain Schnapp, *The Discovery of the Past: The Origins of Archaeology*, trans. I. Kinnes and G. Varndell (London: British Museum Press, 1996), 11–38; Peter Fritzsche, "Chateaubriand's Ruins: Loss and Memory after the French Revolution," *History and Memory* 10.2 (1998): 102–17; Laurent Olivier, *The Dark Abyss of Time: Archaeology and Memory*, trans. A. Greenspan (Lanham, MD: AltaMira Press, 2011), 75–104; and Julia Hell, *The Conquest of Ruins: The Third Reich and the Fall of Rome* (Chicago: University of Chicago Press, 2020).

[18] Barkan, *Unearthing the Past*, 18–19.

[19] Peter Fritzsche, *Stranded in the Present: Modern Time and the Melancholy of History* (Cambridge, MA: Harvard University Press, 2004), 106.

[20] Ibid., 106.

drawing attention to perspectives distant from our own. Historical investigations into more recent responses to ruination – whether of the Renaissance,[21] the French Revolution,[22] or the twentieth century CE[23] – can, from this vantage point, be augmented and further refined by attending to how more ancient communities described their encounters with remnants from ages past. Biblical scholars are especially well-positioned to address such historical questions because the Hebrew Bible is one of the richest sources on ruination that we possess from the ancient world, offering detailed accounts of how communities in the first millennium BCE thought about the ruins that were embedded in their surroundings. Even more, the biblical writings are of particular interest because the ruined landscapes these texts depict are some of the most excavated in the world. This constellation of written references and archaeological remains offers unparalleled insights into how those living in the first millennium BCE experienced ruination, both in what the biblical writings tell us explicitly about these encounters and, more obliquely, in what goes unmentioned within them about ruins that we know, archaeologically, were once in view.

When investigating these ancient accounts, the separate case studies of this work have drawn out modes of temporality linked to remembrance, presence, and anticipation. The thread that binds these experiences together, I argue, is a sense of affiliation and connectedness across the ages that material remains represent in these writings. The meaning of Shiloh's old ruins, as Chapter 2 detailed, is bound up in the Hebrew Bible with a collection of memories recounted about it by later communities who considered Shiloh's past their own. Even five hundred years after its demise, the Book of Jeremiah relates that the ruins of Shiloh could be recalled to unsettling effect (Jer 7:12, 14; 26:6, 9), attesting to an awareness of the ancient site's past and the sense that its fate could be shared, centuries later, by other locations like it. There is little curiosity expressed in these texts about how the ruins of Shiloh relate to the lives of those who once occupied the site in the eleventh century BCE or, further still, to the MBA inhabitants from centuries before. Even accounts

---

[21] So, for example, Barkan, *Unearthing the Past*; Ruth Rubinstein, "Pius II and Roman Ruins," *Renaissance Studies* 2.2 (1988): 197–203; Andrew Hui, *The Poetics of Ruins in Renaissance Literature* (New York: Fordham University Press, 2016).

[22] E.g., Fritzsche, *Stranded in the Present*; Stewart, *The Ruins Lesson*, 221–42; Andreas Schönle, "Modernity as 'Destroyed Anthill,'" in *Ruins of Modernity*, eds. J. Hell and A. Schönle, 89–103 (Durham, NC: Duke University Press, 2010).

[23] Hell, *Conquest of Ruins*, 307–443; W. G. Sebald, *On the Natural History of Destruction*, trans. A. Bell (New York: Modern Library, 2003), esp. 1–104; Julia Hell and Andreas Schönle, eds., *Ruins of Modernity*, 253–356; Andreas Huyssen, "Nostalgia for Ruins," *Grey Room* 23 (2006): 6–21; Caitlin DeSilvey and Tim Edensor, "Reckoning with Ruins," *Progress in Human Geography* 37.4 (2012): 465–85; Bjørnar Olsen and Þóra Pétursdóttir, eds., *Ruin Memories: Materialities, Aesthetics, and the Archaeology of the Recent Past* (London: Routledge, 2014).

about the history of Shiloh's downfall are unclear. Rather, the ruins of Shiloh matter insofar as they function as a place of memory within the biblical writings, calling to mind for later audiences distinct stories about what Shiloh once was and what, through certain misfortunes, this residence of Yahweh had become.

The possibility of ruins to speak to lived experiences across time is also apparent in the themes of presence and anticipation associated with these remains. Chapter 3 considered the afterlife of ruins in biblical storytelling and how older artifacts could continue to haunt the storyteller's present. "To this day," we are repeatedly told, certain ruins were visible to later onlookers, representing a past that somehow survived into their contemporary settings, still able to influence the practices and beliefs of those who came across them later in time. Once more, ruins find little value in these writings for the information they impart about past incidents. Instead, ruins such as those connected to Rachel's tomb (Gen 35:20) or the rock on which the ark once rested near Beth-Shemesh (1 Sam 6:18), among other old objects named in these writings, offered the possibility of coming into contact with former individuals or occurrences that were otherwise lost long ago. Opposed to a sense of distance, then, these accounts foreground a feeling of proximity, or an awareness of how the past is able to persist into the present through the ruins that remain.

And, finally, Chapter 4, too, drew out how ruins, by dint of conveying something about the future, were meaningful to those who came later. The dominant experience of ruination in the Hebrew Bible, I argue, is prospective temporality, or an anticipatory sense that ruins offer some insights into what the future may bring. In the numerous references to the ruins of Jerusalem, what appears in the prophetic writings are both admonitions about the looming destruction of the city and, after its fall, words of hope that one day these ruins would perhaps be ruins no more. This sense of the future is above all connected to the agency of Yahweh – the bearer of both ruin and restoration – who could, at any moment, bring about something new. From this perspective, ruins indexed a sense of time that was contingent and undetermined, pointing forward to a future when the present state of affairs could be suddenly undone.

In stepping back from these biblical accounts, what becomes evident is how distinct their impressions of ruins are from our own. To us, such remains are evidence of "counter lives" – as Fritzsche describes our appraisal of material finds[24] – in which the traces of former populations exemplify the disparities in lived experience that come to expression across the centuries. But for the

---

[24] Fritzsche, *Stranded in the Present*, 104.

biblical writers ruins are more immanent and familiar, binding together previous experiences with present and future ones. Ruins often attest to experiences held in common, this is to say, where the worlds in which Moses erects pillars at Sinai (Ex 24:4) or Joshua sets 'Ai aflame (Josh 8:28) are ones not too distant from the storyteller's own. Time itself is condensed – or, perhaps better, dissolved – in these portrayals of material remains, I have argued, such that ruined sites and artifacts are depicted in ways that are almost timeless, where anachronisms are tolerated and historical developments are muted in order to draw attention to the semblances between former and more recent periods. This is not to deny the rich sense of the past that ruins evoke for the biblical writers, in which certain destroyed sites or old objects can be attributed to the age of Abraham or Moses or the early moments of Israel's life in Canaan. Nor is it to negate the handful of passages when these writings take notice of certain changes that have occurred over the generations. But it is to argue that this vision of the past's continuity with the present is something quite distinct from our own reflections on former periods, absent, as it is, the "temporalization of history" that Reinhart Koselleck identifies as a hallmark of our historical perspective and efforts.[25] The moment we label an artifact as "Iron Age" or "fourth century BCE," we have entered into a universe of assumptions about time and ruins that the biblical writers would not – indeed could not – recognize.

An appreciation of what separates our historical appraisals of ruins from their portrayals in the Hebrew Bible has been indebted throughout to the work of Koselleck. What has been crucial for my purposes is Koselleck's collection of studies pertaining to how perceptions of time were reshaped during a period he labeled the *Sattelzeit*, or an era that stretched roughly from 1750 to 1850 CE.[26] Within this interval, Koselleck documents, time is increasingly described as something "new" by those who lived during these decades – a novelty characterized principally as a sense of time's acceleration that made previous ways of life suddenly distant and unfamiliar in comparison to what was now at hand. In Koselleck's terminology, the "space of experience" was increasingly unbound from a "horizon of expectation" in this period, meaning that the past could no longer serve as a paradigm for how life should be lived in the future.[27] This impression of time brought to the fore an acute awareness of asymmetries

---

[25] Reinhart Koselleck, *Futures Past: On the Semantics of Historical Time*, trans. K. Tribe (New York: Columbia University Press, 2004), 128–54.

[26] Much of this work is brought together in English in two edited volumes, the aforementioned *Futures Past: On the Semantics of Historical Time*, and Reinhart Koselleck, *Sediments of Time: On Possible Histories*, trans. S. Franzel and S. L. Hoffmann (Stanford, CA: Stanford University Press, 2018).

[27] Koselleck, *Futures Past*, 26–42, 255–76.

between past and present, Koselleck writes, or the realization of discontinuities that separated the customs, habits, and worldviews of prior generations from one's own. In this moment of rupture,[28] a discipline of history emerges whose aim is to draw out and examine the differences that have appeared across the ages, a manner of study pursued not in order to return to or emulate the past (i.e., *historia magistra vitae*) but to better understand former ways of life that were now unrepeatable and, as unrepeatable, obscure. In its wake, a discipline of archaeology is born that attends to how dissimilarities in lived experience are preserved in the ruins left behind.[29] A recognition of the diachronic variation in ceramic typologies, the changing morphology of architectural forms, or, most of all, the identification of archaeological strata are the recognition of differences located in time. But it is only in this moment that such differences are found to be historically significant.

By attending to how "the experience of historical time is articulated"[30] in his sources, Koselleck provides a theoretical framework for this investigation and a model for its manner of inquiry – a model insofar as it encourages similar historical studies of other eras apart from that on which Koselleck concentrates his efforts, a study that has been undertaken within these pages and their focus on temporalities of ruination as expressed within the biblical writings. But the more lasting influence of Koselleck's work is its consideration of the semantics of time, as he describes it, or a theory of how temporal experience is organized and made meaningful by those within a given period. That the experience of time is itself a historical phenomenon, conceptualized and ordered in distinct ways by various communities across the ages, is the theoretical apparatus on which this study of ruins has been built.

What this approach affords, I argue, is a deeper and more penetrating explanation for the differences that separate our sense of ruins from those behind the biblical writings. That is, if contemporary archaeological research is underpinned by more recent frameworks of temporality, as Koselleck's work demonstrates,[31] then the absence of similar archaeological interests in antiquity can also be traced, at least in part, to experiences of time and ruination distinct from our own. The prospect of digging down through space to learn about those who lived differently in the past is a predisposition that we hold, derived

---

[28] "The divide between previous experience and coming expectation opened up, and the difference between past and present increased, so that lived time was experienced as a rupture, as a period of transition in which the new and the unexpected continually happened." Koselleck, *Futures Past*, 246.

[29] Fritzsche puts the matter succinctly: "In the nineteenth century, the past was increasingly organized according to temporal and spatial differences." Fritzsche, *Stranded in the Present*, 101.

[30] Koselleck, *Futures Past*, 3.

[31] On this point, see also Gavin Lucas, *The Archaeology of Time* (London: Routledge, 2004), esp. 32–94; Julian Thomas, *Archaeology and Modernity* (London: Routledge, 2004), 1–34.

from a particular experience of time largely removed from how the biblical writings describe the meaning of material remains.

Instead, within the Hebrew Bible ruins convey something about life here and now. The temporalities of remembrance, presence, and anticipation are all centered on this abiding sense that past experiences preserved in material form bear directly on current ones. In part, this phenomenology of time and ruination finds historical import through what it discloses about the ancient mindsets that informed the biblical writings, further elucidating our understanding of the worlds in which these texts were written and how the individuals behind them experienced the past. What this study has demonstrated is that, like us, these nameless scribes lived among landscapes that preserved ruins from long ago, and like us they composed stories and poems about encounters with these remains. But the underlying sense of time mediated through the ruins they depict is something distinct from ours, set apart by the belief that the remnants of more distant eras retain meaningful connections to one's own. That, in the end, these distant eras are not so distant at all. Shiloh's downfall, Rachel's death, and Jerusalem's destruction, among the many other phenomena examined in these chapters, are experienced as something lasting – a time of ruination that can be described as residual and recursive, blurring the boundaries between what was, what is, and what is yet to come.

Such a sensibility, however, is not one that guides historical and archaeological work today. To remember a past affiliated with certain material remains is something distinct, this is to say, from the commitment to contextualize these artifacts within the scope of history, as Zachary Schiffman describes our contemporary efforts,[32] and to feel the past's presence in the remnants left behind is an experience opposed to the sense of distance and disassociation that will come to mark Chateaubriand's journals or Joseph Callaway's reflections on the ruins of 'Ai. Foreseeing something of the time ahead in the ruins one encounters is, furthermore, a perspective so radically at odds with a scholarly preoccupation with what once happened in the Neolithic or Bronze Ages that almost nothing connects them other than the ruins they both hold in view. Indeed, modern historical thought comes into its own, Koselleck remarks, once beliefs about the eschaton and the imminent end of this age are finally abandoned.[33]

An appreciation of the depth of historical time and a sensitivity to historical context are intuitions that are largely absent from the temporalities of ruination expressed in the Hebrew Bible. Removed from these concerns, there is little impetus to unearth older material remains and study them if one believes that

---

[32] Zachary Schiffman, *The Birth of the Past* (Baltimore: Johns Hopkins University Press, 2011), 1–34.
[33] Koselleck, *Futures Past*, 11–17.

CONCLUSION   265

what lies beneath the ground is much the same as what is found above it, only more dilapidated and unsound. Absent our belief that the forward flow of time occasions unprecedented advancements and change, the biblical writers experience ruins that can signify attachments between the past and the present, offering contemporary lessons and reinforcing the bonds of communal identity, at moments even warning of what is to come. The sheer existence of ruins, *that* they could be experienced at certain locations, is enough to derive such meanings from them.

But such attachments are no longer ours. Ruins are now about differences that appear in history, and to excavate is to better understand all that separates one era from the next, and us from those who came before. The disparities across the epochs are so staggering, in fact, that despite exhuming the corpses of the dead and sifting the dirt of their homes, we question whether we can understand their lives at all. We dig, then, not out of some idle curiosity. We dig because time has wrought such change so quickly, as Koselleck might put it, that without these efforts even our fragile connections to those who came before would be lost, we the orphans of forces still quite recent.[34] We dig, in other words, because we must. It is the sign of a predicament, not a solution.

§

It is under the sign of a predicament that the previous chapters have been written. Perhaps this comes to clearest expression in the heading Paul Ricoeur proposes in a prelude to a study of historical knowledge entitled "History: Remedy or Poison?"[35] The question posed by Ricoeur is directed at history's relationship to memory or, better, the knowledge claimed by historical research as it pertains to what a community's shared memories disclose about its past. Already in the work of Maurice Halbwachs, Ricoeur notes, the charge is levied against those "who write history" that their research is undertaken in opposition to the memories that bind a community together. The historian's focus on "the changes, the differences" that mark the passing of time have the effect, Halbwachs writes, of undermining the "tableau of resemblances" that a living memory affords, disrupting, if not shattering, a shared past that connects

---

[34] Olivier writes of dream in which something similar comes to expression in his archaeological work, a sense of "looking for something I can't find because I can't remember what I am after." Olivier, *Dark Abyss of Time*, xiv. Hayden White, in his review of Paul Ricoeur, puts the matter succinctly: In "modernity," we have "consummated the great programs of demystification that has deprived us of the consolations of religion and the certainties of metaphysics." Hayden White, "Guilty of History? The *Longue Durée* of Paul Ricoeur," *History and Theory* 46 (2007): 233–51, 234.

[35] Paul Ricoeur, *Memory, History, Forgetting*, trans. K. Blamey and D. Pellauer (Chicago: University of Chicago Press, 2004), 141–45.

50 Excavation of royal cemetery at Ur, 1900 CE. From C. L. Woolley, *Ur Excavations, Volume II: The Royal Cemetery*. Joint Expedition of the British Museum and of the Museum of the University of Pennsylvania to Mesopotamia, 1927. Plate 8. No known copyright restrictions

generations across time.[36] A similar ambivalence, Ricoeur observes,[37] is found in the works of Pierre Nora and Yosef Yerushalmi and their historical studies of earlier practices of remembrance. Yerushalmi, for his part, will raise these misgivings to a crisis point, when, in the last lecture of his seminal work, *Zakhor*, he writes of an "ironic awareness" that the "very mode in which I delve into the Jewish past represents a decisive break with that past."[38] Later, Yerushalmi will refer to an "unraveling" and a "malady" that has afflicted the community from which he descends, to which the historian "seems at best a pathologist, hardly a physician."[39]

But something deeper is at work in these comments than matters of memory alone. Rather, what memory represents more broadly to these authors is an older, more venerable mode of retrospection, unhinged from contemporary modes of historical inquiry and thus free from the assumptions

---

[36] Maurice Halbwachs, *La collective mémoire*, 2nd ed. (Paris: Presses Universitaires de France, 1968), 78. On this point, see also the discussion of Halbwachs in Chapter 2.

[37] Ricoeur, *Memory, History, Forgetting*, 397–411.

[38] Yosef Yerushalmi, *Zakhor: Jewish History and Jewish Memory*, 2nd ed. (Seattle: University of Washington Press, 1996), 81.

[39] Ibid., 94.

and guiding interests of the historian's work. Ricoeur's question – "history: remedy or poison?" – is, in fact, directed at the question of history's relationship to what came before its modern advent. So it is that Ricoeur turns to Friedrich Nietzsche,[40] the great critic of modernity, who, a century before Yerushalmi, had also detected a sickness (*Krankheit*) that had taken hold of his society, an infirmity linked to what was described as a glut of history, or a fixation on the historical that, in Nietzsche's terms, negates life rather than promotes it.[41] "I believe, indeed, that we are all suffering from a consuming fever of history," Nietzsche writes in this vein, "and ought to at least recognize that we are suffering from it."[42] Enervating in its effect, insatiable in its appetite, "historical culture is indeed a kind of inborn grey-hairedness," Nietzsche comments further, fulfilling Hesiod's ancient prophecy of a generation in which infants are birthed already old, a culture that makes even the youthful and strong suddenly frail.[43] Too much history, too little life. The debilitating, pathological character of historical research finds one of its most eloquent expressions in Nietzsche's essay, tilting the question Ricoeur poses toward the toxic.

History, remedy or poison? The question has hovered in the background of this work, too, where in each chapter certain voices have been brought forward to interrogate the motivations underpinning these studies and to wonder at what has been lost in their pursuit. In Chapter 2, Schliemann's belief in Homer encounters Yerushalmi's faith of the fallen, the historian's research now occupying a space once reserved for the claims of ancient writings and the worldviews they long supported.[44] For Ankersmit, in Chapter 3, the desire for the ecstasy of presence in one's study of the past, of the "union of subject and object" that overcomes the boundaries of time is, instead, stymied by a "professionalized historical writing that stakes everything on pulling them apart as much as possible."[45] Edward Said indicts historical projects such as the *Description de l'Égypte* as exploitations of colonialism laid bare,[46] and Walter Benjamin has visions of a messianic power that would one

---

[40] The title of this prelude with Nietzsche as its focus is "The Burden of History and the Non-Historical." Ricoeur, *Memory, History, Forgetting*, 281–86.

[41] Friedrich Nietzsche, "On the Uses and Disadvantages of History for Life," in *Untimely Meditations*, ed. D. Breazeale, trans. R. J. Hollingdale, 57–124 (Cambridge: Cambridge University Press, 1997), 120–21.

[42] Nietzsche, "Uses and Disadvantages of History," 60.

[43] Ibid., 101. Elsewhere, Nietzsche writes of this debilitating effect of history: "The young man has become so homeless and doubts all concepts and all customs. He now knows: every age is different, it does not matter what you are like." Ibid., 98.

[44] So also Ricoeur comments: "If Koselleck can speak of the experience of history, this is also to the extent that the concept of history can claim to fill the space previously occupied by religion." Ricoeur, *Memory, History, Forgetting*, 300.

[45] Frank Ankersmit, *Sublime Historical Experience* (Stanford, CA: Stanford University Press, 2005), 170.

[46] Edward Said, *Orientalism* (New York: Vintage, 1978), 42–44.

day overturn the "homogeneous, empty time" within which modern history operates, its historians implicated for their love of the powerful and lack of love for the defeated.[47]

To include these voices of antipathy within this work is to allow the ambivalence within Ricoeur's question to be also conveyed across its pages, mirroring Ricoeur's own willingness to "allow this unavoidable suspicion" surrounding history's aims "to express itself again more than one time" within his lengthy study.[48] But for my purposes these voices are also meaningful insofar as their outlooks draw so near at moments to what the biblical writings often convey about the past's relationship to the present and the future. The recent upsurge of interest regarding issues of memory, presence, or the work of Benjamin among historians, this is to say, could be taken as a desire for something beyond what the tools of historicism have long offered. Nietzsche's quotation of Friedrich Hölderlin's reading of Diogenes Laertius would appear to speak to our moment as well: "I have again found here what I have often before discovered, that the transitoriness and changeableness of human thoughts and systems strike me as being almost more tragic than the destinies which alone are usually called real."[49]

But if the reader has made it to these final moments of this book, they realize that no flight from history has been undertaken in this volume. To what destination we would find refuge is not clear. Chapter 1 details how our "historical condition," as Ricoeur put it, is "insurmountable" – a condition that, as such, cannot be suppressed, or at least not if our intellectual labors are to have some integrity and, perhaps, some value. "We make history, and we make histories," Ricoeur writes, "because we are historical."[50]

A response to Ricoeur's question – "remedy or poison?" – may, then, reside in what Hölderlin had already recognized, and what Hayden White also described, as the "tragic" among the modes of possible histories in his famous study.[51] Or at least it is one response offered in this work. How to write otherwise after the events of the twentieth century is difficult to know. "At a time when the promises of the modern age lie shattered like so many ruins,"[52] Andreas Huyssen writes, it is perhaps not surprising that many recent works, including this one, cannot look away, and that a sense of ruin and loss runs deep, even into the histories we try to write about them.

---

[47] Walter Benjamin, "Theses on the Philosophy of History," in *Illuminations: Essays and Reflection*, ed. H. Arendt, 253–64 (New York: Mariner, 2019), 256.
[48] Ricoeur, *Memory, History, Forgetting*, 145. Later, Ricoeur will remark: "Should we now speak of unhappy history? I do not know." Ibid., 500.
[49] Nietzsche, "Uses and Disadvantages of History," 98.
[50] Ricoeur, *Memory, History, Forgetting*, 284.
[51] Hayden White, *Metahistory: The Historical Imagination in 19th Century Europe* (Baltimore: Johns Hopkins University, 1973), 29–30, 108–11, 191–229, 333–56.
[52] Huyssen, "Nostalgia for Ruins," 7.

BIBLIOGRAPHY

Adams, Matthew, Israel Finkelstein, and David Ussishkin. "The Great Temple of Early Bronze I Megiddo." *American Journal of Archaeology* 118 (2014): 285–305.

Agamben, Giorgio. "Time and History: Critique of the Instant and the Continuum." In *Infancy and History: Essays on the Destruction of Experience*, translated by L. Heron, 89–106. London: Verso, 1993.

——— *The Time That Remains: A Commentary on the Letter to the Romans*. Translated by P. Dailey. Stanford, CA: Stanford University Press, 2005.

Ahlskog, Jonas. "R. G. Collingwood and the Presence of the Past." *Journal of the Philosophy of History* 11 (2017): 289–305.

Albright, W. F. "Archaeology and the Date of the Hebrew Conquest of Palestine." *Bulletin of the American Schools of Oriental Research* 58 (1938): 10–18.

Alcock, Susan. *Archaeologies of the Greek Past: Landscape, Monuments, and Memories*. Cambridge: Cambridge University Press, 2002.

Alpert Nakhai, Beth. *Archaeology and the Religions of Canaan and Israel*. Boston: American Schools of Oriental Research, 2001.

Alt, Albrecht. "Jerusalems Aufstieg." *Zeitschrift der Deutschen Morgenländishen Gesellschaft* 79 (1925): 2–19.

——— "Josua." In *Kleine Schriften zur Geschichte des Volkes Israel*, Vol. I, 176–92. Munich: C. H. Beck, 1953.

Amiran, Ruth, and Amir Eitan. "A Canaanite-Hyksos City at Tel Nagila." *Archaeology* 18 (1966): 113–23.

Amiran, Ruth, and Ornit Ilan. "Arad." In *New Encyclopedia of Archaeological Excavations in the Holy Land*, Vol. I, edited by E. Stern, 76–82. Jerusalem: Israel Exploration Society, 1993.

——— *Early Arad: The Chalcolithic and Early Bronze 1B Settlements and the Early Bronze II City: Architecture and Town Planning*. Jerusalem: Israel Exploration Society, 1996.

Amesung, Walter. *Die Sculpturen des Vaticanischen Museums*. Band II, 2. Berlin: Reimer, 1908.

Anderson, Benedict. *Imagined Communities: Reflections on the Origin and Spread of Nationalism*. Revised ed. London: Verso, 2006.

Anderson, J. K. "The Geometric Catalogue of Ships." In *The Ages of Homer: A Tribute to Emily Townsend Vermeule*, edited by J. Carter and S. Morris, 181–92. Austin: University of Texas Press, 1995.

Ankersmit, Frank. *Sublime Historical Experience*. Stanford, CA: Stanford University Press, 2005.

Anonymous. "The Ruin." In *The Complete Old English Poems*, translated by C. Williamson, 582–83. Philadelphia: University of Pennsylvania Press, 2017.

Apel, Dora. *Beautiful Terrible Ruins: Detroit and the Anxiety of Decline*. New Brunswick, NJ: Rutgers University Press, 2015.

Arendt, Hannah. "Franz Kafka: A Revaluation – On the Occasion of the Twentieth Anniversary of His Death." In *Essays in Understanding, 1930–1954*, edited by J. Kohn, 69–80. New York: Harcourt, Brace & Company, 1994 [1944].

——— "Walter Benjamin, 1892–1940." In *Illuminations*, edited by H. Arendt, translated by H. Zohn, 1–55. New York: Schocken, 1968.

Aristotle. *The Parva Naturalia*. Translated by J. I. Beare. Oxford: Clarendon Press, 1908.

Asheri, David, Alan Lloyd, and Aldo Corcella. *A Commentary on Herodotus, Books I–IV*. Edited by O. Murray and A. Moreno. Oxford: Oxford University Press, 2007.

Assmann, Jan. *Das kulturelle Gedächtnis: Schrift, Erinnerung, und politische Identität in frühen Hochkulteren*. München: C. H. Beck, 1997.

Aster, Shawn. *Reflections of Empire in Isaiah 1–39: Responses to Assyrian Ideology*. Atlanta: SBL Press, 2017.

Auden, W. H. "Archaeology." In *Collected Poems*, edited by E. Mendelson. New York: Vintage International, 1991.

———. "Musée des Beaux Arts." In *Poems: Volume 1 – 1927–1939*, edited by E. Mendelson, 338. Princeton, NJ: Princeton University Press, 2022.

Augustine. *Confessions*. Edited by C. Hammond. Cambridge, MA: Harvard University Press, 2016.

———. *Confessions*. Translated by R.S. Pine-Coffin. New York: Penguin, 1961.

Avisar, Reli, Yiftah Shalev, Harel Shochat, Yuval Gadot, and Ido Koch. "'Jerusalem Ivories': Iron Age Decorated Ivory Panels from Building 100, Giv'ati Parking Lot Excavations, and Their Cultural Setting." *Antiqot* 106 (2022): 57–74.

Bach, Alice. "Rereading the Body Politic: Women and Violence in Judges 21." *Biblical Interpretation* 6.1 (1998): 1–19.

Bachelard, Gaston. *The Poetics of Space*. Translated by M. Jolas. Boston: Beacon Press, 1994.

Bakker, Egbert. "Homeric ΟΥΤΟΣ and the Poetics of Deixis." *Classical Philology* 94.1 (1999): 1–19.

Banfield, Ann. *Unspeakable Sentences: Narration and Representation in the Language of Fiction*. 2nd ed. New York: Routledge, 2015.

Barkan, Leonard. *Unearthing the Past: Archaeology and Aesthetics in the Making of Renaissance Culture*. New Haven, CT: Yale University Press, 1999.

Barkay, Gabriel. "Excavations at Ketef Hinnom in Jerusalem." In *Ancient Jerusalem Revealed*, edited by H. Geva, 85–106. Jerusalem: Israel Exploration Society, 1994.

Barkay, Gabriel, Alexander Fantalkin, and Oren Tal. "A Late Iron Age Fortress North of Jerusalem." *Bulletin of the American Schools of Oriental Research* 328 (2002): 49–71.

Barkay, Gabriel, Amos Kloner, and Amihai Mazar. "The Northern Necropolis of Jerusalem during the First Temple Period." In *Ancient Jerusalem Revealed*, edited by H. Geva, 119–27. Jerusalem: Israel Exploration Society, 1994.

Barnes, Annette, and Jonathan Barnes. "Time out of Joint: Some Reflections on Anachronism." *The Journal of Aesthetics and Art Criticism* 47.3 (1989): 253–61.

Barrera, Julio. "Textual Criticism and the Composition History of Samuel: Connection between Pericopes in 1 Samuel 1–4." In *Archaeology of the Books of Samuel: The Entangling of the Textual and Literary History*, edited by P. Hugo and A. Schenker, 119–27. Leiden: Brill, 2010.

Barthes, Roland. "The Reality Effect." In *The Rustle of Language*, translated by R. Howard, 141–48. Berkeley: University of California Press, 1989.

Bassi, Karen. *Traces of the Past: Classics between History and Archaeology*. Ann Arbor: University of Michigan Press, 2016.

Beaulieu, Paul-Alain. *The Reign of Nabonidus King of Babylon 556–539 B.C.* New Haven, CT: Yale University Press, 1989.

Bechar, Shlomit. "Abuse, Reuse, Recycle: The Use of Basalt Orthostats at Hazor in the Bronze and Iron Ages." *Oxford Journal of Archaeology* 40.1 (2021): 65–86.

Becking, Bob. *The Fall of Samaria: An Historical and Archaeological Study*. Leiden: Brill, 1992.

Beit-Arieh, Itzhaq. *Horvat 'Uza and Horvat Radum: Two Fortresses in the Biblical Negev*. Tel Aviv: Emery and Claire Yass Publications, 2007.

Beit-Arieh, Itzhaq, and Liora Freud. *Tel Malḥata: A Central City in the Biblical Negev*. Vol. I. Tel Aviv: Amery and Claire Yass Publications in Archaeology, 2015.

Bekkum, Koert van. "Coexistence as Guilt: Iron I Memories in Judges 1." In *The Ancient*

Near East in the 12th–10th Centuries BCE: Culture and History, edited by G. Galil et al., 525–47. Münster: Ugarit-Verlag, 2012.

Ben Zvi, Ehud. *Social Memory among the Literati of Yehud*. Berlin: De Gruyter, 2019.

Ben-Ami, Doron, and Yana Tchekhanovets. "A New Fragment of Proto-Aeolic Capital from Jerusalem." *Tel Aviv* 42 (2015): 67–71.

Benjamin, Walter. *The Arcades Project*. Translated by H. Eiland and K. McLaughlin. Cambridge, MA: Harvard University Press, 1999.

———. "Franz Kafka: On the 10th Anniversary of His Death." In *Illuminations: Essays and Reflection*, edited by H. Arendt, 111–40. New York: Mariner, 2019.

———. *Selected Writings: Volume I, 1913–1926*. Edited by M. Bullock and M. Jennings. Cambridge, MA: Belknap, 1996.

———. "On Some Motifs in Baudelaire." In *Illuminations: Essays and Reflection*, edited by H. Arendt, 155–200. New York: Mariner, 2019.

———. "The Storyteller." In *Illuminations: Essays and Reflection*, edited by H. Arendt, 83–110. New York: Mariner, 2019.

———. "Theses on the Philosophy of History." In *Illuminations: Essays and Reflection*, edited by H. Arendt, 253–64. New York: Mariner, 2019.

———. "Theologico-Political Fragment." In *Reflections: Essays, Aphorisms, Autobiographical Writings*, edited by P. Demetz, translated by E. Jephcott, 312–13. New York: Schocken, 1986.

———. "Über den Begriff der Geschichte." In *Gesammelte Schriften*, I–2, 693–704. Frankfurt: Suhrkamp, 1980.

Ben-Shlomo, David. "New Evidence of Iron Age II Fortifications at Tel Hebron." In *The Last Century in the History of Judah: The Seventh Century BCE in Archaeological, Historical, and Biblical Perspectives*, edited by F. Capek and O. Lipschits, 63–88. Atlanta: Society of Biblical Literature Press, 2019.

———. "Tell Jemmeh, Philistia and the Neo Assyrian Empire during the Late Iron Age." *Levant* 46.1 (2014): 58–88.

Ben-Tor, Amnon. "The Ceremonial Precinct in the Upper City of Hazor." *Near Eastern Archaeology* 76.2 (2013): 81–91.

———. *Hazor: Canaanite Metropolis, Israelite City*. Jerusalem: Israel Exploration Society, 2016.

———. "Jokneam." In *New Encyclopedia of Archaeological Excavations in the Holy Land*, Vol. III, edited by E. Stern, 805–11. Jerusalem: Israel Exploration Society, 1993.

Ben-Tor, Amnon, and Sharon Zuckerman. "Hazor at the End of the Late Bronze Age: Back to Basics." *Bulletin of the American Schools of Oriental Research* 350 (2008): 1–6.

Ben-Tor, Amnon, Sharon Zuckerman, Shlomit Bechar, and Dalit Weinblatt. "The Late Bronze Age Strata XV–XIII (Strata XV–XIII)." In *Hazor VII: The 1990–2012 Excavations, The Bronze Age*, edited by A. Ben-Tor et al., 66–144. Jerusalem: Israel Exploration Society, 2017.

Ben-Tor, Doron. "Early Iron Age Cult Places – New Evidence from Tel Hazor." *Tel Aviv* 33.2 (2006): 121–33.

———. "Hazor at the Beginning of the Iron Age." *Near Eastern Archaeology* 73.2 (2013): 101–4.

———. "Mysterious Standing Stones." *Biblical Archaeology Review* 32.2 (2006): 38–45.

Ben-Tor, Doron, and Amnon Ben-Tor. "The Iron Age (Stratum "XII/XI"): Stratigraphy and Pottery." In *Hazor VI: The 1990–2009 Excavations: The Iron Age*, edited by A. Ben-Tor, D. Ben-Ami, and D. Sandhaus, 7–25. Jerusalem: Israel Exploration Society, 2012.

Benz, Brendon. "The Destruction of Hazor: Israelite History and the Construction of History in Israel." *Journal for the Study of the Old Testament* 44.2 (2019): 262–78.

Bergson, Henri. *Matière et mémoire: essai sur la relation du corps a l'esprit*. 5th ed. Paris: F. Alcan, 1908.

———. *Time and Free Will: An Essay on the Immediate Data of Consciousness*. Translated by P. L. Pogson. New York: Cosimo, 2008.

Berlin, Andrea. "Power and Its Afterlife: Tombs in Hellenistic Palestine." *Near Eastern Archaeology* 65.2 (2002): 138–48.

Bietak, Manfred. "Avaris and Piramesse: Archaeological Exploration in the Eastern Nile Delta." *Proceedings of the British Academy* 65 (1979): 225–90.

―― *Tell el-Dab'a II: Der Fundort im Rahmen einer archäologish-geographischen Untersuchung über das ägyptishche Ostdelta*. Vienna: Österreichische Akademie der Wissenschaften, 1975.

Biran, Avraham. *Biblical Dan*. Jerusalem: Israel Exploration Society, 1994.

Biran, Avraham, and Joseph Naveh. "An Aramaic Stele Fragment from Tel Dan." *Israel Exploration Journal* 43 (1993): 81–98.

―― "The Tel Dan Inscription: A New Fragment." *Israel Exploration Journal* 45 (1995): 1–18.

Blenkinsopp, Joseph. "The Structure of P." *Catholic Biblical Quarterly* 38.3 (1976): 275–92.

Bloch-Smith, Elizabeth. "Archaeology: What It Can Teach Us." In *The Wiley Blackwell Companion to Ancient Israel*, edited by S. Niditch, 13–27. Malden: Wiley, 2016.

―― "The Cult of the Dead in Judah: Interpreting the Material Remains." *Journal of Biblical Literature* 111.2 (1992): 213–24.

―― "Israelite Ethnicity in Iron I: Archaeology Preserves What Is Remembered and What Is Forgotten in Israel's History." *Journal of Biblical Literature* 122.3 (2003): 401–25.

―― *Judahite Burial Practices and Beliefs about the Dead*. Sheffield: JSOT Press, 1992.

―― "Massebot Standing for Yhwh: The Fall of a Yhwistic Cult Symbol." In *Worship, Women, and War: Essays in Honor of Susan Niditch*, edited by J. Collins, T. M. Lemos, and S. Olyan, 99–116. Providence, RI: Brown Judaic Studies, 2015.

―― "A Stratified Account of Jephthah's Negotiations and Battle: Judges 11:12–33 from an Archaeological Perspective." *Journal of Biblical Literature* 134.2 (2015): 291–311.

―― "Will the Real Massebot Please Stand Up: Cases of Real and Mistakenly Identified Standing Stones in Ancient Israel." In *Text, Artifact, and Image: Revealing Ancient Israelite Religion*, edited by G. Beckman and T. Lewis, 64–79. Providence, RI: Brown University Press, 2006.

Bloch-Smith, Elizabeth, and Beth Alpert Nahhai. "A Landscape Comes to Life: The Iron Age I." *Near Eastern Archaeology* 62.2 (1999): 62–127.

Blum, Erhard. *Studien zur Komposition des Pentateuch*. Berlin: De Gruyter, 1990.

Boast, Robin. "The Formative Century, 1860–1960." In *The Oxford Handbook of Archaeology*, edited by C. Gosden, 47–70. Oxford: Oxford University Press, 2009.

Bober, Phyllis Pray, and Ruth Rubinstein. *Renaissance Artists and Antique Sculpture: A Handbook*. 2nd ed. London: H. Miller, 2010.

Boling, Robert. *Judges*. New York: Doubleday, 1975.

Borger, Riekele. *Die Inschriften Asarhaddons Königs von Assyrien*. Osnabrück: Biblio-Verlag, 1967.

Bornstein, Arye. "Shechem." In *The Oxford Encyclopedia of Bible and Archaeology*, Vol. 2, edited by D. Master, 354. New York: Oxford University Press, 2013.

Bourke, Stephen. "The Six Canaanite Temples of Ṭabaqat Fahil. Excavating Pella's 'Fortress' Temple (1994–2009)." In *Temple Building and Temple Cult: Architecture and Cultic Paraphernalia of Temples in the Levant (2.–1. Mill. B.C.E.)*, edited by J. Kamlah, 159–201. Wiesbaden: Harrassowitz Verlag, 2012.

Bowie, Angus M., ed. *Herodotus Histories: Book VIII*. Cambridge: Cambridge University Press, 2007.

Boyer, M. Christine. *The City of Collective Memory: Its Historical Imagery and Architectural Entertainments*. Cambridge, MA: MIT Press, 1996.

Braudel, Fernand. *Civilization and Capitalism: 15th–18th Century, Volume III*. Translated by S. Reynolds. Berkeley: University of California Press, 1992.

Breed, Brennan. *Nomadic Text: A Theory of Biblical Reception History*. Bloomington: Indiana University Press, 2014.

Bright, John. "The Date of the Prose Sermons of Jeremiah." *Journal of Biblical Literature* 70.1 (1951): 15–35.

Brissaud, Philippe. "Les Principaux résultats des fouilles récentes à Tanis (1987–1997): L'emergence d'une vision nouvelle du site." In *Tanis: travaux récents sur le Tell Sân el-Hagar 1987–1997*, edited by P. Brissaud and C. Zivie-Coche, 13–70. Paris: Noêsis, 1998.

———. "Tanis (Tell San el-Hagar)." In *Royal Cities of the Biblical World*, edited by J. Westenholz, 113–49. Jerusalem: Bible Lands Museum, 1996.

Brissaud, Philippe, Violaine Chauvet, and Isabelle Hairy. "Deux siècles de fouilles à Tanis: Analyse des divers modes d'intervention sur le site." In *Tanis: travaux récents sur le Tell Sân el-Hagar 1987–1997*, edited by P. Brissaud and C. Zivie-Coche, 71–100. Paris: Noêsis, 1998.

Britt, Benjamin. "The Romantic Roots of the Debate on the Buber-Rosenzweig Bible." *Prooftexts* 20.3 (2000): 262–89.

———. *Walter Benjamin and the Bible*. London: Continuum, 1996.

Brueggemann, Walter. *A Commentary on Jeremiah: Exile and Homecoming*. Grand Rapids, MI: Eerdmans, 1998.

Budde, Karl. *Das Buch der Richter*. Freiburg: J. C. B. Mohr, 1897.

———. *Die Bücher Samuel*. Tübingen: J. C. B. Mohr, 1902.

Buhl, Marie-Louise, and Svend Holm-Nielsen. *Shiloh: The Danish Excavations at Tall Sailun, Palestine, in 1926, 1929, 1932, and 1963: The Pre-Hellenistic Remains*. Copenhagen: National Museum of Denmark, 1969.

Bunimovitz, Shlomo. "Area C: The Iron Age I Building and Other Remains." Excavations at Shiloh 1981–1984: Preliminary Report." *Tel Aviv* 12 (1985): 130–39.

Bunimovitz, Shlomo, and Zvi Lederman. "Beth-Shemesh." In *New Encyclopedia of Archaeological Excavations in the Holy Land*, Vol. V, edited by E. Stern, 1644–48. Jerusalem: Israel Exploration Society, 2008.

———. "The Final Destruction of Beth Shemesh and the *Pax Assyriaca* in the Judean Shephelah." *Tel Aviv* 30.1 (2003): 3–26.

———. "Solving a Century-Old Puzzle: New Discoveries at the Middle Bronze Age of Tel Beth-Shemesh." *Palestine Exploration Quarterly* 145.1 (2014): 6–24.

Burke, Aaron. "Canaan under Siege: The History and Archaeology of Egypt's War in Canaan during the Early Eighteenth Dynasty." In *Studies on War in the Ancient Near East: Collected Essays on Military History*, edited by J. Vidal, 43–66. Münster: Ugarit-Verlag, 2010.

———. "The Decline of Egyptian Empire, Refugees, and Social Change in the Southern Levant, ca. 1200–1000 BCE." In *The Archaeology of Forced Migration: Conflict-Induced Movement and the Collapse of the 13th c. BCE Eastern Mediterranean*, edited by J. Driessen, 229–49. Louvain: Presses Universitaires de Louvain, 2018.

———. "Early Jaffa: From the Bronze Age to the Persian Period." In *The History and Archaeology of Jaffa*, Vol. I, 63–78. Los Angeles: Cotsen Institute of Archaeology Press, 2011.

———. *Walled up to Heaven: The Evolution of Middle Bronze Age Fortification Strategies in the Levant*. Winona Lake, IN: Eisenbrauns, 2008.

Burke, Aaron, and Krystal Lords. "Egyptians in Jaffa: A Portrait of Egyptian Presence in Jaffa during the Late Bronze Age." *Near Eastern Archaeology* 73.1 (2010): 2–30.

Burke, Aaron, Martin Peilstöcker, Amy Karoll, George Pierce, Krister Kowalski, Nadia Ben-Marzouk, Jacob Damm, et al. "Excavations of the New Kingdom Fortress in Jaffa, 2011–2014: Traces of Resistance to Egyptian Rule in Canaan." *American Journal of Archaeology* 121.1 (2017): 85–133.

Burke, Peter. *The Renaissance Sense of the Past*. New York: St. Martin's Press, 1969.

Buster, Aubrey. *Remembering the Story of Israel: Historical Summaries and Memory Formation in Second Temple Judaism*. Cambridge: Cambridge University Press, 2022.

Byrne, Ryan. "The Refuge of Scribalism in Iron I Palestine." *Bulletin of the American Schools of Oriental Research* 345 (2007): 1–31.

Cahill, Jane. "Jerusalem at the Time of the Monarchy: The Archaeological Evidence." In *Jerusalem in Bible and Archaeology: The First Temple Period*, edited by A. Vaughn and A. Killebrew, 13–80. Atlanta: Society of Biblical Literature, 2003.

Callaway, Joseph. "Ai." In *New Encyclopedia of Archaeological Excavations in the Holy Land*, Vol. I, edited by E. Stern, 39–45. Jerusalem: Israel Exploration Society, 1993.

———. "Excavating Ai (Et-Tell): 1964–1972." *Biblical Archaeologist* 39.1 (1976): 18–30.

———. "New Evidence on the Conquest of 'Ai." *Journal of Biblical Literature* 87.3 (1968): 312–20.

Campbell, Antony. *1 Samuel*. Grand Rapids, MI: Eerdmans, 2003.

Campbell, Edward. "Shechem." In *New Encyclopedia of Archaeological Excavations in the Holy Land*, Vol. IV, edited by E. Stern, 1349–51. Jerusalem: Israel Exploration Society, 1993.

———. *Shechem III: The Stratigraphy and Architecture of Shechem Tell Balâtah*. Vol. 1. Boston: American Schools of Oriental Research, 2002.

Carr, David. *Experience and History: Phenomenological Perspectives on the Historical World*. Oxford: Oxford University Press, 2014.

Carr, David M. *The Formation of the Hebrew Bible: A New Reconstruction*. New York: Oxford University Press, 2011.

———. "Orality, Textuality, and Memory: The State of Biblical Studies." In *Contextualizing Israel's Sacred Writings: Ancient Literacy, Orality, and Literary Production*, edited by B. Schmidt, 161–73. Atlanta: SBL Press, 2015.

Carroll, Robert. *Jeremiah*. Louisville, KY: Westminster John Knox, 1986.

———. "Psalm LXXVIII: Vestiges of a Tribal Polemic." *Vetus Testamentum* 21.1 (1971): 33–50.

Carruthers, Mary. *The Book of Memory: A Study of Memory in Medieval Culture*. 2nd ed. Cambridge: Cambridge University Press, 2008.

Carvalho, Corinne. "Ezekiel's Tangible Ethics: Physicality in the Moral Rhetoric of Ezekiel." In *The Oxford Handbook of Ezekiel*, edited by C. Carvalho. Oxford: Oxford University Press, 2020.

Case, Megan. "Procuring Virgins, Performing Peace: Reconciliation through the Exchange of Women in Judges 21." *Vetus Testamentum* 70.3 (2020): 396–413.

Casey, Edward. *Remembering: A Phenomenological Study*. Bloomington: Indiana University Press, 1987.

Chadwick, Jeffrey. "Discovering Hebron." *Biblical Archaeology Review* 31.5 (2005): 24–33.

———. "Hebron in Early Bronze III and Middle Bronze Age II: Fortification Walls in Area I.3 of the American Expedition to Hebron (Tell er-Rumeide)." In *Tell It in Gath: Studies in the History and Archaeology of Israel: Essays in Honor of Aren M. Maeir on the Occasion of His Sixtieth Birthday*, edited by J. R. Chadwick et al., 167–86. Münster: Zaphon, 2018.

Chakrabarty, Dipesh. "Postcoloniality and the Artifice of History: Who Speaks for 'Indian' Pasts?" *Representations* 37 (1992): 1–26.

Chateaubriand, François René de. *The Memoirs of François René, Vicomte de Chateaubriand*. Translated by A. Teixeira de Mattos. London: Freemantle, 1902.

———. *Travels in America and Italy*. Vol. II. London: Henry Colburn, 1828.

Chavel, Simeon. "A Kingdom of Priests and Its Earthen Altars in Exodus 19–24." *Vetus Testamentum* 65 (2015): 169–222.

Childs, Brevard. "A Study of the Formula 'Until this Day.'" *Journal of Biblical Literature* 82 (1963): 279–92.

Chopra-McGowan, Cathleen. "Representing the Destruction of Jerusalem: Literary Artistry and the Shaping of Memory in 2 Kings 25, Lamentations, and Ezekiel." Ph.D. diss., University of Chicago, 2019.

Cicero. *On the Orator*. Translated by H. Rackham, LCL 349. Cambridge, MA: Harvard University Press, 1942.

Clark, Elizabeth. *History, Theory, Text: Historians and the Linguistic Turn*. Cambridge, MA: Harvard University Press, 2004.

Clifford, Richard. *The Cosmic Mountain in Canaan and the Old Testament*. Cambridge, MA: Harvard University Press, 1972.

Cline, Eric. *Digging up Armageddon: The Search for the Lost City of Solomon*. Princeton, NJ: Princeton University Press, 2020.

Three Stones Make a Wall: The Story of Archaeology. Princeton, NJ: Princeton University Press, 2017.

Cogan, Mordechai. *1 Kings*. New York: Doubleday, 2001.

"Cross-examining the Assyrian Witnesses to Sennacherib's Third Campaign: Assessing the Limits of Historical Reconstruction." In *Sennacherib at the Gates of Jerusalem: Story, History and Historiography*, edited by I. Kalimi and S. Richardson, 51–74. Leiden: Brill, 2014.

Cogan, Mordechai, and Hayim Tadmor. *II Kings*. New York: Doubleday, 1988.

Cohen, Martin. "The Role of Shilonite Priesthood in the United Monarchy of Ancient Israel." *Hebrew Union College Annual* 36 (1965): 59–98

Collingwood, R. G. *The Idea of History*. Revised ed. Edited by J. Van Der Dussen. London: Oxford University Press, 2005.

Comay, Rebecca. "Benjamin's Endgame." In *Walter Benjamin's Philosophy: Destruction and Experience*, edited by A. Benjamin and P. Osborne, 251–91. Manchester: Clinamen, 1994.

Commission des Sciences et Arts d'Égypte. *Description de l'Égypte, ou, Recueil des observations et des recherches qui ont été faites en Égypte pendant l'expédition de l'Armée française*. 23 vols. Paris: L'Imprimerie impériale, 1809–1828.

Cook, R. M. "Thucydides as Archaeologist." *The Annual of the British School at Athens* 50 (1955): 266–70.

Cooper, Frederick. *Colonialism in Question: Theory, Knowledge, History*. Berkeley: University of California Press, 2005.

Cordier, Louis. "Description des Ruines de Sân." In *Description de l'Égypte, ou, Recueil des observations et des recherches qui ont été faites en Égypte pendant l'expédition de l'Armée française*, Tome 5, 99–134. Paris: De l'Imprimerie impériale, 1809–1828.

Cox, Benjamin, and Susan Ackerman. "Rachel's Tomb." *Journal of Biblical Literature* 128.1 (2009): 135–48.

Creanga, Ovidiu. "The Conquest of Memory in the Book of Joshua." In *The Oxford Handbook of Biblical Narrative*, edited by D. Fewell, 168–79. New York: Oxford University Press, 2016.

Cross, Frank Moore. *Canaanite Myth and Hebrew Epic: Essays in the History of Religion*. Cambridge, MA: Harvard University Press, 1973.

Darby, Erin. *Interpreting Judean Pillar Figurines: Gender and Empire in Judean Apotropaic Ritual*. Tübingen: Mohr Siebeck, 2014.

Davis, Thomas W. *Shifting Sands: The Rise and Fall of Biblical Archaeology*. Oxford: Oxford University Press, 2004.

Day, John. "The Destruction of the Shiloh Sanctuary and Jeremiah VII 12, 14." In *Studies in the Historical Books of the Old Testament*, edited by J. Emerton, 87–94. Leiden: Brill, 1979.

De Groot, Alon, and Hannah Bernick Greenberg. *Excavations at the City of David 1978–1985 Directed by Yigal Shiloh, Vol. VIIA: Area E: Stratigraphy and Architecture*. Jerusalem: Hebrew University of Jerusalem, 2012.

De Miroschedji, Pierre. "Excavations at Tel Yarmouth: Results of the Work from 2003 to 2009." *Comptes-rendus des séances de l année – Académie des inscriptions et belles-lettres* (2013): 759–804.

"Far'ah, Tell el-(North)." In *New Encyclopedia of Archaeological Excavations in the Holy Land*, Vol. II, edited by E. Stern, 433–38. Jerusalem: Israel Exploration Society, 1993.

"Yarmuth: The Dawn of City-States in Southern Canaan." *Near Eastern Archaeology* 62.1 (1999): 2–19.

De Miroschedji, Pierre, Moain Sadeq, Dina Faltings, Virginie Boulez, Laurence

Naggiar-Moliner, Naomi Sykes, and Margareta Tengberg. "Les fouilles de Tell es-Sakan (Gaza): nouvelles données sur les contacts égypto-cananéens aux IVe–IIIe millénaires." *Paléorient* 27.2 (2001): 75–104.

DeGrado, Jessie. "Authoring Empire: Intellectual Engagement with the Neo-Assyrian Empire in the Bible." Ph.D. diss., University of Chicago, 2018.

Dekker, Jan. *Zion's Rock-Solid Foundations: An Exegetical Study of the Zion Text in Isaiah 28:16*. Leiden: Brill, 2007.

DeSilvey, Caitlin, and Tim Edensor. "Reckoning with Ruins." *Progress in Human Geography* 37.4 (2012): 465–85.

Deuel, Leo. *Memoirs of Heinrich Schliemann*. New York: Harper & Row, 1977.

Dever, William. "Archaeological Method in Israel: A Continuing Revolution." *Biblical Archaeologist* 43 (1980): 41–48.

——— "Archaeology and the Fall of the Northern Kingdom: What Really Happened?" In *"Up to the Gates of Ekron": Essays on the Archaeology and History of the Eastern Mediterranean in Honor of Seymour Gitin*, edited by S. W. Crawford, A. Ben-Tor, J. P. Dessel, W. G. Dever, A. Mazar, and J. Aviram, 78–92. Jerusalem: W. F. Albright Institute of Archaeological Research, 2007.

——— *Did God Have a Wife? Archaeology and Folk Religion in Ancient Israel*. Grand Rapids, MI: Eerdmans, 2005.

——— "Iron Age Epigraphic Material from the Area of Khirbet el-Kom." *Hebrew Union College Annual* 40/41 (1969–1970): 139–204.

——— "The Middle Bronze Age 'High Place' at Gezer." *Bulletin of the American Schools of Oriental Research* 371 (2014): 17–57.

——— "The Middle Bronze Age: The Zenith of the Urban Canaanite Era." *Biblical Archaeologist* 50 (1987): 149–77.

Dever, William, and Joe Seger. "A Brief Summary of the Stratigraphy and Cultural History of Gezer." In *Gezer VI: The Objects from Phases I and II (1964–74)*, edited by J. Seger, W. Dever, and S. Gitin, 8–17. Winona Lake, IN: Eisenbrauns, 2014.

Díaz-Andreu, Margarite. *A World History of Nineteenth Century Archaeology: Nationalism, Colonialism, and the Past*. Oxford: Oxford University Press, 2007.

Dietler, Michael. *Archaeologies of Colonialism: Consumption, Entanglement, and Violence in Ancient Mediterranean France*. Berkeley: University of California Press, 2010.

Dietrich, Walter. *The Early Monarchy in Israel: The Tenth Century B.C.E.* Translated by J. Vette. Atlanta: SBL Press, 2007.

——— *Prophetie und Geschichte: Eine redaktionsgeschichte Untersuchung zum deuteronomistischen Geschichtswerk*. Göttingen: Vandenhoek & Ruprecht, 1972.

——— *Samuel*. Teilband I, 1 Sam 1–12. Neukirchen Vluyn: Neukirchener Verlagsgesellschaft, 2011.

Dobbs-Allsopp, F. W. *On Biblical Poetry*. New York: Oxford, 2015.

——— *Lamentations*. Louisville, KY: Westminster John Knox, 2002.

——— "R(az/ais)ing Zion in Lamentations 2." In *David and Zion: Biblical Studies in Honor of J. J. M. Roberts*, edited by B. F. Batto and K. L. Roberts, 21–68. Winona Lake, IN: Eisenbrauns, 2004.

Domanska, Ewa. "The Material Presence of the Past." *History and Theory* 45 (2006): 337–48.

Doolittle, Hilda (H. D.). "The Walls Do Not Fall," in *Trilogy*, 1–60. New York: New Directions, 1998.

Dorsey, David. *The Roads and Highways of Ancient Israel*. Baltimore: Johns Hopkins University, 1991.

Dothan, Moshe. "Tel Mor." In *New Encyclopedia of Archaeological Excavations in the Holy Land*, Vol. III, edited by E. Stern, 1072–74. Jerusalem: Jerusalem Exploration Society, 1993.

Dozeman, Thomas. *Joshua 1–12*. New Haven, CT: Yale University Press, 2015.

Dubovsky, Peter. *The Building of the First Temple: A Study in Redactional, Text-Critical and Historical Perspectives*. Tübingen: Mohr Siebeck, 2015.

Duhm, Bernhard. *Das Buch Jeremia*. Tübingen: Mohr, 1907.

Dyson, Stephen. *In Pursuit of Ancient Pasts: A History of Classical Archaeology in the Nineteenth and Twentieth Centuries*. New Haven, CT: Yale University Press, 2006.

Edrey, Meir, Eric Cline, Roey Nickelsberg, and Assaf Yasur-Landau. "The Iron Age Lower Settlement at Kabri Revisited." *Palestine Exploration Quarterly* 152.2 (2020): 94–120.

Eichrodt, Walter. *Ezekiel: A Commentary*. Translated by C. Quiz. Philadelphia: Westminster Press, 1970.

Eidevall, Göran. *Amos: A New Translation with Introduction and Commentary*. New Haven, CT: Yale University Press, 2017.

Eisenberg, Emmanuel. "Tell Kitan." In *New Encyclopedia of Archaeological Excavations in the Holy Land*, Vol. III, edited by E. Stern, 878–81. Jerusalem: Israel Exploration Society, 1993.

——— "The Temples at Tell Kittan." *Biblical Archaeologist* 40.2 (1977): 77–81.

Eißfeldt, Otto. *Baal Zaphon, Zeus Kasios und der Durchzug der Israeliten durchs Meer*. Halle: Niemeyer, 1932.

——— "Silo und Jerusalem." In *Volume du Congrès, Strasbourg 1956*, edited by P. De Boer, 138–47. Leiden: Brill, 1957.

Epstein, Claire. "An Interpretation of the Megiddo Sacred Area during Middle Bronze II." *Israel Exploration Journal* 15 (1965): 204–21.

Erll, Astrid. "Travelling Memory." *Parallax* 17.4 (2011): 4–18.

Fantalkin, Alexander. "The Appearance of Rock-Cut Bench Tombs in Iron Age Judah as a Reflection of State Formation." In *Bene Israel: Studies in the Archaeology of Israel and the Levant during the Bronze and Iron Ages in Honour of Israel Finkelstein*, edited by A. Fantalkin and A. Yasur-Landau, 17–44. Leiden: Brill, 2008.

Fasolt, Constantine. *The Limits of History*. Chicago: University of Chicago Press, 2004.

Faust, Avraham. *Israel's Ethnogenesis: Settlement, Interaction, Expansion, and Resistance*. London: Equinox, 2006.

——— "Israelite Temples: Where Was Israelite Cult Not Practiced and Why." *Religions* 10 (2019): 1–26.

——— *Judah in the Neo-Babylonian Period: The Archaeology of Desolation*. Atlanta: SBL Press, 2012.

——— *The Neo-Assyrian Empire in the Southwest: Imperial Domination and Its Consequences*. New York: Oxford University Press, 2021.

——— "Settlement, Economy, and Demography under Assyrian Rule in the West: The Territories of the Former Kingdom of Israel as a Test Case." *Journal of the American Oriental Society* 135.4 (2015): 765–89.

——— "The World of P: The Material Realm of Priestly Writings." *Vetus Testamentum* 69 (2019): 173–218.

Faust, Avraham, and Haya Katz. "Tel 'Eton Cemetery: An Introduction." *Hebrew Bible and Ancient Israel* 5 (2016): 171–86.

Faust, Avraham, and Shlomo Bunimovitz. "The Four Room House: Embodying Iron Age Israelite Society." *Near Eastern Archaeology* 66 (2003): 22–31.

——— "The Judahite Rock-Cut Tomb: Family Response at a Time of Change." *Israel Exploration Journal* 58 (2008): 150–70.

Felski, Rita. *The Uses of Literature*. Malden, MA: Blackwell, 2008.

Fenves, Peter. *The Messianic Reduction: Walter Benjamin and the Shape of Time*. Stanford, CA: Stanford University Press, 2011.

Finkel, Irving, and Alexandra Fletcher. "Thinking Outside the Box: The Case of the Sun-God Tablet and the Cruciform Monument." *Bulletin of the American Schools of Oriental Research* 375 (2016): 215–48.

Finkelstein, Israel. *The Archaeology of the Israelite Settlement*. Jerusalem: Israel Exploration Society, 1988.

——— "Conclusion." In *Shiloh: The Archaeology of a Biblical Site*, edited by I. Finkelstein, S. Bunimovitz, and Z. Lederman, 371–72. Tel Aviv: Institute of Archaeology of Tel Aviv, 1993.

——— "Excavations at Khirbet ed-Dawwara: An Iron Age Site Northeast of Jerusalem." *Tel Aviv* 17.2 (1990): 163–208.

——— "Excavation Results in Other Areas." Excavations at Shiloh 1981–1984:

Preliminary Report." *Tel Aviv* 12 (1985): 146–58.

"First Israel, Core Israel, United (Northern) Israel." *Near Eastern Archaeology* 82.1 (2019): 8–15.

The Forgotten Kingdom: The Archaeology and History of Northern Israel. Atlanta: SBL Press, 2013.

"Introduction." In *Shiloh: The Archaeology of a Biblical Site*, edited by I. Finkelstein, S. Bunimovitz, and Z. Lederman, 1–14. Tel Aviv: Institute of Archaeology of Tel Aviv, 1993.

"Jerusalem in the Persian (and Early Hellenistic) Period and the Wall of Nehemiah." *Journal for the Study of the Old Testament* 32 (2008): 501–20.

"Kadesh Barnea: A Reevaluation of Its Archaeology and History." *Tel Aviv* 37 (2010): 111–25.

"Shechem in the Late Bronze and Iron I." In *Timelines: Studies in Honor of Manfred Bietak*, Vol. 2, edited by E. Czerny et al., 349–56. Leuven: Peeters, 2006.

"Summary and Conclusions: Excavations at Shiloh 1981–1984: Preliminary Report." *Tel Aviv* 12 (1985): 162–63.

"What the Biblical Authors Knew about Canaan before and in the Early Days of the Hebrew Kingdoms." Ugarit-Forschungen 48 (2017): 173–98.

Finkelstein, Israel, and Eliazer Piasetzky. "The Iron I–IIA in the Highlands and Beyond: 14C Anchors, Pottery Phases and the Shoshenq I Campaign." *Levant* 38 (2006): 45–61.

Finkelstein, Israel, and Lily Singer-Avitz. "Reevaluating Bethel." *Zeitschrift des Deutschen Palästina-Vereins* 125.1 (2009): 33–48.

Finkelstein, Israel, and Mario A. S. Martin, eds. *Megiddo VI: The 2010–2014 Seasons*. Tel Aviv: Sonia and Marco Nadler Institute of Archaeology, 2022.

Finkelstein, Israel, and Thomas Römer. "Early North Israelite 'Memories' of Moab." In *The Formation of the Pentateuch*, edited by J. Gertz et al., 711–27. Tübingen: Mohr Siebeck, 2016.

Finkelstein, Israel, and Zvi Lederman "Area H–F: Middle Bronze III Fortifications and Storerooms." In *Shiloh: The Archaeology of a Biblical Site*, edited by I. Finkelstein, S. Bunimovitz, and Z. Lederman, 49–64. Tel Aviv: Tel Aviv University Press, 1993.

Finkelstein, Israel, David Ussishkin, and Baruch Halpern. "Archaeological and Historical Conclusions." In *Megiddo IV: The 1998–2002 Seasons*, Vol. II, edited by I. Finkelstein, D. Ussishkin, and B. Halpern, 843–59. Tel Aviv: Emery and Claire Yass Publications, 2006.

Finkelstein, Israel, Shlomo Bunimovitz, and Zvi Lederman, eds. *Shiloh: The Archaeology of a Biblical Site*. Tel Aviv: Institute of Archaeology of Tel Aviv, 1993.

Finkelstein, Israel, Shlomo Bunimovitz, Zvi Lederman, Salo Hellwing, and Moshe Sadeh. "Excavations at Shiloh 1981–1984: Preliminary Report." *Tel Aviv* 12 (1985): 123–80.

Finnegan, Ruth. *Oral Traditions and the Verbal Arts: A Guide to Research Practices*. London: Routledge, 1992.

Fishbane, Michael. "Jeremiah iv 23–26 and Job iii 3–13: A Recovered Use of the Creation Pattern." *Vetus Testamentum* 21 (1971): 151–67.

Fitzmyer, Joseph. *The Aramaic Inscriptions of Sefire*. Revised ed. Roma: Editrice Pontificio Istituto Biblico, 1995.

Flanagan, James, David McCreery, and Hair Nimr Yāsīn. "Tell Nimrin: Preliminary Report on the 1993 Season." *Annual of the Department of the Antiquities of Jordan* 38 (1994): 205–44.

Foley, John. "Memory in Oral Tradition." In *Performing the Gospel: Orality, Memory, and Mark*, edited by R. Horsely et al., 83–96. Minneapolis: Fortress, 2011.

Forster, Michael. *After Herder: Philosophy of Language in the German Tradition*. Oxford: Oxford University Press, 2010.

Herder's Philosophy. Oxford: Oxford University Press, 2018.

Foucault, Michel. *The Order of Things: An Archaeology of the Human Sciences*. London: Routledge, 2002.

Franken, H. J. *A History of Potters and Pottery in Ancient Jerusalem: Excavations by K. M. Kenyon in Jerusalem 1961–1967*. London: Equinox, 2005.

Franken, H. J., and Margreet Steiner. *Excavations in Jerusalem, 1961–1967, II: The Iron Age Extramural Quarter on the South-East Hill*. Oxford: Oxford University Press, 1990.

French, Elizabeth. "Mycenae." In *The Oxford Handbook of the Bronze Age Aegean*, edited by E. Cline, 671–79. Oxford: Oxford University Press, 2012.

Frisch, Amos. "Ephraim and Treachery, Loyalty and (the House) of David: The Meaning of a Structural Parallel in Psalm 78." *Vetus Testamentum* 59.2 (2009): 190–98.

Fritz, Volkmar. "Chinnereth, Tell." In *New Encyclopedia of Archaeological Excavations in the Holy Land*, Vol. V, edited by E. Stern, 1684–86. Jerusalem: Israel Exploration Society, 2008.

―――. *Das Buch Josua*. Zürich: Theologischer Verlag Zürich, 2008.

Fritzsche, Peter. "Chateaubriand's Ruins: Loss and Memory after the French Revolution." *History and Memory* 10.2 (1998): 102–17.

―――. *Stranded in the Present: Modern Time and the Melancholy of History*. Cambridge, MA: Harvard University Press, 2004.

Froeyman, Anton. "Frank Ankersmit and Eelco Runia: The Presence and the Otherness of the Past." *Rethinking History* 16.3 (2012): 393–414.

Frolov, Sergei. "Judah Comes to Shiloh: Genesis 49:10bα, One More Time." *Journal of Biblical Literature* 131.3 (2012): 417–22.

Gadd, C. J. "Inscribed Prisms of Sargon II from Nimrud." *Iraq* 16.2 (1954): 173–201.

Gadot, Yuval. "Iron Age (Strata XII–X6)." In *Aphek-Antipatris II: The Remains of the Acropolis*, 88–110. Tel Aviv: Emery and Claire Yass Publications, 2009.

―――. "The Late Bronze Egyptian Estate at Aphek." *Tel Aviv* 37 (2010): 48–66.

Gafijczuk, Dariusz. "Dwelling Within: The Inhabited Ruins of History." *History and Theory* 52 (2013): 149–70.

Gal, Zvi. *Lower Galilee during the Iron Age*. Translated by M. Josephy. Winona Lake, IN: Eisenbrauns, 1992.

Galor, Katharina, and Hanswulf Bloedhorn. *The Archaeology of Jerusalem: From the Origins to the Ottomans*. New Haven, CT: Yale University Press, 2013.

Ganor, Saar, and Igor Kreimerman. "An Eighth Century BCE Gate Shrine at Tel Lachish, Israel." *Bulletin of the American Schools of Oriental Research* 381 (2019): 211–36.

Gardiner, Alan. "Tanis and Pi-Ra'messe: A Retraction." *Journal of Egyptian Archaeology* 5 (1933): 122–28.

Garfinkel, Yosef, Katharina Streit, Saar Ganor, and Paula Reimer. "King David's City at Khirbet Qeiyafa: Results of the Second Radiocarbon Dating Project." *Radiocarbon* 57.5 (2015): 881–90.

Gaulmier, Jean. *L'idéologue Volney, 1757–1820: contribution à l'histoire de l'orientalisme en France*. Geneva: Slatkine, 1980.

Gelb, I. J. "The Date of the Cruciform Monument of Manishtushu." *Journal of Near Eastern Studies* 8 (1949): 346–48.

Geoghegan, Jeffrey. *The Time, Place, and Purpose of the Deuteronomistic History: The Evidence of "Until this Day"*. Providence, RI: Brown Judaic Studies, 2006.

―――. "'Until this Day' and the Preexilic Redaction of the Deuteronomistic History." *Journal of Biblical Literature* 122.2 (2003): 201–27.

Geraty, Lawrence. "Exodus Dates and Theories." In *Israel's Exodus in Transdisciplinary Perspective*, edited by T. Levy et al., 55–64. New York: Springer, 2015.

―――. "Hesban." In *Oxford Encyclopedia of Archaeology in the Near East*, Vol. III, edited by E. M. Meyers, 18–22. Oxford: Oxford University Press, 1997.

Gere, Cathy. *The Tomb of Agamemnon*. Cambridge, MA: Harvard University Press, 2012.

Geva, Hillel, ed. *Jewish Quarter Excavations in the Old City of Jerusalem Conducted by Nahman Avigad 1969–1982. Vol. I: Architecture and*

Stratigraphy: Areas A, W and X–2, Final Report. Jerusalem: Israel Exploration Society, 2000.

——. "Summary and Discussion of Findings from Areas A, W, and X–2." In *Jewish Quarter Excavations in the Old City of Jerusalem Conducted by Nahman Avigad 1969–1982. Vol. 2: The Finds from Areas A, W, and X–2: The Final Report*, edited by H. Geva, 501–52. Jerusalem: Israel Exploration Society, 2003.

Gibbs, Robert. "Messianic Epistemology: Thesis XV." In *Walter Benjamin and History*, edited by A. Benjamin, 197–214. London: Continuum, 2005.

Gitin, Seymour. "Bronze Age Egyptian-Type Stone Stands from a Late Iron Age IIC Context at Tel Miqne-Ekron." *Eretz-Israel* 33 (2018): 83–90.

——. "Philistia in Transition: The Tenth Century and Beyond." In *Mediterranean Peoples in Transition: Thirteenth to Early Ten Centuries BCE*, edited by S. Gitin et al., 162–83. Jerusalem: Israel Exploration Society, 1998.

Golani, Amir, and Benjamin Sass. "Three Seventh-Century BCE Hoards of Silver Jewelry from Tel Miqne-Ekron." *Bulletin of the American Schools of Oriental Research* 311 (1998): 57–81.

Goossens, G. "Les recherches historiques a l'époque néo-babylonienne." *Revue d'assyrologie* 42 (1948): 149–59.

Goren, Haim. *"The Loss of a Minute Is Just So Much Loss of Life": Edward Robinson and Eli Smith in the Holy Land.* Turnhout: Brepols, 2020.

Gray, John. *I & II Kings.* London: SCM Press, 1980.

Grayson, A. K. *Assyrian and Babylonian Chronicles.* Locust Valley, NY: J. J. Augustin, 1975.

——. "The Walter Art Gallery Sennacherib Inscription." *Archiv für Orientforschung* 20 (1963): 83–96.

Green, Douglas. *"I Undertook Great Works": The Ideology of Domestic Achievements in West Semitic Royal Inscriptions.* Tübingen: Mohr Siebeck, 2010.

Greenberg, Moshe. *Ezekiel 1–20.* Garden City, NY: Doubleday, 1983.

Greenberg, Raphael. *The Archaeology of the Bronze Age Levant: From Urban Origins to the Demise of City-States, 3700–1000 BCE.* Cambridge: Cambridge University Press, 2019.

Greenberg, Raphael, Sarit Paz, David Wengrow, and Mark Iserli. "Tel Bet Yerah: The Hub of the Early Bronze Age Levant." *Near Eastern Archaeology* 75.2 (2012): 88–107.

Greenstein, Edward. "The Formation of the Biblical Narrative Corpus." *Association for Jewish Studies Review* 15.2 (1990): 165–78.

——. "Mixing Memory and Design: Reading Psalm 78." *Prooftexts* 10.2 (1990): 197–218.

Grethlein, Jonas. "Memory and Material Objects in the Iliad and Odyssey." *Journal of Hellenic Studies* 128 (2008): 27–51.

Gribetz, Sarit Kattan, and Lynn Kaye. "The Temporal Turn in Ancient Judaism and Jewish Studies." *Currents in Biblical Research* 17.3 (2019): 332–95.

Groß, Walter. *Richter.* Freiburg im Breisgau: Herder, 2009.

Grummond, Nancy Thompson de. "Belvedere Torso." In *An Encyclopedia of the History of Classical Archaeology*, Vol I, edited by N. de Grummond, 146–48. Westport, CT: Greenwood Press, 1996.

Guillaume, Philippe. *Land and Calendar: The Priestly Document from Genesis 1 to Joshua 18.* New York: T&T Clark, 2009.

Gumbrecht, Hans Ulrich. "Presence Achieved in Language." *History and Theory* 45 (2006): 317–27.

——. *The Production of Presence: What Meaning Cannot Convey.* Stanford, CA: Stanford University Press, 2004.

Güthenke, Constanze. *Feeling and Classical Philology: Knowing Antiquity in German Scholarship 1770–1920.* Cambridge: Cambridge University Press, 2020.

Habicht, Christian. *Pausanias' Guide to Ancient Greece.* Berkeley: University of California Press, 1986.

Hachlili, Rachel. *Jewish Funerary Customs, Practices and Rites in the Second Temple Period.* Leiden: Brill, 2005.

Halbwachs, Maurice. *La collective mémoire*. 2nd ed. Paris: Presses Universitaires de France, 1968.

——. *La topographie légendaire des Evangiles en Terre sainte: Étude de mémoire collective*. Paris: Presses Universitaires de France, 1941.

Halmi, Nicholas. "Ruins Without a Past." *Essays in Romanticism* 18 (2011): 7–27.

Halpern, Baruch. "Touch of Ebal: Tesselated Identity in the Historical Frontier of Iron I." In *Biblical and Ancient Near Eastern Studies in Honor of P. Kyle McCarter, Jr.*, edited by C. Rollston, S. Garfein, and N. Walls, 535–74. Atlanta: SBL Press, 2022.

Halpern, Baruch, and André Lemaire. "The Composition of Kings." In *The Book of Kings: Sources, Composition, Historiography and Reception*, edited by A. Lemaire and B. Halpern, 123–54. Leiden: Brill, 2010.

Halpern, Baruch, and David Vanderhooft. "The Editions of Kings in the 7th–6th Centuries." *Hebrew Union College Annual* 62 (1991): 179–244.

Hamacher, Werner. "'Now': Walter Benjamin on Historical Time." In *Walter Benjamin and History*, edited by A. Benjamin, 38–68. London: Continuum, 2005.

Hamilakis, Yannis, and Jo Labanyi. "Introduction: Time, Materiality, and the Work of Memory." *History and Memory* 20.2 (2008): 5–17.

Haran, Menahem. "Shiloh and Jerusalem: The Origin of the Priestly Tradition in the Pentateuch." *Journal of Biblical Literature* 81.1 (1962): 19–24.

——. *Temples and Temple-Service in Ancient Israel: An Inquiry into Biblical Cult Phenomena and the Historical Setting of the Priestly School*. Winona Lake, IN: Eisenbrauns, 1985.

Hardin, James. *Lahav II: Households and the Use of Domestic Space at Iron II Tell Halif: An Archaeology of Destruction*. Winona Lake, IN: Eisenbrauns, 2010.

Harmanşah Ömür. *Cities and the Shaping of Memory in the Ancient Near East*. Cambridge: Cambridge University Press, 2013.

——. "Upright Stones and Building Narratives: Formation of a Shared Architectural Practice in the Ancient Near East." In *Ancient Near Eastern Art in Context: Studies in Ancient Near Eastern Art in Context: Studies in Honor of Irene Winter*, edited by J. Cheng and M. Feldman, 69–99. Leiden: Brill, 2007.

Harten, Stuart. "Rediscovering Ancient Egypt: Bonaparte's Expedition and the Colonial Ideology of the French Revolution." In *Napoleon in Egypt*, edited by I. Bierman, 33–46. Reading: Ithaca Press, 2003.

Hartman, Geoffrey. *Criticism in the Wilderness: The Study of Literature Today*. 2nd ed. New Haven, CT: Yale University Press, 2007.

Hartog, François. *Regimes of Historicity: Presentism and Experiences of Time*. Translated by S. Brown. New York: Columbia University Press, 2015.

Hasegawa, Shuichi. *Aram and Israel during the Jehuite Dynasty*. Berlin: De Gruyter, 2012.

Hayes, John. "The Tradition of Zion's Inviolability." *Journal of Biblical Literature* 82.4 (1963): 419–26.

Hays, Rebecca W. P. "Trauma, Remembrance, and Healing: The Meeting of Wisdom and History in Psalm 78." *Journal for the Study of the Old Testament* 41.2 (2016): 183–204.

Heidegger, Martin. *Being and Time*. Translated by J. Macquarrie and E. Robinson. London: Blackwell, 1962.

Hell, Julia. *The Conquest of Ruins: The Third Reich and the Fall of Rome*. Chicago: University of Chicago Press, 2019.

Hell, Julia, and Julia Andreas Schönle. "Introduction." In *Ruins of Modernity*, edited by J. Hell and J. A. Schönle, 1–16. Duke, NC: Duke University Press, 2010.

——, eds. *Ruins of Modernity*. Duke, NC: Duke University Press, 2010.

Hendel, Ronald. "The Landscape of Memory: Giants and the Conquest of Canaan." In *Collective Memory and Collective Identity: Deuteronomy and the Deuteronomistic History in Their Context*, edited by J. Ro and D. Edelman, 263–88. Berlin: De Gruyter, 2021.

——. *Remembering Abraham: Culture, Memory, and History in the Hebrew Bible*. Oxford: Oxford University Press, 2005.

Herder, Johann Gottfried. "This Too a Philosophy of History for the Formation of Humanity." In *Philosophical Writings*, edited and translated by M. N. Forster, 272–360. Cambridge: Cambridge University Press, 2002.

Hermann, Virginia. "Appropriation and Emulation in the Earliest Sculptures from Zincirli (Iron Age Sam'al)." *American Journal of Archaeology* 121.2 (2017): 237–74.

Herrmann, Siegfried. *Jeremia: Der Prophet und das Buch*. Darmstadt: Wissenschaftliche Buchgesellschaft, 1990.

Herzog, Ze'ev. "The Fortress Mound at Tel Arad: An Interim Report." Tel Aviv (2002): 3–109.

Heschel, Abraham. *The Prophets*. New York: Harper and Row, 1962.

Hess, Richard. *Israelite Religions: An Archaeological and Biblical Survey*. Grand Rapids, MI: Baker, 2007.

Hillers, Delbert. *Micah: A Commentary on the Book of the Prophet Micah*. Philadelphia: Fortress, 1984.

Treaty-Curses and the Old Testament Prophets. Rome: Pontifical Biblical Institute, 1964.

Höflmayer, Felix. "Egypt's 'Empire' in the Southern Levant during the Early 18th Dynasty." In *Policies of Exchange: Political Systems and Modes of Interaction in the Aegean and the Near East in the 2nd Millennium B.C.E.*, edited by B. Eder and R. Pruszinszky, 191–206. Vienna: Austrian Academy of Science, 2015.

Hölderlin, Friedrich. "Lebensalter." In *Hyperion and Selected Poems*, edited by E. Santner, 190–91. New York: Continuum, 1990.

Holladay, John. *Jeremiah 1: A Commentary on the Book of the Prophet Jeremiah, Chapters 1–25*. Minneapolis: Fortress, 1989.

"Religion in Israel and Judah under the Monarchy: An Explicitly Archaeological Approach." In *Ancient Israelite Religion: Essays in Honor of Frank Moore Cross*, edited by P. Miller et al., 249–99. Philadelphia: Fortress, 1987.

Hornblower, Simon. *A Commentary on Thucydides*. Vol. 1: Books I–III. Oxford: Clarendon Press, 1991.

Hossfeld, Frank-Lothar, and Ivo Meyer. "Der Prophet vor dem Tribunal: Auslegungsversuch von Jer. 26." Zeitschrift für die alttestamentliche Wissenschaft 86 (1974): 30–50.

Hui, Andrew. *The Poetics of Ruins in Renaissance Literature*. New York: Fordham University Press, 2017.

Huizinga, Johan. "De taak der cultuurgeschiedenis." In *Verzamelde Werken*, Vol. 7. Haarlem: H. D. Tjeenk Willink, 1950.

Hundley, Michael. *Gods in Dwellings: Temples and Divine Presence in the Ancient Near East*. Atlanta: SBL Press, 2013.

Hurowitz, Victor. *I Have Built You an Exalted House: Temple Building in the Bible in Light of Mesopotamian and North-West Semitic Writings*. Sheffield: Sheffield Academic Press, 1992.

Huyssen, Andreas. "Nostalgia for Ruins." *Grey Room* 23 (2006): 6–21.

Iakovidis, Spyros. *Late Helladic Citadels on Mainland Greece*. Leiden: Brill, 1983.

Icke, Peter. *Frank Ankersmit's Lost Historical Cause: A Journey from Language to Experience*. New York: Routledge, 2011.

Irwin, Robert. "Volney's Meditations on Ruins and Empires." In *Scholarship between Europe and the Levant: Essays in Honour of Alastair Hamilton*, edited by J. Loop and J. Kraye, 299–317. Leiden: Brill, 2020.

Itkin, Eli. "Post-Destruction Squatter Phases in the Iron IIB–IIC Southern Levant." *Bulletin of the American Schools of Oriental Research* 388 (2022): 51–72.

James, Elaine T. *Landscapes of the Song of Songs: Poetry and Place*. New York: Oxford University Press, 2017.

Jeremias, Jörg. *The Book of Amos: A Commentary*. Translated by D. W. Scot. Louisville, KY: Westminster John Knox, 1995.

Die Propheten Joel, Obadja, Jona, Micha. Göttingen: Vandenhoek & Ruprecht, 2007.

Joannès, Francis. *The Age of Empires: Mesopotamia in the First Millennium BC*. Edinburgh: Edinburgh University Press, 2004.

Joffe, Alexander, Eric Cline, and Oded Lipschitz. "Area H." In *Megiddo III*.

Vol. 1, edited by I. Finkelstein, D. Ussishkin, and B. Halpern, 153–60. Tel Aviv: Emery and Claire Yass Publications, 2000.

Jonker, Gerdien. *The Topography of Remembrance: The Dead, Tradition and Collective Memory in Mesopotamia*. Translated by H. Richardson. Leiden: Brill, 1995.

Kafka, Franz. "The Coming of the Messiah." In *The Basic Kafka*, 182. New York: Washington Square Press, 1979.

Kalimi, Isaac, and Seth Richardson, eds. *Sennacherib at the Gates of Jerusalem: Story, History and Historiography*. Leiden: Brill, 2014.

Kant, Immanuel. "Idea for a Universal History with a Cosmopolitan Purpose." In *Political Writings*, 2nd ed., edited by H. Reiss, translated by H. B. Nisbet, 41–52. Cambridge: Cambridge University Press, 1991.

Katschnig, Gerhard. "The Supportive Voice in the Midst of Solitude and Melancholy: Volney's Genie des Tombeaux et des Ruines." *History of European Ideas* 47:6 (2021): 958–73.

Katz, Hayah, and Avraham Faust. "The Assyrian Destruction Layer at Tel 'Eton." *Israel Exploration Journal* 62.1 (2012): 22–53.

Kawashima, Robert. "Covenant and Contingence: The Historical Encounter between God and Israel." In *Myth and Scripture: Contemporary Perspectives on Religion, Language, and Imagination*, edited by D. Callender, Jr., 51–70. Atlanta: SBL Press, 2014.

Keel, Othmar. *Die Geschichte Jerusalems und die Entstehung des Monotheismus*. Vol. 2. Göttingen: Vandenhoeck & Ruprecht, 2007.

Keel, Othmar, and Christoph Uehlinger. *Gods, Goddesses, and Images of God in Ancient Israel*. Translated by T. Trapp. Edinburgh: T&T Clark, 1998.

Kenyon, Kathleen. *Jerusalem: Excavating 3000 Years of History*. New York: McGraw-Hill, 1967.

Killebrew, Ann. "New Kingdom Egyptian-Style and Egyptian Pottery in Canaan: Implications for Egyptian Rule in Canaan during the 19th and Early 20th Dynasties." In *Egypt, Israel, and the Ancient Mediterranean World: Studies in Honor of Donald B. Redford*, edited by G. Knoppers and A. Hirsch, 309–43. Leiden: Brill, 2004.

Kim, Minchul. "Volney and the French Revolution." *Journal of the History of Ideas* 79.2 (2018): 221–42.

King, Leonard. "The Cruciform Monument of Manishtushu." *Revue d'assyriologie* 9 (1912): 91–105.

Kinney, Dale. "Introduction." In *Reuse Value: Spolia and Appropriation in Art and Architecture from Constantine to Sherrie Levine*, edited by R. Brilliant and D. Kinney, 1–12. New York: Routledge, 2011.

Kirk, G. S. *The Iliad: A Commentary*. Vol. I. Cambridge: Cambridge University Press, 1985.

Kisilevitz, Shua. "The Iron IIA Judahite Temple at Tel Moza." *Tel Aviv* 42 (2015): 147–64.

Kleiman, Assaf. "The Damascene Subjugation of the Southern Levant as a Gradual Process (ca. 842–800 BCE)." In *In Search for Aram and Israel: Politics Culture, Identity*, edited by O. Sergi, M. Oeming, and I. de Hulster, 57–78. Tübingen: Mohr Siebeck, 2016.

Kleiman, Assaf, Margaret E. Cohen, Erin Hall, Robert S. Homsher, and Israel Finkelstein. "Cult Activity at Megiddo in the Iron Age: New Evidence and a Long-Term Perspective." *Zeitschrift des Deutschen Palästina-Vereins* 133 (2017): 24–52.

Kleinberg, Ethan. "Prologue." In *Presence: Philosophy, History, and Cultural Theory for the Twenty-First Century*, edited by R. Ghosh and E. Kleinberg, 1–7. Ithaca, NY: Cornell University Press, 2013.

Kletter, Raz. *Economic Keystones: The Weight System of the Kingdom of Judah*. Sheffield: Sheffield Academic Press, 1998.

The Judean Pillar Figurines and the Archaeology of Asherah. Oxford: Tempus Reparatum, 1996.

Kletter, Raz, and Etty Brand. "A New Look at the Iron Age Silver Hoard from

Esthemoa." *Zeitschrift des Deutschen Palästina-Vereins* 114.2 (1998): 139–54.

Knauf, Ernst Axel. *1 Könige 1–14*. Freiburg: Herder, 2016.

———. *Josua*. Zürich: Theologischer Verlag, 2008.

Knittel, Ann-Kathrin. *Das erinnerte Heiligtum: Tradition und Geschichte der Kultstätte in Schilo*. Göttingen: Vandenhoeck & Ruprecht, 2019.

Knoppers, Gary. "Periodization in Ancient Israelite Historiography: Three Case Studies." In *Periodisierung und Epochenbewusstein im Alten Testament und in seinem Umfeld*, edited by J. Wiesehöfer and T. Krüger, 121–45. Stuttgart: Franz Steiner, 2012.

———. *Two Nations under God: The Deuteronomistic History of Solomon and the Dual Monarchies*. Vol. 2. Atlanta: Harvard Semitic Monographs, 1993.

Koch, Ido. "Religion at Lachish under Egyptian Colonialism." *Die Welt des Orients* 49.2 (2019): 161–82.

———. "Revisiting the Fosse Temple at Tel Lachish." *Journal of Ancient Near Eastern Religions* 17 (2017): 64–75.

———. "Southern Levantine Temples during the Iron Age II: Towards a Multivocal Narrative." *Ancient Judaism* 8 (2020): 325–44.

Kochavi, Moshe. "The Aphek Acropolis in Context." In *Aphek-Antipatris II: The Remains on the Acropolis*, 592–603. Tel Aviv: Emery and Claire Yass Publications, 2009.

———. "The History and Archaeology of Aphek-Antipatris." *Biblical Archaeologist* 44.2 (1981): 75–86.

Koselleck, Reinhart. "Einleitung." In *Geschichtliche Grundbegriffe: Historisches Lexikon zur politisch-sozialen Sprache in Deutschland*, Vol. I, edited by O. Brunner, W. Bonze, and R. Koselleck, XIII–XXVII. Stuttgart: Klett-Cotta, 1972.

———. *Futures Past: On the Semantics of Historical Time*. Translated by K. Tribe. New York: Columbia University Press, 2004.

———. "Historia Magistra Vitae: The Dissolution of the Topos into the Perspective of a Modernized Historical Process." In *Futures Past: On the Semantics of Historical Time*, translated by K. Tribe, 26–42. New York: Columbia University Press, 2004.

———. "Moderne Sozialgeschichte und historische Zeiten." In *Zeitschichten: Studien zur Historik*. Frankfurt: Suhrkamp, 2000.

———. "Neuzeit." In *Futures Past: On the Semantics of Historical Time*, translated by K. Tribe, 222–54. New York: Columbia University Press, 2004.

———. *Sediments of Time: On Possible Histories*. Translated by S. Franzel and S. L. Hoffmann. Stanford, CA: Stanford University Press, 2018.

———. *Vergangene Zukunft: Zur Semantik geschichtlicher Zeiten*. Frankfurt: Suhrkamp Verlag, 1979.

Kosmin, Paul. *Time and Its Adversaries in the Seleucid Empire*. Cambridge, MA: Harvard University Press, 2018.

Kotkin, Joel. *The City: A Global History*. New York: Modern Library, 2005.

Kotrosits, Maia. *The Lives of Objects: Material Culture, Experience, and the Real in the History of Early Christianity*. Chicago: University of Chicago Press, 2020.

Kratz, Reinhard. *The Composition of the Narrative Books of the Old Testament*. Translated by J. Bowden. London: T&T Clark, 2005.

Kuenen, Abraham. *Historisch-kritische Einleitung in die Bücher des alten Testaments*. Band 1. Leipzig: Otto Schulze, 1892.

Kugler, Gili. "Not Moses, but David: Theology and Politics in Psalm 78." *Scottish Journal of Theology* 73.2 (2020): 126–36.

Kuhrt, Amélie. *The Ancient Near East c. 3000–300 BC*. Vol. 2. London: Routledge, 1995.

Kurtz, Paul Michael. "A Historical, Critical Retrospective on Historical Criticism." In *The New Cambridge Companion to Biblical Interpretation*, edited by I. Boxall and B. C. Gregory, 15–36. New York: Cambridge University Press, 2022.

———. "Is Kant among the Prophets? Hebrew Prophecy and German Historical Thought, 1880–1920." *Journal of Central European History* 54.1 (2021): 34–60.

"The Philological Apparatus: Science, Text, and Nation in the Nineteenth Century." *Critical Inquiry* 47.4 (2021): 747–76.

"The Silence on the Land: Ancient Israel versus Modern Palestine in Scientific Theology." In *Negotiating the Secular and the Religious in the German Empire*, edited by R. Habermas, 56–100. New York: Berghahn Books, 2019.

Laato, Antti. *The Origin of the Israelite Zion Theology*. London: T& T Clark, 2018.

Lamon, Robert, and Geoffrey Shipton. *Megiddo I*. Chicago: University of Chicago Press, 1939.

Langdon, Stephen. *Die Neubabylonischen Königsinschriften*. Leipzig: J. C. Hinrichs, 1912.

Langer, Lawrence. *Holocaust Testimonies: The Ruins of Memory*. New Haven, CT: Yale University Press, 1991.

LaRocca-Pitts, Elizabeth. *"Of Wood and Stone": The Significance of Israelite Cultic Items in the Bible and Its Early Interpreters*. Winona Lake, IN: Eisenbrauns, 2001.

Laurens, Henry. *L'expédition d'Egypte: 1798–1801*. 2nd ed. Paris: Seuil, 1997.

Lederman, Zvi. "The Middle Bronze Age IIC Defense System." Excavations at Shiloh 1981–1984: Preliminary Report. *Tel Aviv* 12 (1985): 140–46.

Lehmann, Gunnar, and Ann Killebrew. "Palace 6000 at Megiddo in Context: Iron Age Central Hall Tetra-Partite Residencies and the *Bit-Hilani* Building Tradition in the Levant." *Bulletin of the American Schools of Oriental Research* 369 (2010): 13–33.

Leonard-Fleckman, Mahri. *Scribal Representations and Social Landscapes of the Iron Age Shephelah*. New York: Oxford University Press, forthcoming.

Leuchter, Mark. "Jeroboam the Ephratite." *Journal of Biblical Literature* 125.1 (2006): 51–72.

The Levites and the Boundaries of Israelite Identity. New York: Oxford University Press, 2017.

The Polemics of Exile in Jeremiah 26–45. Cambridge: Cambridge University Press, 2008.

"The Reference to Shiloh in Ps 78." *Hebrew Union College Annual* 77 (2006): 1–31.

Levenson, Jon. *Creation and the Persistence of Evil*. Princeton, NJ: Princeton University Press, 1994.

Sinai and Zion: An Entry into the Jewish Bible. Minneapolis: Winston, 1985.

Levin, Yigal. "Conquered and Unconquered: Reality and Historiography in the Geography of Joshua." In *The Book of Joshua*, edited by E. Noort, 361–70. Leuven: Peeters, 2012.

"Philistine Gath in the Biblical Record." In *Tell es Safi/Gath I: The 1996–2005 Seasons, Part I: Texts*, edited by A. Maeir, 141–52. Wiesbaden: Harrassowitz Verlag, 2012.

Lichtheim, Miriam. "The Report of Wenamun." In *Ancient Egyptian Literature*, Vol. II, edited by M. Lichtheim, 224–30. Berkeley: University of California Press, 2006.

Lipschits, Oded. *The Fall and Rise of Jerusalem: Judah under Babylonian Rule*. Winona Lake, IN: Eisenbrauns, 2005.

"Jerusalem between Two Periods of Greatness: The Size and Status of the City in the Babylonian, Persian, and Early Hellenistic Periods." In *Judah between East and West: The Transition from Persian to Greek Rule (ca. 400–200 BCE)*, edited by L. L. Grabbe and O. Lipschits, 163–75. London: Bloomsbury, 2011.

"Persian Period Finds from Jerusalem: Facts and Interpretations." *Journal of Hebrew Scriptures* 9: Article 2 (2009): 1–20.

"Persian-Period Judah: A New Perspective." In *Texts, Contexts, and Readings in Postexilic Literature*, edited by L. Jonker, 187–212. Tübingen: Mohr Siebeck, 2011.

"Shedding New Light on the Dark Years of the 'Exilic Period': New Studies, Further Elucidation, and Some Questions Regarding the Archaeology of Judah as an 'Empty Land.'" In *Interpreting Exile: Displacement and Deportation in Biblical and Modern Contexts*, edited by B. Kelle, F.

Ames, and J. Wright, 57–90. Atlanta: SBL Press, 2011.

Lipschits, Oded, Yuval Gadot, Benjamine Arubas, and Manfred Oeming. *What Are the Stones Whispering? Ramat Rahel: 3,000 Years of Forgotten History*. Winona Lake, IN: Eisenbrauns, 2017.

Lipschits, Oded, Yuval Gadot, and Manfred Oeming, "Four Seasons of Excavation at Tel Azekah: The Expected and (Especially) Unexpected Results." In *The Shephelah during the Iron Age: Recent Archaeological Studies*, edited by O. Lipschits and A. Maeir, 1–26. Winona Lake. IN: Eisenbrauns, 2017.

Liverani, Mario. *Assyria: The Imperial Mission*. Translated by A. Trameri and J. Valk. Winona Lake, IN: Eisenbrauns, 2017.

——— "The Great Powers Club." In *Amarna Diplomacy: The Beginnings of International Relations*, edited by R. Cohen and R. Westbrook, 15–27. Baltimore: Johns Hopkins, 2000.

Lohfink, Norbert. "Die Priesterschrift und Die Geschichte." In *Congress Volume: Göttingen, 1977*, edited by J. Emerton, 189–225. Leiden: Brill, 1978.

Loud, Gordon. *Megiddo II*. Chicago: University of Chicago Press, 1948.

Lucas, Gavin. *The Archaeology of Time*. London: Routledge, 2004.

Lundbom, Jack. *Jeremiah 21–36*. New York: Doubleday, 2004.

Maeir, Aren. "Assessing Jerusalem in the Middle Bronze Age: A 2017 Perspective." *New Studies in the Archaeology of Jerusalem and Its Region* 11 (2017): *64–*74.

——— "Exodus as a *Mnemo-Narrative*: An Archaeological Perspective." In *Israel's Exodus in Transdisciplinary Perspective: Text, Archaeology, Culture, and Geoscience*, edited by T. Levy et al., 409–18. New York: Springer, 2015.

——— "Introduction and Overview." In *Tell es Safi/Gath II: Excavations and Studies*, edited by A. Maeir and J. Uziel, 3–54. Münster: Zaphon, 2020.

——— "Memories, Myths, and Megalithics: Reconsidering the Giants of Gath." *Journal of Biblical Literature* 139.4 (2020): 675–90.

——— "The Tell es Safi/Gath Archaeological Project 1996–2010: Introduction, Overview, and Synopsis of Results." In *Tell es Safi/Gath I: The 1996–2005 Seasons, Part I: Texts*, edited by A. Maeir, 1–88. Wiesbaden: Harrassowitz Verlag, 2012.

Maeir, Aren, and Louise Hitchcock. "The Appearance, Formation and Transformation of Philistine Culture: New Perspectives and New Finds." In *The Sea Peoples Up-to-Date: New Research on the Migration of Peoples in the 12th Century BCE*, edited by P. Fischer and T. Bürge, 149–62. Vienna: Verlag der Österreichischen Akademie der Wissenschaften, 2017.

Magen, Barbara. *Steinerne Palimpseste: Zur Wiederverwendung von Statuen durch Ramses II und seine Nachfolger*. Wiesbaden: Harrassowitz Verlag, 2011.

Malamat, Abraham. "The Last Kings of Judah and the Fall of Jerusalem: An Historical–Chronological Study." *Israel Exploration Journal* 18.3 (1968): 137–56.

Malpas, Jeffrey. *Place and Experience: A Philosophical Topography*. New York: Routledge, 1999.

Maran, Joseph. "The Presence of the Past: Ruin Mounds and Social Memory in Bronze and Early Iron Age Israel and Greece." In *Nomads of the Mediterranean: Trade and Contact in the Bronze and Iron Ages: Studies in Honour of Michael Artzy*, edited by A. Gilboa and A. Yasur-Landau, 177–98. Leiden: Brill, 2020.

Marchand, Suzanne. *Down from Olympus: Archaeology and Philhellenism in Germany 1750–1970*. Princeton, NJ: Princeton University Press, 1996.

Marchetti, Nicolo. "A Century of Excavations on the Spring Hill at Tell es-Sultan, Ancient Jericho: A Reconstruction of Its Stratigraphy." In *The Synchronisation of Civilisations in the Eastern Mediterranean in the Second Millennium B.C. II*, edited by M. Bietak, 295–32. Wien: Verlag der Österreichischen Akademie der Wissenschaften, 2003.

Mariette, Auguste. "Fragments et documents relatifs aux fouilles de San." In *Recueil de Travaux relatifs á la philologie et á l'archéologie égyptiennes et assyriennes*, Vol. 9, 1–20. Paris: Libraire Emile Bouillon, 1887.

Marom, Nimrod, and Sharon Zuckerman. "Applying on-Site Analysis of Faunal Assemblages from Domestic Contexts: A Case Study from the Lower City of Hazor." In *Household Archaeology in Ancient Israel and Beyond*, edited by A. Yasur-Landau, J. Ebeling, and L. Mazow, 37–54. Leiden: Brill, 2011.

Martin, M. A. S. "Egyptian and Egyptianized Pottery in Late Bronze Age Canaan." *Egypt and the Levant* 14 (2004): 265–84.

Egyptian-Type Pottery in the Late Bronze Age Southern Levant. Vienna: Verlag der Österreichische Akademie der Wissenschaften, 2011.

Matthews, Victor. "Josiah at Bethel and the 'Monument' to the Unnamed Prophet from Judah." *Biblical Theology Bulletin* 50.4 (2020): 200–6.

"Remembered Space in Biblical Narrative." In *Constructions of Space IV: Further Developments in Examining Ancient Israel's Social Space*, edited by M. George, 61–75. New York: Bloomsbury, 2013.

Mazar, Amihai. "Archaeology and the Bible: Reflections on Historical Memory in the Deuteronomistic History." In *Congress Volume, Munich 2013*, edited by C. Maier, 347–69. Leiden: Brill, 2014.

Archaeology of the Land of the Bible 10,000–586 BCE. New York: Doubleday, 1990.

"The Beth-Shean Valley and Its Vicinity in the 10th Century BCE." *Jerusalem Journal of Archaeology* 1 (2021): 241–71.

"The 'Bull Site': An Iron Age I Open Cult Place." *Bulletin of the American Schools of Oriental Research* 247 (1982): 27–42.

"An Early Israelite Settlement Site near Jerusalem." *Israel Exploration Journal* 31 (1981):1–36.

"The Egyptian Garrison Town at Beth-Shean." In *Egypt, Canaan and Israel: History, Imperialism, Ideology and Literature*, edited by S. Bar, D. Kahn and J. J. Shirley, 155–89. Leiden: Brill, 2011.

"The Ladder of Time at Tel Rehov: Stratigraphy, Archaeological Context, Pottery and Radiocarbon Dates." In *The Bible and Radiocarbon Dating*, edited by T. Levy, 193–255. London: Equinox, 2005.

"Tel Beth-Shean: History and Archaeology." In *One God – One Cult – One Nation. Archaeological and Biblical Perspectives*, edited by R. G. Kratz and H. Spieckermann, 239–71. Berlin: De Gruyter, 2010.

"Tel Rehov in the Assyrian Period: Squatters, Burials, and a Hebrew Sea." In *The Fire Signals of Lachish Studies in the Archaeology and History of Israel in the Late Bronze Age, Iron Age, and Persian Period in Honor of David Ussishkin*, edited by I. Finkelstein and N. Na'aman, 265–80. Winona Lake, IN: Eisenbrauns, 2011.

"Tel Reḥov in the Tenth and Ninth Centuries BCE." *Near Eastern Archaeology* 85.2 (2022): 110–25.

"Temples of the Middle and Late Bronze Age and the Iron Age." In *The Architecture of Ancient Israel from the Prehistoric to the Persian Periods*, edited by A. Kempinski and H. Katzenstein, 161–87. Jerusalem: Israel Exploration Society, 1992.

Timnah (Tel Batash) I: Stratigraphy and Architecture. Jerusalem: Hebrew University Press, 1997.

Mazar, Amihai, and Nava Panitz-Cohen. *Timnah (Tel Batash) II: The Finds from the First Millennium BCE*. Jerusalem: Hebrew University Press, 2001.

Mazar, Amihai, and Shmuel Ahituv. "Tel Rehov in the Assyrian Period: Squatters, Burials, and a Hebrew Seal." In *The Fire Signals of Lachish: Studies in the Archaeology and History of Israel in the Late Bronze Age, Iron Age, and Persian Period in Honor of David Ussishkin*, edited by I. Finkelstein and N. Na'aman, 265–80. Winona Lake, IN: Eisenbrauns, 2011.

Mazar, Eilat, and Benjamin Mazar. *Excavations in the South of the Temple Mount: The Ophel of*

Biblical Jerusalem. Jerusalem: Hebrew University Press, 1989.

McCarter, P. Kyle. *1 Samuel*. New Haven, CT: Yale University Press, 1980.

McFarland, Thomas. *Romanticism and the Forms of Ruin: Wordsworth, Coleridge, and the Modalities Fragmentation*. Princeton, NJ: Princeton University Press, 1981.

McKenzie, Steven. *The Trouble with Kings: The Composition of the Book of Kings in the Deuteronomistic History*. Leiden: Brill, 1991.

Megill, Alan. *Historical Knowledge, Historical Error: A Contemporary Guide to Practice*. Chicago: University of Chicago Press, 2007.

Meier, Christian, and Reinhart Koselleck. "Fortschritt." In *Geschichtliche Grundbegriffe. Historisches Lexikon zur politisch-sozialen Sprache in Deutschland*, Vol. 2, edited by R. Koselleck, W. Conze, and O. Brunner, 351–423. Stuttgart: Klett Cotta, 1975.

Melman, Billie. *Empires of Antiquities: Modernity and the Rediscovery of the Ancient Near East, 1914–1950*. Oxford: Oxford University Press, 2020.

Meskell, Lynn. "Memory's Materiality: Ancestral Presence, Commemorative Practice and Disjunctive Locales." In *Archaeologies of Memory*, edited by R. Van Dycke and S. Alcock, 28–55. Malden, MA: Blackwell, 2003.

Milgrom, Jacob. "The Antiquity of the Priestly Source: A Reply to Joseph Blenkinsopp." Zeitschrift für die alttestamentliche Wissenschaft 111 (1999): 10–22.

Leviticus 1–16. A New Translation with Introduction and Commentary. New York: Doubleday, 1991.

Miller, J. Maxwell, and John Hayes. *A History of Ancient Israel and Judah*. Philadelphia: Westminster, 1986.

Minchin, Elizabeth. "Commemoration and Pilgrimage in the Ancient World: Troy and the Stratigraphy of Cultural Memory." *Greece and Rome* 59.1 (2012): 76–89.

Homer and the Resources of Memory: Some Applications of Cognitive Theory to the Iliad and Odyssey. Oxford: Oxford University Press, 2001.

"Spatial Memories and the Composition of the Iliad." In *Orality, Literacy, Memory in the Ancient Greek and Roman World*, edited by E. A. Mackay, 9–34. Leiden: Brill, 2008.

Minor, Heather Hyde. *Piranesi's Lost Words*. University Park: Pennsylvania State University Press, 2015.

Mitchell, Christine. "David and Darics: Reconsidering an Anachronism in 1 Chronicles 29." *Vetus Testamentum* 69 (2019): 748–54.

Moawiyah, Ibrahim, and Siegfried Mittmann. "Zeiraqun (Khirbet El)." In *Archaeology of the Jordan II.2: Field Reports, Sites L–Z*, edited by D. Homès-Rederiq and J. B. Hennesy, 641–46. Leuven: Peeters, 1989.

Montet, Pierre. *Le Drame d'Avaris*. Paris: Paul Geuthner, 1940.

"Tanis, Avaris et Pi-Ramsès." *Révue Biblique* 39.1 (1930): 5–28.

Moorey, P. R. S. "Kathleen Kenyon and Palestinian Archaeology." *Palestine Exploration Quarterly* 111 (1979): 3–10.

Moran, William. *The Amarna Letters*. Baltimore: Johns Hopkins University Press, 1992.

Morris, Ellen Fowles. *The Architecture of Imperialism: Military Bases and the Evolution of Foreign Policy in Egypt's New Kingdom*. Leiden: Brill, 2005.

Morris, Sarah. "Troy between Bronze and Iron Ages: Myth, Cult and Memory in a Sacred Landscape." In *Epos: Reconsidering Greek Epic and Aegean Bronze Age Archaeology*, edited by R. Laffineur and S. P. Morris, 59–68. Liège: Aegaeum, 2007.

Mosès, Stéphane. "The Theological-Political Model of History in the Thought of Walter Benjamin." *History and Memory* 1.2 (1989): 5–33.

Mourad, Anna-Latifa. *Rise of the Hyksos: Egypt and the Levant from the Middle Kingdom to the Early Second Intermediate Period*. Oxford: Archeopress, 2015.

Mowinckel, Sigmund. *Zur Komposition des Buches Jeremia*. Kristiana: Jacob Dybwad, 1914.

Mullins, Robert. "The Late Bronze and Iron Age Temples at Beth-Shean." In *Temple*

Building and Temple Cult Architecture and Cultic Paraphernalia of Temples in the Levant (2.–1. Mill. B.C.E.), edited by J. Kamlah, 127–58. Wiesbaden: Harrassowitz Verlag, 2012.

Mumford, Lewis. *The City in History: Its Origins, Its Transformations, Its Prospects*. New York: Harcourt Brace Jovanovich, 1961.

Müntz, Eugène, ed. *Les Arts á la cour des papes endant le XVe et le XVIe siècle: Recueil de documents inédits tirés des archives et des bibliothèques romaines*. 3 vols. Paris: E. Thorin, 1878–1882.

Myers, David, and Alexander Kaye, eds. *The Faith of Fallen Jews: Yosef Hayim Yerushalmi and the Writing of Jewish History*. Waltham: Brandeis University Press, 2014.

Na'aman, Nadav. "The 'Conquest of Canaan' in the Book of Joshua and History." In *From Nomadism to Monarchy: Archaeological and Historical Aspects of Early Israel*, edited by N. Na'aman and I. Finkelstein, 218–81. Jerusalem: Israel Exploration Society, 1992.

"The 'Discovered Book' and the Legitimation of Josiah's Reform." *Journal of Biblical Literature* 130.1 (2011): 47–62.

"The Exodus Story: Between Historical Memory and Historiographical Composition." *Journal of Ancient Near Eastern Religions* 11 (2011): 39–69.

"Memories of Canaan in the Old Testament." *Ugarit-Forschungen* 47 (2016): 129–46.

"The Northern Kingdom in the Late 10th–9th Centuries BCE." In *Understanding of the History of Ancient Israel*, edited by H. G. M. Williamson, 399–418. Oxford: British Academy, 2007.

Nagar, Yossi. "Human Skeletal Remains." In *Megiddo IV: The 1998–2002 Seasons*, edited by I. Finkelstein, D. Ussishkin, and B. Halpern, 471–72. Tel Aviv: Yass Publications, 2006.

Namdar, Dvory, Alexander Zukerman, Aren M. Maeir, Jill Citron Katz, Dan Cabanes, Clive Trueman, Ruth Shahack-Gross, and Steve Weiner. "The 9th Century BCE Destruction Layer at Tell es-Safi/Gath, Israel: Integrating Macro- and Microarchaeology," *Journal of Archaeological Science* 38.12 (2011): 3471–82.

Naveh, Joseph. "Old Hebrew Inscriptions in a Burial Cave." *Israel Exploration Journal* 13 (1963): 74–92.

Nelson, Richard. *The Double Redaction of the Deuteronomistic History*. Sheffield: JSOT Press, 1981.

Joshua: A Commentary. Louisville, KY: Westminster John Knox, 1997.

Niditch, Susan. "Hebrew Bible and Oral Literature: Misconceptions and New Directions." In *The Interface of Orality and Writing: Speaking, Seeing, Writing in the Shaping of New Genres*, edited by A. Weissenrieder and R. Coote, 3–18. Tübingen: Mohr Siebeck, 2015.

Judges. Louisville, KY: Westminster John Knox, 2008.

Nielsen, Kai-Uwe. *Die Magdalenenklause im Schlosspark zu Nymphenburg*. München: Tuduv Verlag, 1990.

Nietzsche, Friedrich. "On the Uses and Disadvantages of History for Life." In *Untimely Meditations*, edited by D. Breazeale, trans. R. J. Hollingdale, 57–124. Cambridge: Cambridge University Press, 1997.

Nigro, Lorenzo. "The Built Tombs on the Spring Hill and the Palace of the Lords of Jericho ('DMR RH') in the Middle Bronze Age." In *Exploring the Longue Durée: Essays in Honor of Lawrence E. Stager*, edited by J. D. Schloen, 261–76. Winona Lake, IN: Eisenbrauns, 2009.

"The Italian-Palestinian Expedition to Tell es-Sultan, Ancient Jericho (1997–2015): Archaeology and Valorisation of Material and Immaterial Heritage." In *Digging up Jericho: Past, Present and Future*, edited by R. T. Sparks et al., 175–214. Oxford: Archeopress, 2020.

"The 'Nordburg' of Megiddo: A New Reconstruction on the Basis of Schumacher's Plan." *Bulletin of the American Schools of Oriental Research* 293 (1994): 15–29.

"Tell es-Sultan 2015: A Pilot Project for Archaeology in Palestine." *Near Eastern Archaeology* 79:1 (2016): 4–17.

Nora, Pierre. "Between Memory and History: Les Lieux de Mémoire." *Representations* 26 (1989): 7–24.

Noth, Martin. "The Background of Judges 17–18." In *Israel's Prophetic Heritage: Essays in Honor of James Muilenburg*, edited by B. W. Anderson and W. Harrelson, 68–85. London: SCM, 1962.

——. "Bethel und 'Ai." *Palästinajahrbuch* 31 (1935): 7–29.

——. *Das Buch Josua*. 2nd ed. Tübingen: J. C. B. Mohr, 1953.

——. *The Deuteronomistic History*. 2nd ed. Sheffield: JSOT Press, 1981.

——. *The History of Ancient Israel*. 2nd ed. Translated by P. Ackroyd. New York: Harper and Row, 1959.

——. *A History of the Pentateuchal Traditions*. Translated by B. Anderson. Englewood Cliffs, NJ: Prentice-Hall, 1972.

——. "Jerusalem und die israelitische Tradition." *Oudtestamentische Studiën* 8 (1950): 28–46.

——. "Samuel und Silo." *Vetus Testamentum* 13.4 (1963): 390–400.

Ó Murchadha, Felix. "Being as Ruination: Heidegger, Simmel, and the Phenomenology of Ruins." *Philosophy Today* 46 (2002): 10–18.

Olick, Jeffrey, Vered Vinitzky-Seroussi, and Daniel Levy. *The Collective Memory Reader*. New York: Oxford University Press, 2011.

Olivier, Laurent. *The Dark Abyss of Time: Archaeology and Memory*. Translated by A. Greenspan. Lanham, MD: AltaMira Press, 2011.

Ollenburger, Ben. *Zion, City of the Great King: A Theological Symbol of the Jerusalem Cult*. Sheffield: JSOT Press, 1987.

Olsen, Bjørnar, and Dóra Pétursdóttir, eds. *Ruin Memories: Materialities, Aesthetics, and the Archaeology of the Recent Past*. London: Routledge, 2014.

Oren, Eliezer. "Governors' Residencies in Canaan under the New Kingdom: A Case Study of Egyptian Administration." *Journal of the Society for the Study of Egyptian Antiquities* 14 (1984): 37–56.

——. "Tel Sera." In *New Encyclopedia of Archaeological Excavations in the Holy Land*, Vol. IV, edited by E. Stern, 1329–35. Jerusalem: Israel Exploration Society, 1993.

Osborne, James. "Counter-Monumentality and the Vulnerability of Memory." *Journal of Social Archaeology* 17.2 (2017): 163–87.

——. "Secondary and Mortuary Practice and the Bench Tomb: Structure and Practice in Iron Age Judah." *Journal of Near Eastern Studies* 70.1 (2011): 33–53.

Oshima, Takayoshi. *Babylonian Prayers to Marduk*. Tübingen: Mohr Siebeck, 2011.

Papazoglou-Manioudaki, Lena, Argyro Nafplioti, J. H. Musgrave, and A. J. N. W. Prag. "Mycenae Revisited Part 3: The Human Remains from Grave Circle A. Behind the Masks: A Study of the Bones of Shaft Graves I–V." *The Annual of the British School at Athens* 105 (2010): 157–224.

Parpola, Simo, and Kazuko Watanabe, eds. *Neo-Assyrian Treaties and Loyalty Oaths*. Helsinki: Helsinki University, 1988.

Pearce, Robert. "Shiloh and Jer VII 2, 14 & 15." *Vetus Testamentum* 23 (1973): 105–8.

Person, Raymond. "Biblical Historiography as Traditional History." In *The Oxford Handbook of Biblical Narrative*, edited by D. Fewell, 73–83. Oxford: Oxford University Press, 2016.

Petrie, W. M. Flinders. *Tanis, Part I: 1883–1884*. 2nd ed. London: Trübner & Company, 1889.

——. *Tell el Hesy (Lachish)*. London: Palestine Exploration Fund, 1891.

Pétursdóttir, Þóra, and Bjørnar Olsen. "An Archaeology of Ruins." In *Ruin Memories: Materialities, Aesthetics, and the Archaeology of the Recent Past*, edited by B. Olsen and Þ. Pétursdóttir, 3–29. New York: Routledge, 2014.

Phillips, Mark Salber. *On Historical Distance*. New Haven, CT: Yale University Press, 2013.

Pinto, John. *Speaking Ruins: Piranesi, Architects, and Antiquity in Eighteenth Century Rome*. Ann Arbor: University of Michigan Press, 2012.

Pioske, Daniel. "The Appearance of Prose and the Fabric of History." In *The Hunt for Ancient Israel: Essays in Honour of Diana V. Edelman*, edited by C. Shafer Elliott et al., 313–35. London: Equinox, 2022.

——. *David's Jerusalem: Between Memory and History*. New York: Routledge, 2015.

——. "'And I Will Make Samaria a Ruin in the Open Country': On Biblical Ruins, Then and Now." *Revue Biblique* 129.2 (2022): 161–82.

——. "Material Culture and Making Visible: On the Portrayal of Philistine Gath in the Book of Samuel." *Journal for the Study of the Old Testament* 43.1 (2018): 3–27.

——. *Memory in a Time of Prose: Studies in Epistemology, Hebrew Scribalism, and the Biblical Past*. New York: Oxford, 2018.

——. "Prose Writing in an Age of Orality: A Study of 2 Sam 5:6–9." *Vetus Testamentum* 66 (2016): 261–79.

——. "Retracing a Remembered Past: Methodological Remarks on Memory, History, and the Hebrew Bible." *Biblical Interpretation* 23.3 (2015): 291–315.

Plath, Sylvia. "The Colossus." In *The Colossus and Other Poems*, 20–21. New York: Vintage Books, 1957.

Polak, Frank. "The Oral and the Written: Syntax, Stylistics and the Development of Biblical Prose Narrative." *Journal of Near Eastern Studies* 26 (1998): 59–105.

Porter, James. "Ideals and Ruins: Pausanias, Longinus, and the Second Sophistic." In *Pausanias: Travel and Memory in Roman Greece*, edited by S. Alcock, J. Cherry, and J. Elsner, 63–92. New York: Oxford, 2001.

Powell, Barry. *Homer and the Origin of the Greek Alphabet*. Cambridge: Cambridge University Press, 1996.

Powell, Marvin. "Naram-Sin, Son of Sargon: Ancient History, Family Names, and a Famous Babylonian Forgery." *Zeitschrift fur Assyriologie* 81 (1991): 20–30.

Prent, Mieke. "Glories of the Past in the Past: Ritual Activities at Palatial Ruins in Early Iron Age Crete." In *Archaeologies of Memory*, edited by R. Van Dyke and S. Alcock, 81–103. Malden, MA: Blackwell, 2003.

Pressler, Carolyn. *Judges, Joshua, Ruth*. Louisville, KY: Westminster John Knox, 2002.

Pritchard, James. *Palestinian Figurines in Relation to Certain Goddesses Known through Literature*. New Haven, CT: American Oriental Society, 1943.

Proust, Marcel. *In Search of Lost Time*. Translated by C. K. S. Moncrieff, T. Kilmartin, and A. Mayor. New York: Modern Library, 2003.

Rad, Gerhard von. "Die Stadt auf dem Berge." *Evangelische Theologie* 9 (1948/1949): 439–47.

Radstone, Susanna, and Bill Schwarz, eds. *Memory: Histories, Theories, Debates*. New York: Fordham University Press, 2010.

Rawi, F. N. H., and A. R. George. "Tablets from the Sippar Library. III. Two Royal Counterfeits." *Iraq* 56 (1994): 135–48.

Raymond, André. *Égyptiens et Français au Caire 1798–1801*. Cairo: Institut Français d'Archéologie Orientale, 1998.

Ready, Jonathan. *Orality, Textuality, and the Homeric Epics: An Interdisciplinary Study of Oral Texts, Dictated Texts, and Wild Texts*. New York: Oxford University Press, 2019.

Redford, Donald. *The Wars in Syria and Palestine of Thutmose III*. Leiden: Brill, 2003.

Reich, Ronny, and Eli Shukron. "A New Segment of the Middle Bronze Fortification in the City of David." *Tel Aviv* 37 (2010): 141–53.

Reid, Donald Malcolm Reid. *Whose Pharaohs? Archaeology, Museums and Egyptian National Identity from Napoleon to World War I*. Berkeley: University of California Press, 2002.

Ricoeur, Paul. *Memory, History, Forgetting*. Translated by K. Blamey and D. Pellauer. Chicago: University of Chicago Press, 2004.

——. *Time and Narrative*. Vol. I. Translated by K. Blamey and D. Pellauer. Chicago: University of Chicago Press, 1984.

Time and Narrative. Vol. III. Translated by K. Blamey and D. Pellauer. Chicago: University of Chicago Press, 1988.

Rigney, Ann. "Plenitude, Scarcity, and the Circulation of Cultural Memory." *Journal of European Studies* 35.1 (2005): 11–28.

Ristau, Kenneth. *Reconstructing Jerusalem: Persian Period Prophetic Perspectives.* Winona Lake, IN: Eisenbrauns, 2016.

Roberts, J. J. M. "The Davidic Origin of the Zion Tradition." *Journal of Biblical Literature* 92 (1973): 329–44.

——— *The Earliest Semitic Pantheon: A Study of Semitic Deities Attested in Mesopotamia before Ur III.* Baltimore: Johns Hopkins University Press, 1972.

——— *First Isaiah.* Minneapolis: Fortress, 2015.

——— "Yahweh's Foundation in Zion (Is 28:16)." *Journal of Biblical Literature* 106 (1987): 27–45.

——— "Zion in the Theology of the Davidic-Solomonic Empire." In *Studies in the Period of David and Solomon and Other Essays,* edited by T. Ishida, 93–108. Tokyo: Yamakaw-Shuppansha, 1982.

Robinson, Edward. *Biblical Researches in Palestine, Mount Sinai and Arabia Petraea: A Journal of Travels in the Year 1838.* Vol I. Boston: Crocker & Brewster, 1841.

Rofé, Alexander. "The Arrangement of the Book of Jeremiah." *Zeitschrift fur die Alttestamentliche Wissenschaft* 101.3 (1989): 390–98.

Rojas, Felipe. *The Pasts of Roman Anatolia: Interpreters, Traces, Horizons.* Cambridge: Cambridge University Press, 2019.

Rollston, Christopher. "Scribal Education in Ancient Israel: The Old Hebrew Epigraphic Evidence." *Bulletin of the American Schools of Oriental Research* 344 (2006): 47–74.

Rom-Shiloni, Dalit. *Voices from the Ruins: Theodicy and the Fall of Jerusalem in the Hebrew Bible.* Grand Rapids, MI: Eerdmans, 2021.

Rood, Tim, Carol Atack, and Tom Phillips. *Anachronism and Antiquity.* London: Bloomsbury, 2020.

Rose, Charles Brian. *The Archaeology of Greek and Roman Troy.* Cambridge: Cambridge University Press, 2014.

Rosi, Ivanna, and Jean-Marie Roulin, eds. *Chateaubriand, penser et écrire l'histoire.* Saint-Étienne: Publications de l'Université de Saint-Étienne, 2009.

Rubin, David. *Memory in Oral Traditions: A Cognitive Psychology of Epics, Ballads, and Counting-Out Rhymes.* New York: Oxford University Press, 1995.

Rubinstein, Ruth. "Pius II and Roman Ruins." *Renaissance Studies* 2.2 (1988): 197–203.

Runia, Eelco. "Presence." *History and Theory* 45.1 (2006): 1–29.

——— "Spots of Time." *History and Theory* 45.3 (2006): 305–16.

Ryan, Jordan. *From the Passion to the Church of the Holy Sepulchre: Memories of Jesus in Place, Pilgrimage, and Early Holy Sites over the First Three Centuries.* New York: T&T Clark, 2022.

Said, Edward. *Orientalism.* New York: Vintage, 1978.

Sanders, Seth. *The Invention of Hebrew.* Urbana: University of Illinois Press, 2009.

Sandhaus, Débora. "Hazor in the Ninth and Eighth Centuries BCE." *Near Eastern Archaeology* 76.2 (2013): 110–17.

Sapir-Hen, Lidar. "Human–Animal Relationship with Work Animals: Symbolic and Economic Roles of Donkeys and Camels during the Bronze and Iron Ages in the Southern Levant." *Zeitschrift des Deutschen Palästina-Vereins* 136 (2020): 83–94.

Sapir-Hen, Lidar, and Erez Ben-Yosef. "The Introduction of Domestic Camels to the Southern Levant: Evidence from the Aravah Valley." *Tel Aviv* 40 (2013): 277–85.

Saussy, Haun. *The Ethnography of Rhythm: Orality and Its Technologies.* New York: Fordham University Press, 2016.

Sayce, A. H. "Preface." In Heinrich Schliemann, *Troya: Results of the Last Researches and Discoveries on the Site of Homer's Troy,* v–xxx. London: John Murray, 1884.

Schama, Simon. *Landscape and Memory.* New York: Vintage Books, 1995.

Schaudig, Hanspeter. *Die Inschriften Nabonids von Babylon und Kyros' des Großen samt den in ihrem Umfeld entstandenen Tendenzschriften*. Münster: Ugarit-Verlag, 2001.

———. "Nabonid, der 'Archäologe auf dem Königsthron': Zum Geschichtsbild des ausgehenden neubabylonishcen Reiches." In *Festschrift für Burkhart Kienast*, edited by G. Selz, 447–97. Münster: Ugarit-Verlag, 2003.

———. "Nabonidus the Mad King: A Reconsideration of His Steles from Harran and Babylon." In *Representations of Political Power: Case Histories and Times of Change and Dissolving Order in the Ancient Near East*, edited by M. Heinz and M. Feldman, 137–66. Winona Lake, IN: Eisenbrauns, 2007.

———. "The Restoration of Temples in the Neo- and Late Babylonian Periods: A Royal Prerogative as the Setting for Political Argument." In *From the Foundations to the Crenelations: Essays on Temple Building in the Ancient Near East and Hebrew Bible*, edited by M. Boda and J. Novotny, 141–64. Münster: Ugarit-Verlag, 2010.

Schiffman, Zachary. *The Birth of the Past*. Baltimore: Johns Hopkins University Press, 2011.

Schipper, Bernd. "Egypt and Israel: The Ways of Cultural Contact in the Late Bronze and Iron Age." *Journal of Ancient Egyptian Interconnections* 4 (2012): 30–47.

———. *Israel und Ägypten in der Königszeit: Die kulturellen Kontakte von Salomo bis zum Fall Jerusalems*. Göttingen: Vandenhoeck & Ruprecht, 1999.

Schley, Donald. *Shiloh: A Biblical City in Tradition and History*. Sheffield: JSOT Press, 1989.

Schliemann, Heinrich. *Mycenae: A Narrative of Researches and Discoveries at Mycenae and Tiryns*. New York: Scribner, Armstrong, & Company, 1878.

———. *Troja: Results of the Last Researches and Discoveries on the Site of Homer's Troy*. London: John Murray, 1884.

Schliemann, Sophie, ed. *Heinrich Schliemann's Selbstbiographie*. Leipzig: F. A. Brockhaus, 1892.

Schmid, Konrad. "How to Date the Book of Jeremiah: Combining and Modifying Linguistic- and Profile-Based Approaches." *Vetus Testamentum* 68.3 (2018): 444–62.

———. *The Old Testament: A Literary History*. Translated by L. Maloney. Minneapolis: Fortress, 2012.

Schnapp, Alain. *The Discovery of the Past: The Origins of Archaeology*. Translated by I. Kinnes and G. Varndell. London: British Museum Press, 1996.

———. "The Poetics of Ruin in Ancient Greece and Rome." In *The Archaeology of Greece and Rome: Studies in Honour of Anthony Snodgrass*, edited by J. Bintliff and K. Rutter, 382–401. Edinburgh: Edinburgh University Press, 2016.

———. "What Is a Ruin? The Western Definition." *Know* 2.1 (2018): 155–73.

Schniedewind, William. *How the Bible Became a Book: The Textualization of Ancient Israel*. Cambridge: Cambridge University Press, 2004.

———. *A Social History of Hebrew: Its Origins through the Rabbinic Period*. New Haven, CT: Yale University Press, 2013.

Scholem, Gershom. *The Messianic Idea in Judaism*. New York: Schocken, 1972.

Scholem, Gershom, and Theodor Adorno, eds. *The Correspondence of Walter Benjamin, 1910–1940*. Translated by M. Jacobson and E. Jacobson. Chicago: University of Chicago Press, 1994.

Schönle, Andreas. "Modernity as 'Destroyed Anthill.'" In *Ruins of Modernity*, edited by J. Hell and A. Schönle, 89–103. Durham, NC: Duke University Press, 2010.

Schumacher, Gottlieb. *Tell el-Mutesellim*. Vol. I. Leipzig: R. Haupt, 1908.

Schwartz, Barry. "Where There Is Smoke There Is Fire: Memory and History." In *Memory and Identity in Ancient Judaism and Early Christianity: A Conversation with Barry Schwartz*, edited by T. Thatcher, 7–37. Atlanta: SBL Press, 2014.

Sebald, W. G. *On the Natural History of Destruction*. Translated by A. Bell. New York: Modern Library, 2003.

Seger, Joe, and James Hardin. "Cultural and Historical Summary: Synchronic and Diachronic Study of the Fortifications at Gezer." In *Gezer VII: The Middle Bronze and Later Fortifications in Fields II, IV, and VIII*, edited by J. Seger and J. Hardin, 12–36. Winona Lake, IN: Eisenbrauns, 2013.

Seow, Choon-Leong. *Job 1–21*. Grand Rapids, MI: Eerdmans, 2013.

Seth, Suman. "The Politics of Despair and the Calling of History." *History and Theory* 56.2 (2017): 241–57.

Shafer, Ann. "The Carving of an Empire: Neo-Assyrian Monuments on the Periphery." Ph.D. diss., Harvard University, 1998.

Shai, Itzhaq, David Ilan, Aren M. Maeir, and Joe Uziel. "The Iron Age Remains at Tel Nagila." *Bulletin of the American Schools of Oriental Research* 363 (2011): 25–43.

Shalev, Yiftah, Nitsan Shalom, Efrat Bocher, and Yuval Gadot. "New Evidence on the Location and Nature of Iron Age, Persian and Early Hellenistic Period Jerusalem." *Tel Aviv* 47.2 (2020): 149–72.

Shalom, Nitsan, Yiftah Shalev, and Ortal Chalaf. "How Is a City Destroyed? New Archaeological Data of the Babylonian Campaign to Jerusalem." In *New Studies in the Archaeology of Jerusalem and Its Region*, Vol. XIII, 229–48. Jerusalem: Israel Antiquities Authority, 2019 [Hebrew].

Sharp, Carolyn. *Jeremiah 26–52*. Stuttgart: Kohlhammer, 2021.

Shectman, Sarah, and Joel Baden, eds. *The Strata of the Priestly Writings: Contemporary Debate and Future Directions*. Zürich: Theologischer Verlag Zürich, 2009.

Shelley, Mary. *Frankenstein: Or the Modern Prometheus*. London: Penguin Books, 1992.

Shelley, Percy Bysshe. "Ozymandias." In *The Works of Percy Bysshe Shelley*, Vol. II, 62. New York: Gordian, 1965.

Sherratt, Susan. "Archaeological Contexts." In *A Companion to Ancient Epic*, edited by J. M. Foley, 119–41. Malden, MA: Blackwell, 2005.

Sherratt, Susan, and John Bennet, eds. *Archaeology and Homeric Epic*. Oxford: Oxbow, 2017.

Shiloh, Yigal. *Excavations at the City of David, I: Interim Report of the First Five Seasons*. Jerusalem: Hebrew University, 1984.

Siegmund, Andrew. *Die romantische Ruine im Landschaftsgarten: Ein Beitrag zum Verhältnis der Romantik zu Barock und Klassik*. Würzburg: Königshausen & Neumann, 2006.

Simmel, Georg. "Die Ruine." In *Philosophische Kultur: Gesammelte Essais*, 125–33. Leipzig: Kröner, 1919.

Singer, Itamar. "The Middle Bronze Age Fortified Enclosure." In *Ergebnisse der Ausgrabungen auf der Ḫirbet el-Mšaš (Tel Masos), 1972–75*, edited by V. Fritz and A. Kempinski 186–97. Wiesbaden: Otto Harrassowizz, 1983.

Singer-Avitz, Lily. "Household Activities at Tel Beersheba." In *Household Archaeology in Ancient Israel and Beyond*, edited by A. Yasur-Landau et al., 275–302. Leiden: Brill, 2011.

Sjöberg, Ake, and E. Bergmann. *The Collection of the Sumerian Temple Hymns*. Locust Valley, NY: J. J. Augustin, 1969.

Smelik, Klaas. "My Servant Nebuchadnezzar." *Vetus Testamentum* 64.1 (2014): 109–34.

Smith, Daniel. "On Appeals to an Imperfect Past in a Present Future: Remembering the Israelite Wilderness Generation in the Late Second Temple Period." *Journal for the Study of the Pseudepigrapha* 28.2 (2018): 123–42.

Smith, Mark S. *The Memoirs of God: History, Memory, and the Experience of the Divine in Ancient Israel*. Minneapolis: Fortress Press, 2004.

Smith, Mark S., and Elizabeth Bloch-Smith. *Judges 1*. Minneapolis: Fortress, 2021.

Smith, Patricia. "Human Remains from the Babylonian Destruction of 604 B.C." In *Ashkelon I: Introduction and Overview (1985–2006)*, edited by L. Stager, J. D. Schloen, and D. Master, 533–36. Winona Lake, IN: Eisenbrauns, 2008.

"Skeletal Remains from Level VI." In *The Renewed Archaeological Excavations at Lachish (1973–1994)*, edited by D. Ussishkin, 2504–7. Tel Aviv: Yass Publications, 2004.

Smith, S. "Report on a Tablet from Jericho." *Annals of Archaeology and Anthropology* 21 (1934): 116–17.

Soggin, J. Alberto. *Judges*. Translated by J. Bowden. Philadelphia: Westminster, 1981.

Sollberger, Edmond. "The Cruciform Monument." *Jaarbericht Ex Oriente Lux* 20 (1968): 50–70.

Spiegel, Gabrielle. "The Future of the Past: History, Memory, and the Ethical Imperatives of Writing History." *Journal of the Philosophy of History* 8 (2014): 149–79.

——— "The Limits of Empiricism: The Utility of Theory in Historical Thought and Writing." *The Medieval History Journal* 22:1 (2019): 1–22.

Spinoza, Benedict de. *Theological-Political Treatise*. Edited by J. Israel. Translated by M. Silverthorne and J. Israel. Cambridge: Cambridge University Press, 2007.

Stade, Bernhard. "Bemerkungen über das Buch Micha." Zeitschrift für die alttestamentliche Wissenschaft 1 (1881): 161–72.

Stager, Lawrence. "The Archaeology of the Family in Ancient Israel." *Bulletin of the American Schools of Oriental Research* 260 (1985): 1–35.

——— "Forging an Identity: The Emergence of Ancient Israel." In *The Oxford History of the Biblical World*, edited by M. Cogan, 152–71. New York: Oxford, 1998.

——— "The Fortress-Temple at Shechem and the 'House of El, Lord of the Covenant.'" In *Realia Dei: Essays in Archaeology and Biblical Interpretation in Honor of Edward F. Campbell, Jr. at His Retirement*, edited by P. H. Williams, Jr., and T. Heibert, 228–49. Atlanta: Scholars Press, 1999.

——— "Introduction." In *Ashkelon 6: The Middle Bronze Age Ramparts and Gates of the North Slope and Other Fortifications*, edited by L. Stager, J. D. Schloen, and R. Voss, 3–23. North Park, PA: Eisenbrauns, 2018.

——— "The Shechem Temple Where Abimelech Massacred a Thousand." *Biblical Archaeology Review* 29 (2003): 26–35.

Stager, Lawrence, Daniel Master, and David Schloen. *Ashkelon 3: The Seventh Century B.C.* Winona Lake, IN: Eisenbrauns, 2011.

Steiner, Margreet. *Excavations by Kathleen Kenyon in Jerusalem, 1961–1967, Vol. III: The Settlement in the Bronze and Iron Ages*. Sheffield: Sheffield Academic Press, 2001.

——— "The Persian Period Wall of Jerusalem." In *The Fire Signals of Lachish: Studies in the Archaeology and History of Israel in the Late Bronze, Iron Age and Persian Period in Honor of David Ussishkin*, edited by I. Finkelstein and N. Na'aman, 307–17. Winona Lake, IN: Eisenbrauns, 2011.

Stern, Ephraim. *Archaeology of the Land of the Bible*. Vol. II. New Haven, CT: Yale University Press, 2001.

——— *Tel Mevorakh*. Vol. II. Jerusalem: Hebrew University Press, 1984.

Stewart, Susan. *The Ruins Lesson: Meaning and Material in Western Culture*. Chicago: University of Chicago Press, 2020.

Stoler, Anna Laura. "Imperial Debris: Reflections on Ruins and Ruination." *Cultural Anthropology* 23.2 (2008): 191–219.

Streit, Katharina. "Archaeological Evidence for the Presence of Egyptians in the Southern Levant during the Late Bronze Age – A Reappraisal." *Journal of Ancient Egyptian Interconnections* 21 (2019): 68–87.

Suriano, Matthew. *A History of Death in the Hebrew Bible*. New York: Oxford University Press, 2018.

——— "Remembering Absalom's Death in 2 Samuel 18–19: History, Memory, and Inscription." *Hebrew Bible and Ancient Israel* 7.2 (2018): 172–200.

——— "Ruin Hills at the Threshold of the Netherworld: The Tell in the Conceptual Landscape of the Ba'al Cycle and Ancient Near Eastern Mythology." *Die Welt des Orients* 42.2 (2012): 210–30.

Sussnow, Matthew. *The Practice of Canaanite Cult: The Middle and Late Bronze Ages*. Münster: Zaphon, 2021.

Sweeney, Marvin. *1&2 Kings*. Louisville, KY: Westminster John Knox, 2007.

Tammuz, Oded. "Psalm 78: A Case Study in Redaction as Propaganda." *Catholic Biblical Quarterly* 79:2 (2017): 205–21.

Thareani, Yifat. "Imperializing the Province: A Residence of a Neo-Assyrian City

Governor at Tel Dan." *Levant* 48.3 (2016): 254–83.

"The Judean Frontier in the Seventh Century BCE: A View from 'Aroer." In *Unearthing the Wilderness: Studies on the History and Archaeology of the Negev and Edom in the Iron Age*, edited by J. Tebes, 227–65. Leuven: Peeters, 2014.

Thomas, Julian. *Archaeology and Modernity*. London: Routledge, 2004.

Thomas, Rosalind. *Herodotus in Context: Ethnography, Science, and the Art of Persuasion*. Cambridge: Cambridge University Press, 2000.

Thomas, Sophie. *Romanticism and Visuality: Fragments, History, Spectacle*. London: Routledge, 2007.

Thompson, E. P. *The Making of the English Working Class*. New York: Vintage, 1966.

Tiedemann, Rolf. "Dialectics at a Standstill." In *The Arcades Project*, translated by H. Eiland and K. McLaughlin, 929–45. Cambridge, MA: Harvard University Press, 1999.

"Historical Materialism or Political Messianism? An Interpretation of the Theses 'On the Concept of History.'" *The Philosophical Forum* 15.1–2 (1983–1984): 71–104.

Tooman, William. "Ezekiel's Radical Challenge to Inviolability." *Zeitschrift für die alttestamentliche Wissenschaft* 121.4 (2009): 498–514.

Trigg, Dylan. *The Memory of Place: A Phenomenology of the Uncanny*. Athens: Ohio University Press, 2012.

Trigger, Bruce. *A History of Archaeological Thought*. 2nd ed. Cambridge: Cambridge University Press, 2006.

Truc, Gérôme. "Memory of Places and Places of Memory: For a Halbwachsian Socio-Ethnography of Collective Memory." *International Social Sciences Journal* 62 (2011): 147–59.

Tubb, Jonathan. "Tell es-Sa'idiyeh." In *New Encyclopedia of Archaeological Excavations in the Holy Land*, Vol. IV, edited by E. Stern, 1295–1300. Jerusalem: Israel Exploration Society, 1993.

Tucci, Giulia. "Egyptian Royal Statues and Stelae from Late Bronze Public Buildings in the Southern Levant." In *Proceedings of the 9th International Congress on the Archaeology of the Ancient Near East*, edited by S. Bickel, 87–102. Wiesbaden: Harrassowitz Verlag, 2016.

Unsok Ro, Johannes, and Diana Edelman, eds. *Collective Memory and Collective Identity: Deuteronomy and the Deuteronomistic History in Their Context*. Berlin: De Gruyter, 2021.

Uphill, E. P. "Pithom and Raamses: Their Location and Significance." *Journal of Near Eastern Studies* 27.4 (1968): 291–316.

Ussishkin, David. "Area P: The Level VI Temple." In *The Renewed Excavations at Lachish (1973–1994)*, edited by D. Ussishkin, 215–81. Tel Aviv: Tel Aviv University Press, 2004.

"Area P: The Middle Bronze Age Palace." In *The Renewed Excavations at Lachish (1973–1994)*, Vol. I, edited by D. Ussishkin, 140–87. Tel Aviv: Tel Aviv University Press, 2004.

"Area R and the Assyrian Siege." In *The Renewed Excavations at Lachish (1973–1994)*, Vol. II, edited by D. Ussishkin, 695–767. Tel Aviv: Tel Aviv Emery and Clare Yass Publications, 2004.

"The Borders and De Facto Size of Jerusalem in the Persian Period." In *Judah and Judeans in the Persian Period*, edited by O. Lipschits and M. Oeming, 147–66. Winona Lake, IN: Eisenbrauns, 2006.

"The Destruction of Megiddo at the End of the Late Bronze Age and Its Historical Significance." *Tel Aviv* 22.2 (1995): 240–67.

"The 'Lachish Reliefs' and the City of Lachish." *Israel Exploration Journal* 30 (1980): 174–95.

"The Necropolis from the Time of the Kingdom of Judah at Silwan, Jerusalem." *Biblical Archaeologist* 33 (1970): 33–46.

"Notes on the Middle Bronze Age Fortifications of Hazor." *Tel Aviv* 19 (1992): 274–81.

"The Sacred Area of Early Bronze Age Megiddo: History and Interpretation."

Bulletin of the American Schools of Oriental Research 373 (2015): 69–104.

"A Synopsis of the Stratigraphical, Chronological, and Historical Issues." In *The Renewed Archaeological Excavations at Lachish (1973–1994)*, Vol. I, Part I, edited by D. Ussishkin, 50–119. Tel Aviv: Emery and Claire Yass Publications, 2004.

The Village of Silwan: The Necropolis from the Period of the Judean Kingdom. Jerusalem: Israel Exploration Society, 1993.

Uziel, Joe. "Middle Bronze Age Ramparts: Functional and Symbolic Structures." *Palestine Exploration Quarterly* 142.1 (2010): 24–30.

Uziel, Joe, Yuval Baruch, and Nahshon Szanton. "Jerusalem in the Late Bronze Age – The Glass Half Full." In *The Late Bronze and Early Iron Ages of Southern Canaan*, edited by A. Maeir et al., 171–84. Berlin: De Gruyter, 2019.

Vaknin, Yoav, Ron Shaar, Yuval Gadot, Yiftah Shalev, Oded Lipschits, and Erez Ben-Yosef. "The Earth's Magnetic Field in Jerusalem during the Babylonian Destruction: A Unique Reference for Field Behavior and an Anchor for Archaeomagnetic Dating." *PLoS ONE* 15.8 (2020): e0237029.

Van Dyke, Ruth. "Archaeology and Social Memory." *Annual Review of Anthropology* 48 (2019): 207–25.

Van Seters, John. *The Hyksos: A New Investigation*. New Haven, CT: Yale University Press, 1966.

Vaux, Roland de. "Jerusalem and the Prophets." In *Interpreting the Prophetic Tradition*, edited by H. Orlinsky, 277–300. New York: Ktav, 1969.

Veijola, Timo. *Das Königtum in der Beurteilung der deuteronomistischen Historiographie: Eine redaktionsgeschichtliche Untersuchung*. Helsinki: Suomalainen Tiedeakatemia, 1977.

Volney, M. Constantine-François. *Les Ruines, ou Méditation sur les Révolutions des Empires*. Paris: Desenne, 1791.

Voyage en Syrie et en Égypte, pendant les années 1783, 1784, et 1785. Vol. II. Paris: Volland, 1787.

Vukosavovic, Filip, Ortal Chalaf, and Joe Uziel. "'And You Counted the Houses of Jerusalem and Pulled Houses down to Fortify the Wall' (Isaiah 22:10): The Fortifications of Iron Age II Jerusalem in Light of New Discoveries in the City of David." In *New Studies in the Archaeology of Jerusalem and Its Region*, Vol. XIV, edited by Y. Zelinger et al., 1–38. Jerusalem: Israel Antiquities Authority, 2021.

Walcott, Derek. "Ruins of a Great House." In *The Poetry of Derek Walcott 1948–2013*, edited by G. Maxwell, 29–30. New York: Farrar, Straus and Giroux, 2014.

Watzinger, Carl. "Zur Chronologie der Schichten von Jericho." *Zeitschrift der Deutschen Morgenländischen Gesellschaft* 80.2/3 (1926): 131–36.

Weinfeld, Moshe. "Zion and Jerusalem as Religious and Political Capital: Ideology and Utopia." In *The Poet and the Historian: Essays in Literary and Historical Biblical Criticism*, edited by R. Friedman, 93–115. Chico, CA: Scholars Press, 1983.

Weingart, Kristin. "Wie Samaria so auch Jerusalem: Umfang und Pragmatik einer frühen Micha-Komposition." *Vetus Testamentum* 69 (2019): 460–80.

Weippert, Helga. *Die Prosareden des Jeremiabuches*. Berlin: De Gruyter, 1973.

Weitzman, Steven. "Text and Context in Biblical Studies: A Brief History of a Troubled Relationship." In *The Wiley Blackwell Companion to Ancient Israel*, edited by S. Niditch, 67–83. London: John Wiley & Sons, 2016.

Wellhausen, Julius. *Die Composition des Hexateuchs und der historischen Bücher des Alten Testaments*. 3rd ed. Berlin: De Gruyter, 1899.

Westermann, Claus. *Isaiah 50–66: A Commentary*. Translated by D. M. G. Stalker. Philadelphia: Westminster Press, 1969.

White, Hayden. "Guilty of History? The *Longue Durée* of Paul Ricoeur." *History and Theory* 46 (2007): 233–51.

Metahistory: The Historical Imagination in 19th Century Europe. Baltimore: Johns Hopkins University, 1973.

Wiegend, Theodor, ed. *Palmyra: Ergebnisse der Expeditionen von 1902 und 1917.* Berlin: H. Keller, 1932.

Wilcox, Donald. *The Measure of Times Past: Pre-Newtonian Chronologies and the Rhetoric of Relative Time.* Chicago: University of Chicago Press, 1987.

Wildberger, Hans. *Isaiah 13–27.* Translated by T. Trapp. Minneapolis: Fortress, 1997.

Wilson, Ian W. "History and Hebrew Bible: Culture, Narrative, and Memory." *Brill Research Perspectives in Biblical Interpretation* 3.2 (2018): 1–69.

——— . *Kingship and Memory in Ancient Judah.* New York: Oxford, 2017.

Winckelmann, Johann. "Description of the Torso in the Belvedere in Rome (1759)." In *Johann Joachim Winckelmann on Art, Architecture, and Archaeology*, translated by D. Carter, 143–48. Rochester: Camden House, 2013.

——— . *Letter and Report on the Discoveries at Herculaneum.* Translated by C. Mattusch. Los Angeles: Getty Publications, 2011.

Winter, Holly. "Tell el-'Ajjul Palaces I and II: Context and Function." *Palestine Exploration Quarterly* 150.1 (2018): 4–33.

Winter, Irene. "Babylonian Archaeologists of The(ir) Mesopotamian Past." In *Proceedings of the First International Congress of the Archaeology of the Ancient Near East*, Vol. II, edited by. P. Matthiae et al., 1787–1800. Rome: La Sapienza, 2000.

Winter, Jay. "Sites of Memory." In *Memory: Histories, Theories, Debates*, edited by S. Radstone and B. Schwarz, 312–24. New York: Fordham University Press, 2010.

Wohlfarth, Irving. "On the Messianic Structure of Walter Benjamin's Last Reflections." *Glyph* 3 (1978): 148–212.

Wolf, F. A. *Prolegomena to Homer, 1795.* Translated by A. Grafton, G. Most, and J. Zetzel. Princeton, NJ: Princeton University Press, 1985.

Wolff, Hans Walter. *Amos' geistige Heimat.* Neukirchen-Vluyn: Neukirchener Verlag, 1964.

——— . *Dodekapropheton 2: Joel und Amos.* Neukirchen-Vluyn: Neukirchener Verlag, 1969.

——— . *Dodekapropheton 4: Micha.* Neukirchen-Vluyn: Neukirchener Verlag, 1982.

Wolin, Richard. *Walter Benjamin: An Aesthetic of Redemption.* Berkeley: University of California Press, 1994.

Wood, Robert. *The Ruins of Palmyra, Otherwise Tedmor in the Desert.* London: Robert Wood, 1753.

Woolf, Virginia. *Mrs. Dalloway.* New York: Harcourt, Brace & World, 1925.

Wright, G. Ernest. *Shechem: The Biography of a Biblical City.* New York: McGraw-Hill, 1965.

Würthwein, Ernst. *Die Bücher der Könige: 1 Könige 1–16.* Göttingen: Vandenhoek & Ruprecht, 1985.

Yasur-Landau, Assaf. *The Philistines and Aegean Migration at the End of the Late Bronze Age.* Cambridge: Cambridge University Press, 2010.

Yasur-Landau, Assaf, and Eric Cline. "The Four-Dimensional Palace: The Middle Bronze Age Palace of Kabri through Time." In *Space and Time in Mediterranean Prehistory*, edited by S. Souvatzi and A. Hadji, 231–46. New York: Routledge, 2014.

——— . "Looking Ahead: Strategies for Moving Forward and Synthesis of Stratigraphic Sequences." In *Excavations at Tel Kabri: The 2005–2011 Seasons*, edited by A. Yasur-Landau and E. Cline, 335–40. Leiden: Brill, 2020.

Yerushalmi, Yosef. *Zakhor: Jewish History and Jewish Memory.* 2nd ed. Seattle: University of Washington Press, 1996.

Ypi, Lea. "Commerce and Colonialism in Kant's Philosophy of History." In *Kant and Colonialism: Historical and Critical Perspectives*, edited by K. Flikschuh and L. Ypi, 99–126. Oxford: Oxford University Press, 2014.

Zertal, Adam. "An Early Iron Age Cultic Site on Mt. Ebal: Excavation Seasons 1982–1987." *Tel Aviv* 13–14 (1986–1987): 105–65.

Zevit, Ziony, *The Religions of Ancient Israel: A Synthesis of Parallactic Approaches.* London: Continuum, 2001.

Zimmerli, Walter. *Ezekiel 1: A Commentary on the Book of the Prophet Ezekiel, Chapters 1–24.* Translated by R. Clements. Philadelphia: Fortress Press, 1979.

Zimmerman, Reinhard. *Künstlichen Ruinen: Studien zu ihrer Bedeutung und Form.* Wiesbaden: Reichert, 1989.

Zorn, Jeffrey. "Jeremiah at Mizpah of Benjamin (Tell en-Nasbeh): The Archaeological Setting." In *The Book of Jeremiah: Composition, Reception, and Interpretation*, edited by J. Lundbom, C. A. Evans, and B. Anderson, 69–92. Leiden: Brill, 2018.

———. "Tell en Nasbeh: A Re-Evaluation of the Architecture and Stratigraphy of the Early Bronze Age, Iron Age, and Later Periods." Ph.D. diss., University of California, Berkeley, 1993.

Zuckerman, Sharon. "Anatomy of a Destruction: Crisis Architecture, Termination Rituals and the Fall of Canaanite Hazor." Journal of Mediterranean Archaeology 20 (2007): 3–32.

———. "'The City, Its Gods Will Return There . . .': Toward an Alternative Interpretation of Hazor's Acropolis in the Late Bronze Age." *Journal of Near Eastern Studies* 69.2 (2010): 163–78.

———. "Ruin Cults at Iron Age I Hazor." In *The Fire Signals of Lachish: Studies in the Archaeology and History of Israel in the Late Bronze Age, Iron Age, and Persian Period in Honor of David Ussishkin*, edited by I. Finkelstein and N. Na'aman, 387–94. Winona Lake, IN: Eisenbrauns, 2010.

———. "The Temples of Canaanite Hazor." In *Temple Buildings and Temple Cult*, edited by J. Kamla, 99–125. Wiesbaden: Harrasowitz Verlag, 2012.

Zwickel, Wolfgang. "Die Altarbaunotizen im Alten Testament." *Biblica* 73.4 (1992): 533–46.

SUBJECT INDEX

'Ai, 35–36, 64, 133, 185, 188
Abraham, 74, 189
Absalom, 65, 187, 190
Agamemnon, 89, 90, 92, 143
Ahijah, 139
Ahijah the Shilonite, 116
Albright, W. F., 151
Alt, Albrecht, 124–25
    Ortsgebundenheit, Theory of, 124, 132
Altdorfer, Albrecht, 68–71, 250
    Alexanderschlacht, 68–71
anachronism, theory of, 72–76
Ankersmit, Frank, 7, 193–96
    sublime historical experience, 194
Aphek, 166, 175, 177
Arad, 33–35, 62, 70, 171, 174
Archaeology of Presence, 156
    The Dead, 157–62
    The Displaced, 163–67
    The Empires, 175–81
    The Gods, 167–75
Arendt, Hannah, 240
Aristotle, 129
Aroer, 62
Ashdod, 179
Ashkelon, 37
Auden, W. H., 1, 13, 253
    "Archaeology," 1
Augustine, 15, 156
Avaris, 149

Babel, Tower of, 65
Babylon, 65
Barkan, Leonard, 1–4, 258
Bassi, Karen, 189
Bench Tombs, 157–62
Benjamin, Walter, 17, 211, 240–49
    angel of history, 241, 246, 249, 251
    the messianic, 243–46
    Theses on the Philosophy of History, 17
Bethel, 54, 59, 67, 76, 137
Beth-Shean, 47–50, 59, 164, 170, 176, 177
Beth-Shemesh, 164
Bietak, Manfred, 151
Bloch-Smith, Elizabeth, 11, 190

Bull Site, 171
Burke, Aaron, 42

Callaway, Joseph, 84
Carmel, 65
Casey, Edward, 128, 136, 138
Chakrabarty, Dipesh, 201
Chateaubriand, François René de, 28, 77–81
Collingwood, R. G., 76
Comay, Rebecca, 244, 245, 249
Cordier, Louis, 147–49

David, 65, 74, 190
Delphi, 135
Description de l'Égypte, 147, 198
Dietrich, Walter, 113
Djanet, 151
Doolittle, Hilda (H. D.), 203

Ekron, 54
En-Gedi, 62

Faust, Avraham, 58, 166, 171
Felski, Rita, 12, 192
Finkelstein, Israel, 97, 99, 100, 102
Flinders, Petrie, 83–84
Fritzsche, Peter, 78–80, 259

Garden Tomb, Jerusalem, 158
Gardiner, Alan, 151
Gath, 55–58, 64, 137, 181
Gezer, 38, 42, 178
Gilgal, 65
Giloh, 54
Greenberg, Raphael, 36, 40

Halbwachs, Maurice, 125–27, 132, 143, 156
    La Mémoire Collective, 126
    La topographie légendaire des Évangiles en Terre Sainte, 125
Haran, Menahem, 122
Hartog, François, 11, 93
Hazor, 37, 50–52, 59, 64, 70, 164, 166, 168, 174
Hebron, 38, 39, 45, 62, 73, 178, 181
Herder, Johann Gottfried, 13

Herodotus, 135, 143, 186, 188
Heshbon, 62, 67, 70
Hissarlik, 88
Hölderlin, Friedrich, 205, 268
Horvat Uza, 62
Huizinga, Johan, 194, 196
Huyssen, Andreas, 10, 268
Hyksos, 149

Iliad, 91, 137

Jaffa, 47, 175
Jericho, 38, 43–44, 62, 64, 133
Jerusalem, 46, 60, 64, 149, 157, 165, 178
   history and archaeology of, 212–21
Josephus, 149
Josiah, 66, 76

Kadesh Barnea, 62, 67
Kant, Immanuel, 81, 241
Khirbet Abu et-Twein, 165
Khirbet ed-Dawwara, 54, 136
Khirbet el Qom, 178
Khirbet ez-Zeraqun, 33
Khirbet Qeiyafa, 54
Klee, Paul, 240
Kleinberg, Ethan, 155
Knittel, Ann-Kathrin, 121
Koselleck, Reinhart, 14–15, 28, 77, 81, 93, 262
   die Geschichte selber, 82
   Sattelzeit, 28, 77, 81
   temporalization of history, 67

Lipschits, Oded, 179, 218
Loud, Gordon, 254

Maeir, Aren, 57, 140
Maništušu, Cruciform Monument of, 21–23
Mariette, August, 149
Mask of Agamemnon, 90, 91
Mazar, Amihai, 37–38
McCarter, P. Kyle, 113
Megiddo, 54, 168, 174, 253–56
Memory and Ruins, 131–43
   Competition of Memory, 138
   On Forgetting, 140
   Persistence of the Past, 135
   Remembering What Never Was, 131
migdal temples, 168–70
Mizpah, 179, 181, 233
Montet, Pierre, 150
Moses, 66, 149, 189
Mt. Ebal, 172, 189
Mycenae, 89–92, 134, 143
   Lion Gate, 89

Nabonidus, 21–29, 75, 258
Nebuchadnezzar II, 24

Niditch, Susan, 112
Nietzsche, Friedrich, 17, 87, 267
Noth, Martin, 110, 116, 122

Oresteia, 91

Palmyra, 205–8
Pausanias, 92, 188
Pella, 168
Petrie, Flinders, 149
Pi-Ramesses, 150, 152
Piranesi, Giovanni Battista, 207
Plath, Slyvia, 88
Pompeii, 28, 77–79
presence, theory of, 155, 156, 193–97

Rachel's tomb, 154, 155
Ramat Rahel, 179, 181
Ramesses II, 177
Rassam, Hormuzd, 21
Ricoeur, Paul, 10, 14, 16, 29, 82, 86, 128, 133, 145, 265, 267, 268
   historical condition, 86
Robinson, Edward, 83

Said, Edward, 197–98, 201, 267
Saul, 65, 189
Schaudig, Hanspeter, 26–27, 75
Schiffman, Zachary, 11, 72, 73
Schliemann, Heinrich, 83, 88–93, 143
Seti I, 177
Shalmaneser III, 179
Shechem, 37, 44, 45, 54, 67, 137, 168, 178
Shelley, Mary, 205
Shelley, Percy, 20, 205
   Ozymandias, 21
Shiloh, 38, 44, 54, 57, 64, 181, 260
   Archaeology of, 94–104
   in Book of Jeremiah, 117–19
   in Book of Joshua, 106–9
   in Book of Judges, 109–12
   in Book of Kings, 116–17
   in Book of Samuel, 112–16
   in Psalm 78, 119–21
Simmel, Georg, 10, 193
Sinai, 66
Sippar, 21–24, 75, 86
Smith, Mark, 140
Soggin, Alberto, 112
Spiegel, Gabrielle, 6, 198
Stewart, Susan, 10

Tanis, 147–53
Tel Beth Yerah, 31
Tel Dan, 171, 174
Tel Dan inscription, 75
Tel el-Hesi, 175
Tel Eton, 178

SUBJECT INDEX

Tel Haror, 41
Tel Jemmeh, 179
Tel Jokneam, 178
Tel Kabri, 40, 42
Tel Kinrot, 178
Tel Lachish, 38, 40, 51, 60, 164, 175
Tel Malhata, 43
Tel Masos, 43
Tel Mevorakh, 170
Tel Mor, 176
Tel Moza, 171
Tel Nagila, 38, 51
Tel Rehov, 54, 164
Tel Sera', 175
Tel Yarmuth, 31, 33
Tell el-Ajjul, 175
Tell el-Far'ah (North), 31
Tell es Sakan, 33
Tell es-Saidiyeh, 164
Tell Jemmeh, 179
Tell Kitan, 51
Tell Kittan, 170, 174

Tell Nimrin, 42
Thucydides, 92, 134
Thutmose III, 175
Tiglath-Pileser III, 58, 179
Timnah, 37, 165
to this day, language of, 183–89
Tomb of Pharaoh's Daughter, 161
Torso Belvedere, 1–4
Troy, 89, 91, 143
Tyre, 65

Uphill, E. P., 152

Volney (Constantin-François de Chasseboeuf), 203–8

Walcott, Derek, 146
White, Hayden, 268

Yerushalmi, Yosef, 145, 266

Zion traditions, 222–23

SCRIPTURE INDEX

Genesis
  8:20, 189
  11:8, 65
  12:7–8, 189
  13:18, 189
  21:32, 74
  23:1–20, 191
  24:10, 74
  26:1, 74
  28:18, 190
  33:20, 189
  35:1, 189
  35:1–7, 189
  35:19, 155
  35:20, 154, 261
  35:40, 16
  48:7, 155
Exodus
  1:11, 150
  12:37, 150
  17:15, 189
  23:24, 190
  24:4, 66, 189, 190, 262
  34:13, 65
Leviticus
  19:4, 174
  26:1, 174
  26:30, 65
Numbers
  13–14, 27
  13:22, 45, 147
  21:1–3, 64
  21:14–15, 73
  21:25–30, 67
  33:3, 150
  33:40, 34
Deuteronomy
  1:44, 64
  2:12, 74
  7:5, 190
  7:25, 174
  12:2, 174
  13:16, 197
  13:17, 64
  26:1–14, 27
  27:15, 174
Joshua
  4:1–9, 185
  4:5, 190
  4:5–7, 66
  5:2–12, 123
  5:9, 183
  6, 44, 133
  6:20, 65
  7:26, 185
  8, 133
  8:28, 124, 185, 262
  8:30, 66, 189
  10:3, 5, 33, 134
  10:13, 73
  10:27, 65
  10:36–39, 134
  10:41, 67
  11:13, 63
  11:21, 45
  12:11, 33
  12:14, 34
  14:15, 73
  15:35, 33
  18:1, 108, 138
  18:8, 108
  18:10, 108
  19:46, 47
  19:51, 108, 138
  21:29, 33
  22:9–34, 108
  22:10, 66, 108, 189
  22:12, 108
  22:19, 138
  22:27–28, 189
  24:1, 25, 109
  24:26, 191
Judges
  1, 27, 52
  1:1, 110
  1:10, 73
  1:11, 73
  1:16, 34

Judges (cont.)
   1:17, 64
   1:22–26, 57, 67
   2:2, 65
   3:19, 191
   6:24, 63, 66, 185
   6:25, 65
   8:17, 65
   9, 52, 67, 137
   18:3, 94
   18:30–31, 111
   18:31, 109
   20:18, 26, 137
   21:12, 109, 111, 112, 138
   21:19, 95
   21:21, 138

1 Samuel
   1:3, 112, 177
   1:7, 24, 115
   1:9, 20, 112
   1:10, 2, 66, 155
   2:11–36, 113
   2:12–17, 22–25, 114
   2:12–36, 122
   2:22, 114
   3:3, 113, 114, 115
   4:1–7 114
   4:4, 12, 113
   4:11, 138
   6:18, 63, 184, 261
   7:2, 115
   7:5–12, 115
   7:15, 115
   7:16, 123
   7:17, 189
   9:9, 73
   13:21, 74
   14:3, 113, 116
   14:35, 189
   15:12, 65, 190
   21, 57
   22:20, 116
   27, 57

2 Samuel
   3:32, 66
   5:6–9, 46, 210
   5:18–25, 114
   6, 57
   6:17, 115
   7:6, 115
   7:13, 16, 224
   8:3, 65, 190
   8:16–18, 177
   12:20, 74
   15, 57
   18:8, 66
   18:18, 187, 190
   20:25, 116
   24:21, 189

1 Kings
   2:26, 116
   2:27, 113
   3:1, 177
   9:6–9, 209
   9:8, 65
   12:19, 184
   13:32, 74
   14:1–8, 117
   14:2, 116
   14:4, 116, 138
   14:23, 190
   16:24, 74
   18:30, 189

2 Kings
   2:22, 188
   10:26, 190
   10:27, 65
   12, 181
   17:34, 40, 73
   18:4, 65
   19:25, 231
   21:1–17, 212
   22:14, 218
   23:5, 174
   23:15, 65, 76
   23:17, 66
   23:26–27, 212
   24:3, 212
   25:1, 3, 217
   25:1–21, 212
   25:8, 218
   25:9–10, 218
   25:10, 65
   27:10, 190

Isaiah
   1:21–16, 225
   5:8–10, 225
   5:17, 64, 210
   7:9, 227
   8:18, 230
   8:19, 160
   10:12, 225
   10:20–22, 229
   13:20, 166
   14:25, 225
   17:1, 239
   17:3, 64
   17:12–14, 225
   19:11, 147
   19:19, 190
   25:2, 231
   25:12, 64
   29:5–6, 225
   29:7, 229
   30:25, 65
   34:13, 64

37:18, 180
37:26, 231
43:19, 240, 248
44:26, 15, 233, 237
45:4, 231
49:18–19, 236
51:3, 16, 211, 237
52:9, 236
58:12, 63, 93
61:4, 63, 236
61:11, 236
64:10, 65
64:11, 235
65:18, 236
Jeremiah
  2:14, 147
  2:15, 59
  4:5–8, 210
  4:6, 230
  4:23, 26, 232
  5:1–17, 212
  6:6, 212
  7:4, 8, 14, 227
  7:8, 247
  7:12, 15, 95, 104, 118, 145
  7:12–14, 58, 117, 118, 260
  7:14, 118
  7:16–34, 212
  7:17–26, 175
  8:4–17, 212
  9:9, 228
  9:10, 228
  14:13–18, 212
  18:7, 248
  18:7–10, 232
  21:11–14, 212
  22:4–5, 228
  22:6–7, 228
  22:11–30, 212
  25:1–14, 228
  25:11, 180
  26:1, 117
  26:6, 9, 15, 115, 117, 118, 210, 260
  26:7–11, 226
  26:8, 11, 119
  26:9, 95, 118
  26:17–19, 226
  26:20–24, 226
  29:11, 238
  30:18, 63, 64, 238
  31:15, 154, 155
  31:17, 236, 238
  31:21, 191
  33:10–11, 236
  33:11, 237
  39:1–14, 61, 229
  40:7–12, 219
  41:4–5, 130
  41:5, 117, 171, 197, 234
  43:7–9, 147
  44:6, 63
  44:15–19, 175
  46:18, 239
  47:5–7, 228
  48:18, 64
  51:37, 239
  52:1–16, 212
Ezekiel
  4:1–3, 229
  4:1–8, 209
  5:8, 230
  5:10, 14, 229
  5:11, 212
  6:6, 210
  8:6–17, 212
  8:7–18, 175
  9:1–11, 212
  9:5, 230
  10:2, 230
  11:23, 230
  14:1–5, 175
  14:23–33, 219
  26:4, 239
  26:9, 65
  26:20, 161
  30:14, 147
  33:24–27, 166
  36:35, 16, 211, 236
  36:36, 237
  39:15, 191
Hosea
  3:4, 190
  10:14, 64
  12:12, 65
Joel
  1:17, 210
Amos
  5:15, 229
  6:2, 58, 210
  7:9, 65, 207, 210
  9:11, 15, 63, 237
Jonah
  1:3, 47
Micah
  1:6, 9–16, 224
  3:10, 224
  3:11, 225, 244
  3:12, 64, 224
  5:10, 210
Zephaniah
  1:15, 210
  3:6, 231
  3:12–13, 229
  3:16, 65

Haggai
    1:6, 235
    2:3, 171, 220
Psalms
    7, 93
    9, 63
    46:6, 224, 230, 231
    48:3, 223, 229
    48:3–6, 223
    48:13–15, 223
    69:35, 238
    72:12, 240
    74:3, 63, 235, 238
    74:12, 235
    76:3–6, 223
    76:6–7, 230
    78:2–3, 130
    78:12, 147
    78:59, 120
    78:60, 94, 115, 138
    78:60–64, 120
    78:62–63, 120
    78:68, 94
    78:69, 120
    79:1–5, 235
    79:8, 212
    89:41, 231
    105, 27
    132:10–18, 224
    132:13, 230
    132:14, 223, 239
Job
    3:14, 63
    38:7, 236
Ruth
    4:7, 73
Lamentations
    1:4, 234
    2:2, 64
    2:15, 234
    4:13–14, 212
Ezra
    3:2, 189
    3:7, 47
    3:13, 235
Nehemiah
    2:3, 17, 63
    2:13–16, 220
    6:15, 220
    12:37, 71
1 Chronicles
    4:30, 64
    11:4–9, 210
    16, 35, 74
    29:7, 74
2 Chronicles
    2:16, 47